OBLIQUE DRAWING

Writing **Architecture** series

A project of the Anyone Corporation; Cynthia Davidson, editor

OBLIQUE DRAWING

A HISTORY OF ANTI-PERSPECTIVE

MASSIMO SCOLARI

introduction by
JAMES S. ACKERMAN

THE MIT PRESS

CAMBRIDGE, MASSACHUSETTS

LONDON, ENGLAND

Translated from the Italian by Jenny Condie Palandri.

This translation was made possible in part by a grant from the Graham
Foundation for Advanced Studies in the Fine Arts.

MIT Press books may be purchased at special quantity
discounts for business or sales promotional use.
For information, please email special_sales@mitpress.mit.edu
or write to Special Sales Department, The MIT Press,
55 Hayward Street, Cambridge, MA 02142.

This book was set in Filosofia and Trade Gothic by The MIT Press.
Printed and bound in the United States of America.

Library of Congress Cataloging-in-Publication Data

Scolari, Massimo, 1943–

[Disegno obliquo. English]
Oblique drawing : a history of anti-perspective / Massimo Scolari ;
introduction by James S. Ackerman.
p cm—(Writing architecture)
Includes bibliographical references and index.
ISBN 978-0-262-01774-9 (hardcover : alk. paper) 1. Axonometric
projection. 2. Oblique projection. 3. Drawing—Technique. — I. Title.
NA2711.S3613 2012
741.01'8—dc23
2011052651

10   9   8   7   6   5   4   3   2   1

CONTENTS

INTRODUCTION
James S. Ackerman

I have long admired Massimo Scolari as an artist, teacher, and writer whose originality of perception is coupled with an impressively wide-ranging knowledge of the philosophy, learning, and arts of the Western tradition. His independence from the fashions of the academic and intellectual establishment guides us to discoveries that have remained clouded by our acceptance of approved approaches, giving his insights uncommon vitality. And yet Scolari, as much as any professional scholar, is a master of historical research; whatever his subject, he penetrates the foundation of related accumulated knowledge. The discursive endnotes in this volume expand the message of the text, not in a pedantic fashion, but by demonstrating that in order to get to the core of an investigation, we must absorb the contributions of our predecessors to further our own understanding—or misunderstanding—of the past. Characteristic of Scolari's work, these notes—in contrast to standard procedure—are illustrated with images that constitute another level of reference, which expands on that of the text.

Scolari's studies orbit around the theme of visual and conceptual representation, and approach that theme as a manifestation of the ideological and philosophical orientations of different cultures. Scolari considers images not just as a form of art but as a form of thought, a projection of a way of life. This is most vividly articulated in the chapter bearing the name of the book, "Oblique Drawing," which begins with an extended investigation of representation in ancient Egypt—a tightly integrated society with the worldview of a closed and relatively unchanging culture in which writing, symbol, and depiction were intertwined. For all its preoccupation with the afterlife, Egypt represented the world more truthfully than other cultures, though not without ideographic conventions for adjusting to the flatness of paintings and reliefs. Greek and early Roman artists worked in a more open society and reported what they observed as well as the events of mythology (which Plato vigorously opposed), often with striking optical persuasiveness. Arab writers and artists, who preserved many of the

Greek illustrated texts, and their medieval followers in the Aristotelian tradition responded to an atmosphere of philosophical/theological uncertainty, which disrupted the coherence of the object and led to a diagrammatic image that disregarded the viewer. The iconic character of Byzantine imagery also frustrated the efforts of observers to place themselves in relation to the icon or narrative.

The radical theology of the Franciscans in the Trecento promoted a new engagement of the artist with visual experience: Giotto and his contemporaries made the picture into a stage and the viewer a member of the audience. A century later the humanist Leon Battista Alberti built the foundation of artists' perspective on the concept of the picture as the intersection of a "pyramid" of visual rays originating in the object and converging on the viewer's eye.

As the subtitle of this book suggests, the majority of the chapters examine alternative—nonperspectival—techniques of presenting objects seen or imagined by draftsmen and painters for expressive and instructional purposes. Viewers in modern Western societies usually read ancient and medieval examples of oblique drawing as stepping-stones toward perspectival representation and modern examples as arbitrary geometrical distortions.

One-point perspective, built on the principles of ancient and medieval geometrical and optical texts, became paradigmatic for modern viewers. It plays a subliminal role in many of these studies because Scolari's intention is to illuminate alternatives to its obfuscating dominance during the last five centuries. Though familiar, one-point perspective distorts. Traditional artists' perspective requires the viewer to remain in a fixed position, seeing with only one eye, when actually our perception of depth is entirely dependent on the different position of two constantly moving eyes. We are so attuned to the artist's perspective that other types of projection appear to distort their subjects; bodies or structures presented in axonometric projection seem to the viewer raised on perspectival images to grow larger as they recede to the rear. Indeed, it is not always possible to establish a rear or a front in such images: when we look steadily at the transparent cubes in "Demonstration Figures," for example, what we first see as the rear face (in figures 6.6–6.9) shifts to the front, while the inner faces of the lateral sides become outer faces.

The methods of drawing discussed here have much in common, but each of Scolari's studies has a unique approach, which I shall characterize here.

"Elements for a History of Axonometry" provides a foundation for the other essays related to oblique drawing. According to *The Thesaurus of Art and Architecture of the Getty Research Center*, axonometry "refers to all forms of parallel projection, particularly where at least one of the three spatial axes is inclined to the plane of projection or picture surface. It is often used to refer to projections depicted as if a plan were drawn to scale, and the plan is then tilted at a 45-degree angle to provide a third dimension, typically height, which is drawn to the same scale as the plan. This system for projection depicts both the plan and volume simultaneously and with a consistent measurement, without the distortion caused by the converging lines of one-point perspective."

The essay underscores Scolari's basic thesis that the illusionistic perspective that constituted the standard representational technique from the Renaissance until the early 1900s (and that is used even today by many non-avant-garde modern and contemporary artists) is not the only, or even the best, representation of objects in the world. While perspective purports to reproduce an object or a scene as it appears to an observer in a particular position, it gives a distorted impression of size and extension, particularly with regard to elements at a distance from the hypothetical eye of the viewer. Axonometric projection, by contrast, preserves, in scale, the actual measurements of objects it represents in breadth, height, and depth, as receding lines do not converge. It therefore is suited to the depiction of things that have to be constructed, such as buildings and machines, though it is less satisfactory for irregular and diffuse objects.

"Drawing in *Paralleli Modo*" is a short amplification of the study of axonometry that addresses the terminology of parallel projection historically. I was intrigued to find that Piero della Francesca differentiated *perspettiva* (as based on optics) from *prospettiva* (as based on conic representation) and that the terms *axonometry* and *oblique axonometric projection* were coined as late as the mid-nineteenth century.

Scolari elevates these geometrical/optical considerations to a higher level by tracing their philosophical roots, initially to the Platonic tradition and to Plotinus in particular, who dismissed illusionism as the mere shadow of reality and exhorted readers and listeners to seek the fundamental qualities of things, accessible to the mind's eye. Thus the object depicted in parallel projection was seen as closer to nature than the one clothed in appearances.

In sharp contrast to the philosophical motivations that had prompted the use of parallel projection in antiquity and the Middle Ages, its employment by the designers of fortifications ("The Soldierly Perspective") and machines ("Machinations") was a purely practical matter. Their drawings were addressed to specialists and responded to the need for precise measurement and descriptive effectiveness. They were not interested in developing a philosophical foundation for their work.

The character of warfare changed radically in the late fifteenth century when Charles VIII of France invaded Italy with mobile cannons that easily demolished the tall square towers and flat walls that had protected cities from attack by military machinery in the era before the discovery of gunpowder. A wholly new type of defensive system had to be devised, one that not only would be less vulnerable to artillery attack but also could provide ample platforms upon low-lying bastions to accommodate mobile defensive cannons. Soulless machines of destruction became the driving force behind the design of defensive fortifications. The military architect—who had to calculate the trajectory of missiles and the angles of masonry and rubble most likely to deflect or absorb them—had to be a geometer and a ballistics expert, and had to provide precise measurements for every element of the plans and elevations. Fortification designs were executed in parallel projection so as to convey exact measurements in all dimensions. Gradually, over the course of the sixteenth century, architects—who had conceived defensive systems at the end of the 1400s with attention to beauty as well as to effectiveness—yielded this part of their practice to military specialists and theorists with battle experience whose aim was to protect their fellow soldiers and the citizens of towns under attack.

In "Machinations," Scolari traces the early history of the representation of machines and mechanisms, a field dominated by craftsmen whose low social status prevented their work from gaining the recognition accorded to geometrical and optical illustrated texts. The cultural and practical importance of machines was recognized by Vitruvius, who devoted his entire tenth book to the subject, emphasizing war machines in particular but providing few illustrations, none of which have survived. The mechanical texts of antiquity and the Middle Ages emphasized application over theory. Their illustrators made no attempt to suggest a particular point of view; they represented the elements of machines rather than how they functioned, often flattening them against the picture plane and focusing primarily on parts with which the machinist consulting their drawings was unlikely to be familiar. Post-Renaissance viewers—even specialists in the field—found many such drawings to be unreadable: a recent editor of *Machinationes* by Heron of Alexandria had all of the ancient illustrations redrawn because they were seen to be deformed and out of perspective.

The chapter "Demonstration Figures" examines illustrations found in manuscripts and printed books of cubes and other geometrical solids from antiquity to the Enlightenment. Scolari finds frequent confusion and errors related to a subtle problem in the evolution of axonometric projection, which had not previously affected modern discussions of representation (though it was discussed in Proclus's *A Commentary on the First Book of Euclid's Elements*). It results from the conflict between the abstract/ideal character of propositions in Euclidian geometry (for example, a point is that which has no part; a line is breadthless length, etc.) and the function of mathematical calculation to record concrete and practical measurements and proportions, which transforms the abstract into the concrete.

Two of the chapters, "Spatial Illusionism in Pompeian Wall Paintings" and "The Jesuit Perspective in China," depart from the technical orientation of the preceding by focusing on the role of oblique drawing in art.

Certain encaustic paintings of the Hellenistic period in the environs of Pompeii attracted Scolari's attention because at first sight they seemed to him to be examples of one-point perspective of a kind not found in other antique images. He first challenges Erwin Panofsky's influential theory that Pompeian illusionism was based on a form of perspective in which lines receding from the picture plane converge on a number of points along a vertical axis, like bones radiating from the spine of a fish. Scolari argues that a convincing representation of three-dimensional depth does not require the use of any systematic perspectival construction; indeed, even after the invention of *costruzione legittima* in the fifteenth century, artists almost always departed from its rules in some way. His attention focuses on a wall painting in the Villa dei Misteri (Villa of Mysteries) in Pompeii that represents a three-bay columnar niche. At the rear of each bay we see the persuasive illusion of a coffered barrel vault apparently receding into the space. Scolari examines and illustrates three hypotheses about the point of view chosen to construct the illusion and concludes that none of them works consistently, because the depiction, apart from assuring that the lines of the coffers and of the architectural orders converge on a central point, is achieved subjectively.

I suppose that Scolari was attracted to the efforts of sixteenth- and seventeenth-century Jesuit missionaries in China to import Western religious images to help convert the Chinese to Christianity in part because they unequivocally failed, demonstrating how Renaissance perspective was not universally relevant. The pictures, illustrating Bible stories and other common devotional compositions, observed Renaissance rules of perspective. The Chinese could not read them, not only because they were accustomed to parallel projection, but because most of their own images focused on landscape—flora and fauna—not on gatherings of people, structures, or other rectilinear forms. They read shadows in the Jesuits' prints and paintings as stains. Like the Platonists, Chinese artists sought to appeal to the spiritual rather than to the descriptive powers of imagery. An acute insight into the differences in approach may be found in a citation for a Chinese painters' manual of the seventeenth century, *The Mustard Seed Garden Manual of Painting*.

The architectural model is the subject of two investigations, one general, "The Idea of Model," and one specific, "Brunelleschi's Model for the Dome of Santa Maria del Fiore and the Gherardi Drawing."

The first provides a three-dimensional foil for the studies of drawing and painting I have discussed. Models have played an important role in the building process since the late Middle Ages, particularly in preparation for the construction of large structures, but their function has been quite different from that of architectural drawings. Because architects have to work out definitive solutions initially in plan, they rarely get involved with models until the later stages of design; like the building itself, the model (unless it is a rough sketch of massing) cannot be started until the plan is fixed; architects then normally assign the construction of models to assistants or specialists. A primary reason for the production of models is the need to elucidate designs for those who are inexperienced in reading plans and sections (for example, a body of citizens, or a patron). Scolari also points to a practical function that is rarely discussed: models make it possible to study solutions to complicated construction problems. Prior to the twentieth century, models seldom represented the environment of buildings; consequently, they rarely were made for programs of military defense, which had to be highly responsive to the topography of their sites.

The second of these chapters has two parts. The first proposes evidence of Brunelleschi's authorship of the surviving model of the cathedral dome, and the second addresses a highly technical issue raised by the drawings and explanatory notes made on a sheet of parchment by Brunelleschi's contemporary, humanist Giovanni di Gherardo Gherardi. Gherardi's drawing has been analyzed by the most qualified contemporary Brunelleschi scholars with varying conclusions. The issues are so complex that I am unqualified to judge among these conclusions, especially without having seen the original, but Scolari's interpretation seems to me to demonstrate exceptional ingenuity and to warrant our support.

What I find most illuminating in this book is Scolari's multifaceted pursuit of his fundamental thesis that, from their earliest visual representations, natural and imagined objects—especially buildings, geometrical bodies, tools, machines—have been shaped philosophically and ideologically. At any given moment in history, the reader of images starts from the presumption that there is one proper technique with which to convey observations or conceptions from maker to viewer, from one person to another, and from one time to another. Scolari's studies vividly demonstrate what diverse forms of representation humankind has devised and how each one reveals something that is lacking in the others.

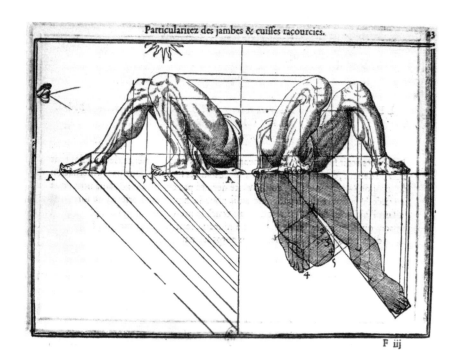

1.1
Jean Cousin the Younger, from *Livre de portraicture* (Paris, 1571).

1.2
Fragment of a krater from Taranto, fourth century BC.

1

ELEMENTS FOR A HISTORY
OF AXONOMETRY

For over half a century Erwin Panofsky's *Perspective as Symbolic Form*[1] has dominated studies of visual representation. A vast literature has discussed the theses it contains, contradicting or amplifying them, but never shifting attention from the main theme: central projection, or perspective. To some this might seem justified, given the extraordinary importance of the Italian Renaissance in the history of Western culture, but the hegemony of perspective has prevented consideration of other equally important methods of representation. Even a summary examination of the history of representation in the West will show how parallel projection has alternated with central projection at least twice in the past two thousand years. It can be found in representations on classical Greek vases, in frescoes in Pompeii, in Byzantine mosaics, and in the Italian Renaissance, and it can be found in the return of parallel projections in the historical avant-garde.[2]

The Demonstration Figures

The use of parallel projection by Leonardo da Vinci and the authors of the Codex Coner during the perspective-oriented Renaissance is significant, as it proves the continuity of a method of representation other than the pictorial view. Although Leonardo had a firm grasp of the laws of perspective, even if he had to violate them with the aerial perspective, he seems to have given precedence to the older method of parallel projection in many of his sketches. Parallel projection appeared in Western culture as early as the fourth century BC and has remained the predominant form of representation in China, where it is often found together with convergent projection in some transitional moments. Giotto's work is a typical example of the fifteenth-century "rediscovery" of perspective. The appearance of parallel projection in Leonardo's work obviously cannot be explained by his uncertain preparation in other techniques or by the quick execution of sketches. Rather, it seems he chose it because it was better suited to representing the actual space of an object rather than an object in space.

1.3
Landscape with *aediculae*, painting on
marble, first century BC, Herculaneum.

1.4
St. Lawrence on his way to martyrdom,
mosaic, fifth century AD, Ravenna,
Mausoleum of Galla Placidia.

Whatever the case may be, the drawings of Leonardo, Conrad Kyeser, and Taccola go beyond pure representation due to of the accentuation of mechanical-functional elements. They tend to straighten out the conical nature of perspective by retaining the parallelism and measurability found in Vitruvian orthogonal projections and wooden models, but they use the very old tradition in a new way—as a three-dimensional proof of functioning and buildability. This is a result that could not be achieved with perspective, and by the time construction had begun on the great sixteenth-century work sites, Vitruvian *iconographia* and *orthographia* had regained their primacy in architectural drawing.

Thanks to Alberti and Piero della Francesca, by the beginning of the sixteenth century a theoretical and technical code had already been formulated for perspective, but there is no explicit mention of parallel projection in any Renaissance text before the second half of the sixteenth century. However, Luca Pacioli[3] and Niccolò Tartaglia[4] used it widely for proofs in solid geometry. Oronce Finé went even further, reproducing on the edges of his oblique figures the metrics (measurements) from which axonometrics took its name three hundred years later.[5] It is almost as if parallel projection had been given as the only way to precisely work out geometric proofs. In geometry, parallel lines must appear as such for they must satisfy both the eye and the reasoning of spectators. Flat and solid figures must remain objective and retain in representation as much of their geometric qualities as possible, even to the detriment of perspectival "realism." One hundred years later Descartes wrote about this problem: "In following the rules of perspective, we represent circles better with ovals than with other circles or squares with rhomboids instead of squares ... in that to be more perfect in images or to better represent an object, they lose their semblance entirely."[6] Only Girard Desargues's invention of projective geometry was able to bring the oval back to the realm of pure geometry as the "conic section." But in the century in which perspective achieved the height of its figurative and theoretical peaks, applied geometry (*geometria pratica*) still maintained a different, pre-perspective status. In almost all the texts concerned with solids or their proofs, oblique parallel projections appear alongside the classical *ichnographiae*.

At the end of the first half of the sixteenth century, geometry was not the only field that demanded more accurate possibilities of representation. To provide workmen with clear instructions on how to cut timber and stone, Philibert de l'Orme wrote a treatise, and the literature of stereotomy began.[7] Cosmography once more adopted Ptolemy's applied geometry and produced

1.5
Leonardo da Vinci, sketch of a winch for
lifting weights. Milan, Biblioteca Ambrosiana,
Cod. Atlantico, folio 8v b.

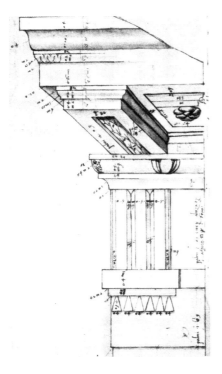

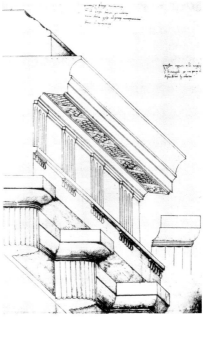

1.6
Fra Giocondo, drawing of a Doric trabeation discovered in Borgo. Florence, Uffizi Gallery, U.A. 1632.

1.7
Andrea Palladio, detail of the Pons Nomentanus in Rome. London, Royal Institute of British Architects, v. x, folio 16r.

1.8
Mariano di Jacopo called Taccola, detail of a wheeled cart with sail, from *Liber tertius de ingeneis ac edifitiis non usitatis* (1433). Florence, Biblioteca Nazionale, Cod. Palatinus 766, folio 27r.

the famous Mercator projection. Military architecture also broke away from the composed Renaissance perspective because it demanded a rapid measurability that the technique could not provide.

Military Perspective

After 1550, the theme of war was no longer addressed by general treatises but by bona fide literature. New techniques of war and the Turkish invasion syndrome stimulated the pursuit of impregnability. Dozens of treatises on fortifications offered warring princes of Europe the secrets of an architecture whose only ornament was its geometric impenetrability. It was no longer a question of designing ideal fortresses, but of building efficient bulwarks in the defense of kingdoms and principalities. The nobleman Diego Gonzales de Medina Barba,[8] subject of Philip III of Spain for whom defense was "allowed by the Catholic point of view [*catolicamente permetida*]," pointed out that the precision of the drawing was vital because "an imperfection of a line could mean the loss of an army." Great architects had traditionally devoted themselves to these defensive works, but at this point a new class of experts, the soldier-engineers, joined them. The soldiers contrasted the practice of war with theoretical projects, and placed little faith in seductive perspective drawings. The dogged march of death made rapid descriptions necessary. A bullet's lethal trajectory had to be measured with the same precision as the bulwarks that were built to deflect it. The *ars mechanica* of war, like the practice of applied geometry (*geometria pratica*), used techniques other than perspective.

In 1564, a work explicitly countering parallel projection with Renaissance central projection was published.[9] It was the result of a collaboration between the king of France's Superintendent of Fortresses, Jacomo Castriotto, who was killed at Calais shortly before the work's publication, and his friend Girolamo Maggi, who met the same fate ten years later at the hands of the Turks at Famagusta. They were innovators: "No one should expect to see the method or rules of perspective in these works; mainly, because it is not part of a soldier's profession to produce them, and secondly, because the foreshortening involved would remove too much from the plans, whereas the entirety of these works lies in such plans and outlines as shall be called 'soldierly perspective' [*prospettiva soldatesca*]."[10] The woodcuts that accompany their text are perfect examples of military axonometry, although they are improperly defined as perspectives. For almost three hundred years, all English and

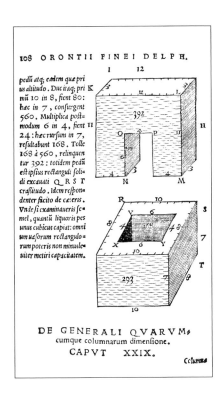

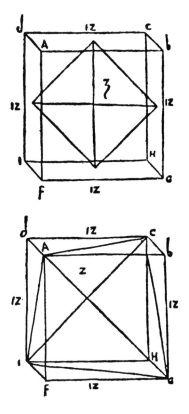

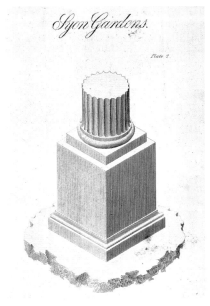

1.9
Oronce Finé, *De geometria pratica* (Strasbourg, 1544).

1.10
Luca Pacioli, *Divina proportione* (Venice, 1509).

1.11
Joseph Jopling, *The Practice of Isometrical Perspective* (London, 1842), plate 2.

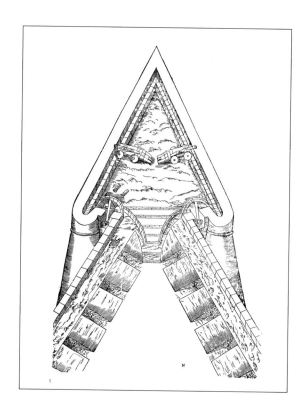

1.12
Girolamo Maggi and Jacomo Castriotto, from
Della fortificazione delle città (Venice, 1564).

1.13
Bonaiuto Lorini, from *Delle fortificazioni*
(Venice, 1597).

French works continued to call oblique parallel projection "perspective."[11] Marking the different nature of perspective were adjectives that emphasized its traits of simplicity and practicality.[12]

Lorini called this new method the "more common perspective [*prospettiva più comune*],"[13] describing it in this way: "Perspectives have to show their own height from a close distance; thus they are all formed of parallel lines both for the height and the width of any building whatsoever, though placed perpendicular to its plane … drawing lines to infinity so that they fall perpendicular and remain parallel." In his original proposal for a soldier's dagger-regulus,[14] Bartolomeo Romano described a spherical perspective in which the "measured parts shall give the right distances, which the oval form would not do because of the foreshortening its parts produce." Giovan Battista Belici (Belluzzi), who was firmly convinced that "the soldier must also be a theoretician," used parallel representation because "we need to see the thing whole, distinct, clear; one can find the truth precisely with compasses."[15] He favored axonometry over perspective, because in war "one single view does not serve, since the whole has to be shown."

Treatises written over a fifty-year period demonstrate the primacy of military perspective in the actual design of fortresses. Jacques Perret de Chambéry, "Gentleman of Savoy," wrote an elegant treatise (dedicated to King Henri IV of France, who entered Paris triumphantly in 1594) in which almost all of the fifty-four plates engraved by Thomas de Leu are military perspectives.[16] By this time, the procedure seems to have been taken so much for granted that Perret limited himself to explaining how one could obtain all the measurements on the plane and in perspective simply by keeping the dividers "sur l'echelette" (at a reduced scale).

With the outbreak of the religious wars of the seventeenth century, writings on the military and perspective were dominated by the Minims and Jesuits, great confessors to kings and princes, who sensed the topic's political and cultural importance. Renaissance perspective survived in that bloody and colorful century by evolving from the mystery of the anamorphosis of Père Niceron, *La perspective curieuse* … (Paris, 1638) to Padre Pozzo's solid treatise, *Perspectiva pictorum* … (Rome, 1693–1700). At the same time, it was seized by *l'esprit de géométrie* and incorporated into mathematics. This paved the way for the technical legitimation of parallel projection, which became the accredited method of representation for engineering and science.

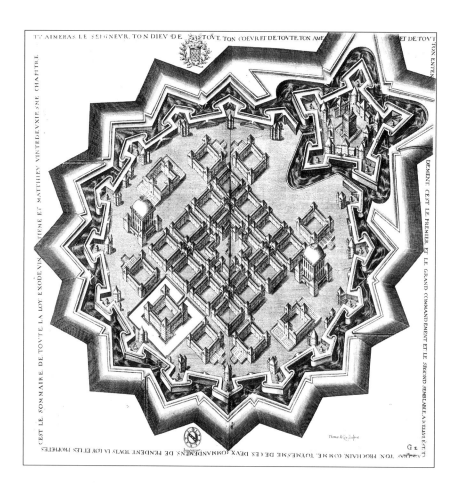

1.14
Jacques Perret, *Des fortifications et artifices,
architecture et perspective* (Paris, 1601).

Vision and the Fundamental Principle of Parallel Lines

Although it is relatively easy to study the application and elaboration of parallel projection in the course of the sixteenth century and to speculate on its subterranean continuity, from the vase painting of Magna Graecia through Byzantine mosaic art to late medieval painting and beyond, it is less easy to locate its theoretical and technical beginnings. If we accept Panofsky's thesis, we can easily understand the birth of Renaissance perspective and see if its nucleus has any residual elements that can lead us backward, any obsolete remains of the stages it replaced.

After stripping perspective of all its symbolic aspects, we are left with Euclid's optical and geometrical formulations. Two of these have been of particular interest since classical antiquity: the theory of vision (the visual pyramid) contradicted by the school of Democritus (although it played a very important role in Renaissance perspective), and the fifth postulate of parallel lines, which D'Alembert called "the scandal of geometry."

Formulating the first theory of vision, Euclid explained the mechanism of vision by saying that visual rays sent out by the eye form a "visual pyramid," which played such an important role in Renaissance *prospettiva*. This theory was not fully accepted by the Latin tradition until the end of the fourteenth century, when optics freed its body of disciplines from all metaphysical and physical interpretation. Significantly, Euclid's mechanism was unknown in the Chinese world, where parallel oblique projection was the only form of representation.

Franco Alessio[17] showed that the application of geometry to optics in the Latin tradition took place within a period of two hundred years, starting with the Oxford school of Robert of Lincoln at the beginning of the thirteenth century. The various works of perspective that flourished at the time favored the Arabic formulations of the tenth and eleventh centuries, especially those by Alhazen and Al-Kindi, over the optics of Euclid and Ptolemy. The works of Roger Bacon and Witelo concentrated on psycho-physiological theories of the Arabic school and ignored the more abstract and geometrical precepts of the Euclidean Greek school. Their interpretations ascribed philosophical and gnoseological significance to the Arabic texts, which were basically scientific in nature. Perspective stopped being merely a science and became *the science*, the door and the key to all sciences ("scientia quae est porta et clavis omnium scientiarum"). In this way light (*lux*) became "the original essence of the created being, the truth and the reason of the unity, which produces space and time." Light summed up within itself the supreme condition of all physical events.[18]

The theological consequences of this position are easy to infer, and reference may be made to Alessio's essay for further discussion of the subject. What concerns us is its influence on pre-Renaissance oblique representations. Alhazen maintains, in the second book of his *Thesaurus opticae*,[19] that an understanding of the world is not determined by Euclidean visual rays (visual pyramid) but by rays emanating from things and carrying their qualities (*species*) to the eye. In *De multiplicatione specierum* (thirteenth century), Roger Bacon claims that "the universe from each of its points radiates influences in all directions, rays and *species*, so that each point is *per se* an active center, a sort of eye sending *species* over the entire universe and receiving them from the entire universe." No human eye orders this world, for it is composed of an infinity of radiant points where space, to use an expression of the philosopher Proclus, is nothing more than "thinner light"; it is not anthropomorphic, it has no privileged points but only directions. In this view of the world, neither convergent representation nor even the idea of a meeting point of the visual rays was possible. Biagio Pelacani da Parma removed any remaining doubts about the matter in *Quaestiones*, written in 1380. He explains that visual rays, which philosophers called *species*, are not mathematical rays; they have dimensions and therefore they cannot converge in one point.

The discovery of perspective brought the Euclidean visual pyramid once more into the center of representation and stopped any further theorizing about parallel projection for almost a hundred years. But, as with military perspective, it was the problem of measuring that caused parallel projection to be reconsidered in the middle of the sixteenth century. This time the subject was not the metaphysical *lux* of thirteenth-century perspectives but rather the physical light of the sun created by God.

In 1551, Oronce Finé[20] once more took up the gnomonic tradition and linked shadow indissolubly to measurement. He observed that "if the said shadow of the sun is precisely at 45 degrees, then all shadowy bodies are equal to their shadows whether right-side round or reversed." A few years later, Gemma Frizon explained how to "find the height of anything by its shadow" and observed that when the sun is at its zenith "the shadows of all objects are equal to those objects."[21] Thus both the plan and the elevation could be measured by shadows, but for the measurement of the elevation, the projection of the sun's rays had to occur obliquely. This oblique shadow is merely the oblique axonometric representation of the body, which, at 45 degrees, becomes an isometry (later called cavalier axonometry).

Before these observations could be reflected in artists' representations, two mathematicians—Guidobaldo del Monte and François d'Aguilon—had to sweep the field clear of all perspectival prejudice. Guidobaldo del Monte, in his first commentary on Juan de Rojas's *Planisphere*, pointed out how the author avoided explaining where the eye must be placed while at the same time deducing everything from perspective; while his master, Frizon, claimed that "oculos in infinitum (si fieri potest) absistat." But, del Monte asked himself, "aliquid ex perspectiva ortum ducere, oculum vero infinita distantia absistere? Hoc nimirum ipsi perspectivae repugnat."[22]

It is clear at this point that parallel projection has nothing to do with perspective, despite the fact that the eye, at an infinite distance, remains the causal center of representation. In perfectly describing the isometric projection of the cube in a hexagon (which Jean Cousin had already drawn in 1560),[23] d'Aguilon talks of "Orthograficae proiectiones" as being that method "in quo oculos a re infinite abesse supponitur" and which can be applied not only to the celestial sphere "sed etiam aedificia quaecumque libuerit describenda occurrunt." But he also claims that "in orthographicis proiecturis radios ducere convenit parallelos" and since they "numquam concurrunt ... ac proinde in orthographicis proiectionibus radij paralleli ducendi sunt, *nulla habita oculi ratione*."[24] Thus the way was definitively opened to the reaffirmation of parallel projection as conceptually different from conical projection. In 1625, Pietro Accolti wrote a book with the evocative title *Lo inganno degl'occhi* (The deception of the eyes) in which he applied parallel projection to the problem of shadow. The theory of shadow was resolved by casting light on a shadow and discovering that it was a representation. Accolti was concerned with the practices of painting and claimed that "the evidence of sight (upon which painting depends) teaches us that shadows of things are cast parallel to the plane, they being at an infinite distance from the Sun. Thus we are able to represent any object as it appears to the Sun's eye. Therefore speculating we understand that the Sun can not ever see the shadow side of objects ... it can see only those parts that are illuminated and can not, on the contrary, see those that remain in shadow.... So we may say that this kind of drawing, being a representation of the Sun's eye, can be done using lines and parallel sides, that never meet at any perspectival converging point."[25]

After almost two hundred years, the concept was coming full circle. Anti-Euclidean parallel projection was returning, not as an all-embracing meta-physical force, but as a means to measure the world and represent it. Indeed, in Desargues's projective geometry, all symbolic connotations were removed

Corps ʃolide.

Plan   Perʃpectif.

Ligne   Terre.

Plan   Geometrial.

E Cube ainʃi dreʃʃé ʃus la pointe, comme deʃia ay parlé cy deuant, fait ʃon plan Geometrial à ʃix faces, comme eʃt icy au
plan mis au deʃʃouz de la ligne Terre, 1. 2. 3. 4. 5. 6: & auʃʃi
party des ʃections Geometriques, comme pouez voir en ce
quarré Geometrial, merqué g. h. i. k, reduires le Perʃpectif en
la maniere cóme les reigles cy deuant miʃes le demonʃtrent,
& le corps ʃolide du Cube, eʃleué ʃus la platte forme Perʃpectiue, merqué des
meʃmes lettres & chiffres, cóme le Geometrial & Perʃpectif facillement & ayʃe-
ment vous le fera entendre, comme pouez voir par ces petites lignes punctees,
prenants leur origine du plan Perʃpectif, leʃquelles eʃtants ʃi bien concatenees
peuuent parler, ʃeullemét à les voir, encor' meʃmes qu'il n'y euʃt aucune deʃcri-
ption & traité fait.

P iij

1.15
Jean Cousin the Elder, orthogonal projection
of the cube (isometric axonometry), from
Livre de perspective (Paris, 1560).

from the "eye of the Sun" and parallel projection became the instrument of exact representation.

The second point, the question of parallel lines, must now be examined. In Renaissance central projection, straight lines parallel to the plane of projection remained parallel by convention, as did lines perpendicular to the ground plane. This maintenance of parallelism is what we might call the Achilles' heel of Euclid's *Elements*: it makes the opposite of the fifth postulate a provable theorem. Proclus, who was the last director of the Platonic Academy in Athens,[26] was perfectly aware of this, and in his very fine *Commentary upon the First Book of Euclid's Elements* he wrote: "Even if the straight lines of the fifth postulate get closer and closer the further into the distance they run, there is no sign of their meeting." Proclus still kept faith with Euclid's lemma, but not everyone agreed. Panofsky said, "According to Kern ... there was a controversy in antiquity and particularly in the Middle Ages over whether 'parallels running off into the distance appear to converge in a single point or not.'"[27] Witelo's *Optica* argued against the theory of the vanishing point ("lineae videbuntur quasi concurrere"), and Panofsky claimed that the concept of the vanishing point could not be fully expressed since the concept of limit was absent and was, in fact, not formulated until the beginning of the seventeenth century by Desargues. In reality, Witelo was against Euclid's theory of vision but was not opposed to Euclid's geometry, which had nothing to do with the problems of representation. However, it is significant that Proclus's confirmation was followed by half a millennium of parallel projection, while the confirmation *per absurdum* expressed by the Jesuit Girolamo Saccheri at the beginning of the eighteenth century led, unintentionally of course, to the non-Euclidean formulations of Carl Gauss, Nikolai Lobachevski, and János Bolyai. These theories were in turn taken up by El Lissitzky as a theoretical explanation for his pictorial concept, which was, in fact, perfectly Euclidean.[28]

As can be seen, the geometrical question of parallel lines penetrated deeply into the mechanism of representation and often affected its figuration. Parallel projection was used to detach early images from the human eye during the first thousand years of the Christian era, when the dawning spirituality of the religion was deeply imbued with Neoplatonism. In Byzantine art, the glittering light of the gold background that projected oblique figures was cast onto the plane of the mosaic. However, these representations were used not only for their optical and geometrical effect, but also because they interpret the opposition to Hellenistic-Roman realism. This opposition had its roots in the thinking of the Neoplatonist philosopher Plotinus (203–270 AD), but was also alive to the mystical and spiritual stimuli that united paganism and early Christianity.

Plotinus and the Problem of Depth

The works of Plotinus were collected in fifty-four treatises and arranged in six *Enneads*, of which the first and the fifth deal with aesthetic problems.[29] For Plotinus, an image was the reflection of the thing that, in accordance with the Stoic principle of universal sympathy, shared the same nature as its model. The purpose of an image was not merely to reproduce the appearance of an object, but rather, to understand the *nous*, the intellect, and through it the universal soul. Yet the necessarily abstract images of art are meant neither to pique aesthetic pleasure nor imitate the appearance of reality nor provide moral teachings. Plotinus therefore found it necessary to establish the conventions today known as the statutes of representation. They stated that to achieve knowledge of the *nous*, the observer had to be acquainted with the physical nature of vision: this was the only way to perceive the message of the work correctly. In considering the problems of vision, in particular the reduction of distant dimensions and the weakening of color in distant objects, Plotinus claimed that the only view faithful to the true sizes and tones of color was the one very close to the eye, which represented the object in its completeness. Only this view made it possible to see things in detail and correctly assess measurements and overall size. Distant objects were indeterminate and thus imperfect; all objects therefore had to be represented in the foreground, in the very fullness of light, with exact colors, and in all their detail and without shadows. This meant avoiding depth, since depth entailed shadow or obscurity and thus empty matter. According to Plotinus, the eye had to become "equal and similar to the object observed in order to contemplate it … one can never see the sun without becoming similar to it, and a soul can never contemplate beauty without being beautiful itself." This form of interpenetration was not possible with the "eye of the body" but only with the "inner eye." The importance of this claim is obvious: when seventeenth-century optics correctly resolved the geometrical problem of vision, it found that the "eye of the body" was only a channel of vision and that perception really began from the retina: what can really see is the "inner eye."

Similar arguments were advanced by mystics before Plotinus and by Christian theologians after him, but his claims are important because they were applied to the problem of representation. They implied that the space between the observer and the object was annulled, and thus also the point of view. Plotinus said that "there is no point at which one can fix one's own limits and say: this is as far as I am up to here." He claimed that perception "clearly takes place where the object is ... to see, it is necessary to lose consciousness of one's own being, it is necessary in some way to stop seeing."

Plotinus's ideas did not have a direct influence on the painting of his day, but they certainly affected representation up until the Middle Ages. Their anti-perspectival characteristics, together with their breadth of philosophical conception, allow us to extend the symbolic scope of the limits that four-teenth-century optics put on fifteenth-century painting. At the same time, it is worth pointing out that parallel projection should have avoided the forma-tion of depth by avoiding convergence, leaving aside the Euclidean "eye of the body." It would have been possible to see the geometry of real measure-ments and understand how the "eye of the sun" was bound to represent it without shadows. The fact that this happens beyond vision is what Plotinus described as "becoming equal and similar to the object." From the fifteenth century onward, the inner eye, freed of its fixed mysticism and the symbolic insularity of painting, moved to become the place of exact knowledge, where measurement shatters the seduction of the gaze.

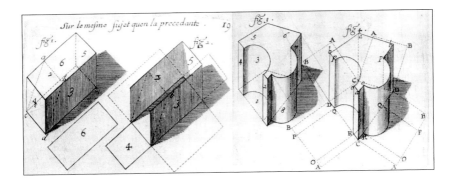

1.16
Abraham Bosse, *Traité des pratiques géométrales et perspectives* ... (Paris, 1665), page 19.

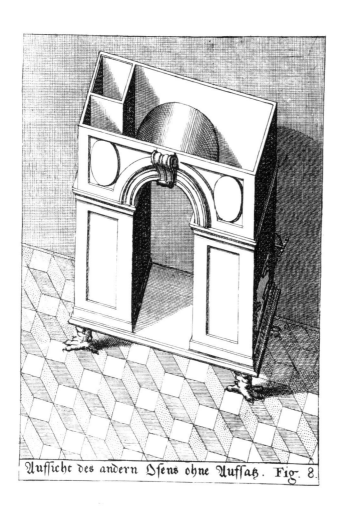

Aufsicht des andern Ofens ohne Auffatz. Fig. 8.

1.17
Stove in "military perspective." L. C. Sturm,
*Ausführliche Anleitung zu der gantzen civil
Baukunst ...* (Wolfenbüttel and Amsterdam,
1699).

Notes

1. Erwin Panofsky, "Die Perspektive als symbolische Form," in *Vorträge der Bibliothek Warburg* (Hamburg, 1924–1925). Italian translation, *La prospettiva come "forma simbolica" e altri scritti*, ed. Guido D. Neri with notes by Marisa Dalai (Milan: Feltrinelli, 1961). English translation, *Perspective as Symbolic Form*, trans. Christopher S. Wood (Cambridge: MIT Press, 1991).

2. See the preface of Bruno Reichlin in *Alberto Sartoris*, exh. cat. (Zurich and Lausanne, 1978); and Yve-Alain Bois, "Metamorphosis of Axonometry," *Daidalos*, no. 1 (1981): 41–58. The arguments that the two authors put forward on "axonometry as a symbolic form" in connection with the historical avant-garde seem highly debatable. Use of the "axonometric method" (van Doesburg) is simply the signal for a different methodology and certainly does not register new systematics. Although perspective was emerging as a symbolic form at the same time as it was being codified during the Renaissance, the axonometry that was "rediscovered" in the 1920s had already concluded its course of scientific codification at least a half century earlier. Apart from the studies by William Farish, Thomas Sopwith, Joseph Jopling, Giovanni Codazza, and Quintino Sella (see the chapter "Drawing in *Paralleli Modi*" in this book), see the seminal work by Julius Weisbach, "Die monodimetrische und axonometrische Projectionsmethode," *Polytechnische Mitteilungen* 1 (Tübingen, 1844). For oblique axonometry see the definitive account given by Karl Pohlke, *Darstellende Geometrie* (Berlin: Gaertner, 1860). The essay by Yve-Alain Bois attributes the first geometrical explanation of axonometry to Christian Rieger's *Perspectiva militaris* (1756), and does not take into account sixteenth-century treatises or the works of François d'Aguilon (see note 24 below); Jean Dubreuil, *La perspective pratique* (Paris: chez la Veuve François L'Anglois, 1651), especially the chapter "De la perspective militaire ou élévations géométrales," 161–171; or Abraham Bosse, *Traité des pratiques géométrales et perspectives* (Paris: chez l'Auteur, 1665), 65–87.

3. Luca Pacioli, *Divina proportione* (Venice: Paganino de' Paganini, 1509).

4. Niccolò Tartaglia, *Questiti et inventioni* (Venice: Venturino Ruffinelli, 1546).

5. Oronce Finé (Orontius Fineus), *Liber de geometria pratica ...* (Strasbourg: Knobloch per Georgium Machaeropoeum, 1544).

6. René Descartes, *Discours de la methode pour bien conduire sa raison ... Plus la dioptrique* (Leyden: imprimerie de Jan Maire, 1637), 113.

7. Philibert de l'Orme, *Le premier tome de l'architecture* (Paris: F. Morel, 1567). For a concise exposition of stereotomy up to the time of Guarini, see Werner Müller, "The Authenticity of Guarini's Stereotomy in his *Architettura Civile*," *Journal of the Society of Architectural Historians* 28, no. 3 (October 1968): 202.

8. Diego Gonzales de Medina Barba, *Examen de fortificación hecho por Don Diego Gonzales de Medina Barba, natural de Burgos* (Madrid: en la imprenta del licenciado Varez de Castro, 1599), 5.

9. Girolamo Maggi and Jacomo Castriotto, *Della fortificazione delle città* (Venice: Rutilio Borgominiero, 1564).

10. Ibid., II, 43.

11. William Farish uses the term "isometrical perspective" in presenting his "invention, which is none other than an isometrical orthogonal projection of the classic cube along the diagonal leading from opposite corners." See "On Isometrical Perspective," *Transactions of the Cambridge Philosophical Society*, no. 1 (1822): 4–9. After Meyer called this type of projection "axonometry" (M. H. Meyer and C. T. Meyer, *Lehrbuch der axonometrischen Projectionslehre* [Leipzig: Haessel, 1852–1862]), we find

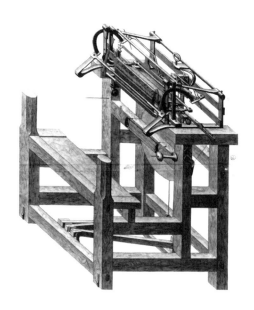

1.18
Jean-Claude Hindret, *Album du métier à faire des bas*, drawing in "soldierly perspective" made on Colbert's orders around 1664. Paris, Bibliothèque Nationale, Cabinet des Estampes Lh. 32. The album was used by Diderot for his *Encyclopédie*.

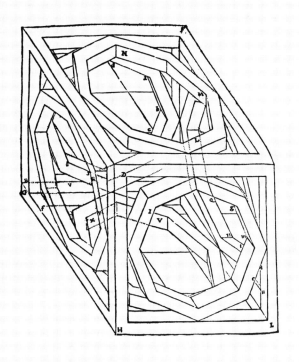

1.19
Pietro Accolti, *Lo inganno degl'occhi. Prospettiva pratica* (Florence, 1625), page 140.

the same imprecisions in successive treatises; Joseph A. Adhémar, *Traité des ombres: théorie des teintes, des points brillants et de la perspective cavalière* (Paris: Armand Colin, 1874–1875), and Nicolas Breithof, *Traité de perspective cavalière* (Paris: Gauthier-Villars, 1881).

12. For example, the term "cavalier perspective" must almost certainly derive from the word "cavalier" as Luigi Marini defined it: "a circular or polygonal elevation ... which dominates the other parts of the fortress ... like a man on a horse, a cavalier, who by virtue of his elevated height can survey all that surrounds him." Luigi Marini, *L'architettura militare di F. Marchi* (Rome: da torchi di M. de Romanis, 1810), 41.

13. Bonaiuto Lorini, *Delle fortificazioni* (Venice: Rampazzetto, 1597), 32–34.

14. Bartolomeo Crescenzio, *Proteo militar di Bartolomeo Romano, diviso in tre libri* (Naples: Gio. Iacomo Carlino e Antonio Pace, 1595), 104.

15. Giovan Battista Belici (Belluzzi), *Nuova inventione di fabbricar fortezze* (Venice: M. Meletti, 1598), 1–6.

16. Jacques Perret, *Des fortifications et artifices, architecture et perspective de Jacques Perret gentilhomme Savoysien. Thomas Le Leu sculpsit* (Paris: Jacques Perret, 1601).

17. Franco Alessio, "Per uno studio sull'Ottica del Trento," *Studi Medievali*, no. 2 (1961): 445–504.

18. Ibid., 467.

19. Alhazen's *Book of Optics* was known in the Christian West long before the translation by Gherardo da Cremona in 1175. Neoplatonist in derivation, it took up the theory of Democritus's *scorze* in contrast to the Euclidean theory.

20. Oronce Finé, *La sphère du monde proprement ditte cosmographie* (Paris: Imprimerie de M. de Vascosan, 1551), 43.

21. Gemma Frizon, *Les principes d'astronomie* (Paris: chez Guillaume Cavellat, 1556), 89.

22. Guidobaldo del Monte, *Planisphaeriorum universalium theorica* (Pesaro: apud Hieronymum Concordiam, 1579), 11, 57.

23. Jean Cousin, *Livre de perspective* (Paris: Imprimerie de J. Le Royer, 1560), iij. As far as we know, this orthogonal projection must be considered the first "isometric axonometric" of the cube in a printed book. Loria attributes this primacy to Kepler in the imperfect figure on pages 58 and 180 of book v, chapter 1 of the *Harmonices mundi* (Linz: sumptibus Godofredi Tampachil Bibl. Francof. Excudebat Ioannes Plancus, 1619) From Gino Loria, *Storia della geometria descrittiva* (Milan: Hoepli, 1921), 412.

24. François d'Aguilon, *Opticorum libri sex* (Antwerp: ex Officina Plantiniana, apud viduam et filios Io. Moreti, 1613), 503.

25. "Insegnandoci il testimonio del senso visivo (al quale unicamente è sottoposta la pittura) manda l'ombre sue, parallele sul piano ... con la infinita distanza del luminoso degli opachi ... così restiamo capaci potersi all'occhio nostro, in disegnar far rappresentazione di quella precisa veduta di qualsivoglia dato corpo, esposto all'occhio (per così dire) del Sole quale ad esso Sole gli si rappresenta in veduta: onde si come specolando intendiamo il Sole non vedere giammai alcuna ombra degl' opachi, e superficie, ch'egli rimiri e illustri, così tutte quelle, che vengono in sua veduta, intendiamo restare lumeggiate e per il contrario tutte le altre a lui ascose restare ombreggiate....Così intendiamo dover essere il suddetto disegno, per rappresentazione di veduta del Sole, terminato con linee, e lati paralleli, non occorrenti a punto alcuno di Prospettiva." Pietro Accolti, *Lo inganno degl'occhi* (Florence: P. Cecconcelli, 1625), 143.

26. Justinian closed down the Academy in 529 AD.

27. Panofsky, *Perspective as Symbolic Form*, 103, n. 22.

28. El Lissitzky, "Kunst und Pangeometrie," in Carl Einstein and Paul Westheim, eds., *Europa Almanach* (Potsdam: Gustav Kiepenheuer, 1925).

29. Even as they adopt a different point of view, the considerations made here are broadly based on the interpretation made by André Grabar in his fundamental essay, "Plotin et les origines de l'esthétique medievale," *Cahiers Archéologiques* 1 (1945): 15–34.

1.20
Rudolf Skuhersky,
*Die orthographische
Parallelperspektive*
(Prague, 1858).

2.1
Paul Klee, *Uncomposed Figures in Space*,
1929. Belp Private Collection. Copyright
SIAE, 2005.

2

SPATIAL ILLUSIONISM IN POMPEIAN WALL PAINTINGS

The Bauhaus, Weimar, 28 November 1921. The subject of Paul Klee's lecture is perspective. He explains to his students that "the point of the entire procedure is simply to be able to exercise control," and that "accurate perspective drawing has no merit whatsoever, if for no other reason than anybody can do it." A few years earlier, Klee had seen perspective disintegrate in the paintings of the Parisian Cubists, which enabled him confidently to state, "There is absolutely no necessity for a single viewpoint. For some time now, though not that long, we have been able to do without."[1]

In 1928, Walter Gropius resigned as director of the Bauhaus. The crafts-based, conservative program of Thuringia was replaced by the industrially based establishment in Hessen where, in 1925, Gropius had built his "Cathedral of the Future." In Dessau the historical avant-garde intermixed with the aseptic-social tendencies of its new director, Hannes Meyer. Klee held a course titled Contributions to a Pictorial Theory of Form (*Beiträge zur bildnerischen Formlehre*), and here, under the heading "Deviation from the Form," Klee gave his students forewarning of the theme of "stray centers," or "stray viewpoints." A year later, he painted *Uncomposed Objects in Space* (1929), in which the entire composition seems governed by linear perspective. In reality, the vanishing point is dislocated to multiple "stray centers" and the perspective is so off center that it could not even be classified as axial or "fishbone" perspective, the latter term having been used by Erwin Panofsky two years before to describe ancient perspective.[2]

In his famous lecture at the Warburg Institute, Panofsky had considered what kind of perspective was used in antiquity, and especially how the sophisticated optics of the classical world had conditioned the practice of ancient perspective, considered antithetical to linear perspective. Panofsky made a brilliant series of links between the optical concepts of antiquity and the work of its artists. The representation method he posited was a complicated spherical perspective that could be schematized in a "fishbone" pattern, in which the points of convergence were aligned on a vertical axis.

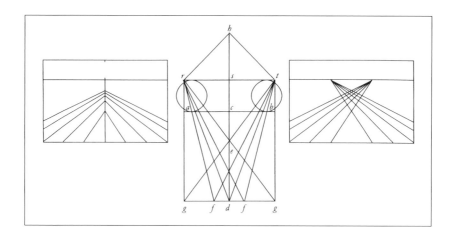

2.2
Panofsky's "fishbone" (left) and Witelo's
axis of receding points according to
binocular vision (center and right).
From Dominique Raynaud, *L'hypothèse
d'Oxford* (Paris, 1998), page 56.

2.3
François d'Aguilon, *Opticorum libri sex*
(Antwerp, 1613).

Klee probably had no direct knowledge of Panofsky's ideas, but he was very familiar with linear perspective, although he chose for artistic reasons not to use it. So, in his watercolor *Uncomposed Objects in Space*, Klee uses converging parallelepipeds to create an apparently unitary composition even though there is no single viewpoint, just several "stray centers" that are not plotted along a vertical axis. In geometrical terms, this is the exact opposite of the Chinese pictorial method, in which the oblique drawing controls the narrative sequence, which is then conveyed onto paper scrolls in an almost filmic sequence.[3] In this way, Klee avoids fixing a human viewpoint within what he defined as the "muddiness of reality." In the 1929 watercolor, a palpable sense of depth is suggested by the combination of the convergence of stray lines and a Leonardesque "lessening light," which plunges the center of the composition into darkness. It would be wholly inappropriate to criticize Klee's painting for its lack of perspectival precision, or to question whether the recession of parallelepipeds in space is correctly executed or not. The illusion is obtained by means of a simple compositional procedure. Clearly, Klee considers the method of pictorial representation to be akin to the musical pentagram, a device for ordering notes that in no way dictates how they are to be composed. The converging stray viewpoints are like harmonic columns that are traversed by melodies, which control in this way the whole composition of the painting. Klee would go on to explore these means further, building an oeuvre that traces the delicate filigree of the human spirit like an X-ray rendition.

Even at the height of Renaissance perspective inquiry, there are many more examples of works that bend the rules of linear perspective than of works that adhere rigidly to them. And often the former are more pictorially interesting than the latter, precisely because of the tendency of perspectival representation to compromise the overall balance of a composition, plunging the whole work into a cone-shaped catastrophe.

But for the viewer, what is the nature of the relationship between Klee's painting and everyday visual experience? In environments that are greatly geometric, such as cities, the apparent convergence of the architectural elements and the straight lines of the streets signal that one is moving through three-dimensional space. The edges of a street may only be seen as parallel in an axonometric representation: if they appear as parallel in real life as well, this means that what is being viewed—and this is only possible from a single viewpoint—is in fact an anamorphic construction. Such a geometrical contrivance sets out deliberately to trick the eye, like the Ames room or a camouflage device. Optical illusions of this kind have always been used in scenography in order to suggest the wide regular spaces of an urban scene within the very shallow space of a stage. Plato makes mention of similar devices being used to create beauty that is only apparent,[4] and Vitruvius refers to these corrections by the term *temperaturae* when applying them to architecture. But since these optical illusions have almost always, from their very beginnings, been created for the pleasure of subsequent recognition, the intelligent observer has never felt the need to repudiate them. After all, illusion is the most desirable gift of pictorial representation and, as Lucretius explained, "From little signs, we conjecture great systems, and we end by being ourselves deceived by the illusion."[5]

Standing in front of a famous colonnade, the author of *De rerum natura* notes,

> A portico,
> Albeit it stands well propped from end to end
> On equal columns, parallel and big,
> Contracts by stages in a narrow cone,
> When from one end the long, long whole is seen,
> Until, conjoining ceiling with the floor,
> And the whole right side with the left, it draws
> Together to a cone's nigh-viewless point.[6]

This is a perfect description of Proposition 12 in Euclid's *Optics*.[7] Lucretius observes that as he moves his eyes gradually toward the far end of the colonnade, the colonnade disappears toward the point of the cone. While giving no clue as to where he noticed this phenomenon, Lucretius does indicate the manner: *paulatim*—by degrees, little by little—"it draws / Together to a cone's nigh-viewless point [*trahit angusti fastigia coni*]." That point, which is appropriately designated in English with the term *vanishing point*, is very distant and the eye cannot perceive it; there is, therefore, no reason to represent it.[8]

Nowhere in the known Latin literature is it written that the point of the cone coincides in the picture with the vanishing point of the orthogonals leading to it; nor is the viewing distance of a painting ever defined. Lucretius is not a scientist and his observation is not addressed to specialists. The poet relates what he sees, as well as what he expects to see and recognize in a painting, according to the concept of *mimesis*. From this activity he derives a simple and immutable pleasure, based on the convictions that, in the infinite space of matter, everything already exists and nothing comes from nothing. Lucretius is not even a philosopher; his is no ideological judgment of appearance or of representation, and he is content to remain with his body and mind enveloped in the reality of phenomena. Nor does he go as far as the great technician of these matters, Vitruvius, who found himself obliged to shortcut when it came to articulating certain complex questions and difficult terms, which he considered to be incomprehensible to most people anyway.[9] Vitruvius's synthetic style of writing could only be understood by those who truly needed to understand his techniques. To this day, experts are unable to explain what exactly is meant by the term *scaenographia*, or understand the role of Agatharchus in Athenian theater, or imagine what was contained in the writings on scenography, which Proclus would link to a catoptric art and which made its images "not seem disporportionate or shapeless when seen at a distance or on an elevation."[10]

Proposition 5 of Euclid's *Optics* establishes that "equal quantities unequally distant [from the eye] appear unequal, the one lying closer to the eye always appearing larger." But in answer to the question of the ratio of this variance, Euclid supplies no hard and fast rule. In fact, Proposition 8 says that "equal lengths placed on the same straight line in a noncontingent fashion and at unequal distances from the eye appear unequal." Ancient painters found a practical way of overcoming this obstacle by successively reducing the distances between transversals by one-third, a method that continued to be used until well into the Renaissance period. The reason for this is that someone who knows how to paint knows that there is always a measure of inaccuracy in evaluating distances and dimensions within the visual field. Furthermore, as the viewer moves forward, a troubling visual absurdity becomes evident: "the space between parallel lines appears unequal when viewed from a distance."[11] The fifteenth-century perspective painters reproduced this phenomenon in their frescoes by means of steeply inclined orthogonal lines. The Chinese painter-literati, on the other hand, were careful never to introduce such exaggerations into their refined watercolors.

If the visual space is modified by the nonproportionality of the evaluation of distances by undefined angles, it nevertheless remains true that everything within it seems to converge by degrees (*paulatim*)[12] toward a center. Given the indeterminate nature of this perception, there is only one geometrical certainty that is easily transferable onto the pictorial surface: the convergence of lines that, in reality, are parallel. And to the painter it is of little consequence whether this convergence ends in an *obscurum coni acumen* or in an "almost at infinite" point or in a precise point on the painting. After all, Alberti never so much as mentioned this embarrassing issue, and two centuries would have to pass before a more precise definition was supplied by Guidobaldo del Monte and Girard Desargues.

If the convergence of Lucretius's colonnade is the element that most characterizes its depth, then it will be enough to move it into the center of the picture, ordering the composition of the architectural elements along the straight lines that fan out from the center point. As far as the relative sizes of the elements are concerned, it is simple to look with one eye at the apparent size of the visible objects, starting from those in the foreground. The system of aligning the eye with the stylus or brush and in turn with the real object in fact contains the three elements necessary and sufficient for a practical perspectival method. It is a method that allows the painter, with certainty and rapidity, to order proportionately each object's height in relation to its distance from the observer. In antiquity, the painter observed the convergences and transferred them onto his painting at arm's length without feeling any need to reflect on what system he was using, however simple it might appear: two similar triangles, one cathetus coinciding with the stylus and the corresponding cathetus being the height of the object covered by the stylus. In this transference procedure, the observed dimensions and the real dimensions are obviously seen from the same viewing angle. The approximation of the viewing angle is reproduced in the certain geometry of the pictorial representation without any need to acknowledge its perspectival nature.

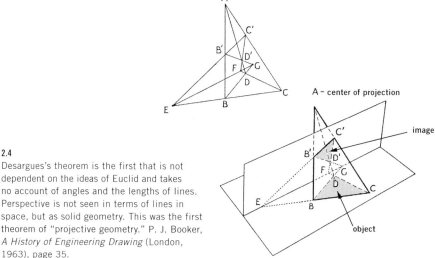

2.4
Desargues's theorem is the first that is not dependent on the ideas of Euclid and takes no account of angles and the lengths of lines. Perspective is not seen in terms of lines in space, but as solid geometry. This was the first theorem of "projective geometry." P. J. Booker, *A History of Engineering Drawing* (London, 1963), page 35.

In fact, the painter's body constitutes in itself a tool for perspective drawings. When a culture decides to portray in a painting that which appears to a person's sight rather than what is there in reality, the body is the most immediately available system of comparison. The painter's body becomes a tool for interpreting the object in space, and the obvious means of translation onto the physical painting is Euclidean geometry, which by no accident is also cited in Islamic art as a synonym of *drawing*.[13] The move toward the formulation of a method that established a set of rules is the result of an elevation in the status of the artist and a consequent will to give a theoretical basis to his work. There was, in fact, no requirement for this in the *techné*-based approach of antiquity, and it would not have improved in the least the artist's ability to render the visible world in his painting. Besides, the language of the *technítes* and the whole technical terminology at use in artists' workshops rarely found its way into learned texts, which tended always to keep practical issues at arm's length, even at the risk of making their authors seem unskilled workers (*idiótai*) compared to those with experience (*graphikói*).[14]

Since the discussion here is limited to certain works and their immediate cultural context, it does not seem necessary to reexamine the very learned debate on "the question of perspective in antiquity" that followed the 1961 publication in Italy of Panofsky's study. Nor does the present discussion wish in any way to widen the heuristic or deepen the hermeneutical methods of previous authors. Although it may seem to narrow the scope of our inquiry, the only reference text that will be alluded to with any certainty here will be Lucretius's *De rerum natura* (*On the Nature of Things*). Observations on Euclid's *Optics* clearly form the backdrop to this work, but there is no explicit mention of pictorial representation or of planar intersection of the visual cone, which can be found only in the refined world of Apollonius of Perga's conic sections. Moving forward in time, Ptolemy's[15] observations, which were only twenty years old when the "Pompeian painting" period was drawing to a close (around 120 AD), are fascinating but of little help.[16]

Let us now consider the examples from the Villa Poppaea at Oplontis near Pompeii and the famous fresco with triple barrel vaults in the Villa of the Mysteries at Pompeii.[17] The first thing we notice is that all of these compositions have a painted architectural framework that extends over the whole painted surface of the fresco. On top of this *scaenae frons* is painted a simple convergence of lines, which evoke the presence of a colonnade. The impression of depth is entrusted to the shadows of those elements that project from the architectural elevation and to the receding lines that appear in small areas

2.5
Fresco 1 on Wall A of Room E2 of the
Villa Poppaea, Oplontis: width 8.8 m,
height 5.7 m.

2.6
Fresco 2 on Wall B of Room E1 of the
Villa Poppaea, Oplontis: width 6.9 m,
height 4.1 m.

2.7
Fresco 3 on Wall B5 of Room H2 of the
Villa Poppaea, Oplontis: width 4.6 m,
height 2.8 m.

2.8
Fresco 4 on Wall A4 of Room H2 of the
Villa Poppaea, Oplontis: width 4.5 m,
height 2.9 m.

2.9
Fresco 5 on Wall A of Room H1 of the
Villa Poppaea, Oplontis: width 2.5 m,
height 3.4 m.

2.10
Fresco 6 in Alcove B, Cubiculum 16 (Maiuri),
the Villa of the Mysteries: width 2.4 m,
height 3 m.

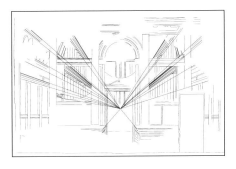
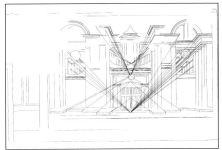
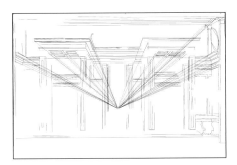
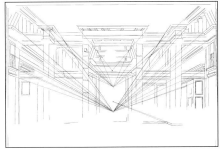
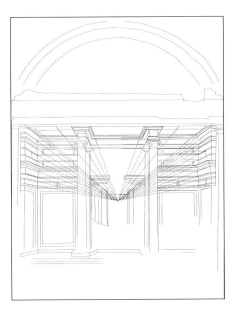
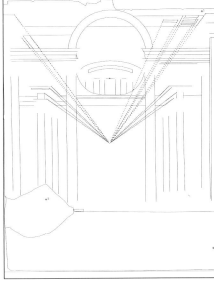

above it. When the central portion of the scene is not hidden by a wall, the parallels receding toward the center are covered by *thóloi* or by a dark area, a fig leaf, which even Renaissance painters will not be ashamed to have recourse to fourteen centuries later.

The remains of Pompeii represent a remarkable body of artistic achievement produced over a period of about two hundred years. To this day, there is no certain indication, in either pictorial or literary form, of the existence of a perspective system in painting during the Greco-Roman period.

It is worth noting, however, that given the very advanced scientific levels of the works of Aristarchus of Samos, Archimedes, Euclid, Apollonius, and the Democritean school, classical antiquity had at its disposal a body of optical-geometrical knowledge that it used in order to resolve the problem of perspective in the theater. On the other hand, the relationship between scientific elaboration and its application in painting today is perhaps comparable to the total absence of a relationship between a software designer making programs for the modeling of solids and a common user: in each case there are two parallel worlds that do not communicate but that inhabit the same space at the same time and use the same instruments. If a point of contact ever existed, it must have been in the art of stage design. Given the importance of the theater in the Greek city-states, it is hard to believe that the objections of the philosophers could have been so strenuous as to prevent the application of geometrical optics to such simple problems as theatrical representation. For this reason, before looking at the results of the analysis of the fresco in Villa of the Mysteries, three points should be addressed.

First, in looking at a supposedly perspectival pictorial representation, it is almost impossible to deduce the nature of the physical structure that it describes without knowledge of certain geometrical elements. Any shape drawn on a two-dimensional plane may correspond to an infinite number of real objects. The example of Jean Dubreuil shows clearly how a monocular vision may lead to extraordinary misunderstandings as to the nature of the observed object. A table devised by François d'Aguilon demonstrated the dual viewpoint hypothesis, which a recent study improbably proposed as an explanation of Panofsky's "fishbone" system.[18]

Second, in a pictorial representation, space is immediately evoked by a composition of converging lines. To obtain this impression, one has only to draw a series of elements progressively receding back into space, and no knowledge of the methods of linear perspective are necessary to do this.

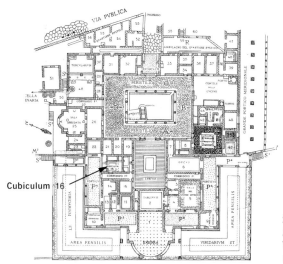

Cubiculum 16

2.11
Amedeo Maiuri, floor plan of the
Villa of the Mysteries at Pompeii.
Pompei (Rome, 1931), page 79.

2.12
Coffered vault in Alcove A, Cubiculum
16 (Maiuri), first century AD. Villa
of the Mysteries, Pompeii.

2.13
Fresco in Alcove A, Cubiculum 16, first
century AD. Villa of the Mysteries, Pompeii.

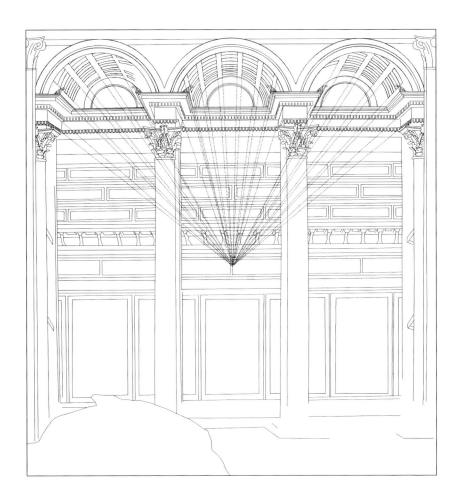

2.14
Alcove A, Cubiculum 16. Digital elaboration
from photogrammetric survey.

Third, it is not very important to know whether the painters who worked in the House of Livia on the Palatine in Rome or at the House of Nero's wife Poppaea at Oplontis represented the end of a glorious Greek-Hellenistic tradition or were novices setting out on a modest Rome-based career. They were certainly very good painters, conscious of their own excellence, aware of fashions, and alert to the whims of their potential clients. And it doesn't seem very meaningful to justify their lack of rigor in perspectival representation in terms of their technical decadence: perhaps one might simply assume that they were unaware of it, or that they found it too complicated, which is the case with many painters today. What I want to underline here is the necessity of maintaining a methodological alignment of the extant works with the descriptions of Lucretius. The interpretation of a work seems acceptable until such time as the center of gravity of critical thought falls within the work's interior, and thus into its space and its time. Each subsequent movement toward the exterior risks a loss of meaning and leads inevitably to the work no longer being used as an object of inquiry, but instead to demonstrate a thesis.

The fresco in Alcove A in Cubiculum 16 (in Amedeo Maiuri's numeration) in the Villa of the Mysteries[19] is among the smallest of the seven we have examined: it is 230 centimeters wide by 300 centimeters high. The theatrical character of the painted architecture is particularly evident in this work. Four metal ties hold the Corinthian columns at a distance from the wall with "incrustation style" decorations. This method of affixing painted wings and isolated wooden elements is characteristic of stagecraft. This cubiculum, which contained the bed, is surmounted by a coffered barrel vault, the curved framework of which shares the same geometrical characteristics as the painted, coffered, triple-barreled vaults. Together with the more famous fresco of the House of Livia on the Palatine, the fresco in Cubiculum 16 is perhaps the most studied example and the one most often cited as evidence in defense of the use of linear perspective in antiquity, as opposed to Panofsky's hypothesized spherical perspective. This is because both of these frescoes present in a particularly evident fashion a set of lines that are seemingly perpendicular to the pictorial plane and converge toward a single point. Careful inspection of the painting in Alcove A reveals that the three semicircular sections of the vaults are aligned with a deviation of less than two centimeters on the same line that runs along the upper part of the trabeation. The receding lines of the coffers all meet at a single, central point, at a height of 165 centimeters from the present-day floor. Careful analysis of the squared decorative panels or coffers[20] in each vault has revealed that they number seven in depth and seven around the circumference of the intrados. On the basis of a photogrammetric survey, Camillo Trevisan has built for the author a three-dimensional digital model, and three hypotheses as to the perspectival scheme have been formulated:

First hypothesis: the viewing distance is equal to half of the width of the fresco so that the optical cone of the observer can take in almost the whole of the fresco except for the lower section, which has its own, different vanishing point, slightly lower compared to that of the principal cone.

Second hypothesis: the viewing distance is equal to the width of the fresco.

Third hypothesis: the viewing distance is equal to three times the width of the fresco.

None of these three perspectival schemes would produce an image comparable to the existing one. For the barrel vaults to appear as they do in the fresco there would need to be three different viewpoints aligned with the top of the pillars supporting the vaults, and each would have to be observed at a distance equal to half of the width of the fresco. In this way, the half-circles at the back of the vaults would appear as in the fresco, aligned horizontally on the same line as the viewpoints. The lines of convergence from the coffers should actually have three different vanishing points rather than a single one at a height of 165 centimeters from the floor, as the painter has effectively suggested.

A second, though unlikely, way of obtaining the same pictorial representation of the three vaults is illustrated in the diagram in figures 2.18 and 2.19, which shows how the vaults would have to be constructed in order for us to see them with a central perspective from a single viewpoint and with their vanishing point coinciding with the central point of the fresco. These hypothetical vaults, which diverge and extend upward, have the same depth as regular vaults according to the basic digital model. The distance from the viewpoint to the vanishing point is equal to two-fifths of the width of the wall. But this perspectival arrangement only corresponds to the painted image if the coffers have an irregular construction, as shown in the illustration.

From the foregoing, the following conclusions may be drawn: the upper part of the fresco has a geometric construction that satisfies compositional requirements and has a remarkably illusionist feel. The painter's only concern has been to make the receding lines from the architectural elements jutting out toward the spectator center on a single vanishing point in the painting. The proposed geometrical construction shows how the vaults might have been located in depth by means of a simple procedure that could be carried

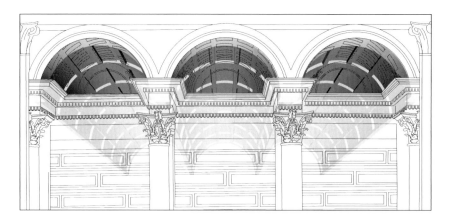

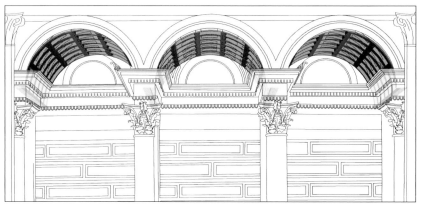

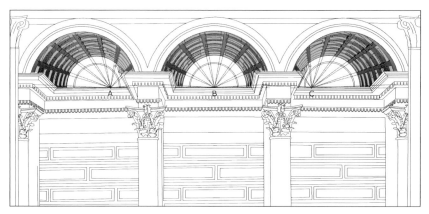

2.15–2.17
First, second, and third hypotheses.

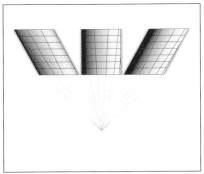

2.18, 2.19
How the vaults should be configured
according to the perspective shown in
the fresco.

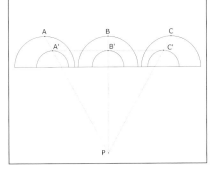

2.20
Geometric construction for positioning
the half-circles at the back of the
barrel vaults.

out directly on the wall. As is evident in the geometrical diagram in figures 2.18 and 2.19, the painter has first chosen an appropriate size for the central semicircle and has then simply reproduced it on either side, moving it to the left or right and making sure that the line from point A to point P meets the arch at its highest point. The construction is valid for whatever position P is in. Analysis of the other frescoes does not show the characteristic "fish-bone" perspective system theorized by Panofsky. The points of convergence arranged vertically along a central axis are necessary in order to avoid too steeply recessing lines in the upper and lower part of the fresco. In this way, the "stray centers" help mitigate the compositional rigidity that would have resulted from a single vanishing point, exactly as Paul Klee would find eighteen centuries later.

Notes

1. Paul Klee, *Beiträge zur bildnerischen Formlehre*, ed. Jürgen Glaesemer (Basel: Schwabe, 1979), 1:14–15.

2. Erwin Panofsky, *Perspective as Symbolic Form* (1924–1925), trans. Christopher S. Wood (Cambridge: MIT Press, 1991).

3. The linear perspective system of Western art and the axonometric or parallel system of Eastern art are manifestations of two different world viewpoints and two different conceptions of the art object. In the former, the artist is at the center of nature; in the latter it is nature that is central while the artist is only the interpreter, the go-between. In Western art, the manipulation of form is acceptable for the sake of beauty, while Oriental art demands total respect for the natural form and for the calligraphic gesture that poetically evokes its essence.

4. Plato, *Sophist* 235d–236c.

5. "Deinde adopinamur de signis maxima parvis ac nos in fraudem induimus frustraminis ipsi." Lucretius, *De rerum naturae* 4.816–817.

6. Ibid., 4.426–431. Translation by William Ellery Leonard.

7. The optical cone faithfully follows Euclid's second Premise: "The figure contained in the visual rays is a cone whose point is at the eye and whose base is the edge of the object." It is twice mentioned here and what Lucretius sees obeys the laws of Euclidean optics. Euclid, *Optics*, Premise 2.

8. According to Beyen, the direct source for the passage in Lucretius regarding the vanishing point in space is Epicurus; indirectly the sources Democritus and the anonymous author of an *aktinographia* (treatise on rays) and of a *peri zographias* (treatise on the art of painting) who according to Plutarch described sectioning the optical cone parallel to its base. Plutarch, *De communibus notitiis adversus Stoicos* 39.3. Cf. H. G. Beyen, "Die antike Zentralperspektive," *Jahrbuch des deutschen archäologischen Instituts* 54 (1939): 47–72.

9. "But this cannot be the case with architectural treatises because those terms which originate in the peculiar needs of the art give rise to obscurity of ideas from the unusual nature of language. Hence while the things themselves are not well known, and their names not in common use, if, besides this, principles are described in a very diffuse fashion without any attempt at conciseness and explanation in a few pellucid sentences, such fullness and amplitude of treatment will be only a

hindrance, and will give the reader nothing but indefinite notions. Therefore, when I mention obscure terms, and symmetrical proportions of members of buildings, I shall give brief explanation, so that they may be committed to memory: for thus expressed, the mind will be enable to understand them the more easily." Vitruvius, *The Ten Books on Architecture*, trans. Morris Hicky Morgan (Cambridge: Harvard University Press, 1914), 5.2.

10. Proclus, *A Commentary on the First Book of Euclid's Elements*, trans. Glenn R. Morrow (1970; Princeton: Princeton University Press, 1992), 33. Proclus was the last director of the Platonic Academy of Athens; he died in 485 AD.

11. Euclid, *Optics*, Proposition 6.

12. *Paulatim* means "little by little" or "gradually."

13. In Islamic art, the pictorial skills of the famous Mani are still linked to the figure of Euclid, both in geometrical and in optical terms: "Shapur is said to excel Mani in painting and Euclid in drawing." Priscilla Soucek, "Nizami on Painters and Painting," in Richard Ettinghausen, ed., *Islamic Art in the Metropolitan Museum of Art* (New York: Metropolitan Museum of Art, 1972), 11.

14. Lucian, *Zeuxis or Antiochus* 3.5.

15. In Ptolemy's *Optics* the perspective process is clearly expounded with regard to the reflection of images on the surface of mirrors: "In all mirrors we find that if, on the surface of any one of them, we mark the points in those places where objects appear and we cover them, the form of the object will not appear in any way. But when, one after the other, we uncover them and look at the parts we have uncovered, the marked points will appear and instantaneously also the form of the object, according to the original direction of the visual rays. And if we turn tall, straight objects perpendicularly to the surface of the mirror at a moderate distance, the reflected image and the same objects that one sees directly outside will appear on a single straight line. From both of these experiences the object must appear in the mirror on the point of intersection between the visual ray and the perpendicular line that falls from the object onto the mirror." *L'Ottica di Claudio Tolomeo da Eugenio Ammiraglio di Sicilia, scrittore del secolo XII, ridotta in latino sovra la traduzione araba di un testo greco imperfetto* … , ed. Gilberto Govi (Turin: Stamperia Reale della ditta G. B. Paravia e C di I. Vigliardi, 1885), 82–83.

16. According to Alix Barbet, Pompeian perspective developed over the course of two generations: the last

three Second Styles from 100 BC to 20 BC; the Third Style from 15 BC to 40 AD; the Fourth Style from 50 AD to 90 AD. See Alix Barbet, *La peinture murale romane. Les styles décoratifs pompéiens* (Paris: Picard, 1985), 273.

17. This study originated from research undertaken at the beginning of the 1980s together with Camillo Trevisan, who at the time was a research assistant for the Theory and History of Representational Methods course conducted by the author. On that occasion, a photogrammetric survey was carried out in the Villa of the Mysteries and in the Villa Poppaea at Oplontis. The analyses did not, however, give rise to any relevant data, but led to serious reservations about the spherical perspective method proposed by Erwin Panofsky. The problem was set aside in the hope that further studies might bring about a comparison of the compositional techniques of a more extensive group of works. It goes without saying that any errors that might emerge from the present study are the sole responsibility of the author.

18. Dominique Raynaud, *L'hypothèse d'Oxford. Essai sur l'origine de la perspective* (Paris: Presses Universitaires de France, 1998), 54–61.

19. Amedeo Maiuri, *Pompei* (Rome: Libreria dello Stato, 1931), 78, fig. 15.

20. It has been assumed, through the analysis of a series of Pompeian examples, that the coffers in the vaults are square-shaped.

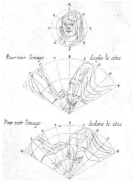

2.21, 2.22
Jean Dubreuil, *Troisième et dernière partie de la perspective pratique* (Paris, 1649), pages 147 and 121.

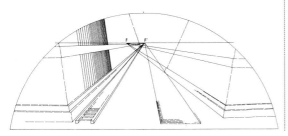

2.23
Paolo Uccello, *The Flood*, reconstruction of perspective scheme with two vanishing points. Dominique Raynaud, *L'hypothèse d'Oxford* (Paris, 1998), figure 22.

3.1
Base of the statue of Djoser with
inscription showing titles of Imhotep.
Egyptian Museum, Cairo. JE 49889.

3.2
Base of the statue of Djoser showing the
king's feet standing on nine bows (enemies).
The three lapwings (*rekhyt*) at his feet
symbolize the common people. Egyptian
Museum, Cairo. JE 49889.

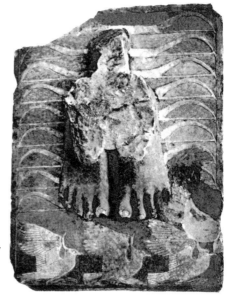

3

OBLIQUE DRAWING

Ancient Egypt was centripetal: it neither expanded like Rome nor established colonies like Greece. Its physical boundaries were like the waters of the Nile, without beginning or end, and its political boundaries were unimportant, for the king was universal ruler. This belief was reiterated during the Feast of the Jubilee (*heb-sed*) when the king fired arrows into the four corners of the universe. In the course of this impenetrable ritual, the royalty would take possession of the north-south axis of the river course and the east-west axis of the sun.[1] Egypt's sovereignty, however, was contested by the inhabitants of the arid border regions, the Asians, the Libyans, and the Nubians. These enemies of Egypt are traditionally represented by the symbol of the nine bows,[2] which appears both in statues of the pharaoh, where they are trampled under his feet, and on the inner soles of his sandals.

In order to keep the nine bows at bay, the kings had to keep moving the frontiers of the world away from Egypt: to the east toward the land of the Euphrates, to the south toward the third Nubian cataract as far as Napata,[3] and to the west toward the coast of Libya. In this way, royalty kept the representation of territorial unity stable, preventing chaos from prevailing and allowing the waters of the Nile to form a black ribbon of mud along the edges of the red desert.

Egypt's real obsession was not the conquest of new lands but keeping together its own: the northern lands (the cobra, *wadjet*) had to be kept united with those of the south (the vulture, *nekhbet*) so that the irrigation of the fields could be controlled and the two lands might be allowed to breathe together, as in the hieroglyph *sema* which united the heraldic plants of the south and the north on either side of the throne.[4] The people (*rekhyt*) knew that the king guaranteed justice and cosmic balance, that the river current would always carry the boats toward the Delta, and that the constant north wind would blow them toward Aswan, where there are the last falls in the Nile's course. They knew that at the beginning of every year the river would burst its banks and that the sun Ra would accompany the king on his last journey, to be born together with him again and for "millions of years" to come.[5]

In the Black Earth country (*kemet*),[6] cyclical time was always reset from the beginning, and symbols took on a significance and density of meaning that is unthinkable in later Western culture. Nature accompanied the life of the Egyptian in a journey around himself, without craving for truth or for conquest, an earthly journey to which the *Song of the Harpist* did not, as might be imagined from the splendid funeral accoutrements, invite conclusion. Every Egyptian knew all too well that there is no return from death.[7] This is why the son built a decorous tomb in order to "render the name of the living father,"[8] and why Sinuhe returned to Egypt in order to be "saved from death":[9] it is difficult to imagine anything less mysterious or more human. So it comes as no surprise that Ineni announces the death of Tuthmosis I in the simplest terms: "The king, arrested from life, going forth to heaven, having completed his years with gladness of heart";[10] nor are we disappointed by the calm composure with which he announces the accession of his heir: "The Hawk [Horus] in the nest [appeared as] the King of Upper and Lower Egypt, Okheperenre [Tuthmosis II], he became King of the Black Land and ruler of the Red Land, having taken possession of the Two Regions in triumph."[11]

Were it not for the difficulty of hieroglyphic script, the figures in the temples and tombs would also seem like tranquil memorial elegies, stone encyclopedias in which are inscribed cosmogonies, accounts of voyages and battles, lists of kings, and "formulas for going out in the day time."[12] Impenetrable for most, the figurative culture of Egypt is striking for an extraordinary coherence and precision that has no equal in the history of humanity. It underwent very few outside influences, and most of these involved technical innovations, such as the Asiatic chariot in the New Kingdom. On the other hand, it radiated far and wide: its characteristic features are to be found along the eastern coast as far as Ebla, while the fascinating cult of the magician Isis reached Rome and even Paris.[13] Even the Ptolemaic conquerors had their portraits done in the Egyptian style, and when Napoleon's scientists returned to France, they brought with them not just a drawn description of ancient Egypt but also a style that would become known as the *retour d'Egypte*.[14]

Over the course of her three-thousand-year history, Egypt seems continually to return to where she began without appearing to have grown or progressed.[15] Her divinities showed men the rules, the rites, and the forms of life. They were rewarded with excellence of execution and constant repetition of stylistic choices through time: qualities that explain the inimitable

3.3
Hunting in the desert, tomb of Raemkai,
Fifth Dynasty. Metropolitan Museum
of Art, New York, Rogers Fund, 1908.
Accession number 08.201.1g.

3.4
Deciphering hieroglyphic inscriptions,
by Henry George Fischer, *L'écriture
et l'arte de l'Egypte ancienne* (Paris,
1986), pp. 27–28 and figure 2.

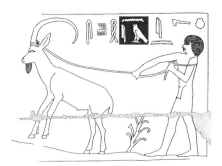

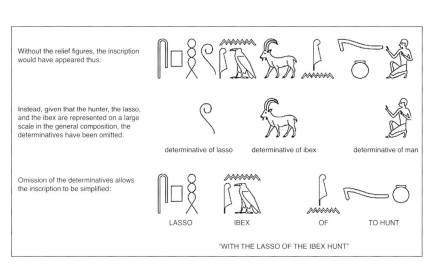

Without the relief figures, the inscription
would have appeared thus:

Instead, given that the hunter, the lasso,
and the ibex are represented on a large
scale in the general composition, the
determinatives have been omitted:

determinative of lasso   determinative of ibex   determinative of man

Omission of the determinatives allows
the inscription to be simplified:

LASSO   IBEX   OF   TO HUNT

"WITH THE LASSO OF THE IBEX HUNT"

essentiality of the Egyptian style. A painter-scribe knew that to be worthy of remembrance in the future and to earn the trust of the king he had to attain a level similar to that of the best works of the past and offer them again as if for the first time.[16] Like hieroglyphic script, the figures in the tombs always looked to the beginning of the phrase, where the meaning was formed: every temple was a representation of the very first building; every elevation was the first tumulus; every living king was Horus; every bride was the sister Isis; every dead king was Osiris.[17] This is why the noble Ineni felt he was measuring himself against the fathomless greatness of his predecessors, declaring that he had completed "a work such as the ancestors had not done."[18] Within this concept of regeneration and renewal, death was seen as an essential component of life rather than as an annihilation. The apostle Paul will have no qualms about using the same idea at the dawning of Christian thought: "That which thou sowest is not quickened, except it die."[19]

Everything in Egypt was powered by a mysterious dynamism that kept the pulse of the world in equilibrium; despite appearing immobile, this world was constantly being transformed. Wavering between representation and life, between reality and magic, this equilibrium culminated in that sharp hieroglyphic figuration, with its orthogonal distinctness of outline, its rare frontal views, and its absence of points of view and foreshortening.[20] In Egyptian art, everything that existed had to be included in the representation according to the principle of maximum evidence. Dwelling in the hieroglyphs in the darkness of the tombs are the dangerous scorpion or the horned viper, which the prophylactic statues attempted to exorcise. In order to prevent them emerging from the shadowy rows of script and endangering the afterlife of the king, the scribe mutilated them, depriving them of their deadly venom.

No other culture experienced the representation of the world with such veracity, and none has attempted belief in the illusion of life after death with such joyous knowingness. It would almost seem that, in comparison to how the life of man was represented pictorially, his actual life was limited to a series of theatrical scenes, part of a drama in which frail bodies were temporarily clothed in the unchanging forms of hieroglyphs. How else can we explain the belief that the multiform spectacle of life was created by "divine words" (*medw neter*)[21] and that once they had been spoken by Ptah, these words had the magic power to create things, stamping their shape onto inert matter? By way of a sublime yet difficult *aporia*, words entered into signs and they became the world. Within those signs the things of the world converse, even without sounds. So in Egypt everything moved forward while looking back-

3.5, 3.6
Statue representing Hemiunu, a high-ranking dignitary, architect, and relative of King Khufu (Cheops), Fourth Dynasty, discovered in the *serdab* of the mastaba of Giza (G4000). Next to his feet is an inscription containing his titulary: "Member of a restricted circle, high official, vizier, keeper of the seals, attendant at the city of Nejhen, representative of every inhabitant of Pe, priest of Bastet, of Shesmetet, of Ram of Mendes, guardian of the Apis bull and of the White bull beloved by his king, elder of the Palace, priest of Thoth, beloved by his king, member of the court, overseer of the royal scribes, priest of the goddess Pantera, director of the Singers of Upper and Lower Egypt, overseer of the king's works, son of the same body of the king (relative), Hemiunu." (Translation by James P. Allen.) Pelizaeus Museum, Hildesheim.

3.7
Djoser during the feast of *Heb-sed*. Saqqara, South Tomb.

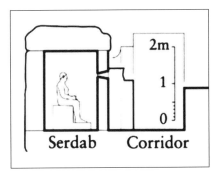

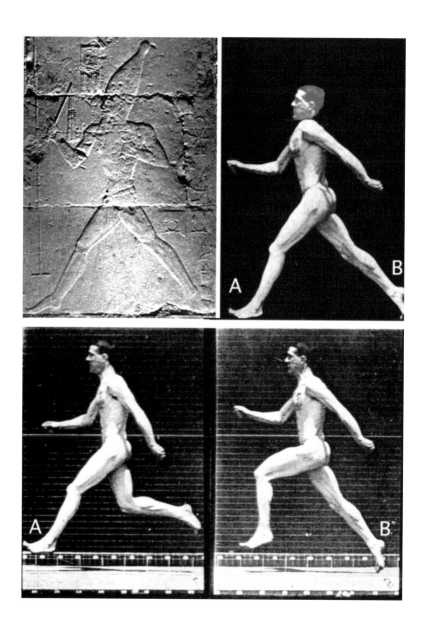

3.8
Comparison of Djoser running (above left)
and Eadweard Muybridge's photograms
(below). The image above right is a composite
of the legs taken from photograms A
and B, which demonstrates that Djoser is
not running.

ward toward a primordial chaos that had already expressed the pronounce-able and had already generated the totality of all things. It is a fascinating idea that, thousands of years later, will reemerge in the words of the apostle John: "In the beginning was the Word, and the Word was with God, and the Word was God."[22]

The Egyptian artist enjoyed a social status that was incomparably superior to his Greek equivalent.[23] The *scribe of contours* lived within the sphere of the sacred and was answerable to one man only: the king, son of Ra. He worked on the shadow line that divided the hidden from the evident, the eternal from the everyday, the living sacred from the sacred that was dead. He was a magi-cian who created images in which the balsam of eternity passed into form, who created substitute entities capable of providing consolation for the pre-carious nature of earthly life. The hieroglyphs that he drew were not simply a form of writing, for they expressed things that could not be translated in their entirety into any other language. Translations leave in their wake a dust cloud of images that have a life of their own and may combine with each other according to a kind of logic that is far beyond the acronym or the rebus.[24] Egyptian written culture was evocative and full of the kinds of emotions that only images can transmit, yet it also had the immediacy and profundity of myth. The scribe wove together figures, synecdoches, and sounds in a series of juxtapositions that Jean-François Champollion defined as monstrous, and that resulted in an inextricable and enduring transmutation of correspon-dences that are untranslatable within the spectrum of alphabetic writing.

The figures of the dead in the tombs ignore the observer. Their existence is not dependent upon a third party but implicates the text to which they be-long. Those who must observe, such as the statue of the deceased peering out from the *serdab* at those bringing offerings, remain hidden from view. The extraordinary statues of the architect Hemiunu and of Djoser sat waiting in these cells in which a tiny hole allowed communication between the dead and the living.

In contrast, figures carved in relief on walls are immersed in the text[25] and look only upon their own meaning. So extreme is their bone-muscle torsion that the naturalness of their pose, which they exhibit so disarmingly, is nonetheless improbable.[26] This twisting position allows their bodies to be anchored to an anthropometrical-structural grid modulated on the position of the hairline, the nose, shoulders, hips, knees, and ankles.[27]

In reality, it is not the body but the combinatory capacity of hieroglyphic script that bestows meaning and allows the transfiguration of the king into

Horus, Thoth, or Osiris. The variation of attributes comes about within the writing itself and not as a result of morphological modifications of the person. This is seen clearly in the sarcophagus chamber of Tuthmosis III, in which the father Ra is not the sun but the Great All: "He is the one and only god that has divided himself up into millions of gods … he whose forms are his becoming."[28] Despite the schematic character of their postures, the bodies on the walls seem normal, just as the activities they are engaged in and the lists of offerings seem normal. But even a brief analysis demonstrates inconsistencies, which are very evident: the feet and hands are shown from the same sides; the head is wedged tightly between the shoulders; the eye is represented frontally on a face shown in profile; the chest is drawn in three-quarters profile with a belly button but only one nipple; the upper lip is rotated in comparison to the lower; and then there is the unexpected elongation of the body, which, after the Fifteenth Dynasty, produces figures that are more slender than those of the Middle Kingdom. Rarely does the observer stop to notice these anomalies because the body is portrayed in much the same way as a piece of writing in which the impression of the whole is more powerful than each single part. As a result, the elements of the body strike the mind more than the eye. The task of composing various parts on the bone and muscle canvas is absolutely coherent with Egyptian art's hieroglyphic approach to representing the human body: the body does not portray a living organism but an ideogram, with all the dislocations and rotations that the principle of maximum evidence imposes on a lucid exposition. A symbol, like a letter of the alphabet, is unimpaired by distortion and possesses the fortunate characteristic of persisting through time, notwithstanding different handwriting or an incorrect reading posture. Thanks to the directional equivalency of its meaning, the body may be clothed in those attributes that most appropriately confer information about its social status. Thus the body's representation becomes the control center of the scenes, governing the hierarchies of size, and gestures of submission, deference, and of service; above all it becomes a point of reference for the directionality of the texts that surround it. This is particularly evident in the registers of the tombs of the Old Kingdom[29] where there is no unity of time and space, which can be confusing for the observer who does not relate them to the diachrony of a list. A process akin to this is seen in the Egyptian phonetic system whereby vowels (weak in the northern Semitic languages) are assigned the necessary inflections but shift only minimally the general meaning, which is bound instead to the unchanging framework of consonants.

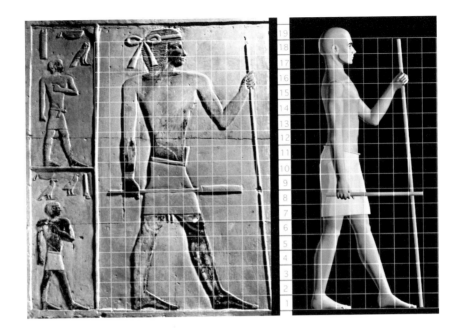

3.9
Comparison between the figure of Neferi,
Fourth Dynasty (Giza PM50), and a
modern mannequin posed as if walking at
a solemn gait.

The artist in Egypt[30] aimed to create something that did not exist *at the origins*, and to create it for reasons and according to procedures not contained in any extant text. Leaving aside the idea of originality, one thing seems clear enough: Egyptian artists had a remarkable ability to capture the essential forms of objects and of living things and to breathe life into them through a few millimeters of relief. After almost six millennia, the stela of Djoser in the South Tomb at Saqqara raises an embarrassing question: who could do better than this and why? What makes the observer feel like an intruder in this place is the fact that the noble figure that appears before his eyes truly does exist, and it moves. It belongs not to the world of appearances, but to the world of living beings. Djoser comes to a halt when he is lit by a raking light, but then he continues running in darkness toward an eternity "of millions of years," brushing as he does so against buildings that tower thirty meters above his head and that have been miraculously constructed in stone by Imhotep for the first time in the history of humanity. The sculptor of these stelae has succeeded in creating actual substitutes of the living being, admirably fulfilling one of the requisites of the painter in ancient Egypt, which was to "preserve life," conferring the breath of life upon his effigies by means of the ceremony of the opening of the mouth. In contrast, the Greek artist-craftsman practiced no such magic, and limited himself to "describing life": he was a *zoográphos*.[31] Perhaps this is why no Greek architect ever had his name sculpted next to that of his sovereign, as Imhotep did: "sole companion of the king of Higher and Lower Egypt, Djoser, the Horus-Netjerikhet."[32]

According to Greek tradition, the plan used by Daedalus for constructing the Cretan labyrinth was discovered in the tomb of an Egyptian pharaoh.[33] Daedalus also seems to have appropriated from Egypt the art of statuary with disunited legs (walking figures) and applied eyes. Imhotep was deified in the Hellenistic era and has even been identified with Asklepios, the god of medicine. For this and other reasons, Philip of Opus writes that there is no doubt of Greece's debt to Egypt, but that the merit of refining and bringing to a fruitful conclusion the premises laid down by the Egyptians belongs to the Greeks.[34] Twenty-one centuries later, Giacomo Leopardi would find himself unable to attribute the same merit to modernity, for "everything has been perfected since the time of Homer, but not poetry."[35] The same poetry of Homer guided the decisions of Alexander the Great. After the conquest of Egypt, the white-haired poet appeared to him in a dream and indicated the place where the city of Alexandria should be founded,[36] just as Gudea had received advice from God about the form of the temple of Lagash.[37] If, for Alexander, the poet of the Iliad was a "very knowledgeable architect," for Plato he was a dangerous trickster. Plato's judgment, as expressed in the *Republic*, leaves us in no doubt: among those myths that ought to be dispensed with, he says, are first and foremost "those narrated by Homer, by Hesiod and other poets, who have recounted and continue to recount false myths to men."[38] Upon returning from the unhappy political experiment of Syracuse, Plato seems to interrupt the dialog between the "I" and the world: man does not see with his eyes, but *through* his eyes. Primitive dialog, bereft as it was of analysis and conclusions, left man immersed in events, in direct contact with the experience of everyday reality. But the downward plunge of philosophical thought into the emotive depth of myth brings to light a third interlocutor: the mind that retreats from the world in order to reason through the senses, to establish laws and predict their behaviors.[39] Although it continues to "proclaim and elaborate a poetic form of truth," the mythical dimension retreats before philosophy, which instead sacrifices the immediate perception of the world to the truth of science (*epistéme*).[40] And when, in the fifth century BC the government of "the best" (*áristoi*) came into conflict with that of "the equal" (*homói*), discussions about democracy promoted literacy among citizens and mythological themes were replaced by domestic and theatrical themes.[41] Despite being swallowed up by philosophy, myth resisted, and it reappears whenever man is unable even to explain his being in the world. In fact, myth enunciates truths that philosophy is unable to assert, truths that may only be made apparent by means of the beauty of form.[42]

It is precisely in that beauty, which protects forms from harm, that Homer's heroes sail, traveling the regions of myth and the meanders of the human soul. In Arnold Böcklin's painting *Odysseus and Calypso*, Ulysses gazes in the direction of home, as in all the *nóstoi*, and Calypso offers to turn him into a god. He only has to conceal his quest, give up his identity, forget Penelope and Ithaca, return no longer as the hero. But amnesia is not Ulysses' style, nor Hypnos his god. Calypso is unable to hold back the myth that flows toward Homer's lyric.

The heroes of Homer return, and those of Alexander leave for a journey with no return, to disappear at the margins of a kingdom that has forgotten its confines. Deprived of the *pólis*, the Greek soldier takes refuge in the mysteries of Cybele and Isis. The centrality of the Homeric hero disintegrates in the famous mosaic of the battle of Issus where the defeated Darius is the central figure.[43] It is his fate, not Alexander's, that is recounted in the story of Curtius Rufus: "The two armies were so close to one another that ... swords touched faces. The frightened and the cowardly could no longer retreat ...

3.10
Arnold Böcklin, *Odysseus und Kalypso*, 1883.
Kunstmuseum, Basel.

Darius towered high above in his chariot, the sight of him inciting not only his own men to defend him, but also the enemy to attack him."[44] It is a scene that seems to celebrate adversity, the fate of those who fly too high above the others, the arbitrary will of the goddess Fortune. Nor did Tyche[45] come to the aid of Alexander, who died shortly before his teacher, Aristotle.

The severe style of the Periclean era was by this time only a faded memory. In the reclining heads of the funeral stelae, grief is consigned to the intimate circle of the family. An exaggerated expressivity is rampant, and that heroic steadfastness in the face of death and with regard to the tragedy of one's destiny, which used to prevail in earlier works, has all but disappeared. Plot takes precedence over individual character. Menander's characters shift the action from the dramatic conflicts of the *pólis* to the chatter and the impetuous gestures of the family arena. This is the world we see represented in Apulian vase paintings of the fourth century BC, which depict actors on stages surmounted by coffered ceilings. It was in such little theaters as these that the touring companies performed before the rich heirs of Alexander "such comical verses that one is moved to helpless laughter."[46] Tyche ensured that the dominant note in life was uncertainty and, after the death of Alexander, the true obsession of the Greek world became the inescapable nature of Fate.[47] Life, explained Epicurus when he opened his school in Athens, was a series of haphazard events. At the same time, the Stoics asserted that the universe is governed by a cosmic mind and that everything moves according to an inscrutable process.

This undermining of the ethical and juridical certitudes cultivated by the Greek city-states resulted in *autárkeia*. The world of imperial Rome was shot through with it, together with other philosophies of life that pagan curiosity incorporated unhesitatingly into its pantheon. Autarchy seemed, for dawning Christianity, to be the one and only existential condition. Cast out from the civilization of the empire, which, for the Christian, is subordinate to the kingdom of heaven, isolated in the autarchy of catacomb society, and unsure of his credo, the Christian chose poverty and felt pity for the centurion who opened the gates of the kingdom of heaven for him. His passivity rendered futile the centurion's cruelty and persecution for, as Paul wrote in his first epistle to the Corinthians, "He that hath suffered in the flesh has ceased from sins."[48] Up until the fourth century, the depictions of these martyrs found in the catacombs are very simple: they include the worshipper, a few strands of vine, and some symbols and patterns that had filtered through from popular tradition.

3.11
Scene in a *naiskos*, Apulian,
fourth century BC. Private
collection.

3.12
Ajax attacking Cassandra,
krater, fourth century BC.
Museo Nazionale, Naples.

3.13
Frons scenae with actors,
Fourth Style (after 62 AD).
House of Pinarius Cerialis,
Pompeii.

3.14
Drinking contest between
Dionysus and Heracles,
mosaic, end of second to
beginning of third century.
University Art Museum,
Princeton.

In contrast, the Roman left home in order to seek honors, riches, and kingdoms. He believed in the glory and the honor of the *civis romanus*; he made sacrifices to the gods; and there was no credo that prohibited him from enjoying earthly pleasures or forbade irony at the expense of his own pantheon: "nullos esse deos, inane caelum," joked Martial.[49] On his return, a *pompa triumphalis* awaited him in which individual heroism was bound inextricably to the interests of the *res publica*. He was portrayed as imposing, immobile, imperial. Yet without the sharp Greek sense of *éthos*, Roman figures sank into a heavy *res*, a materialism that Pliny imputed to a lack of introspection and analytical refinement: "Indolence has corrupted the arts, and since our spirituality is no longer represented in our portraits, similarly the classical perfection of the body is neglected."[50] Nonetheless, the artistic testimony left to the world by the fates of Pompeii and Herculaneum is extraordinary. All trace of the great style of Greek painting has vanished, and the frescoes carried out between the first century BC and the eruptions of Vesuvius in 63 AD and 79 AD demonstrate a high level of excellence in the depiction of people and things.[51]

For Christians, the journey took place in the precipitous silence of the intimate being. In the course of their transient experience of earthly life, they sought neither power nor knowledge: they replaced a pagan religiosity of life with "religiosity as detachment from life."[52] Just as "the soul resides in the body but does not belong to the body," as the Neoplatonist Salustius wrote, so Christians "reside in the world, but do not belong in the world."[53] The Christian's earthly life is, in a certain sense, a duty to be carried out, a *leitourghía*, or, as Marcus Aurelius more stoically put it, "an obligatory service carried out by the flesh."[54] Like Seneca, the believer displayed an exasperated *displacentia sui* for the encumbrance of a body that imprisoned his soul with unpleasant necessities.[55] But his journey toward the kingdom of heaven was accompanied by hymns and incense, by repentance and expiation, and at the end of time he could look forward to death's defeat and to the resurrection of the flesh.

Aristotle considered most dreams to be false; however, popular science, in its ever-obliging way, portrayed all philosophical doubt as useless. For pagans, dreams are a magic way of gaining access to the squabble-wracked world of the gods, of diagnosing ills, predicting the future, and revealing the enigmas created by psychopompal divinities. An apparition in a dream is an image that carries on a dialog with the sleeper, an *éidolon* of the person that vanishes into thin air, emitting a feeble cry, "like a wisp of smoke," such as Patroclus uttered when Achilles attempted to embrace him in a dream.

Ancient as it is, divination is an art[56] the Christian does not practice, at least not officially. He is afraid of the dark Underworld from which the black dog, the rat, and the gigantic Ethiopian emerge. He is afraid of the "messages of temptation from Satan's tribe of daemons,"[57] and believes that no dream can foretell divine providence. He is, instead, predisposed to ecstasy and to the annunciations that, by means of allegories and strange signs, indicate the path he should follow. This path leads him infallibly to the holy Word within him: *in interiore homine habitat veritas*. Detached from the world, he prays and flees from all knowledge not present in the Gospels. With the advancement of Christianity, the extraordinary heritage of classical culture stalled, losing its dynamism and energy. The mechanism of ancient science stalled definitively in the sands of Palestine, becoming a monument to its own immobility, one of the spoils of Egypt. It became possible for Claudianus Mamertus to calmly observe that "thanks to faith, the quiet believer inherits the fruits of science and harvests the fruits of labors in which he took no part."[58] St. Augustine made such appropriation possible by means of the "spoils of Egypt" principle, whereby words are separated from facts, virtue from *gentes*, and form from content. Theologically inert and subordinate to faith, classical culture offered itself as higher education to those Christians suffering from cultural solitude. Reduced to *summae* and fragments, the little that remained flowed into the profane history that Christianity, with its obstinate detachment from the world, had created. Just as the storytelling world of the Greeks had been overwhelmed by the constructive world of the Romans, so the Roman world's hold was now slackened and disarticulated by Christian love, which invited men to "love not the world, nor the things of the world."[59]

It was the end of antiquity, in which justice (*maat*) was guaranteed by the pharaoh, clemency by the Roman emperor, and truth by the Greek philosopher. The germination of myths was stilled by a credo that was, by its very nature, exclusive, repudiating *concupiscentia oculorum* together with everything else that imperial culture had loved and brought to bear: the beauty of form, the perfection of execution, and the immortality of the art work.[60] Classicism slowly faded from the memory of the Christianized pagans, while such concepts as honor and heroism, which had lent dignity to man's destiny, lost their meaning. After Constantine, the march of Christianity was unstoppable, and the virile pagan world succumbed irredeemably to the coming of God. The faithful followed the dogmas of the Church and entered unhesitatingly the *ab aeterno* world of revelation that offered to those minds dazzled by faith a set of rules and an explanation for their existence. For those who had been educated in classical Greek philosophy, "faith was the lowest rung of knowledge, the mental condition of the ignorant,"[61] and certainly little or nothing would have come down to us of the great store of classical literature, philosophy, and science had the curiosity of the culturally refined Arabs, the feared and detested warrior Islam, not intervened.

All this has an explanation that goes beyond the facile cultural expropriation encouraged by Augustine and disparaged by Tertullian. The appropriation of classical culture did not mean developing it or sharing in its *sophía*. The more it appeared devitalized and without the potential for development, the more acceptable it was. It was as if all antique thought had closed within itself the beginning and the end of all speculation. For this reason, says Augustine, "morbid" knowledge and the mania for experimentation that incites us to "scrutinize the secrets of nature … is absolutely useless."[62] It is also in vain because, as Justin remarked in his *Apologia secunda pro Christiani*, "Everything that has been said righteously among men is the property of us Christians."[63] It was therefore not the task of the Christian world to seek anything: "For us," wrote Tertullian, "curiosity is no longer necessary after Jesus Christ, nor research after the Gospels."[64]

The elaboration of a theory and the formulation of a method are necessary when one seeks a truth or tries to solve a problem, but the Christian world had no need to find a truth or supply solutions to the great questions of life. The truth was revealed by books and by prophets. For this reason, the fathers of the church did not develop specific discourses on mechanical arts, art, or architecture, except Augustine, who borrowed them from the classical tradition.[65]

But for one last time, classicism spoke through Plotinus, projecting the dazzling intelligence of his thought toward an indistinct future. The ethical and aesthetic conception of the Egyptian-born philosopher brought back a sense of what lay behind things: what proportions should a beautiful color have? Why do "perceptible beauties, images and shadows … descend into matter, order it, and then move us by their appearance?"[66] As a poet once said to a painter who was unable to render Bissula's beauty with wax and colors, "Let the color of the air be the color of her face."[67] What is hidden behind perceptible beauty is an internal quality that cannot be explained by Pythagorean relationships in terms of *arithmós*, or by means of the properties of numbers. In the *Theaetetus*,[68] the essence of beauty was bound by incommensurability to the irrational, and the golden mean to the perfection of the Platonic solids.[69] In Plotinus, a quality without number illuminates the thing and bestows upon it a beauty that may be perceived only by he who, in symmetrical fashion, already possesses it.

When Augustine, the most important Christian thinker, asked himself what beauty is, the answer he gave was more Greek than that given by Plotinus a century previously. Then, on the night of 24 April 387, Ambrose baptized him in Milan, and everything changed. Augustine abandoned the Pythagorean conception of musical relationships and moved closer to Plotinus's aesthetic-gnoseological theory. His classical ideal of *numerus* lost its mathematical centrality and moved toward an idea of quality that emerged from the relation among parts and from rhythm. The aesthetic experience became a device for reaching everything that is obscured by the senses—"eternal beauty" (*pulchritudo aeterna*). This was only possible if the observer was prepared for the vision of beauty and ready to ascend to imperceptible harmonies by means of perceptible ones.[70]

For Augustine, however, supreme beauty was invisible and therefore impossible to reproduce. The love of beauty (*philokalía*) that had enthralled him as a young man turned into open iconoclasm in his *Confessions*. Claudianus, his contemporary, felt himself at a loss when faced with the meekness of the Christian world and the slow disintegration of the pagan one: classical heroism had been diluted into soft, feminine portraits, while in the *Laus Serenae*, Ulysses' various adventures were reduced to a mere frame in which to show off Penelope's chastity.[71] Plotinus's idea of the image being illuminated from within was obscured by Augustine in the name of faith. After him, Western painters were seized by figurative hypochondria. A painterly tradition survived in the imperial themes of Byzantium, but space had contracted inexorably, and the dogmas of the church finally paralyzed the frontal viewpoint of believers.

In the ancient east, there was no aesthetic theory separate from practice. Religion itself could not be expressed by a belief in dogmas and was unable, therefore, to produce heresies; it could only take action on cults, promoting some at the expense of others. In Greek religion, too, there were no restrictive dogmas governing representation, while philosophy elaborated a theory of the beautiful that was independent of the world of *techné*. Such an attitude separated the freedom of intellectual *otium* from the material necessity of *negotium*, relegating the work of art to the world of manual labor, but failing to produce a cogent argument where artistic practice was concerned. Plato's critique of the art of appearances coincided with the moment in which Hellenistic illusionism rendered the third dimension even more vertiginous.

That philosophers regarded painters with a certain amount of envy is not in doubt. As Lucian put it, words are a "tenuous picture,"[72] and notwithstanding

Plato's considerable authority, his determined condemnation had no effect on representation. In the same way, the non-Euclidean conceptions of Carl Gauss and János Bolyai were unable to condition the representational methods of the early nineteenth century: certainly they did not influence Théodore Géricault when he painted the *Raft of the Medusa*. Nor did they manage to distort Euclidean optics at the beginnings of photography. It is equally evident that the artists of Santa Maria Maggiore in Rome and of the later Ravenna cycles were closer to Plotinus than to Augustine, who should have been their natural confessional point of reference.[73]

When a method of representation becomes habitual, when it has managed to thoroughly penetrate the culture that has chosen it and makes use of it, its resistance to change becomes greater. And no philosophical or scientific theory can stop it from being used if this is not reinforced by political or religious expediency, as was the case in Byzantine iconoclasm, in the Islamification of Orthodox churches, or in the oleographic realism of twentieth-century dictatorships. The centralization of powers usually leads to a unification of methods of representation, achieved by means of shared iconographical programs and stereotyped stylistic rules: this is what happened in the case of the Egyptian canons, in the proportional rules of Polykleitos, and in the "three circles" scheme of Byzantine painting.[74] This phenomenon has advantages and disadvantages and, as it spreads, it superimposes itself on local schools and on various other traditions, which then have difficulty maintaining their own independent visibility within the framework of official modes of representation.

The tendency of methods of representation to resist substitution is reflected in the way that antiquity is regarded by the modern age. It often comes about that an antique representation is reproduced in the manner of modernity, to the point that the figurative outcome derived from ideological choices may be read as an error or a formal amnesia. To modernity, the anti-illusionism of Christian art may seem like a deficiency, and Greek illusionism like an aesthetic contradiction. Richard Krautheimer has observed that for the men of the Middle Ages who required the holy sepulchre to be portrayed *ad similitudinem*, all figures with more than four sides were circular, or were comparable to a circle.[75] The medieval architect wasn't interested in imitating a model in its actual forms, as an architect of today would do, but was instead concerned with reproducing *typice*[76] and *figuraliter*. The relationship between a copy and the original was therefore not one of exact mirroring. In antiquity this mirroring was a guarantee of originality: all statues of Greek provenance were considered Greek originals, because they were perfect copies of previous models. Thus the fact that during the medieval period there was a total lack of such mirroring must be seen not as a defect, but as a culturally significant fact. It is often more useful to examine the deficiencies or the limits that emerge during the course of an iconographical analysis in terms of their possible meanings rather than in the more rewarding and instinctual terms of an aesthetic judgment. The most fundamental and typical aspects of a culture are revealed in its limitations, even when that culture has expressed itself elsewhere in innovations and discoveries that the modern conception of progress considers to be more deserving of attention.

It thus becomes possible to understand how the devaluation of the transient, a sensibility shared by pagans and Christians alike, is not a diminution of previous art, but simply the consolidation of a difference. A novel and coherent approach comes into being, playing down naturalistic elements and leading to the abandonment of classical precision, now perceived as a manifestation of imperial arrogance.[77] This may be seen in funerary art where the impoverished subject matter of both Christian and pagan necropolises is explored hurriedly and perfunctorily. Louis Bréhier has shown how, notwithstanding this distancing from the pagan world, many Christian themes were derived from the pagan world: Christ is clothed in the robes of the sun god Apollo; the ascent of the soul takes the form of Icarus; victory over temptation is Ulysses tied to the ship's mast; Christ is in the guise of Orpheus with the animals; the lamb and the fish become symbols of the Messiah;[78] the circle of the disciples around Aristotle becomes the group of apostles around Christ. The examples are numerous, but they all lead to one conclusion: pagan representational methods transport Christian themes into a world that is more spiritual, less descriptive, more synthetic, and pared of excess. And although some Christian imagery such as the lamb and the anchor is replaced, from the fourth century onward, by the figures of worshipers, the more complex themes remain symbolically represented, such as the Holy Spirit taking the form of a dove, the most appropriate form for representing the third entity of the Trinity.

Usually, the replacement of a method of representation comes about over a long period of time. And it often happens that the preceding method survives intact in the language of disciplines or styles that have adopted it as a symbolic form. This results, for example, in the disproportion of painted figures found in popular Roman art migrating to the Christian world, along with the faith of the converted pagan painters.[79] Martial commented that if the fish sculpted by Phidias were to have been placed in water, they would have swum.[80] Whereas

3.15
The gate of Jerusalem,
mosaic, c. 435. Santa Maria
Maggiore, Rome.

3.16
Bethlehem, mosaic, 1140.
Santa Maria in Trastevere,
Rome.

on the contrary, the expectation of a future life inherent in the new pagan and Christian mysticism brought about a representational way that eschewed the vivacity of naturalistic description. The lively scenes of a world animated by porticos, *tholoi*, gardens, and fountains gave way to the desiccated life of Christianity, devoid of shadows, of belongings, and of movement. Far away, in the last proconsular pagan villas of Numidia and Piazza Armerina in Sicily, even the Syrian and Alexandrian mosaicists struggled to maintain a point of view from within the gummy mutability of late-illusionistic representation.

Beginning in the year 375, Rome was repeatedly invaded, and for the next hundred years the simple abstractions of barbarian decorations eroded the semblance of classical physiognomy. After Augustine, a fatal quiet descended on the sciences. Justinian closed the Platonic school in Athens and prohibited the Isis cults at Philae.[81] The premature death of Boethius put an end to his plans to translate philosophical treatises and precluded any possibility of rebirth for Western scientific culture until the thirteenth century.[82] In the empty *Palatium* of Theodoric in Sant'Apollinare Nuovo in Ravenna, the hands of the dignitaries on the mosaic columns recall the end of the Arian reign that had condemned Boethius. Although Justinian and Theodora never set foot in Ravenna, their beautiful portraits in San Vitale celebrate the return of Byzantine orthodoxy. The new rulers survey the Italian lands from afar, with the same impassibility that they exhibit in the hippodrome of Constantinople, representing "the image of the world and of its order" in which "victories are the marks of destiny."[83] Lack of interest on the part of the Christian West was counterbalanced by the growth in Arabic translations, which, from the end of the ninth century, consigned what remained of Greek philosophy and science to Islam. And while the Byzantine *scriptoria* maintained the tradition of classical texts, in the Christian West the only books that circulated were textbooks, such as the one by Theophilus, who defined himself in the *Schedula diversarum artium* as a "monk by profession."[84]

After Justinian, the authority of Greek culture was reinforced. Greek replaced Latin as the language of Byzantium and, after the seventh century, took its place alongside Arabic in Palestine and Egypt. Greek logic slipped into the language of the Christians of the East along with scientific terminology, thus offering the instruments of argumentation against heresy and its confutations. It seemed that painting was abandoning the world. It was a more devastating loss than the prohibition imposed by Byzantine iconoclasm.[85] Indifference toward naturalism was stronger than prohibition because it seduced the soul even before the imagination. The third dimension was

3.19
Theodosius I and his
court, c. 390–393.
Base of an obelisk in
Hippodrome, Istanbul.

3.20
Christian basilica,
mosaic, provenance
unknown, c. fifth
century. Musée du
Louvre, Paris.
Ma3676.

3.17
Palace of Theodoric,
mosaic, before 526.
Sant'Apollinare in
Classe, Ravenna.

3.18
Palace of Theodoric,
detail of hand on
column, before 526.
The figures were
destroyed after Emperor
Justinian's reconquest.
Sant'Apollinare in
Classe, Ravenna.

rejected in favor of the concrete space of man, with his lifespan of pain and devotion. This slowed down the perception of homogeneous space, which was finally compressed into the recesses of the soul by prayer, but unexpectedly reopened the flat space of myth, which Greek philosophy had repressed.[86] The reappearance of Hellenistic features in monumental religious painting in the areas of Byzantine influence would have to wait for the eleventh century. From the third century until Giotto, save for a few exceptions,[87] the representation of depth is achieved with so-called parallel perspective, which we prefer to call oblique drawing.[88] In its simplest form, oblique drawing sets two viewpoints side by side, dispenses with shadows, emphasizes outlines, and avoids those gradations of tone that suggest the corporeality of the third dimension.

Even though he was a pagan, Plotinus's description of Christian anti-illusionism was superior to that of any of the church fathers: "Colors do not render objects smaller, although they fade when large objects diminish in size." This meant that no objects were to be placed at a distance in the background, because their colors would consequently be faded, and "when every object is not clearly seen, it is no longer possible to measure … and know the total size." The painter had to vary his colors and clearly define outlines: "Objects of the same appearance and of a uniform hue deceive us … for our eye … runs over them without finding any differences that permit it to pause." No detail should be omitted from the representation that would detract from the clarity and the measure of the composition.[89] Painters were to refrain from including their own shadows or those of others, nor were they to indulge in those optical diminutions that Plato compared to confused speech.[90] They were to transcribe clearly and fit onto the page whatever images were chosen by the liturgists. The Christ Pantocrator was to appear in the cupola; the Virgin in the apse, surrounded by the holy liturgy and the communion of the apostles; the saints and the twelve principal feasts of the church in the nave; the Last Judgment in the entrance; the life of Mary in the narthex.[91]

The symbolic simplicity of Christian thought did not eschew dogma, but pictorial representation rightly avoided it, instead using it out of earshot, like a powerful magnet guiding the simple parts of the narration. In the foreground, the painter placed what was immediately comprehensible and easily visualized. Mosaic figures, evenly lit in the Roman past, and later evenly lit in Ravenna, recount the only possible story to the faithful.

Evangelization was also a problem of power and survival, especially in the face of frequent schisms and given the ease with which empires crumble. Those pagans who converted were not always rich and influential like Ambrose.

In a letter to the bishop of Marseilles, Gregory the Great[92] declared himself opposed to the adoration of images, but also to their destruction. This subtle aporia realigned faith with the course of history. On the eve of iconoclastic frenzy, the church could deny the adoration of images while at the same time leaving the art of icon painting to the Byzantine monasteries, where it reinforced quietism and offered a theater of memory for the Christian masses: it goes without saying that the images, conceived as a sublimation of writing, were absolutely necessary for the creation of the Christian *mythos*.

When, after a hundred years of amnesia, iconoclasm ended and theological legitimacy was once more restored to images, the great illustrated encyclopedia of Western history got under way once more. With the *renovatio* of Charlemagne, image-making changed direction, becoming a polemical badge against the iconophile tendencies of the Eastern empire. Having lost the holy places to Islam, the king of the Franks sought consensus in Rome and did not permit sacred images to be used, as they were in Constantinople, as badges of orthodoxy. They could, however, usefully illustrate people and events that the scriptures were unable to describe for the purposes of education and in order to recall the *res gestae*.[93] But in the *Capitulare de imaginibus*, the distancing from Byzantine iconophilia did not lead to a retrieval of Plotinus's vision, despite the West's renewed interest in Platonism through the offices of an Irishman, Johannes Scotus Eriugena. Images were not a stopping-off point on the road to reaching the intelligible; they were concrete history that instinctively produced admiration for Roman classicism, within which the imperial icon of Charlemagne could be fitted in a suitably Christian manner. The antiquarian-inspired works of the Carolingian *scriptoria* sought to remember the past and beautify the present. At Aquisgrana (Aachen), figurative elements that are more Greek than sacerdotal reappear and hint at three-dimensionality, marking a definitive departure from the flat, arabesque-filled pictorial style of the Irish monasteries.

Once freed from the rigors of theology, painting brought to the service of its Christian subject matter those techniques of scientific illustration that were to be found in the margins of manuscripts on geometry and cosmology, where they elucidated the concepts under discussion.[94] The pictorial freedom of the manuscript annotators shifted representation toward a hyperrealistic dimension, to the point where the underlying geometrical forms were distorted. This is seen clearly in Isidore of Seville's cube of the elements,[95] in which the geometrical figures lose the characteristics of solids, despite the caption reminding the reader that "this three-dimensional form is drawn

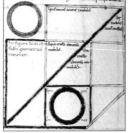

3.21
Master of Registrum Gregorii, Gregory in his study, c. 984. Stadtbibliothek, Trier. *Registrum Gregorii*, unique folio.

3.23
Representation of the world as a solid figure (*cubus elementorum*), in three different manuscripts of Isidore of Seville's *De natura rerum*: tenth-century manuscript, Bibliothèque Nationale, Paris, Cod. Lat. 6413, folio 4v; twelfth-century manuscript,

3.22
Depiction of the crucifixion alongside an iconoclast covering an image of Christ, ninth century. Historical Museum, Moscow, Chludov Psalter.

British Library, London, Cott. Tiberius C.I, folio 6v; eighth-century manuscript, Biblioteca Apostolica Vaticana, Rome, Cod. Vat. Fondo Rossiano 247, folio 60r.

according to geometric rules";[96] the cube is flattened out and becomes simply an orchestration of the surface, which is filled in and decorated.

The Christian preferred theological teaching over the methodology of the *trivium* and the *quadrivium*. But since he considered images to be an effective tool for proselytizing, it was imperative that he solve the problem of the embarrassing iconoclasm of the book of Genesis. Tools adequate to the task were to be found in the vast repertoire of classical culture. Christian thought derived an articulated hierarchy of concepts from the Aristotelian idea of teleology or development, and these progressively materialized into images. These reflections of intelligible reality, taken from the Old Testament and from the Gospels, covered the walls of churches and revealed to the faithful the grandiose nature of the divine.[97] The relationship between prototype and image was calibrated by Theodore the Studite and John of Damascus on the basis of the relationship between God the Father and Christ his Son and, descending the conceptual hierarchy, between the body of man and his soul. At long last, God and his image coincided,[98] so that each act of adoration before His image seemed capable of calling the divine into being.

The invectives of *De pudicitia,* in which Tertullian had branded the arts an invention of the devil,[99] were by now a distant memory. The images created by painters were free from uncertainty about the double nature of Christ. Created on the basis of authentic sources and likeness, pictorial representation embarked on a relationship with the prototype in the same way as a shadow is cast on the ground by a body.[100] Not only was the shadow the immaterial revelation of the prototype, it also divulged the deep bond between Christian representation and the Greco-Roman world, together with the Mediterranean world in general.

In classical Greek, the shadow (*skiá*) is the actual origin of painting itself, of conformity and of measure.[101] Greek tradition makes recourse to the shadow to provide a basis for the invention of drawing.[102] The first painters began by creating a contour (*perigrafé*), with a "line outlining the shadow of man [*umbra hominis lineis circumducta*]," as Pliny described it, recalling the Egyptian "contours scribe."[103] The shadow fixed the figure in an attitude that showed it off to its best advantage, in profile, like the evanescent, dark impression of a seal magically representing its being. But for Plato, shadow drawing (*skiagraphía*) depended for its effect on the weakness of our senses. As in the myth of the cave, the shadow was synonymous with hypocrisy and inexactitude.[104] The *skiagraphía* expressed only the external features, while the contents were obscure and unpredictable; this is why Aristotle compared it to the deliberative style that used chiaroscuro in order to have a powerful effect on the audience seated at some distance from the orator.[105]

In *The Pyramid Texts* "[the dead king's] horror is darkness," while in *The Book of Going Forth by Day* a veritable phobia of the underworld is apparent. However, for some reason the shadow figure, represented metonymically by a hieroglyph in the form of an umbrella, has the meaning of "procreative force" (*shut*). Like the *ba* and the *ka* of the deceased, man's shadow also is a manifestation of his being.[106]

In war it becomes synonymous with the king who defines himself as "the shadow who protects his soldiers"; in the Amarnian era, the temple of Aton was designated as "the shadow of Ra." For the Christian too, the shadow possessed a vital energy. We learn from the Acts of the Apostles that Peter cured the sick by touching them with his shadow.[107] And, as witness to the life-giving significance of the shadow, the Greeks believed that anyone who entered the temple of Zeus Lykaios was fated to lose his shadow and die within the year. The Muslims believed that only demons and dead people possessed no shadow, despite the warning of the sublime al-Biruni that at midday, when the sun is at its zenith, "men walk on the backs of their own necks."[108]

The causal link between being and the shadow that proves its vitality spread throughout the Mediterranean world by means of Egyptian Monophysitism, Christian and Muslim monotheism, and Greek pantheism. But when the shadow ceased being projected and became instead simply an absence of light, then it evoked the gloomy atmosphere of the underworld or the unenviable condition of the artisans who were "forced to live in the shadows" (*skiatrapheisthai*), huddled around the hearth like women.[109] In classical painting, shadow is shown as tonality of color; it was an indicator of depth and adhered to bodies. For Plotinus and for the Christians of the fourth century, however, the shadow concealed, stained, and obscured painted works. In this, their judgment recalls that of the Chinese emperors who were vexed by the stains that defaced the paintings presented to them by the Jesuits.[110] For the Christian, shadow was not, as Leonardo defined it, a "lessening of light."[111] Rather, shadow led the eye into the dark corner of matter where the devil was concealed; to peer into that obscurity, even though it was only a painted representation, could mean to meet his gaze without realizing it, and thus to be lost.

In Christian iconography, the sacred image tended to isolate itself from worldly events by choice. Its destination was not the theater or the imperial stage but the light of revelation. To this day, the Madonna of Torcello appears like a cardboard cut-out, looming alone in a field of golden light, all the more

3.24
The deceased as a shadow, tomb of Arinefer,
Twentieth Dynasty, c. 1150. Deir el Medina,
in situ.

Byzantine for the absence of angels and saints, all the more angelic for the presence of the Last Judgment on the opposite wall. From this moment on, phobia of the world began to decrease and figures resumed their slow progress across the narrative cycles of the sacred scriptures. In the Byzantine Balkans and to the north of Greece, mosaics gave way to painted decorations that extended even to the lower parts of walls, formerly decorated with stone. The figures turned to face the faithful, who could almost look them in the eye. A rediscovered Greek sense of space governed the earth-colored brushstrokes, while the greater available surface area permitted the iconography of the narrative cycles to be greatly enriched. At Daphni, in Attica, the *Christ Baptized in the Jordan* has plastic qualities redolent of classical sculpture, and there is an animation of expression never before seen in mosaic cycles. This *páthos* is visible in the faces of the figures and animates the tender gaze of the Madonna upon her child, climaxing at Gorno Nerezi in Macedonia in the church of St. Panteleimon, in the first depiction of the agonizing pain around the body of the dead Christ.[112] The exploration of such themes broke the spell of ecstasy, engendered a shared sense of devotion and participation, and brought the sacred closer to the life of the common people, just as the life of St. Francis would, a few centuries later.

The illustrated classical texts, which had been transferred onto the parchment manuscripts of Greek papyri since the first century of the modern era, became an iconographical storehouse for painters and mosaicists. In this majestic transposition of illustrative types, it was above all the more useful manuscripts on scientific themes that managed to pass through the net of iconoclastic prohibitions and come to the attention of Islamic culture. The intrinsic necessity of scientific illustration rendered it independent of time and finite space, normally indicated by the flat line of the earth. A cube has no memory, and as a Platonic symbol of the earth, it was well served by the church's declared lack of interest in science. And when the cube came to be expressed on a flat surface, did it not reproduce the form of the Christian cross? Before this cross flowed a whole repertory of postures, geometric shapes, and diagrams, their *auctoritas* spreading throughout a world that hovered on the edge of conversion; it touched the imagination of the Christian painters confused by the disputes about Christ and hampered by visual amnesia, as well as by the decline of classical precision.

Architectural elements, isolated and monolithic, began to make their appearance in the decorations of Byzantine churches, but without the importance they had had in the frescoes of the Second and Fourth Pompeian Style.

3.25
Prayer book of Otto II, Mainz, eleventh
century. Gräflich Schönbornsche
Bibliothek, Pommersfelden. Codex 2940,
folio 26v.

3.26
John the Evangelist from Gospels of Saint
Medard de Soissons, early ninth century.
Bibliothèque Nationale, Paris. Cod. Lat. 8850,
folio 180v.

3.27
Baptism of Christ, mosaic, 1100. Church,
Daphni Monastery.

3.28
Pietà, fresco, 1164. Church of St. Panteleimon,
Gorno Nerezi, Macedonia.

The figures of the *pictor imaginarius*,[113] which stood before the *frons scaenae* of Pompeii, now waited immobile behind the scenes. Twelve centuries would have to pass before they would be able to reveal themselves to the public, dressed in the humble monk's habit of St. Francis. In the meantime, the walls of churches offered the faithful a Christological narration in which the third dimension had been deactivated.[114] The principal characters look impassibly upon their sanctity while the others crowd around the scene looking at each other in three-quarters profile, leaving ample space for the emotion of the spectator.[115] There are no seaports, rivers, woods, and shepherds, as in the Roman *megalographiae*.[116] A back wall pushes all of the figures to the foreground of the proscenium arch, together with their architectural assemblages.

The occlusive nature of this wall is unrelieved by any articulation of the sort provided by the Pompeian *frons scenae*. Wedged up against it, with their sides at an oblique angle, are the thrones and niches that box in the figures.[117] These revolving architectural assemblages seem like mysterious focusing mechanisms, set up in order to garner meaning and orchestrate the conversation among the various figures. There is no pretense on the part of these buildings as big as cities, and cities as small as buildings, to actually exist in space or to constitute urban space: they simply serve to suggest the idea of a city described in the *Corpus agrimensorum romanorum*, with its lozenge-shaped towers of containment.[118]

The refined isolation of these forms results in a fragmentation of the composition and therefore of space. They act as background, frame, separations. This means that the depiction withdraws from the judgment of a unitary vision. As compositional elements, these architectural assemblages act like *caesurae*, and they also lend a rhythmic quality to the succession of scenes. Deliberate disproportion of scale rules out any return to Greek illusionism. This syncopated mode of portrayal is influenced by the changes that came about in the West, starting in the twelfth century. Latin translations of Greek originals began to substitute Arabic versions, and scientific manuscripts containing the works of Euclid, Apollonius, Archimedes, Galen, Hippocrates, Ptolemy, and Heron began to circulate once again.[119] The exegesis of Averroes broke in upon the scene, bringing Aristotle into the schools of the arts, where his influence may even be found in some school's statutes. It was the beginning of the polemic against peripatetic theses and of suspicion of the compliance of scholastic Thomism with those "Arab" philosophies. One result was certainly obtained: Latin Averroism, with its notion of double truth by means of the *quaestiones*, opened the door to rational thinking.

3.29
Conversion of St. Paul, with models of cities similar to those contained in the *Corpus agrimensorum romanorum*, ninth century. Biblioteca Apostolica Vaticana, Rome. Cod. vat. gr. 699, folio 83v.

3.30
The city of Ankara, *Tabula Peutingeriana*, twelfth to thirteenth century, from a fourth-century original. Österreichische Nationalbibliothek, Vienna. Cod. vind. 324.

3.31
Ambrogio Lorenzetti, *Coastal City*,
mid-1300s. Pinacoteca Nazionale,
Siena.

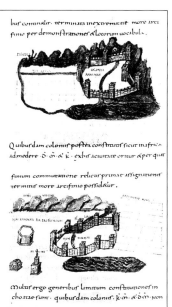

3.32
Corpus agrimensorum romanorum, sixth century. Herzog August Bibliothek, Wolfenbüttel. Cod. guelf. 36.23, Aug. 2°, folio 62v.

3.33
Hyginus Gromaticus, *Corpus agrimensorum*, ninth century. Biblioteca Apostolica Vaticana, Rome. Cod. pal. lat. 1564, folios 88r to 89r.

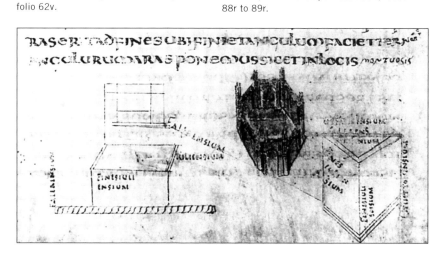

3.34
Corpus agrimensorum romanorum, sixth century. Herzog August Bibliothek, Wolfenbüttel. Cod. guelf. 36.23, Aug. 2°, folio 60r.

3.35
Heron, *Metrics*, eleventh-century copy.
Topkapi Library, Istanbul. MS Cost.
Pal. Vet. 1, L.I., folio 52r.

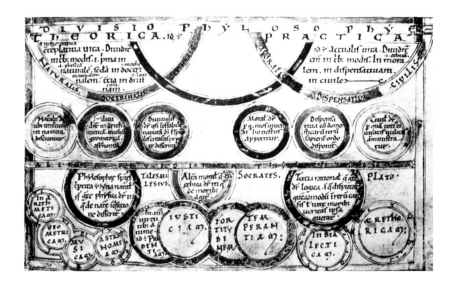

3.36
Classification of the sciences, twelfth
century. St. John's College, Oxford.
OX SJ 17, folio 7r.

3.37
The enrollment for taxation before Quirinius,
mosaic, fourteenth century. Church of
Kharié-Djami, Istanbul.

The deluge of Aristotelian thought brought about a more consistent approach to the classification of knowledge, with the elaboration of dichotomies and *distinctiones*. In the distinctions and enumerations that followed, the *sýmbolon* technique, whereby a figure also represented a truth, began to lose ground. Uncertainty also began to erode the solidity of pictorial representation that divided and distinguished, fragmented and enumerated, irradiated and recomposed. In the attempt to keep all knowledge together and conduct the algid beauty of the past to the Christian present, artists made recourse to geometrical diagrams which ordered and enclosed every aspect of knowledge in the ramifications of the *arbor virtutum* (tree of virtues), in relation to the *cubus elementorum* (cube of elements), in the radiant *rotae* (wheels), and in the hard squares of opposition (see the illustration from Isidore of Seville's *De natura rerum* in figure 3.23). By this logic and in this compositional context, the painter had no way of fixing upon one viewpoint, which was the necessary fulcrum for penetrating the interior of his depiction: Augustine's "credo ut intelligam" was to remain a necessary and sufficient condition for Christian knowledge.

In Byzantine pictorial representation the spectator himself commands nothing. Indeed, it is he who is observed from an infinite distance, by parallel visual rays that are without beginning or end, without interest or pity. The frontally depicted eye of a Byzantine Christ follows him everywhere, like the *Veronica* that fixes Nicholas of Cusa in his studio in Brixen while Constantinople fell into the hands of Mehmet II.[120] As this eye peers out of *the window of apparition*,[121] an infinite distance separates the sacred from the world that admires it. It is the same distance that is stamped on the face of Christ, whose "firmness of feature never relieved by a smile"[122] owes a debt to classical models and whose immobile calm derives from the rightness of His being. The instantaneous fusion of the severe Periclean profile with the hierarchical Byzantine one produces an impassive quality, which will return with full force in the perspectival clarity of Piero della Francesca.

Everything else is in flux. Figures enter and exit the third dimension according to the profound impulses of their spirits, to the will of kings and the beliefs of peoples. Sometimes thought and image part company and contradict each other, giving rise to those returns which confound the classifications of historians and reveal the unpredictable paths of ideas. The illiterate faithful look upon the impassive faces of saints, of the just, and of infants,[123] and their eyes follow the causal link of the images accumulating on the walls of the churches. They are moved by the solemn calm of the mystery play; the meanings of those

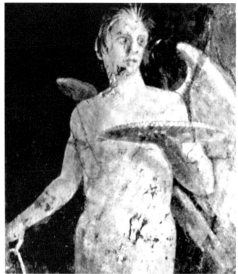

3.38
Carnee Painter, dance scene,
Apulian krater, fourth century.
National Museum, Taranto.

3.39
Winged demon, encaustic painting from
the Fannius Sinistor Villa at Boscoreale,
end of first century. Musée du Louvre,
Paris. P.23.

3.40
Detail of *asaroton* (unswept floor)
mosaic, second century AD. Villa
sull'Aventino, Rome.

gold-drenched stories are lost on them but they nonetheless feel touched by divine grace. From the depths of classical religiosity, Pindar lectures them: "Ephemeral beings! Of what does each one of us consist? Man is a shadow dream. But when the Gods direct a ray of light upon him, a brilliant splendor enfolds him and his existence becomes as sweet as honey."[124] And in that golden ray, which confuses the storyline and puts thought to flight, the Christian faithful feel themselves moved and transfigured.

In the second half of the fourth century BC, Apulian vase painting registered the conquest of depth, and the flat space of myth gave way to the domestic tensions that flare up in the chorus of Menander. In the same way, toward the end of the thirteenth century, the portrayal of the great Christological themes was replaced by that of the lives of the saints. When Franciscanism tore spectators' eyes from the flat plane of liturgy to that of earthly life, painters found themselves having to combine the lives of the saints with those of the merchants (*mercatores*). It was the beginning of what might be described as the descent of the point of view. From the infinite distance of parallel perspective, pictorial representation converged, perforating the veil that concealed reality behind the symbol: somebody looked inside the scene and traced the line of the horizon. On the stained glass windows of Chartres cathedral, secular donors had their portraits inserted along with their names, in the manner of an ex-voto.[125] Something of the ancient world's participation in the sacred was rekindled: a thousand years earlier it had been witnessed by the frescoes of Dura Europos, the floors of the paleo-Christian churches of Syria, and the church of St. Dimitrios at Salonika.[126] Artists were now asked to offer to the church the talent conceded to them by God so that the sacred might be brought closer to the common people.

Dante's vernacular Italian opened the impenetrable culture of the monasteries to laypeople, and the divine became diluted in the life of the saints. The abacus schools introduced Arabic numerals and positional notation to mercantile arithmetic. Cities flourished once more, and the sacred slowly released its hold on profane thought. The stories recounting the life of the saint, set side by side in the spatial boxes of Giotto and Duccio, could be enjoyed visually, and painting was freed from the spatial amnesia in which Byzantine painting had been stuck. Now, an impalpable golden dust was settling in the cubically constructed world of Giotto, where figures and architecture once more appropriated shadow, using it to mold the folds of drapery and projections on facades. The sketchy lines of shadow scratched into Roman-style drapery yielded to a shadow that vibrated among the heavy robes of merchants and was generated by light falling from a solid sky. That shadow, which for Plotinus represented matter, marked the passage from the dazzling light of gold-filled backgrounds to the corporeality of the new pictorial representation. Painted figures stepped down from the architectonic structures that framed them and entered into real life.

Development and change held no interest for the world of Christian pictorial representation in the early Middle Ages. Outside of the Scriptures there was no such thing as a time independent of the events of Sacred History. Time belonged to God and had no direction of its own, except toward God. The infinite time of meditation was no longer merely a "dilation of the soul," as Augustine defined it in his *De civitate Dei*. The circular time of the monasteries, whose rhythm was given by the heads of the Cistercian and Benedictine confraternities, became *chronos* and entered the real world. Machines were invented that, by means of the extraordinary mechanical workings of levers and gears, were able to calculate the wealth of bankers, weave the forecasts of profit with those of astrology, remember dates of death and birth, and order the festivities of city life. This return to the affairs of the earth dilated the space surrounding bodies to the point where even the places of the *res gestae* were included: Dante's wood, Petrarch's streams, and the orderly countryside produced by Sienese good government. In the first half of the fourteenth century, religious art regulated the eternal flow of divine time with the horological expertise of Giovanni Dondi.[127] His *Astrarium* was closer to antiquity and to Leonardo than to the ideas of the late Middle Ages, and it heralded the modern age.

In the conglomerates of the Byzantine painting of the Paleologan period, several images of the same building were often stuck together, with the interiors joined to the exteriors. It was a way of leading the spectator beyond specific places, toward a mystic space and an interior time. The architectural structures that, like small-scale models, gave cadence to the painted episodes became urban landscapes, receding into the background and positioned at an angle to make room for figures "on a stage which is the whole earth where men have in many places set up their stages."[128] The figures seem impatient to leave the sacredness of space-light in order to enter space-place. When Giotto shows the back of a crucifix in the *Manger at Greccio*,[129] it is clear that the ecstasy associated with the frontal view is finished forever. Painting now enters houses, it distinguishes between inside and outside, front and back, and marks the difference between motion and stillness.

Occamism[130] freed the new physics from the insidious bonds of metaphysics and in so doing delivered empirical investigation to the realm of science.

According to Pietro d'Abano, who studied philosophy and the Arabian sciences in Paris, everything that was not revelation was a matter for investigation: *de naturalibus naturaliter*.[131] When Pietro died in 1318, Giotto had only recently completed the Scrovegni Chapel. By this time theology seemed separate from philosophy, which continued to investigate the world by means of the insidious technique of the *quaestio*.[132] Lorenzetti's first attempts in the *Annunciation* shift the eye from the high ceiling, which was supposed to suggest depth, to the floor, which has a single vanishing point.[133] Not only is it a marker of depth but, together with the ceiling, it also defines a space.

Man rediscovered the mark of the divine in the world around him;[134] there was nothing that could not be investigated, observed, and represented. This led to a rediscovery of the forms of nature that had been rendered abstract by the symbol: "The eye of the intellect teaches you," Nicholas of Cusa writes in his *De querendo Deum*, "that, in a small piece of wood and in this tiny stone, or in bronze, or in a mass of gold, or in a grain of mustard or of millet, are stored up all the potential forms of all artificial bodies. In everything, in fact, it is certain that there exists the circle, the triangle, the tetragon, the sphere, the cube, and every geometrical shape."[135]

Man encountered the divine through sight, the most deceptive and immediate of his senses.[136] It was at last possible for art to use the eyes of the body without relapsing into a disgraceful *concupiscientia oculorum*. The task of artists was to observe and make visible the works of nature with a precision that is the distinguishing mark of the science and art of the Renaissance. The body of man, mirror of the universe in ancient Oriental tradition,[137] fashioned in the image and likeness of God according to Christianity, was now the embodiment of the perfection of the harmonic laws that the *numerus* made visible and expressible. In the all-consuming search for proportion and measure, the rediscovery of Vitruvius and Plato aided architects in bringing about a harmonious marriage between the universe, the body, and architecture along the lines of that proposed by Galen.[138] Thirteenth-century optics had deprived *lux* of its divine connotation.[139] Geometrical optics, purged of all metaphysical connotations, now prepared to make the journey that would bring *perspectiva communis* or *naturalis* back within a strictly Euclidean sphere. For the Gospels, God was "the light of the world," and he was also the space of himself: thus light created and maintained all things. For Robert Grosseteste, light was the prime bodily form and the first principle of motion. In order to become acquainted with the study of this divine *autodiffusione* of light, classical geometrical optics returned to the jurisdiction of the philosophers while its refined geometrical mechanism made itself available to the experimentation of the fourteenth century.

In the first decade of the fifteenth century in Rome, Brunelleschi and Donatello[140] were applying their optical-geometrical notions to measure building elevations from a distance. Techniques handed down from antiquity by way of Leonardo Fibonacci and Biagio Pelacani da Parma were retrieved once more for the indirect measuring of inaccessible sites.[141] Distances were represented as visual rays extending from the standpoint of the observer to the highest points of a building. Straight lines, angles, measurements, and some special magic, which it is impossible to reconstruct with precision, transformed that inert physical support into an optical plane: similar triangles establish a proportional relationship between the heights of an object and its representation on the plane, and defeat *more geometrico* the nonproportion-ality between optical angles and distances. The Euclidean passage between optics and representation, between angular perspective and flat perspective, is thus achieved. The role played by Ptolemy's *Geography* or his *Optics*[142] in this renewed method of representation is unclear. Certainly whole chunks of classical geometry and optics were moving without theological impediment toward that mechanism that slips through the hands of Donatello and Brunelleschi while they are measuring the antiquities of Rome with verified (*certificata*) vision.[143]

3.41
Giotto, *The Crucifix of St. Damian*, before 1300. Upper Church of St. Francis, Assisi.

3.42
Giotto, *Manger at Greccio*, detail showing rear view of crucifix, before 1300. Upper Church of St. Francis, Assisi.

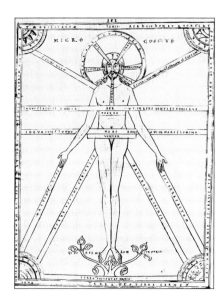

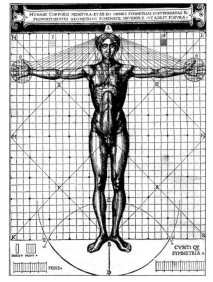

3.43
Solomon of Constance, man as microcosm,
1165. Bayerische Staatsbibliothek, Munich.
Latin codex 13002, folio 7v.

3.44
Man as the measure of the Earth. Cesare
Cesariano, *De architectura* (Como, 1521),
page 49.

3.45
Incipit: "Quando la tua divina mente et
deità imperatore Cesare." Cesare Cesariano,
De architectura (Como, 1521), page 1.

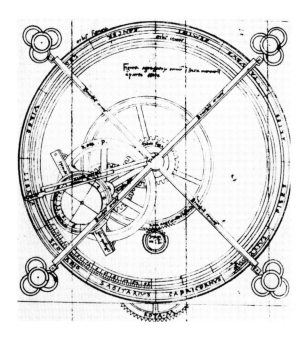

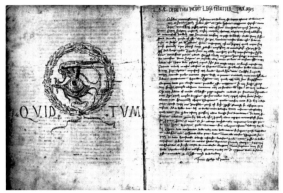

3.46
Giovanni Dondi, *Astrarium*, 1365–1380.
Biblioteca Capitolare, Padua. Codex D 39.

3.47
Leon Battista Alberti, *De pictura*, dedication
letter to Brunelleschi. Biblioteca Nazionale,
Florence. Ms. II.IV. 38, c. 120.

On 7 July 1436, Leon Battista Alberti sent the manuscript of his *De pictura*, written in vernacular Italian, to his friend Brunelleschi, inscribing it with a dedication that expresses humanity and gratitude: "I desire that you before all others should correct my faults, so that I will not be savaged by my detractors."[144] By means of the division of the visual pyramid by a single plane, that which was seen became that which was represented, and the extraordinary *koiné* of the Renaissance began. Space once again opened out onto the theater of the world, and perspective offered the West what convention had turned into the most realistic method of representation.[145] Perspective, having a viewpoint that framed it and showed it off in all its beauty, became the most suitable symbolic form for representing the world. Line was no longer a mere container of areas of color, as it had been in late antique drawings, nor was it used simply to wrinkle the folds of drapery, as in the Gothic period; now it innervated space with fragile filaments of Euclidean geometry and measured out the whole world.

On 12 October 1492, Columbus discovered America. Piero della Francesca lay dying. In Venice, where he taught for the last period of his life, Giorgio Valla was translating and publishing a large number of ancient codices. Classicism comes back once more to regain attention, uniting itself firmly with modernity.

Notes

1. See the stela discovered by Schiapparelli in 1910 at el-Gebelein (Aphroditopolis; in old Egyptian, per-Hathor), preserved in the Egyptian Museum of Turin. No Egyptian document gives a full explanation of the Jubilee feast. In the Papyrus Harris, the longest and most important papyrus to have come down to us, there is merely a description of the gifts Ramesses III presented to gods and men during the celebration of thirty years of his reign. James Henry Breasted, *Ancient Records of Egypt*, 5 vols. (London, 1988), 4:169, §335.

2. See the footstool of Tutankhamun's ceremonial throne representing four "enemies" on one side and five on the other, an asymmetrical arrangement that is unusual for Egyptian art (Cairo, Egyptian Museum, JE 62030). Cf. Mohammed Saleh and Hourig Sourouzian, *Catalogue officiel. Musée égyptien du Caire* (Mainz: Verlag Philipp von Zabern, 1987), index 181.

3. It would appear that the armies of the pharaoh never went further than the total length of Egypt: Tuthmosis III went as far as Carchemish on the Euphrates in a journey of the same number of kilometers as those separating the Delta from the first cataract at Aswan. Legendary expeditions repulsed the Hyksos to the north, reestablishing the unity of Egypt. Ramesses II defeated the Hittites at Quadesh, the Libyans and the "Sea Peoples" in the western Delta, and to the south the Nubians of Kerma between the first and second cataract. These military expeditions also served to keep open the roads along which goods necessary to the royal court were transported. This was the aim of the expedition to Punt (Somalia?) made by Hatshepsut, who procured gold (*electrum*), incense, and the eagerly sought-after myrrh, a resin gum (*Commiphora*) used in embalming. Curiously, these are the same gifts as were brought to the infant Jesus by the three kings. Also imported from Punt were "perfumed woods," ebony, eye color (*kohl*), manna (the hardened sap of *Fraxinus* or secretions provoked by insects on *Tamarix* and *Artemisia*, today used by the Bedouin of Arabia), ostrich feathers, panther skins for priests, and monkeys. In the reliefs of Deir el-Bahri, the ships arriving at Bab el-Mandeb are greeted by an obese queen who proclaims: "Hail to you, *king of Egypt, female sun* that shines like the solar disc" (italics added). The Egyptian texts describe the expeditions to Punt from the time of the Fourth Dynasty onward.

3.48
Schist vase, predynastic period. Egyptian Museum, Cairo.

3.49
The Queen of Punt, temple of Queen Hatshepsut at Deir el-Bahri, Eighteenth Dynasty. Egyptian Museum, Cairo.

3.50
Implement used for the mouth-opening ceremony, tomb of the scribe Khâehmat, also known as Mahou (epoch of Amenhotep III). Necropolis of Sheikh abd el-Gurna, tomb 57.

4. The hieroglyph *sema* (union) represents the two lungs and trachea and signifies "to unite." See the alabaster perfume holder discovered in Tutankhamun's tomb on which the hieroglyph *sema* unites the papyrus, emblem of Lower Egypt, with the lily, emblem of Higher Egypt (Cairo, Egyptian Museum, JE621114). Cf. Saleh and Sourouzian, *Catalogue officiel. Musée égyptien du Caire*, index 190.

5. When he died, the king embarked on a journey during which he underwent the rigors of truth (*maat*) before the court of the kings. The journey to the kingdom of the "Westerners" began with the ceremony of the opening of the mouth, which brought about the rebirth of the king by giving him back his voice. The king then defeated the infernal enemies and dominated the natural elements. After his regeneration he emerged from the tomb and, transfigured, appeared in the eastern sky, having made the twelve transformations carried out by Ra during the course of the day. He crossed the sky in a solar vessel and visited the souls of the holy places (Hermopolis, Heliopolis, Buto, Ierakonpolis). He then returned to the necropolis where he was judged by the forty-two divinities of the tribunal of Osiris (*psicostasia*). If the tribunal judged him fit, he became *justified*, otherwise he was devoured by one of the few monsters in the Egyptian pantheon. Having been solarized, he traveled through the complicated geography of the underworld, recognized all the gods, all the names of Osiris, the names of the seven doors and of the twenty-one gates of his kingdom, and of the relatives of the genie-guardians. At the end of the night he was born like a new sun (*kheper*) and joined Ra on his daily journey. The journey ended with a rebirth, just as in the rite of the jubilee when the king was alive. The most important collections of texts that accompany the king on his underworld journey are known by titles that differ depending on their arrangement: *Texts of the Pyramids, Texts of the Sarcophagi*. The formulae were codified and given book form only in the Saitic era. In 1842 Karl Richard Lepsius published a collection of them in 165 chapters with the title *Book of the Dead*. Champollion had already titled it *Funeral Rites*. In 1886 Henri Naville brought together all the papyri from the Eighteenth to the Twentieth Dynasty, publishing a version called the *Bible of the Ancient Egyptians*. In 1898, Wallis Budge published a collection in which he included texts from as late as the Ptolemaic era. It had 190 chapters, and to the title of *Book of the Dead* he added that used by the Egyptians:

Formulae for Going Forth during the Day. See Alberto Siliotti and Christian Leblanc, *Nefertari e la valle delle regine* (Florence: Giunti, 1993), 124–125.

6. The Arab word *alkimiya* is derived from *kemet* ("black mud" in ancient Egyptian). In sixteenth-century European culture this became the word *alchemy*.

7. "Nobody comes from there to tell us of their [past generations'] condition, to tell us of their needs, or to soothe our hearts until such time as we too arrive in that place where they have gone." *The Harpist's Song in the Tomb of King Antef*, London, British Museum, Papyrus Harris 500. This is a poem of the First Intermediate Period (2200–1800 BC), a Ramesside Period copy of which has come down to us (1600–1100 BC). Cf. Edda Bresciani, ed., *Letteratura e poesia dell'antico Egitto* (Turin: Giulio Einaudi, 1969), 119–121.

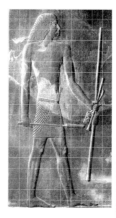

3.51, 3.52
Drawings of wooden panels depicting Hesire, high official of King Djoser, seated and standing, Third Dynasty. Egyptian Museum, Cairo.

3.53
Wooden panel depicting Hesire, high official of King Djoser, standing, Third Dynasty. Egyptian Museum, Cairo.

3.54
The deceased's shadow. Egyptian Museum, Cairo.

3.55
Djoser during the feast of *Heb-sed*. Saqqara, South Tomb.

8. Heinrich Schäfer, *Principles of Egyptian Art* (Oxford: Clarendon Press, 1986), 17. Alan Gardiner has made a careful study of Egyptian literature, judging it to be the work "of a people in love with life, joyful, blessed with an artistic sense, penetrating but devoid of depth of feeling and without idealism." Cf. Gardiner, *Egyptian Grammar* (1927; Oxford: Oxford University Press, 1994), 24. Cf. also Henry George Fischer, *L'écriture et l'art de l'Égypte ancienne* (Paris: Presses Universitaires de France, 1986).

9. This is a tale of the Middle Kingdom describing loyalty to King Amenemhat I (Eleventh Dynasty). Returning from an expedition against the Libyans together with the future Sesostris I, Sinuhe finds himself listening by chance to the announcement of the murder of Amenemhat I. Terrified, he flees toward the east and finds refuge with a local prince. The tale ends with Sinuhe's return to his homeland after wandering in the lands of "those who run in the sand" (Palestine). The narrative exalts the benevolence of the king and describes the plan to save Sinuhe from death: the construction of his tomb in Egyptian territory. When the king allows Sinuhe to return to Egypt, he makes him this promise: "You will be given the night with oils [castor oil and not olive oil like the men who walk in the desert] and bandages [made] by the hands of Tait. A procession will be held in your honor on the day of your inhumation. An anthropoid sarcophagus of gold, with a head of lapis lazuli; a sky shall be above you, inside the sarcophagus. You will be pulled along by oxen and musicians will precede you. The dance of the *mw.w* will be danced at the door of your tomb. The list of offerings will be read out, sacrifices will be made at your stela. Your pilasters shall be built of white stone among the tombs of the king's sons. You shall not die in a foreign land." Sinuhe replies, "This clemency that has saved me from death is beautiful indeed!" And upon his return, he declares, satisfied, "A pyramid in the midst of the pyramids was built for me. The chief of the pyramid stonecutters took possession of the plot, the chief of the planners planned, the chief sculptor sculpted, the directors of works in the necropolis busied themselves. All the furnishings that it is customary to put inside the tomb were organized as necessary. I was assigned funerary priests; a funerary garden was made for me in a place where there were cultivated lands, to the south toward the city, as befits a best friend. My statue was covered in gold and the skirt was of gold." Cf. Bresciani, *Letteratura e poesia dell'antico Egitto*, 167ff., and Alan Gardiner, *Egyptian Civilization* (Turin: Einaudi, 1971), 122

and 131. The *mw.w* may have been the ancient kings of Buto who greeted the deceased at the entrance of the necropolis with a dance. This ritual was carried out in a temporary pavilion, depicted in a tomb of Paheri from the Eighteenth Dynasty (el-Kab, tomb 3).

10. Ineni was "hereditary prince, noble, chief of all the works at Karnak; superintendent of the dual house of silver and gold; guardian of the seals of all the contracts of the House of Amon; conservator of the dual grain stores of Amon." He was a high-ranking official of the Eighteenth Dynasty during the reign of Amenhotep I, Tuthmosis I, II, III, and Hatshepsut. Breasted, *Ancient Records of Egypt*, 2:18, §43, and 2:44, §108.

11. Ibid., 2:47, §116.

12. Up until the Fifth Dynasty (King Unas), monuments were for the most part devoid of epigraphs. It wasn't until Egyptian civilization began to become aware of a decline that hieroglyphs started to appear on monuments, literally covering them, as if to escape from *damnatio memoriae*. For an example of this graphic frenzy, in which the hieroglyphic signs are increasingly compressed during the Ptolemaic era through lack of space, see the walls of the temples of Esna, Edfu, and Dendera.

13. The cults of Isis were introduced to Rome under Sulla, together with the widely known work of Nechepso-Petosiris, an astrological compendium of Alexandrian provenance (second century BC?). In order to halt the spread of neo-Egyptian rites, the Roman Senate was obliged to repeatedly destroy the temples dedicated to Isis in 58, 54, and 50 BC. Cf. Geminos, *Introduction aux phénomènes*, ed. Germaine Aujac (Paris: Belles Lettres, 1975), xxx–xxxi. For the persistence of the cult of the curly-headed Isis during the sixteenth century, see Jean Seznec, *The Survival of the Pagan Gods* (Princeton: Princeton University Press, 1961), 244–245 and 292. For the cult of Isis in general, see Jurgis Baltrusaitis, *La ricerca di Iside, saggio sulla leggenda di un mito* (Milan: Adelphi, 1985).

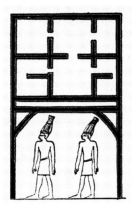

3.56–3.58
The dance of the *mw.w* in the Tomb of Paheri, Eighteenth Dynasty. Necropolis of El-Kab, tomb 3.

14. On 17 July 1799, a few days before the Battle of the Pyramids, Michel-Ange Lancret announced that officer Pierre Bouchard had found, near el-Rashid (in the Nile Delta), a piece of black basalt with an inscription in three languages. On 2 Fructidor of the year 7 of the French Republican Calendar (19 August 1799), the *Courier d'Egypte* informed all scholars of Egyptology that the stone contained three texts: one written in hieroglyphs, one in Syriac (actually Demotic), and one in Greek. Copies were made and distributed to all the European scientists before the fall of Alexandria and the resultant seizure of the stone, which was removed to England in February 1802. The stone, which must originally have been half a meter longer, is 118 cm long, 77 cm wide, 30 cm thick, and weighs 762 kg. Ordered in the ninth year (27 March 196 BC) of the reign of Ptolemy V Epiphanes, it contains a decree issued by priests to honor the concessions made to the temples. A copy of this decree in Demotic, Greek, and hieroglyph was to have been placed in every temple close to the statue of the king. Ernest Alfred Wallis Budge published it for the first time in 1889 with the title *Easy Lessons in Egyptian Hieroglyphics with Sign List*. See also Carol Andrews, *The Rosetta Stone* (London: British Museum, 1981), 17–21, which contains a transcription of the stela. Jean-François Champollion's *Lettre à M. Dacier relative à l'alphabet des hieroglyphs phonétiques* appeared in 1822, three years after the research of Thomas Young was published in London in the 1819 *Supplement to the Fourth Edition of the Encyclopaedia Britannica*. Champollion was familiar with the studies of Sylvestre de Sacy and Johan David Åkerblad, who were responsible for having identified the proper names in the hieroglyphic section of the stone. On 27 September 1822, Champollion was thirty-two years old and exhausted from the long labor of deciphering: the eight pages of his memorial to Dacier, who read it before the Academy, opened the door to three thousand years of Egyptian history for the West. The results of the Napoleonic scientific expeditions were remarkable: Claude-Louis Berthollet's *Observations sur la natron* prepared the way for chemical physics, showing the effects of pressure, heat, light, and the concentration of reagents in chemical reactions; twelve naturalists, among them Geoffroy and Savigny, radically changed the taxonomical notions of Cuvier, drawing attention to the study of morphology; François Michel de Rozière elaborated fifteen tables, which were to bring mineralogy definitively within the scope of geology; Dominique

Jean Larrey, the inventor of field surgery—Wellington admired his work at Waterloo—made important clinical descriptions of tropical diseases. Between 1809 and 1828 the monumental *Description de l'Egypte, ou recueil des obser-vations et des recherches qui ont été faites en Egypte pendant l'expédition de l'armée française, publié par les ordres de sa Majesté l'Empereur Napoléon le Grand*, was published, made up of ten volumes in folio and two volumes of maps: it contained 837 copper plate engravings, fifty of which were in color. A third atlas was dedicated solely to the topography of Egypt and Palestine (47 plates). Nine volumes of text accompanied the graphic works. Cf. *Monuments de l'Egypte. L'édition impériale de 1809* (Paris, 1988).

15. The world of Egyptian pictorial art has nothing in common with the contemporary one. Frankfort noted that "anyone seeking 'speculative thought' in the ancient documents will discover that there is very little in the written sources which is deserving of the name of 'thought' in the strict sense of the term….Speculative thought transcends experience but only because it attempts to explain it, to unify and coordinate it. Speculative thought attempts to buttress the chaos of experience so that the bare bones of its structure be revealed—an order, a coherence, a meaning." Henri Frankfort and Henriette A. Frankfort, "Myth and Reality," in *La filosofia prima dei greci. Concezioni del mondo in Mesopotamia, nell'antico Egitto e presso gli Ebrei* (Turin: Einaudi, 1963), 15.

16. It is significant that Khaemwese, one of the sons of Ramesses II, showed an "antiquarian" interest in the last king of the Fifth Dynasty (Unas) that went beyond the evident aim of restoring Old Kingdom beauty to the Seti era; as High Priest of Ptah at Memphis he carried out restoration work on a pyramid there and added a hieroglyph inscription in memory of Unas on its south side. The pyramid of Unas is particularly important from a cultural point of view, for it was the first to have the Texts of the Pyramids inscribed inside it.

17. For the legend of Osiris, see George Hart, *Egyptian Myths* (London: British Museum, 1990), passim.

18. The inscription on a tomb at Abd el-Gurna, partly transcribed by Brugsch and now lost, read: "I inspected the excavation of the cliff-tomb of his majesty alone, no one seeing, no one hearing. I sought out the excellent things upon ___ I was vigilant in seeking that it was excellent. I made fields of clay, in order to plaster their tombs of the necropolis; it was a work such as the ancestors had not done which I was obliged to do there ___ I sought out

3.59
The jackal Wepwawet,
"opener of the ways," and
the Buto cobra Wadjet
on the banner representing
the king's placenta (?).
Saqqara, Djoser funeral
complex, South Tomb.

3.60
"Vegetating" Osiris. Egyptian
Museum, Cairo.

for those who should be after me. It was a work of my heart, my virtue was wisdom; there was not given to me a command by an elder." Breasted, *Ancient Records of Egypt*, 2:43, §106.

19. 1 Corinthians 15:36. Written for the Christians of Corinth by Paul at Epheseus at Easter of 57 AD.

20. There are very few cases in Egyptian art where the face is depicted frontally: in the ideogram "face" (*her*) and "eye" (*iret*); in depictions of the divinity Bes, a good-natured monster; in the figures of people in unusual poses, such as a woman giving birth. For all other portrayals of animate beings, the principle of the most evidence holds true, which is usually translated into the profile view. In the case of an advancing figure, it is always the far leg that leads. The exception to the rule of the profile view are the hieroglyphs representing the owl, the tortoise, the lizard, the scarab beetle, the fly, the millipede, the scorpion, and the cow, such as the goddess Hathor. Gardiner, *Egyptian Grammar*, s.v. From the beginning of the sixth century BC in Greece, the frontal position was used in figures for representing states of alteration, ugliness, or death, such as in the famous Attic cup with Achilles killing Penthesilea (470 BC, Munich, Staatliche Antikensammlungen).

21. It is useful to remember here that "the 'Hieratic,' or aniconic script, devoid of the magical powers inherent in figures, was written in ink on papyrus, thus becoming one of the principal instruments of the administration, and later, of bookmaking. On the other hand, hieroglyphs, with their figures vested with special powers, were strictly bound to the world of ritual, and suitable therefore for inscriptions destined to 'last forever,' mainly on stone.... The derivation of the signs of hieratic script from the signs of hieroglyphic script is typological and not evolutionary, and is almost certainly linked to the birth of the first texts." Alessandro Roccati, "La nascita della scrittura (IV e III millennio)," in Anna Maria Donadoni Roveri and Francesco Tiradritti, eds., *Kemet. Alle sorgenti del tempo* (Milan: Electa, 1998), 57.

22. John 1:1–4.

23. In Egypt the painter-scribe belonged to the sphere of the sacred; the writing of hieroglyphs was considered the noblest profession in comparison to others carried out in close contact with materials. See on this subject, "La gloria degli uomini saggi è eterna," a scholastic text from the Ramesses era, Eighteenth Dynasty, in Bresciani, *Letteratura e poesia dell'antico Egitto*, 301–302. The statue of Intishedu, scribe and "carpenter of the boats of Neith, known to the king," was discovered in his *serdab* together

with three other statues, which portray him at different ages. The figure is shown in the pose of a dignitary or sovereign, with the right hand holding a handkerchief. The statue, discovered in 1990 in the Western cemetery of Giza, is now preserved in the Egyptian Museum in Cairo (JE 98945). Cf. *Egyptian Art in the Age of the Pyramids* (New York: Metropolitan Museum of Art, 1999), 300–301. According to Zahi Hawass, the tombs of the pyramid builders of Giza also made "democratic" use of a small pyramid similar to that of the king.

24. Hieroglyphic script is based on redundancy. Next to logograms (ideograms), which express what they portray, there are also twenty-four monoconsonant phonograms, erroneously defined as the Egyptian alphabet, which serve as phonetic complements for bi-and tri-consonant hieroglyphs. The monoconsonant signsare constructed according to the principle of acrophony, that is to say, where the sound of a sign is drawn from the picture of the object whose name begins with that sound. Homophone signs, however, are distinguished from each other with the use of mute determinatives, which indicate the class they belong to (man, mineral, etc.). Egypt never renounced the use of hieroglyphs, although it could easily have adopted alphabetic writing, because "les hiéroglyphes sont étroitement liés à la langue égyptienne et non pas, comme on le croit volontiers, à des idées qui pourraient se traduire en n'importe quelle langue." Jean Capart, *Je lis les hiéroglyphes* (Brussels: J. Lebègue, 1946), 5. The concept of scribe was expressed with three hieroglyphs meaning: his tools (*sesh*), a house (*per*), and life (*ankh*). Henri Sottas and Etienne Drioton, *Introduction à l'étude des hiéroglyphes* (1922; Paris: Librairie Orientaliste, 1989), 63.

25. See the example of integration in which the text does not mention the figures of the hunter and the hunted *ibex*, since they are represented as "large" ideograms. Fischer, *L'écriture et l'art de l'Égypte ancienne*, 27–28, fig. 2. The example shows clearly how the hieroglyph developed out of a miniaturization of certain elements of the scene, which, like ideograms or phonograms, became written signs by a process of acronymy. This mechanism is clear from the dawn of writing, as in the Narmer Palette.

26. The Egyptian obsession with the duration and persistence of identity meant that a person was not identified by his character but by means of the attributes of his status, which were worn on his body: hieroglyphic emblems in the true sense of the term. The Egyptian gods were also identified by their hieroglyphic emblems, which were often worn on the head. Usually, portraits of

kings and queens tended toward an ideal of perfection of the human body, starting from their individual characteristics, with the exception of portraits from the Amarna period (Amenhotep IV, later Akhenaten), in which the characteristics of the physiognomic portrait were emphasized, a tendency already present in the statues of Amenhotep III. Cf. the two statues of the scribe Amenhotep (son of Hapu), represented with folds on his belly when he is a youth and thin when he is an old man (Eighteenth Dynasty, 1403–1365 BC, Cairo, Egyptian Museum, JE 44861, JE 38368 = CG 42127).

27. Egyptian artists developed a very sophisticated representational system. The Egyptian construction grid predated the figure in exactly the same way that the Renaissance perspectival box predated the composition of the scene. The squared module corresponded to the height of the ankle from the ground and the main points of the body had their position fixed beforehand with regard to the squared off grid. Thanks to this system, which made no allowance for "interpretations," different parts of the same statue could be sculpted independently and in workshops that were at some distance from one another. The attraction of this objective mode of representation was documented at a later date by Diodorus Siculus, who cites an episode in which two artists (Telekles and Theodorus) attempted to sculpt separately—one at Samos and the other at Ephesus—a statue of Apollo Pythius according to the Egyptian canon. The achievement of classical proportions (Old Canon) came about between the Fifth Dynasty and the First Intermediate Period. They reappeared in the Eighteenth Dynasty after the expulsion of the Hyksos and from the beginnings of the Twenty-fifth Dynasty until the end of the Third Intermediate Period, when there was a feminization of the male figure. During the Old Kingdom, guidelines were used, which in the Sixth Dynasty were traced to the height of the knee. From the Twelfth Dynasty (tomb of Serenput II at Qubbet el-Hawa) until the end of the Third Intermediate Period, a grid of eighteen squares was used for the standing figures (from the foot to the hairline) and of fourteen for seated figures. Only in the Amarnian period do we find twenty squares between the foot and the hairline. After the Twentieth Dynasty, the figures became taller, so that the knee was at the height of six and three-quarters squares and the head at the nineteenth square. With the Twenty-fifth Dynasty the number of squares changes from eighteen to twenty-one for standing figures (from foot to eyelid) and seventeen or sixteen for sitting figures.

Concerning the controversial relationship between the old and new canons, Gay Robins presents a convicing explanation, according to which Egyptian proportions conform to those of the living body. In fact, the royal cubit of 52.5 centimeters could not have been the measurement from the tips of the fingers to the elbow because it would have meant the existence of people around 180 cm tall, for which there was no parallel at that period. A plausible statue may instead be obtained by keeping the same measurement, but in relation to the small cubit of 45 cm. Rather than posit a change in the measuring system, Robins hypothesizes that at the basis of the change in rule there was the desire to move from a squared module of 1⅕ palms to a grid square of one palm, that is to say, ⅙ of the small cubit: this would have meant a shift from a grid square of 9 cm to one of 7.5 cm. If the two grids are superimposed, quadrant 5 corresponds to 6, 10 to 12, and 15 to 18; while quadrant 18 corresponds exactly to quadrant 21⅜ in the new canon. Apparently the new grid was obtained by multiplying the old quadrant by ⁶⁄₅. It must be borne in mind that the change of proportion that is observed in different epochs does not always result in a change to the grid square. Often the ancient grid continues to be used in the New Kingdom, when the proportions of the figures change, while figures with proportions that are very close to those of the Old Kingdom are sometimes drawn with a late (style) grid of twenty-one quadrants. The grid system and proportions are not synonymous, therefore, and there is a certain elasticity in the application of the rules. For an update of the traditional theories of Iversen and Lepsius, see Gay Robins, *Proportion and Style in Ancient Egyptian Art* (Austin: University of Texas Press, 1994), passim. The standard unit of measurement in ancient Egypt was the royal cubit (*meh-njsut*), such as the basalt one from Ptahmose, which measures 53 x 3.3 x 2.2 cm (Eighteenth Dynasty, 1539–1292 BC, Leyden, Rijksmuseum van Oudheden). Usually the royal cubit is equal to 52.5 cm and is subdivided into twenty-eight fingers (in the Djoser complex at Saqqara, Lauer calculated a measurement of 52.5 cm). Several lesser measurements are also marked on the instrument: a "small cubit" of twenty-four fingers, an arm of twenty, a foot of sixteen, a large hand span of fourteen, a small hand span of twelve, a fist of six, a hand of five, a palm of four fingers. From the first to the sixteenth finger the intervals are further subdivided in "fractions" of ½, ⅓, and so on, up to ¹⁄₁₆, more or less the equivalent of 1.16 millimeters. The *remen*, which corresponds to half of the diagonal of the quadrant of a

3.61
Statue of the scribe
Amenhotep, son of Hapu,
as a young man,
New Reign. Egyptian
Museum, Cairo.

3.62
Tomb of Neferseshemptah,
Old Kingdom. Egyptian
Museum, Cairo. H. Schäfer,
Principles of Egyptian Art
(Oxford, 1986), plate 31.

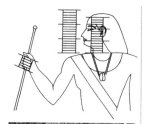

3.63
Comparison between ancient and new canons: six-finger palm and five-finger palm. Gay Robins, *Proportion and Style in Ancient Egyptian Art* (Austin, 1994), page 167.

3.64
Djoser running during the Jubilee feast, detail. Note the reticulate of twenty-one quadrants at the top, which was superimposed on the stela in the Saite period for the purposes of copying. Saqqara, stela in the tomb beneath the step pyramid.

3.65
Self-portrait of Senenmut. Deir el-Bahri, tunnel of tomb TT353.

cubit, equals 19.79 fingers, which falls exactly within the finger subdivided into ten parts, and is therefore measurable. The ruler was generally made of wood or stone and bore good wishes dedicated to its owner. See *The Sense of Art in Ancient Egypt* (Milan, 1990), 121–123, list 71.

28. In the *Litany of Re* in the tomb of Tuthmosis III (KV 34) at Biban el-Moluk, the sun is invoked with seventy-five different names.

29. See Nadine Cherpion, *Mastabas et hypogées d'Ancien Empire. Le problème de datation* (Brussels: Connaissance de l'Egypte ancienne, 1989).

30. In Egypt the painter was a high-ranking worker who received a salary. Although he was bound to the pharaoh, he could also carry out work on private tombs. A stela from the necropolis of Abydos (Eleventh Dynasty, about 2000 BC, Paris, Louvre) exemplifies very well the characteristics of the Egyptian painter-scribe. Sculpted by Irtisen for himself and his family, his text reads, "I am one who knows the secrets of the hieroglyphs and the way to celebrate religious ceremonies. I have applied every sort of magic without leaving out anything, because I am an artist who excels at his art and who has reached the peak of what he has learned. I know the rules of movements and the proportions of the calculations, know how to work in intaglio and in relief, according to what must be set in and what must be given prominence, so that a body is in the right place. I know how a male figure goes and a female figure comes, the attitude of a bird in a trap, the action of one who strikes a prisoner, while one eye looks at the other, the gaze of the terrified enemy, the way the arm is raised of he who strikes a hippopotamus, and the movement of one who runs. I know the proportions of the colors and their elements, and I do not allow them to be burnt by fire or faded by water. These things were revealed only to me, and to the eldest son of my body, because God [= king] ordered that he be taught these things. I saw what came out of his hands when he worked with every sort of precious metal, silver and gold to begin with, as well as with ivory and ebony." Sergio Pernigotti, "Le 'arti minori' nell'Antico Egitto," *Archeo* 71 (1991): 66. In three thousand years of Egyptian history, the only list of architects that has come down to us was left by Khnumibra on the walls of the Wadi Hammamat. Dating from the fifth century, the list begins with Kanofer (2700 BC), father of Imhotep, and ends with the same author. Kazimierz Michałowski, *L'arte dell'antico Egitto* (Milan, 1990), 580. Among the architects mentioned are Amenhotep, son of Hapu (Theban Tomb 73=TT 73), who declares himself

to be a great lover of antique books and writes: "My master has nominated me director of several works; I have fixed the name of the king for all eternity, I have not imitated what was done in the past, I have created for him a mountain of quartzite ... nobody has done that since the time of the reordering of the world.... I was the director of works for his statue ... forty cubits high" (Breasted, *Ancient Records of Egypt*, 2:375, §917); Ineni (TT 81), prefect of Thebes who built the tomb of Tuthmosis I and the fourth and fifth pylon of Karnak; Hapunaseb, "nobleman, priest *sm* at Heliopolis, governor of the city, vizier, superintendent of the temples," and when he built the tomb of Tuthmosis II he was made "chief" (*hery*) of the House of Amon at Karnak (ibid., 2:161–162, §389); Senenmut (TT 71 and TT 353), "architect of all the queen's works [Hatshepsut]," "chief of the Guards of the King's daughter [Neferura], Governor of the Royal palace, Superintendent to the royal apartments." The portrait of Senenmut appears in the funerary temple of the queen at Deir el-Bahri and in the sloping adit of one of her two tombs, the one placed beneath the area of the temple (TT 353). For the story of Senenmut, see Peter F. Dorman, *The Monuments of Senenmut* (London: Kegan Paul International, 1988). The other people listed, whose work is known, are: Bek, architect of Akhenaten, who in his tomb defined himself as "he who was nominated assistant to the same Pharoah" and in a rock inscription at Aswan declares himself to be "chief of the sculptors of the great monuments to the king in the house of Aton in Akhetaton [Tell el-Amarna], son of the chief sculptor Men, born from the woman Royenet";

3.66
"Reserve" head, Fourth Dynasty. Kunsthistorisches Museum, Vienna.

3.67
Amenhotep I's royal cubit (top) and that of his vizier (bottom), c. 1550 BC.

Tuthmosis, the royal sculptor whose works discovered at Tell el-Amarna include plaster casts of living people and the beautiful colored bust of Nefertiti, now in Berlin. "Art" and "skill" are written as the hieroglyph ⌂ which is found in the form of an ideogram 𓎛𓏏𓏠 for *hemet*, meaning "art, technical skill, craft." Gardiner, *Egyptian Grammar*, 518, hieroglyph U 24. In the Old Kingdom 𓎛𓏏 *hemet* was a homophone meaning "woman" or "wife." The hieroglyph in the form of a vase is a determinative of the class "recipients full of water," and it also appears as a determinative in "vulva" and "absurdly" 𓍱 (*hem*). If we examine the composition of the triliteral hemet ⌂ "art, skill," we note that it is composed of three interesting hieroglyphs. The first is a tool for making holes in stone, used by vase makers and sculptors; the second is a bread, or a pestle for grinding pigments (*t*), used by painters; the third is a roll of papyrus, determinative for all the abstract words that refer to writing and thought. Several meanings seem to coexist within the expression "art."

31. Carpenter gives a good definition of the Greek architect: "In the parent language *architektōn* literally-signifies no more than 'builder-in-chief' or the French chef d'atelier. In view of the fact that the normal plan for a fifth-century temple was dictated by established tradition and the architect was free to realize the plan only in terms of one of the two accepted columnar styles, the Doric and the Ionic (to which a Corninthian variant of Ionic was added later), it was not his province to devise a novel plan or invent new schemes of construction and decoration. Rather than that, it was his appointed role to supply his corps of skilled workmen (who first and foremost were expert marble cutters) with schedules of measurements and, on occasion, with full-size carved patterns to be duplicated over and over until they had amassed the store of identically shaped blocks in the required quantity. Thereafter it was his task to supervise the hoisting into place and the precise fitting and the firm fastening of all these blocks in the correct arrangement of the Order. Quite literally, and with all the implications adhering to the term, the Greek *architektōn* was the Master Builder." Rhys Carpenter, *The Architects of the Parthenon* (Harmondsworth, UK: Penguin, 1970), 107. In the age of Pericles a workman was paid one drachma a day, while architects received two and a half drachmas. From 309 to 304 BC, architects were paid three and a half drachmas a day. See Lydia De Novellis Spaventa, *I prezzi in Grecia e a Roma nell'Antichità* (Rome: Ditta tipografia Cuggiani, 1934).

32. In the text *Aegyptiaca*, which was preserved thanks to the transcriptions of Josephus Africanus and Eusebius (*Epitome*), Manetho states that Imhotep lived during the reign of Djoser and that he was active as a physician, master stonemason, and writing expert. See *Manetho*, trans. William G. Waddell (London and Cambridge: Loeb Classical Library, 1980), 41–43. The hieroglyphs on the base of the lost statue of Djoser, discovered by Jean-Philippe Lauer beyond the south wall of the Saqqara complex, describe Imhotep's titles in the following terms: "Chancellor of the King of the North; Chief Official of the King of the South; Regent of the Great Castle; hereditary noble, Grand Priest of Heliopolis; Im-hotep [who comes in peace]; Sculptor and Stonecutter [builder]." Cf. Raymond Weill, "Un temple de Noutirkha-Zosir à Héliopolis," in *Monuments nouveaux des premières dynasties* (Uppsala, 1911), 9–35; Gaston Maspero, "La IIIème Dynastie manéthonienne et le dieu Imouthès," in *Etudes de mythologie e d'archéologie égyptiennes* (Paris: E. Leroux, 1916), 124–142; Cecil M. Firth, "Excavations of the Service des Antiquités at Saqqara (November 1926–April 1927)," *Annales du Service des Antiquités de l'Egypte* 27 (1925): 105–159; Jamieson B. Hurry, *Imhotep: The Egyptian God of Medicine* (1926; Chicago, 1987); Raymond Weill, "Roi Neterkhet-Zeser et l'officier Imhotep à la pyramide à degrés de Saqqarah," *Revue de l'Egypte Ancienne* 2 (1929): 100–121; Cecil M. Firth, "Les nouvelles fouilles de la pyramid à degrés," *Revue de l'Egypt Ancienne* 3 (1931): 4–19; Cecil M. Firth and James E. Quibell, *Excavations at Saqqara: The Step Pyramid* (Cairo, 1935); Jean-Philippe Lauer, *Fouilles à Saqqarah. La Pyramide à degrés. L'Architecture*, 2 vols. (Cairo, 1936); Jean-Philippe Lauer, *Fouilles à Saqqarah. La Pyramide à degrés. Compléments* (Cairo, 1939); Herbert Ricke, "Bemerkungen zur Ägyptischen Baukunst des Alten Reichs II," in *Beiträge zur Ägyptische Bauforschung und Altertumskunde*, vol. 4 (Zurich, 1944), 61ff; Herbert Ricke, "Bemerkungen zur Ägyptischen Baukunst des Alten Reichs II," in *Beitrage zur Ägyptische Bauforschung und Altertumskunde*, vol. 5 (Cairo, 1950), 92–97; Kurt Sethe, "Imhotep. Der Asklepios der Aegypter. Ein vergötterter Mensch aus der Zeit des Königs Doser," in *Untersuchungen zur Geschichte und Altertumskunde Aegyptens*, vol. 2 (Hildesheim, 1964); Dieter Wildung, *Imhotep und Amenhotep. Gottwerdung im alten Ägypten* (Munich and Berlin, 1977); Sergio Donadoni, "Imhotpe," in *Enciclopedia universale dell'arte* (Novara, 1982).

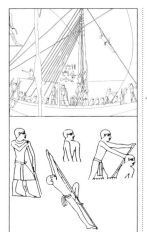

33. The labyrinth mentioned may have been the one in front of the pyramid of Amenemhat III at Hawara, also described by Herodotus. It is thought that the complex of administrative buildings subdivided by province (*nòmoi*) was situated there.

34. Plato, the teacher of Philip of Opus, had said: "We Greeks truly master all that we assimilate from the barbarians, but in doing so we bring it to the highest state of perfection" (*Epinomis* 987e). Egypt was also famous in antiquity for its medical and surgical tradition. In the *Odyssey* Homer comments that "of the Egyptians, each is a medical expert more than any other in the world" (*Odyssey* 4.231). *Paián*, or Peony, is a real person, physician to the gods of Olympus (*Iliad* 5.401). For Homer, *Paián* is "he who cures." *Lessico ragionato dell'Antichità Classica* (1898; Bologna, 1989), s.v. Later it becomes the nickname for the divinities that bring health, such as Apollo, Asklepios, Dionysus, and Thanatos. As confirmation of this ability, which was undoubtedly closely connected with the handling of corpses, Herodotus adds one more very modern characteristic: "Each physician is physician of one disease, not more. Everywhere therefore is full of physicians: there are physicians of the eyes, of the head, of the teeth, of the illnesses of the belly, of illnesses that are hard to identify" (Herodotus, *History* 2.84).

35. Giacomo Leopardi, *Zibaldone di pensieri* 1, 58 (Milan: Mondadori, 2003), 93.

36. Alexander took a copy of the *Iliad* with him everywhere in a silver casket looted from the tent of Darius III after the victory at Issus: "Homer, [Alexander] commented, was admirable for many things: among others for being a very knowledgeable architect, and it was undoubtedly he who was responsible for giving the order to plan the form of the city in harmony with surrounding nature.

3.68
Above: Mastaba of Akhethetep, east wall, Fifth Dynasty (Nyuserre). Musée du Louvre, Paris.

Below: Mastaba of Akhethetep, examples of body postures with and without rotation of torso.

3.69
The depiction of the sun's rays in a window of the Ptolemaic Temple of Dendera.

3.70
Senenmut with an architect's measuring rope and Neferura, daughter of Hatshepsut, Eighteenth Dynasty. Musée du Louvre, Paris.

In the absence of white earth, barley flour was used to trace out the contours, and on the plain which was of a black color, they drew a wide circle inside of which were straight lines that touched the circumference. In this way the form of a *chlamys* [short military cloak] was formed, with the lines running from its hem and the whole of the isthmus was contained within it. Alexander was satisfied with the drawing" (Plutarch, *Life of Alexander and Caesar* 2.26).

37. The diorite statue representing Prince Gudea of the Sumerian city of Lagash (c. 2000 BC) is preserved at the Louvre. A drawing tablet rests on his knees, with a ruler and a stylus; the plan of a temple is drawn on the tablet.

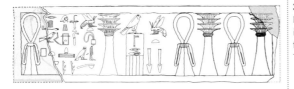

3.71
Reproduction of the inscription on the base of the lost statue of Djoser, Third Dynasty.

3.72
Writing tablet and stylus from the lap of the statue of Prince Gudea of Lagash, third millennium BC. Musée du Louvre, Paris.

38. Plato, *Republic* 377d.

39. Plato, *Theaetetus* 184b–d. The Platonic problem of distinguishing between that which is and that which appears to be, between copy and appearance, is evinced in an example cited by Pliny (*Natural History* 34.65). Lysippus, sculptor to Alexander the Great, "used to say that they [the ancients with their square-shaped statues] showed men as they were and he instead showed them how they appeared to the eye." In the *Republic*, Plato shows impatience with the very language of geometry, which was evolving in order that its practitioners could express themselves more clearly. The question raised by Plato in the myth of the cave comes up again with regard to *mimesis*. One must not go in search of the arts with the sole aim of seeking pleasure, but rather to seek that unique art that expresses a similitude with beauty, and not with the most pleasing sort but with the most right: the criterion of rightness implies a perfect adherence to the imitation of the original (*Laws* 667c–669c). In the dialog of the *Sophist* the problem is further articulated and the basis laid for the fundamental aporia of Western pictorial representation: appearance or reality (*Sophist* 235d–236c). The struggle against the deceptiveness of appearances and the impressions transmitted by the senses led Plato to deny that the visual arts had any superior efficacy where knowledge was concerned. Socrates, whose thought was transmitted through the citations of Plato and Xenophon (*Memorabilia* 3.10.1–10.2), asked the painter Parrasius: "Is not painting the representation of what one sees?… And when you depict models of beauty, since it is not easy to find a man who is perfect in all his parts, you put together the most beautiful details of each individual and in that way you make the whole body seem beautiful." Not only bodies may be reproduced but the soul may also be made manifest through the eyes, or rather by means of the expression of the face. Such an approach, in a certain sense functionalist, is very distant from the mathematical and proportional conception of the Pythagoreans. Like Protagoras, Socrates maintained that beauty is relative, and that it is to be found where there is an adaptation to its purpose. Plato, of course, could not deny the whole of art, and he thus introduced a distinction. If the works are carried out with *sophia*, and are geometrically correct, then they are acceptable: "Since in all of them there is grace and the absence of grace. And ugliness and discord and inharmonious motion are nearly allied to ill words and ill nature, as grace and harmony are the twin sisters of goodness and virtue and bear their likeness" (*Republic* 401a).

40. See *La filosofia prima dei greci*, 21, 15–43. For Jean-Pierre Vernant, myth is "a canvas upon which oral narrative and written literature are embroidered. If myths can vary from one version to another without the balance of the general system being affected, it is because the plot is not so important … as the categories that are transmitted implicitly from the stories as a whole." Myth is often refuted by Plato, for instance in his description of a type of reasoning that, undermined by its internal contradictions, self-destructs like a *mýthos* (*Philebus* 14a); or when he observes, through the mouthpiece of Socrates, that *mýthos* is not something that has to do with him but with poets—those same poets who are expelled from the city as liars in the *Republic*. Aristotle, however, "recognizes that in myth there is an element of divine truth" and is therefore forced to admit that, by implication, "it prefigures philosophy." Jean-Pierre Vernant, *Mito e società nell'antica greca* (Turin: Einaudi, 1982), 210–213.

41. Cook links the progressive disappearance of mythological scenes, which in the Hellenistic era becomes definitive, to the spread of literacy. See Robert M. Cook, *Greek Painted Pottery* (London: Methuen, 1960), chapters 5–7. The Neoplatonist Salustius maintained, however, that myths were useful because they "incited men to seek and impeded laziness of mind." Saturninus Secundus Salustius, *Sugli dèi e il mondo* 3.1, ed. Riccardo Di Giuseppe (Milan: Adelphi, 2000).

42. Vernant writes that, given the impossibility of applying reason to the irrationality of becoming or to the concept of Good, Plato "accorded myth a position of some eminence in his writings, as a means of expressing, at one and the same time, that which is within and outside of the bounds of philosophical language proper." Vernant, *Mito e società nell'antica Grecia*, 210.

43. Work of the first century discovered in the House of the Fawn at Pompeii. It is derived from an original by Philoxenos of Eretria (Eubea), which was painted for King Cassander at the end of the fourth century BC.

44. "The Macedonians threw themselves together with their king upon that squad of horsemen. The massacre turned into a bloodbath. Around Darius's chariot were strewn the most famous generals, struck down by glorious death under the eyes of their king, lying face down where they had fallen fighting, and with wounds to their breasts … commanders of great armies every one. Around them were heaped crowds of unknown foot soldiers and cavalrymen. Among the Macedonians too there were wounded: few, it must be said, but of the bravest.

Alexander was lightly wounded on the right thigh by the point of a sword. The horses that pulled Darius's chariot, wounded by spears and maddened by pain, had begun to shake off their yoke and topple the king from his chariot. He, fearing that he would fall alive into the hands of his enemies, jumped down from the chariot, leapt into the saddle of the horse in his retinue that had been harnessed to the chariot for this purpose, and so that he not be recognized during his flight by his royal insignia, he cast them down ignominiously." Q. Curtius Rufus, *Life of Alexander the Great* 3.2. Plutarch is less emphatic and does not blame Darius for his flight: "So far from allowing himself to be outflanked, he [Alexander] stretched his right wing much further out than the left wing of his enemies, and fighting there himself in the very foremost ranks, put the barbarians to flight. In this battle he was wounded in the thigh, Clares says, by Darius, with whom he fought hand to hand. But in the account that he gave Antipater of the battle, though indeed he owns he was wounded in the thigh with a sword, though not dangerously, he takes no notice of who it was that wounded him. Nothing was lacking to complete this victory, in which he overthrew more than a hundred and ten thousand of his enemies, but the taking of Darius, who very narrowly escaped by flight." Plutarch, *Alexander* 2.20.

45. Polybius (*Histories* 29.21.3–6) recalls that one of the most famous Greek writers, Demetrios of Phaleron, had composed a treatise titled *Tyche* (Fortune).

46. Aristophanes, *Frogs* 42–43.

47. Praxiteles had sculpted a *Tyche* for the sanctuary of the Goddess near the temple of Aphrodite at Megara (Pausanias, *Guide to Greece* 1.43.6). For the *baroque* movement in the Hellenistic period, cf. Jerome J. Pollitt, *Art in the Hellenistic Age* (Cambridge: Cambridge University Press, 1986).

48. Indeed, St. Paul goes on to explain, "The sting of death is sin; and the strength of sin is the law" (1 Corinthians 15:56).

49. Martial, *Epigrams* 4.21.

50. "Artes desidia perdidit, et quoniam animorum imagines non sunt, negleguntur etiam corporum" (Pliny, *Natural History* 35.5). Pliny upholds the ethical function of the images of ancestors and of the spoils of enemies that were hung outside and around the threshold. This was in order that the new purchaser of the house would be forced to keep before his eyes the great spirits of the past, "so that the house continued to triumph in eternity, even when its owner changed." Ibid., 35.7.

51. See Agnès Rouveret, *Histoire et imaginaire de la peinture ancienne* (Rome: École française de Rome, 1989), and Adolphe Reinach, *La peinture ancienne. Recueil Milliet* (Paris: Macula, 1985).

52. Salustius, *Sugli dèi e il mondo*, 25

53. *Epistola ad Diognetum* 6.1. Cf. Salustius, *Sugli dèi e il mondo*, 24. The Emperor Julian, who was a friend of Salustius, abandoned Christianity in 351 and restored the cult of the Sun.

54. Marcus Aurelius, *Meditations* 6.28. Marcus Aurelius cited among the great fortunes of his life that of having known the work of Epictetus, who preached "detachment from the world, disdain for pleasure, pain, and death, asceticism and the overcoming of all passion in order to live in the grace of God." Marcus Aurelius, *I ricordi*, ed. C. Carena (Turin: Einaudi, 1968), ix.

55. Seneca, *On Tranquillity of Mind* 2.7–10. Cf. Plato, who brings back the Orphic or Pythagorean idea of the body as the prison of the soul: "That we men are in a sort of prison" (*Phaedon* 62b).

56. The interpretation of dreams was practiced in ancient Egyptian culture (Chester Beatty papyrus III, London, British Museum, EA10683/3). A papyrus that belonged to Qen-her-khepeshef (Nineteenth Dynasty, 1254–1190 BC), derived from an older one, begins with the words, "If a man sees himself in a dream." The elements of the dream are preceded by "good" or "bad," depending on their presumed effect. The interpretation was based on homophony: if someone dreamed white bread (*hedj*), then his face would light up (*hedj*) with joy. Cf. *Les artistes du Pharaon. Deir el-Medineh et la Vallée des Rois* (Paris, 2002), 135, n. 77.

57. James Hillman, *The Dream and the Underworld* (New York: Harper and Row, 1979), 88. For the Christian hereafter in Byzantium, see also Robert Fossier, *Storia del Medioevo. I nuovi mondi 350–950* (Turin: Einaudi, 1984), 121.

58. Claudianus Mamertus in *De statu animae*, cf. Emile Bréhier, *La filosofia del Medioevo* (Turin: Einaudi, 1980), 30. On 7 June 362, the Emperor Julian forbade Christians to teach rhetoric because it was part of the classical *paidéia* and he did not think it right that Christians could make money by teaching a thing in which they did not believe.

59. Dodds quotes the words of the *Epistle to Diognetus*: "They [the Christians] live in their own countries, but are like foreigners; they share all the duties of citizens, and suffer all the limitations of foreigners, all foreign coun-

tries are their homelands, and all countries for them are foreign" (*Epistola ad Diognetum* 5.5). Cf. Eric R. Dodds, *Pagani e cristiani in un'epoca d'angoscia* (Florence: Nuova Italia, 1988), 19.

60. The *acribia* that Plutarch attributed to the Polykleitian canon: the perfect imitation of nature, "when with clay one gets to the nail … and perfection is obtained with many numbers and by attending to the smallest detail." Plutarch, *Quaestiones conviviales* 2.636c.

61. Robin Lane Fox, *Pagans and Christians* (New York: Knopf, 1987), 31.

62. Augustine, *Confessions* 35.

63. See the chapter on *Scolastica*, in Dagobert D. Runes, *Dizionario di filosofia* (Milan: A. Mondadori, 1982).

64. "Nobis curiositate non opus est, post Christum Jesum; nec inquisitione, post Evangelium." Tertullian, *Liber de praescriptione haereticorum*, c.7, plates 11 20–21. Cf. Eduard J. Dijksterhuis, *Il meccanismo e l'immagine del mondo* (Milan: Feltrinelli, 1980), 124. After 207, Tertullian's severity led him to become embroiled in an argument with the Catholic church. *De pudicitia* dates from this period. He also opposed women's fashions, the arts, and civil professions.

65. The fathers of the church were opposed to technical innovation, and even artistic precision was seen as a pagan *luxuria*, so it is no surprise that Cyprian reports a decline of "skill in the arts" (*Ad Demetrianum* 3.9). Cf. Giusto Traina, *La tecnica in Grecia e a Roma* (Bari: Laterza, 1994), 57.

66. Borrowing from the lost Polykleitian canon, Plotinus writes: "Everybody, so to speak, states that visible beauty consists of symmetry among the parts, each with the other and all together, to which are added beautiful hues, thus … beauty consists in their symmetry and their measure; for those … beautiful colors, like the light of the sun, are without beauty, for they are simple and their beauty does not come from the symmetry of their parts." *Enneads* 1.6, 1.21–33, and 3.35.

67. "Ergo age, pictor, puniceas confunde rosas et lilia misce, quique erit ex illis color aeris, ipse sit oris." Ausonius, *Ad pictorem de Bissulae imagine*, fourth century. Cf. Carlo Carena, ed., *I poeti latini della decadenza* (Turin: Einaudi, 1988), 49.

68. Plato, *Theaetetus* 147d–148b.

69. The five so-called Platonic solids were not invented by Plato (*Timaeus* 31c–32b; 55c, 55d–56c). The Pythagoreans studied the cube, the pyramid, and the dodecahe-

dron. Later, the mathematician Theaetetus added the octahedron and the icosahedron. Cf. Thomas L. Heath, *A History of Greek Mathematics*, vol. 1 (New York: Dover Publications, 1981), 162. According to Heron of Alexandria, Archimedes discovered thirteen semiregular solids inscribable within a sphere. For a careful study of Greek geometry, and in particular of polyhedrons, see Bartel L. van der Waerden, *Science Awakening*, ed. A. Dresden (Groningen: Noordhoff, 1954), 173–179. See also Arpad Szabo, *Les débuts des mathématiques grecques*, trans. M. Federspiel (Paris: Vrin, 1977).

70. Plotinus, *Enneads* 1.6, 3.31.

71. Claudianus, *Laus Serenae Reginae uxoris Stilichonis* 25–33.

72. See Lucian of Samosata, *The Hall* 21. Plato cannot help remarking, "For sight is the most acute of the senses allowed to our body; yet it cannot see thought. What extraordinary loves we would have if thought could assure us of a clear image of itself to contemplate" (*Phaedrus* 251d). Jacob Burckhardt rightly noted that "painting celebrated those myths from which philosophy sought to free the Greek conscience. Speculative thought was the enemy of the splendid and multiform world of the image and may even have felt itself to be in competition with it, to the extent that the lack of discourse about the figurative arts may even be explained in part as being due to envy." Burckhardt, "Die Griechen und ihre Künstler," in *Vorträge. 1844–1887* (Basel, 1919), 202–214. Although the paintings on panels have been lost, Plato's condemnation is indirectly indicative of the high level of illusionism that had been reached by the fifth century in painting and scene painting. Pliny writes that the first to introduce painted panels on stage was Sophocles (*Natural History* 35.77); the "shadow maker" (*skenografos*) Agatharchus's name recurs in Vitruvius (*De architectura* 7.*praef*.2), where he is identified as the most eminent scene painter. An interesting analysis of the term was carried out by Pierre Gros, "La scaenographia dans les projets," in *Le dessein d'architecture dans les sociétés antiques* (Strasbourg, 1984), 232–253.

73. André Grabar, "Plotin et les origines de l'esthétique médiévale," in *Cahiers Archéologiques* 1 (1945): 15–34.

74. For the three circles scheme in the *Manual of Mount Athos*, cf. Erwin Panofsky, *Il significato delle arti visive* (Turin: Einadi, 1962), 82–85.

75. Richard Krautheimer, "Introduction to an Iconography of Mediaeval Architecture," *Journal of the Warburg and Courtauld Institutes* 5 (1942): 1–33.

76. For the imprint of the holy face (*mandylion*), cf. Tania Velmans, "Aspects du conditionnement de l'artiste byzantin: les commanditaires, les modèles, les doctrines," in Xavier Barral i Altet, ed., *Artistes, artisans et production artistique au Moyen Age*, vol. 2, *Commande et travail* (Paris: Picard, 1987), 88–91.

As regards the idea of type, see the Greek term *týpos*, which von Blumenthal analyzed in its various meanings of "blow," "mark," "cast," "mold," and "impression," concluding that the prevalent meaning for the word *týpos* is "relief," both in the literature and in inventories. Herodotus describes how the Egyptians would deliver the corpse of a dead relative to embalmers "who have a model (*týpos*) built in wood in the form of a man [*anthropoid sarcophagus*], and when it is completed they put the corpse inside it" (*Histories* 2.86). The *týpos anthropoeidès* is therefore the man-shaped model and may only indicate a "hollow form in the shape of a man." Of particular interest is the meaning that was subsequently attributed to *týpos*: "a formless object, a coarse figure," referring to a blocked out statue in the rough. The use of *týpos* in this sense is found in the *Physical Poem* by Empedocles, where he writes of the birth of man, "In the beginning shapeless *týpoi* emerged from the earth" (fr. B' 62, 4, according to Hermann Diels, rev. Wilhelm Kranz, *Die fragmente des Vorsokratiker* [Berlin, 1951]), which Diels has interpreted thus: "In the beginning there emerged clods of earth that were piled up in shapeless mounds." The concept of imprecision and incompleteness present in the term *týpoi* (prototypes) was able further to develop the meaning of "roughed out sculpture" found in Plato, the only case in the classical period in which it appears with the meaning of models for statues: "A sketch (*týpos*) and the forms of the penalties having been enunciated, examples were supplied to the judges" (*Laws* 876e). Finally, *týpos* is found in the sense of "general shape or type," having the same meaning as in modern language, where it also includes its negative meaning of "opposite," "reverse," or "double." Albrecht von Blumenthal, "Typos und Paradeigma," in *Hermes* (1928): 391–414. It should be noted that *týpoi* is also translated as "whole moulds" in Empedocles, *Frammenti e testimonianze*, ed. A. Tonelli (Milan: Bompiani, 2002), DK 62, and as "finished molds" in Empedocles, *Poema fisico e lustrale*, ed. C. Gavalotti (Milan: Mondadori, 1975), fr. 62. The idea of a wax mold as a *týpos* is found in Philo of Alexandria: "When a city is founded … sometimes an architect is present who studies the mild climate and the prosperity of the site, and describes to himself first of all almost all the parts of the future city: the temples, the gymnasiums, the prytaneums, the squares, ports, quays and alleys, the foundations of the walls and of the houses and of the other public buildings. *Thus having gathered within his own soul the mark of every separate thing, as in a wax mould*, he carries within himself an intelligible city, the features of which are awakened thanks to an innate memory that accentuates its characteristics; so, like a good worker (*demiourgós*), and keeping the model fixed in his mind, he begins to build it in stone and wood, assimilating to each incorporeal idea the corporeal essences." Traina, *La tecnica in Grecia e a Roma*, 71 (italics added).

77. It was customary for the families of the Roman *nobilitas* to have wax molds made of the faces of deceased family members. These were then brought to funerals in order to demonstrate the antiquity and importance of their *gens*, a custom derived from the Greek courts. For the continuity between Greek and late antique art, cf. Ranuccio Bianchi Bandinelli, "Virgilio Vaticanus 3225 e Iliade Ambrosiana," in *Archeologia e cultura* (Milan and Naples: Ricciardi, 1961).

78. Cf. Louis Bréhier, *L'art chrétien* (Paris: Librairie Renouard, 1928). See: Christ as the sun god Apollo in the necropolis beneath St. Peter's in Rome (third century?); Christ as Orpheus with the animals in the catacomb of Domitilla; the disciples in a circle around Aristotle in the catacombs of via Latina, which becomes the group of apostles around Christ in the Hypogeum of the Aureli.

79. The funerary relief of a circus magistrate (c. 120–140 AD) preserved in the Deposito del Museo Laterano in Vaticano may be compared with the marble bas-relief of the circus races (c. 180–190 AD) in the Museo Archeologico di Foligno. Cf. Ranuccio Bianchi Bandinelli, *L'arte romana nel centro del potere* (Milan: Rizzoli, 1981), 263, fig. 294, and 290, fig. 324.

80. "Artis Phidiacae toreuma clarum / Pisces aspicis: adde acquam, natabunt" (Martial, *Epigrams* 3.35).

81. The last remnants of the Egyptian religion survived on the island of Philae. Near the temple of Isis is a temple dedicated to Augustus, one dedicated to Trajan, and an entrance with the name "Diocletian's door." In the southern zone, near the chapel to the god Mandulis, is the chapel dedicated to Imhotep, the architect of Djoser (Third Dynasty), deified in the age of Ptolemy as Asklepios. Two Christian churches also coexisted among these buildings. After the suppression of the pagan cults, the atrium of the temple was transformed into a church and its images were destroyed. The island also preserves the last testi-

3.73
The charioteer Porphyrios,
fourth century. Archaeological
Museum, Istanbul.

mony of hieroglyphic script, dating from 28 August 394. The last inscriptions in demotic on the island of Philae date from 452: "Words spoken by the god Mandulis." After this, ancient Egyptian script disappears forever.

82. Cassiodorus writes that Theodoric commissioned Boethius to build a hydraulic clock and a solar clock for Gundobald, king of the Burgundians. Boethius was the only man to have "drawn from the very fount of the sciences those arts which are commonly exercised without knowledge of them ... in order to make the scientific laws of the Greeks part of Roman culture" (*Letters* 1.45). Cf. Boethius, *La consolazione di Filosofia*, ed. Alessandro Caretta and Luigi Samarati (Brescia: La Scuola, 1985), ix.

83. Fossier, *Storia del Medioevo*, 114. The Egyptian obelisk erected in the hippodrome of Constantinople was brought there by the emperor Julian in 390. On its base are two groups of sculptures portraying Theodosius I and his court. Ranuccio Bianchi Bandinelli, *Roma: La fine dell'arte antica* (Milan: Rizzoli, 1981), 352–355. This may be compared with the monument to the charioteer Porphyrios at the Archaeological Museum of Istanbul (fourth century) and the monument to the charioteer Quiriacus at Carthage a century later, now preserved in the Louvre, Paris (*Mosaïques romaines et paléochrétiennes du Musée du Louvre* [Paris: Editions de la Réunion des musées nationaux, 1978], 77). A chronological comparison of the depiction of charioteers is particularly useful to verify the progressive flattening of space. See the charioteer in the Basilica of Junius Bassus, and the later *Flight of Alexander the Great* on the Porta di Sant'Alipio in St. Mark's Basilica in Venice.

84. Elizabeth Gilmore Holt, *Storia documentaria dell'arte. Dal Medioevo al XVIII secolo* (Milan: Feltrinelli, 1977), 3–8.

85. Iconoclasm lasted, with few interruptions, from 724 to 843. For a rapid review of the principal texts, see Cyril Mango, *The Art of the Byzantine Empire: Sources and Documents* (Englewood Cliffs, N.J.: Prentice-Hall, 1972), and the fundamental text by André Grabar, *L'Iconoclasme byzantin* (Paris: Flammarion, 1984).

86. Islam was also hostile to painters, defined as the worst of men because they create in competition with the Creator. To possess an image corresponds to usury or to the possession of a dog, whose presence prevents the Angel of Pardon from entering the house.

87. Illusionism reappears, although only sporadically, in the summer residence of the bishops of Milan at Castelseprio (sixth-ninth centuries) and in the church of

3.74
The charioteer Quiriacus, Carthage, fifth to sixth century. Musée du Louvre, Paris. Ma1798.

3.75
Basilica of Junius Bassus, *The Consul in the Circus*, 331–350. Palazzo del Drago, Rome.

3.76
Apulian vase, c. 380 BC. Ruvo.

3.77
Charioteer, silk serge, Byzantium, eighth century. Cathedral Treasury, Aachen.

3.78
The flight of Alexander the Great, Byzantine relief, eleventh century. St. Mark's Basilica, Venice.

Santullano built by Alfonso II at Oviedo. The Castelseprio frescoes are probably the work of a painter of "Hellenistic" culture of the sixth-seventh centuries. See Raffaella Farioli Campanati, "La cultura artistica delle regioni bizantine d'Italia dal VI all'XI secolo," in *I bizantini in Italia* (Milan: Credito Italiano, 1982), 196–206.

88. In the absence of a documented theorization of representational methods in a pre-Renaissance context, it is inappropriate to speak of *parallel perspective*. It seems more appropriate to use the term *oblique drawing* in order to indicate the result of the graphic operation carried out on a physical support, whereby two or three contiguous views of the object are represented alongside each other in a straightforward paratactical fashion in order to represent its three-dimensionality. The same effect can be obtained by judicious choice of the view of the object that is to be represented. In some cases the third view chosen is the interior view, as in the representations of Christian basilicas at the close of the fifth century in Africa, or in the later "section" of the Basilica of St. Mark's in Venice, dating from the thirteenth century. See *Mosaïques romaines et paléochrétiennes du Musée du Louvre*, 150 and 152. See also Sergio Bettini, *Mosaici antichi di San Marco a Venezia* (Bergamo: Istituto italiano d'arti grafiche, 1944), plates XCII–XCIII. Another circumstance in which the term *oblique drawing* is appropriate is in relation to the diverging lines of so-called inverse, or reverse, perspective. Following on from Wulff's ideas on the subject, Liliane Brion-Guerry writes that "ce n'est pas un témoin extérieur à la scène qui les regarde, mais tel personage à l'intérieur de l'espace de représentation." As a theory, it seems outlandish, even if we bear in mind the theories of Plotinus on the self-identification of the subject with the object to be represented. See Brion-Guerry, "Vision intérieure et perspective inversée," in *Zeitschrift für Ästhetik und allgemeine Kunstwissenschaft* 2 (1966): 174–193, and in particular 185; Oskar Wulff, "Die umgekehrte Perspektive und die Niedersicht," in *Kunstwissenschaftliche Beiträge August Schmarsow gewidmet* (Leipzig: K. W. Hiersemann, 1907), 1ff. In small-sized paintings such as illuminated manuscripts, this phenomenon may be explained by a prevarication of the composition on the appearances of the *visio*. In wall painting, however, a phenomenon comes about whereby the artist drawing two parallel lines is subjected to an automatic optical correction: standing on scaffolding close to the wall, the painter must, in order to continue to see the parallel lines while he is executing them, open out the one that is furthest away from him. The pedestal of the

Madonna at Torcello is slightly divergent, but, if observed from a point closer to the wall, thanks to the effect of anamorphosis, the sides of the rectangle become parallel. In listing the reasons why perception is not always truthful, Alhazen and Witelo point out that errors of judgment may be induced "if one is in an unsuitable position." Władysław Tatarkiewicz, *Storia dell'estetica* (Turin: Einaudi, 1979), 2:299–300. Panofsky judges that the thesis of Wulff "must be rejected on principle." Erwin Panofsky, *Perspective as Symbolic Form*, trans. Christopher S. Wood (Cambridge: MIT Press, 1991), 114, n. 30. On the subject of receding parallel lines which seem to diverge instead of converge, Ten Doesschate refutes Wulff's hypothesis and, explaining it as an "underestimation of perspective foreshortening" posits that the painter had gone about drawing the solid using a model in space as his starting point. Gezienus ten Doesschate, *Perspective: Fundamentals, Controversials, History* (Nieuwkoop: De Graaf, 1964), 69–72. This explanation appears complicated if one thinks of the repetitive nature of the footstools and tables appearing throughout Byzantine iconography. Normally the receding sides are literally opened out on the left or the right in order to leave undisturbed, or to include one of the feet; or in order better to "bind" the figure to the table. At this point, we should recall certain circumstances characteristic of post-iconoclastic Byzantine painting. The first is that the context in which painters worked had nothing to do with depicting landscapes or seen objects but was a matter of reproducing from a repertory, from books and from cartoons. It was a task in which no visual verification was carried out and it was easy for misunderstandings to arise, especially when the artist passed from a small drawing to its enlargement on the wall. Compare the relative iconography and relationship between illuminated books and the mosaics of St. Mark's Basilica in Venice. Ernst Kitzinger, "The Role of Miniature Painting in Mural Decoration," in Kurt Weitzmann, ed., *The Place of Book Illumination in Byzantine Art* (Princeton: Art Museum, Princeton University, 1975). Furthermore, mosaics were executed on the basis of models in which all decisions regarding what was to be depicted and how had already been taken, so when the mosaicist proceeded to actually executing the work, a phase in which no deep thought was necessary, it was easy to commit errors of interpretation or to feel legitimized in taking pictorial shortcuts. A good example of this type of laxity is provided by the comparison of two mosaics portraying an identical theme: the *Hospitality of Abraham* in San Vitale in Ravenna and that in

Santa Maria Maggiore in Rome. The phenomenon known today as the Schroder effect in axonometric drawing has, in the space of a century, led the mosaicist of San Vitale to confuse the position of the feet. Another example of careless execution is found in the twelfth-century mosaic of the *Last Supper* in the Basilica of St. Mark in Venice, where in the oblique perspective of the footstools, the receding lines are executed with such deliberate vagueness that it almost amounts to studied "sprezzatura" *ante litteram*. The second circumstance that should not be overlooked, despite its apparent simplicity, is that in different epochs, artist-artisans are not always capable of overcoming problems of execution with the same level of ability and the same success. Thus a simple lack of skill may sometimes be erroneously interpreted as a specific iconological intention or as a stylistic choice.

89. "Seen from a distance, objects appear reduced and close together, however far apart they may be. Within easy range, their sizes and the distances that separate them are observed correctly" (Plotinus, *Enneads* 2.8; 1.29–48).

90. See note 15 in the chapter "Demonstration Figures."

91. Compare the Christ Pantokrator in the cathedral of Cefalù (1148) with that in the Palatine Chapel in Palermo (1143–1151).

92. Gregory the Great, *Epistulae* 11.13.

93. "Ad memoriam rerum gestarum et venustatem parietum" (*Libri Carolini* III, 16). Cf. Tatarkiewicz, *Storia dell'estetica* 2:124.

94. The references for these figures are: the schemes of the Alexandrian cosmographers for representing the universe, the year, man, and the microcosmos; the chorus of angels and the circular diagrams for the meetings of the tribes or the apostles; the medical treatise of Dioscorides or Oppian's treatises on hunting; the calendars with the personifications of the months and relative seasonal activities; the descriptions of cities in the Roman Empire contained in the *Notitia dignitatum imperii romani*; those of Boethius on the liberal arts or of Prudentius on the battle between vices and virtues (*Psychomachia*).

95. Isidore of Seville, *De natura rerum*. Boethius and Cassiodorus were the great pagan encyclopedists who promoted the rebirth of Greek culture during the reign of Theodoric. The bishop Isidore in Visigothic Spain and the Venerable Bede in Britain were the most authoritative Christian representatives of encyclopedism. Cf. William H. Stahl, *La scienza dei romani* (Bari: Laterza, 1991), 255–307.

3.79
Hospitality of Abraham,
mosaic, early sixth century.
San Vitale, Ravenna. Note
the awkward positioning
of the feet and the circular
loaves.

3.80
Hospitality of Abraham,
mosaic, early fifth century.
Santa Maria Maggiore,
Rome.

3.81
Christian basilica, mosaic
of unknown origin, c. fifth
century. Musée du Louvre,
Paris. Ma3677.

3.82
Domes seen in section,
mosaic, thirteenth century.
St. Mark's Basilica, Venice.

3.83
Hospitality of Abraham, icon,
fourteenth century. Bénaki
Museum, Athens.

3.84
Mosaic from Tabarka showing
a basilica, c. 400. Bardo
Museum, Tunis.

96. "Haec figura solida est secundum geometricam rationem." See John E. Murdoch, *Album of Science: Antiquity and the Middle Ages* (New York: Scribner, 1984).

97. The siege of Constantinople of 717 coincided with the beginning of iconoclastic policy on the part of Leo III (717–741), which was continued by Constantine V (741–775). Unlike the total prohibition imposed by the Jewish and Islamic cultures, Byzantium permitted the image of the emperor together with those of animals, trees, and hippodromes. This decision was underpinned by the simultaneous negation of the incarnation, that is, of the dual nature—human and divine—of Christ, and in this way it created fertile territory for those heresies separating the divine from the human: Arianism, Monothelism, Nestorianism, and Monophysitism. Gerhart B. Ladner, *Images and Ideas in the Middle Ages* (Rome: Edizioni di storia e letturatura, 1983), 1:73–111.

98. "For all practical purposes, the image is the God," wrote John Wilson with regard to the Egyptian divinities. He may also have been thinking of the way in which the icon offers access to the world of the divine. John A. Wilson, "L'Egitto," in *La filosofia prima dei greci*, 85.

99. The idea that the artist is a sort of magician, an intermediary between the real world and the divine one, is very old. For Plato, "All which is demonic is between God and the mortal…. God does not have contact with man; only by means of the demonic is there a relationship and conversation between men and gods, both in the waking state and during sleep. And the man who is expert in such relationships is the demonic man, and compared to him, those who are expert in the arts or crafts are but manual laborers" (*Symposium* 202d–203a).

100. According to Theodore the Studite, the "relation between the Prototype and its image … is analogous to that between God the Father and Christ His Son. The prototype, in according with Platonic ideas, is thought of as producing its image of necessity, as a shadow is cast by a material object or the print of a signet ring." Otto Demus, *Byzantine Mosaic Decoration* (London: Routledge and Kegan Paul, 1976), 5–6.

101. Regarding the idea that the parallel rays of the sun produce parallel shadows, see Peithon's polemic against Euclid in the book of Serenus of Antinoe (fourth century BC). Peithon used the shadows of a colonnade to define the parallels. Cf. *Le livre du cylindre et le livre de la section du cône*, ed. P. ver Eecke (Paris: Blanchard, 1969). For the relationships between the theory of shadows and catoptrics, see Arthur E. Haas, "Antike Lichtheorie,"

3.85
Plan and elevation of a temple dedicated to Sobek, papyrus, Ptolemaic era. Egyptian Museum, Cairo. Bulaq papyrus n1, J.95572.

3.86
Dioscorides, author and illustrator, with Epinoia, goddess of thought and invention. Biblioteca Apostolica Vaticana, Rome. MS. Chigi F.VII.159, folio 236v.

Archiv für Geschichte der Philosophie 20 (1906–1907): 345–386. Cf. the chapter "Skiagraphies" in Rouveret, *Histoire et imaginaire de la peinture ancienne*, 13–63.

102. Greek tradition recounts the legend of the daughter of a vase maker of Corinth, Butades, who traces the outline of her lover's shadow on a rock.

103. Herodotus frequently uses the noun *typos* to indicate Egyptian incised reliefs such as the propylaea with incised figures that was built by the successor of Mikerinos (Menkaura) for Efesto (*Histories* 2.136), or in the sanctuary of Bubastis (*Histories* 2.138), or in the "labyrinth" of Amenemhat III at Hawara (*Histories* 2.148). The Egyptian scribe employed to cut the "divine words" (*medw neter*) into the walls of the temples, either in high relief or incised relief, is called a "drawer of outlines." Plato, who loved Egyptian art as a true "art of copying," singled out hieroglyphs as examples of unchanging beauty that have to be repeated without variation (*Laws* 656d–657a). Pliny wrote that "[painting] was born from the tradition of tracing the outline of the shadow cast by a human" (*Natural History* 35.15). In Greek, the word *perigrafe* (outline, sketch, draft) signifies "profile" and derives from the term *Perigrafa podoin*, or "the marks of two feet." Plato uses it in the sense of "sketch, traced from the exterior." Thus *perigrafe* also indicates the contour line of a drawing (*Laws* 6.768c).

104. Cf. Plato, *Republic* 523b, 602d; *Parmenides* 165c–d. An anonymous poet of the fourth century created a strange personalization of shadow in *De umbra*: "I like always to fasten myself in the damp / and rootless, I stretch out immense branches / He who accompanies me will in no way hold me back, / while I may grab hold of my fellow traveler. / To he who sees me from afar I shall show a precise outline / but if that person be close to me he will never see me" (Carena, *I poeti latini della decadenza*, 93).

105. Aristotle, *Rhetoric* 1414a. In contrast to the *bones artes* of Cicero (*De oratore*), painting was relegated until the time of Thomas Aquinas to membership in the *artes serviles*.

106. The human being is represented by five elements: the actual body; the shadow, which represents the procreative force; the *ba*, which is the "animated force" corresponding to the soul (hieroglyph of the pelican); the *ka*, which is the sum of the qualities of the individual and which corresponds to the soul (hieroglyph of raised arms); the *akh*, which is a supernatural quality that is obtained after death and corresponds to the spirit of the person (hieroglyph of the ibis). See Gardiner, *Egyptian Grammar*, 173. During the reign of Amenhotep III the

immaterial and intangible part of the god was conceived as a shadow. For the correspondence between "the shadow of Ra" and the temple of Aton, see Breasted, *Ancient Records of Egypt*, 2:418–419, §879, 2:360, §955, 2:393, §§1017–1018.

107. "They brought forth the sick into the streets, and laid them on beds and couches, and at the least the shadow of Peter passing by might overshadow some of them … and they were healed every one" (Acts 5:15–16).

108. Roberto Casati, *La scoperta dell'ombra* (Milan: Mondadori, 2000), 125; see also the useful annotated bibliography. In equatorial Africa, people avoid going out of doors at midday because, in the same way as spirits, their body casts no shadow. In the 1960 Luchino Visconti film, *Rocco e i suoi fratelli* (Luca episode), Rocco remembers that before a house is built, the foreman must throw a stone on the shadow of the first passerby, because a sacrificial victim is needed in order to ensure that the house will be solid. In ancient Mesopotamia and Egypt, the custom of making sacrifices and creating deposits in the foundations has been demonstrated archaeologically in the perimeters of temples. In modern times, this has all been reduced to the ritual of "laying of the first stone." The problem of the shadow in painting has been dealt with by Thomas DaCosta Kaufmann, "The Perspective of Shadow in the History of the Theory of Shadow Projection," *Journal of the Warburg and Courtauld Institutes* 38 (1975): 258–287; Ernst H. Gombrich, *Ombre* (Turin: Einaudi, 1996); Michael Baxandall, *Shadows and Enlightenment* (New Haven: Yale University Press, 1995).

109. "You speak well, Critobulus, the so-called manual crafts are discredited, and rightly enjoy no esteem in the cities. They filthy the body, both of the workers and of those who direct them, they force people to remain sitting and to stay in the shadows, and there are even some who are forced to pass the whole day by the hearth: when the body loses its vigor, the spirit also weakens" (Xenophon, *Oeconomicus* 4.2). For the unmanly nature of the artisan as opposed to the strong nature of those who practice agriculture and war, see ibid., 6.4.

110. See note 15 of the chapter "The Jesuit Perspective in China" in this book.

111. An idea that originated with the Franciscan John Peckham, teacher at Oxford and Paris and later archbishop of Canterbury: "In hoc autem differt umbra a tenebra quia umbra est lux diminuita." John Peckham, *Perspectiva communis* 25.525. Cf. Egidio Guidubaldi, ed., *Dal "De luce" di R. Grossatesta all'islamico "Libro della scala"* (Florence:

L. S. Olschki, 1978), 161; for the critical edition, see *John Peckham and the Sciences of Optics. Perspectiva communis*, ed. David C. Lindberg (Madison: University of Wisconsin Press, 1970), 102.

112. On this return of classicist tendencies in Byzantine monumental painting, see Ennio Concina, *Le arti di Bisanzio* (Milan: B. Mondadori, 2002), 229–237. The author wishes to thank Ennio Concina for conversations in Venice on this and other subjects.

113. See the figure of the actor in the fresco of the house of Pinarius Cerialis at Pompeii (after 62 AD). Cf. Alix Barbet, *Le peinture murale romane* (Paris: Picard, 1985), 182 passim. The *pictor imaginarius* inserted the figures after the geometrical composition had been completed on the wall. According to the edict of Diocletian (301 AD), the work of the *pictor imaginarius* cost double that of the *pictor parietarius*. The absence of figures in the Second Style might indeed be due to the costs involved. See August Mau, *Geschichte der decorativen Wandmalerei in Pompeji* (Berlin: Reimer, 1882). For a depiction of the painter's studio, see the sarcophagus of Kerch (Crimea) dating from the second century, on which the artist is portrayed heating a tool for encaustic painting (*cestrum* or *cauterium*); in front of him is a box with two hinged lids, subdivided into twenty compartments for the colors, similar to that of the painter Pausias as described by Varro: "For just as Pausias and the other painters of the same school have larges boxes with compartments for keeping their pigments of different colors ..." (*De re rustica* 3.17). On the wall hang images of soldiers armed with shields, and a square, framed portrait. The easel is almost identical to a modern one. See Maria Nowicka, "Le sarcophague de Kertch," in *Au royaume des ombres. La peinture funéraire antique* (Paris: Réunion des Musées Nationaux, 1999), 68. See also Reinach, *La peinture ancienne. Recueil Milliet*, 15.

114. For the composition of architectural scenes, see Tania Velmans, "Le rôle du décor architectural et la représentation de l'espace dans la peinture des Paléologues," *Cahiers Archéologiques* 14 (1964).

115. "If the frontal view is most appropriate for saints, and the profile for powerful men, then the three-quarters view belongs above all to beauty ... in the sense, that is, of the richness of spiritual movements." Pavel Florenskii, *Lo spazio e il tempo nell'arte* (1923–1924; Milan: Adelphi, 1995), 125.

116. *Megalographiae* are paintings of figures with a definite subject: "figures of the gods or detailed mytho-

logical episodes, or the battles at Troy, or the wanderings of Ulysses" (Vitruvius, *De architectura* 7.5.2). Pliny attributes to the painter Studio, or Ludio, "the elegant painting of walls, where he painted villas, ports and gardens, woods, sacred copses, forests, hills, canals, beaches" (Pliny, *Natural History* 25.116–117).

3.87
The artist's studio, sarcophagus from Kerch (Crimea), second century. Hermitage Museum, St. Petersburg.

117. The tradition of using architectural elements to separate different scenes or characters, already present in the classical world, may be observed in the Baptistery and on the Porta di Sant'Alipio in St. Mark's in Venice. See the fragment that reproduces scenes from the life of Achilles, probably transferred from a drawing on a papyrus roll (Palazzo dei Conservatori, Rome). Cf. Kurt Weitzmann, *Illustrations in Roll and Codex: A Study of Origin and Method of Text Illustration* (Princeton: Princeton University Press, 1947), 102–103.

118. *Corpus agrimensorum romanorum*, in Wolfgang Milde, ed., *Mittelalterliche Handschriften der Herzog August Bibliothek Wolfenbüttel* (Frankfurt: V. Klostermann, 1972). Two manuscripts of this collection of authors and relative illustrations are still extant. The one preserved in the Biblioteca Apostolica Vaticana dates from the ninth century (MS. Palatinus Latinus 1564); the other, in the Herzog August Bibliothek in Wolfenbüttel, dates from the sixth century (MS. Guelf. 36.23 Augusteus 2). The codex Palatino was compiled in 450 AD, but the illuminations date from the sixth century. O. A. W. Dilke, *Greek and Roman Maps* (Ithaca: Cornell University Press, 1985); *Das Kartenbild der Renaissance*, exh. cat. (Wolfenbüttel: Herzog August Bibliothek, 1977). By way of correcting an earlier hypothesis, André Grabar has noted that the miniatures present in manuscripts dating from around the ninth century offer

actual images of the sanctuaries of the Holy Land. On the Greco-Roman architectural landscape, see Michael I. Rostovtzeff, "Die hellenistische römische Architeturlandschaft," *Mitteilungen des Kaiserlich Deutschen Instituts* 26 (1911): 1–185. For the images taken from land-surveying manuscripts, see the example of the mosaic in the Palatine Chapel in Palermo, *L'entrata del Cristo a Gerusalemme*, dating from the twelfth century.

119. See Stahl, *La scienza dei romani*, 318–319. For the complex system of translations operating in the *scriptoria*, see Leighton D. Reynolds and Nigel G. Wilson, *Copisti e filologi. La tradizione dei classici dall'antichità ai tempi moderni* (Padua: Antenore, 1987).

3.88
Scenes from the life of Achilles. Palazzo dei Conservatori, Rome.

120. Nicholas of Cusa, who finished writing his *De visione Dei* in 1453, the year of the fall of Constantinople, describes thus the phenomenon of the all-seeing eye: "Among the works of man that the image of the all-seeing makes most fitting for our aim is that of a face painted in such a way as to seem that it is looking at everything all around itself." Nicholas of Cusa cites several works of art that have this all-seeing eye, such as a painting by Roger van der Weyden (now lost), which used to be in Brussels. The effect is seen in portraits where the sitter is portrayed frontally with his eyes looking straight ahead: "From whatever position the viewer looks at it, that face will seem to have its eyes turned on him alone." He is here referring to a painting of Veronica, which hung in his study in Bressanone (*De visione Dei*, preface 2, 3–15). Cf. Nicholas of Cusa, *Scritti filosofici*, ed. Giovanni Santaniello (Bologna: Zanichelli, 1965), 263.

121. The Window of Appearance was a type of balcony upon which the pharaoh appeared before his subjects; it is a typical feature of the New Kingdom. It was situated in the palace beyond the first pylon of the temple, where the pharaoh resided during the main religious festivals. One example still visible is at Medinet Habu, between the palace and the funeral temple of Ramesses III. Traces of this palace may also be seen in the Ramesseum at Luxor. Cf. Alexander Badawy, *Ancient Egyptian Architectural Design: A Study of the Harmonic System* (Berkeley: University of California Press, 1965), 177; Alexander Badawy, *Le dessin architectural chez les anciens égyptiens* (Cairo: Imprimerie Nationale, 1948), 112–114 and plate 108; Christian Leblanc, "Conception et plan du temple," in *Les monuments d'Eternité de Ramsès II* (Paris: Réunion des Musées Nationaux, 1999), 64–76.

122. Plutarch describes Pericles thus: "The firmness of feature, never softened by a smile, his grace of bearing, his manner of draping his robes which kept them from untidiness, and a tone of voice which, no matter how heated his discourse, was unchanging, and other similar attitudes so that any who came near him were filled with amazement" (Plutarch, *Parallel Lives*, "Pericles and Fabius Maximus," 5). In the *Persians*, Queen Atossa asks, "And do they hold their shining arrows ready in the notch [as Asiatic peoples did]," to which the leader replies: "No, they fight immobile, armed with shields and spears." Thus Aeschylus announces to the queen of the Persians the terrifying stillness of the Greeks "who neither serve nor obey any man" (Aeschylus, *Persians* 254–257). The wealthy twenty-year-old Pericles himself was the *chorêgos* in the first performance of *The Persians* in 472 BC.

123. In relation to the foreshortened faces, see the penetrating analysis by Pavel Florenskii: "Our knowledge and contemplation of an object leads us to refute these unexpected angles, in that they impoverish the object, depriving it of all that is most substantial in it; [angulations] which, in any case, characterize not so much the object as the point of view of the artist or the person contemplating the object." Florenskii, *Lo spazio e il tempo nell'arte*, 103–108.

124. Pindar, *Pythian* 7.71–72. Cf. Vincenzo Cilento, *Saggi su Plotino* (Milan: Mursia, 1973), 308.

125. See in the cathedral of Evreux the stained glass window with the portrait of Peter of Navarre, count of Mortain, kneeling before the Virgin. Georges Duby, *Le basi di un nuovo umanesimo 1280–1440* (Geneva: Skira; Milan: Fabbri, 1966), 25.

126. In the pagan temples and the synagogue of Dura Europos (third century), the names of donors appear in several of the wall paintings executed by different artists. Michael I. Rostovtzeff, *Dura Europos and Its Art* (Oxford: Clarendon Press, 1938), 75, 82, 114. On the figure with the square "nimbus" (living person), which appears in the synagogue, and on the problem of the "donor," cf. Ladner, *Images and Ideas*, 115–170 and 1012–1020; André Grabar, *Le vie della creazione nell'iconografia cristiana* (Milan: Jaca Book, 1983), 255. For the church of St. Demetrius, in which, unusually, the saint and the donor faithful are depicted side by side, see André Grabar, *La peinture byzantine* (Geneva: Skira, 1953), 50–51.

127. Giovanni Dondi, *Tractatus astrariis. Johannis de Dondi paduani civis astrarium* (c. 1350), facsimile of the Padua manuscript and French trans. Emmanuel Poulle (Padua and Paris, s.d.). The *astrarium*'s mechanism was heptagonal because the number of known planets was seven. But according to Dondi, the universe was ordered in such a way that everything depended on a sole motor, and it was the twenty-four-hour motor that was responsible for making all the rest move. In 1260, Campano da Novara had built a series of instruments for reproducing the theories of Ptolemy on the movement of the planet. Dondi carried out the mechanization proposed by Campano, completing his task after fifteen years of work. The year of reference for the study of the movements was 1365. The astrarium disappeared in the second half of the sixteenth century. Of the three Latin versions of the text left by Dondi, version A (Padua, Biblioteca Capitolare, MS D39) is without doubt Dondi's own copy. Cf. also Carlo M. Cipolla, *Le macchine del tempo* (Bologna: Il Mulino, 1981).

128. Plotinus, *Enneads* 3.1–9, trans. A. H. Armstrong (Cambridge: Loeb Classical Library; London: William Heinemann, 1980), 93.

129. See the detail of the crucifix seen from behind in the *Manger at Greccio* in the Upper Church of St. Francis at Assisi (before 1300).

130. William of Ockham opposed the theory of the *species* and was the first to postulate action at a distance. For medieval thinking on space matters, see Massimo Parodi, *Tempo e spazio nel medioevo* (Turin: Loescher, 1981).

131. His teachings are based on Ptolemy's *Almagest*, which centers astrological research on mathematical astronomy (eccentrics and epicycles), rather than on the homocentric approach of philosophers. The heliocentric theory of Aristarchus of Samos was never taken into consideration by the Latin writers of classical times during

the first thousand years of Christianity. Despite this, the geo-heliocentric system of Heraclides of Pontus was reposed by Pietro d'Abano in his *Lucidator astrologiae* (1310), and contradicted the geocentric approach of Aristotle and Ptolemy. This contributed to the transmission of the theory of heliocentric orbits to Copernicus's time. Stahl, *La scienza dei romani*, 226–227. See also Carlo Maccagni, "Le scienze nello studio di Padova e nel Veneto," in *Storia della cultura veneta. Dal primo Quattrocento al Concilio di Trento* (Vicenza: Neri Pozza, 1981), 140.

132. When Scholasticism began to be a spent force, the technique of discussion whereby one person asked questions and the other answered was born: the *quaestio*. This method allowed delicate problems to be probed without negating the assumptions of theology.

133. The spatial box is completed by the floor. In Apulian vase painting of the fourth century BC, the coffered ceiling had denoted theatrical space. This method was continued in illuminated manuscripts until the ninth century; see the *Preaching of Joshua* in the Grandval Bible (c. 840, London, British Museum). For the ceilings in the aedicules with "fishbone" vanishing lines or simply in oblique drawing, see Arthur D. Trendall and Alexander Cambitoglou, *The Red-Figured Vases of Apulia* (Oxford: Clarendon Press, 1978), vol. 1, plates 142, 4; 150, 1–2; 151, 3; 155, 4; vol. 2, plates 324, 1; 325, 2; 334, 1–2; 358; 362.

134. Ernst Cassirer, *Individuo e cosmo nel Rinascimento* (Bari: Laterza, 1974), 108–109.

135. Nicholas of Cusa, *Scritti filosofici*, 2:73.

3.89
Joshua and the people of Israel, Grandval Bible, c. 840. British Museum, London. Add. 10546, folio 25*v*.

3.90
Valentinus Engelhart,
Institutiones mechanicae,
c. 1550. Österreichische
Nationalbibliothek,
Vienna. Handschriften,
Codex 15438.

136. "Seeing becomes an artistic construct of man according to rational rules, and recognizing becomes a perceptive-mathematical knowledge." Graziella Federici Vescovini, "Biagio Pelacani," in *Filosofia, scienza e astrologia nel Trecento europeo. Biagio Pelacani Parmense* (Padua: Il Poligrafo, 1992), 50. On Pelacani, see Biagio Pelacani da Parma, "Le questioni di perspectiva di Biagio Pelacani," *Rinascimento* 1 (1961).

137. In Eastern tradition, man is the mirror of the microcosm and his various parts relate to the macrocosm. This is a variant of the biblical idea that man was created in the image of God. See Salomo di Costanza, *Commentario* (Munich, Bayerische Staatsbibliothek, Cod. Lat. 13002, f. 4.0). Cf. Otto Pächt, *Book Illumination in the Middle Ages* (Oxford: Oxford University Press, 1986), 156.

138. "The substance of the bones is for animals the same as so-called tentpoles are for tents and walls for houses." Galen, *De anatomicis administrationibus*, 1.2.218.

139. Cf. the chapter "Elements for a History of Axonometry" in this book.

140. Antonio Manetti described the system of relief used by Donatello and Brunelleschi in Rome: "Together they made rough sketches of almost all the buildings of Rome, and of many places outside it, measuring the widths and heights as they were able, arbitrating and making sure, together with the lengths, etc. And in many places they had parts of the buildings taken apart so that they could see them and check them and their qualities, whether they were square or how many corners they had, or if they were perfectly round or oval or what shape, and thus, where they were able to conjecture, the heights, by measuring the elevations from base to pediment, from the foundations and offsets to the roofs of the buildings. And they wrote it all down on strips of parchment left over from squaring off sheets of paper, with an abacus number and character that only Filippo himself could understand." Antonio Manetti, *Vita di Filippo Brunelleschi*, ed. Domenico De Robertis, intro. Giuliano Tanturli (Milan: Il Polifilo, 1976), 67–68. A manuscript of the twelfth-thirteenth century attributed to Johannes Anglicus of Montpellier contains a very lucid demonstration of the use of similar triangles, the quadrant (*quadrans vetus*) and the mirror for determining the measurements of inaccessible sites. Cf. Murdoch, *Album of Science*, 186, §152.

141. On this problem, see Vagnetti's note on the *Septima distinctio* by Fibonacci and the instrument used by Leon Battista Alberti for his survey of Rome. Luigi Vagnetti, "Mieux vaut voir que courir 1," in *Cartes et figures*

de la terre (Paris: Centre Pompidou, 1980), 242–247. See also Leonardo Fibonacci, *La pratica di geometria volgarizzata da Cristoforo di Gherardo di Dino, cittadino pisano*, ed. Gino Arrighi (Pisa: Domus Galileana, 1966).

142. From this moment on, a large number of astrolabes were built and it became the fashion to "take elevations" in order to "make notes." Cf. Jean-Gabriel Lemoine, "Brunelleschi et Ptolémée," *Gazette des Beaux Arts* 51 (1958). The translation of Ptolemy was the most important scientific event of the fifteenth century, after the translation into the vulgar tongue of the *Trattato della sfera* by Nicole Oresme (1376).

143. See the *questiones perspectivae* by Giorgio Pelacani da Parma, in which "The perception of the figure as a solid … is determined by means of a calculation founded on the measurement of a straight line, that is, of the distance between the nearest or farthest points of the surface of the solid object from the eye." See Graziella Federici Vescovini, *Studi sulla prospettiva medievale* (Turin: Giappichelli, 1965), 259–260.

144. See the dedication to Filippo Brunelleschi, in Leon Battista Alberti, *De pictura*, ed. Cecil Grayson (Rome; Bari: Laterza, 1975), 8.

145. On the concept of "realism," see Nelson Goodman, *I linguaggi dell'arte* (Milan: Saggiatore, 1976), 35–42.

4

THE IDEA OF MODEL

The architectural model is perhaps one of the oldest tools for architectural design, but it is also one of the least preserved and studied. When it has survived to testify to an architectural ambition, it is often the sole representation of a procedure that in the conceptual sense has ended and that will always remain unknown. Any doubts we may have about how to interpret it, however, are swept aside by its sheer attractiveness as an object, thanks to the presence of a quality it has always shared with the art of building itself: that of being definitively the best representation of architecture. It is because of this quality that it has served as an initiatory tool for generations of architects who, by crafting objects in the form of miniature architectures, have prepared for building on a large scale. Yet in its role as a miniature isomorph of the building, the model has on occasion simulated stability where in fact there was none, and it has also concealed many a compositional and distributional uncertainty. It is for this reason that the Vitruvian theory of architecture insists on a sharp distinction between the model and the ideation, with the former being relegated to the material dimension of *techné*.

In his description of the various stages of architectural planning, Vitruvius indicates three *species dispositionis*,[1] or three types of drawings, as being necessary for the representation of architecture. They are listed in a context limited to the planning stages and regard the plan and elevations. No mention is made of the model, which in Greek tradition was considered the product simply of manual skill.[2] However, its use is frequently alluded to in Greek documentary sources, along with drawings in orthogonal projection, written building contracts (*syngraphái*), and drawings (*anagraphái*). Greek models, usually fashioned in wax or wood, were called *paradéigmata*[3] and they were normally included as part of the overall cost of the work, with no special recognition accorded to their conception.[4] It is not known if *paradéigmata* continued to be used in Roman times, nor do we have any proof of their existence in late antiquity.

The votive model, whether actual or a representation, was widespread long before Vitruvius dedicated his treatise to Caesar Augustus. Examples can already be found among the burial objects included in ancient Egyptian and Etruscan tombs, and they also appear in Mesopotamian reliefs as well as in descriptions of the Roman Pompa Triumphalis.[5] Roman coins dating from the late imperial period depicting the emperor holding the model of a temple (*neokóros*) have been cited as antecedents of the "donor bearing model of a church" theme, which recurs in Christian basilicas from the sixth century onward.[6] But the only definite instance in which a model is mentioned in direct relation to an architectural plan is in a sixth-century document relating to the abbey of Saint Germain d'Auxerre. Despite the explicit reference to its construction, this remains too isolated an example from which to conclude regarding whether this was a late example of an antique tradition or an early example of a new one.[7]

As far as we know, there is almost no reference in the literature to the use of models until the thirteenth century. It may be supposed either that their use was so taken for granted as to have been regarded not worthy of mention, or that for many hundreds of years the model was simply considered to be superfluous in the presence of traditional Vitruvian method of representation, or of written descriptions.

Only around the second half of the fourteenth century in Tuscany do models reappear in a significant number in the written sources. They are included as part of a planning process that is always the same and that is described in detailed contracts in which existing buildings were also used as models for imitating.[8]

The research into optics and geometry and the study of the antique that characterized so much of Florentine culture at the beginning of the fifteenth century seem at first not to have had much influence on preexisting Gothic architectural procedures. Their eventual abandonment contributed greatly to defining the figure of the new Renaissance architect, for whom the architectural model took on a wholly new character and role. To the citizen committees who were not always capable of visualizing the effect of the finished building solely from drawings, the model was a guarantee, along the lines of a copyright, of the originality of the solution. Like "writing for illiterates,"[9] the model communicated the planned building in a very concrete, tangible way, offering the possibility of comprehension at a glance, without demanding any special ability for abstract thought of the sort required by ichnographic and orthographic drawings. Its seduction lay in its implicit promise to represent what was to come, and to inflame the observer with *libido aedificandi*.

There is no doubt that the fifteenth-century architect's *viva voce*, or spoken instructions, exceeded in importance other aspects of a merely executive, material nature thanks to those intellectual qualities that Alberti had made a requisite and that constitute the real distinction between these architects and similar figures in classical tradition. This is easily seen by comparing the sum paid to the Greek architect Komodion for a model with that paid almost twenty centuries later to Antonio da Sangallo for the model of St. Peter's: a price is put on the Renaissance artist's ideation, and it is paid for separately from the actual building of the model, not together with it.[10] The commencement of the great building projects of the sixteenth century brought about a necessary specialization of roles, imposing a change in the architect's professional demeanor. In addition, the increasing familiarity of his relations with his patron had fostered an ever-growing separation between the conceptual phase of the project and the practical phase of the construction site. It was imperative that the complex building instructions, at this point no longer transmitted *viva voce*, reach the workmen on site with the greatest possible precision. It was in response to this necessity that there was a move away from using autograph drawings in the first two decades of the sixteenth century, in favor of the orthogonal drawing (*trasparente e in pulito*), that was so typical of the Raphaelesque circle.[11] This shift from the autographic fifteenth-century "antiquarian" drawing to the allographic type of drawing used in archaeological relief made it possible to control the various building sites, which were often very far away.[12]

It is difficult to say if models also addressed the problem of structural stability. The Florentine masters of the abacus certainly contributed to calculating loads and quantities in the construction of the Florentine cathedral. Mindful of the disastrous experiences of the Gothic era, fifteenth-century building practice erred on the side of caution, either by overcompensating structurally or by building models in brick that so nearly approximated the designed building that it was also possible to evaluate any problems of stability that might occur.

Our picture of the history of the model in the fifteenth century is not precise enough for us to draw definitive conclusions. However, the archival and biographical sources as well as the few bibliographical references to the subject supply enough evidence for us to attempt some theoretical considerations on the Renaissance architectural model.[13]

There is frequent mention in the Florentine documents, especially those regarding the building of Santa Maria del Fiore in Florence, of the use of models, some of which were carried out by Brunelleschi. Vasari writes that "he secretly executed models and mechanisms for work on the dome but still spent time on scaffolding with the other artisans. It was then that he played the prank of *The Fat Woodcarver* (*Novella del grasso legnaiuolo*), and often amused himself by going to help Lorenzo Ghiberti polish something on his doors."[14] No other citation so effectively describes the personality of Brunelleschi. His native Tuscan wit, his familiarity with work of a technical nature, the sarcasm implicit in the phrase "he often amused himself" describe the spirit in which he lent a hand to his rival Ghiberti. Above all, it allows us a glimpse of that same Gothic secrecy with regard to his technical innovations, which is also apparent in his exhortation to his friend Taccola: "Do not share your intentions with others."[15] This reserve was no doubt due to the magnitude of the tasks he undertook, as well as a natural response to the envy of his closest competitors. It is again apparent in Antonio Manetti's *Life of Filippo Brunelleschi*, where the author recalls that while planning the Barbadori house, Ser Filippo "did not want to build a model," but preferred instead to give orders directly to the builders "using only drawings and by word of mouth."[16] Even when circumstances rendered it necessary, his model was never a faithful representation of his actual design. Manetti is very explicit on this point. Describing Brunelleschi's models, he comments that "there was little to be seen where matters of symmetry were concerned," and that they showed only "the principal walls and how they related to some other members, without ornament or any indication of the capitals or architraves, the friezes or cornices."[17]

Clearly, Brunelleschi's models served a very basic purpose: they indicated the layout of the parts as a whole and their structure, but gave very little idea of the overall design, so that "the model maker was unable to understand all of its secrets."[18] Important instructions were given in person, by word of mouth, thus leaving a wide margin of freedom for alterations to what had not been said.

Up to this point, the model had constituted a limit beyond which it was not permitted to go. It acted as a kind of three-dimensional contract upon which oaths often had to be sworn, and in this way it stood guard against the sort of transgressions that often occurred in the absence of the master builder or the architect. Yet paradoxically it was precisely the model's durability that led to its disappearance. Any significant modifications to the design necessitated the execution of a new model and the destruction of the preceding one.

The widespread use of a design plan in the second half of the fifteenth century also contributed to changes in the model's role and its size. The rediscovery of Vitruvius brought the clear-cut geometries of Gothic design back within the context of Vitruvian orders, articulating them through his *species dispositionis*, or types of drawings. The model tended increasingly to abandon its purely presentational role and to lose, as may be seen in the case of Palazzo Strozzi, all authority as a reference tool during the building work.[19]

Alberti offers us a measure of the rapid changes to which architectural planning in the fifteenth century was subjected. It was due to his influence that the architect's role was elevated beyond any involvement in the manual aspects of the profession: his task was basically theoretical, and consisted of ensuring the requisites of solidity and functionality, which *concinnitas* imparted to the separate parts of the building, according to some precise rule, so that they correspond to one another in appearance (*symmetry* in Vitruvius). It was not appropriate, therefore, for him to build the models with his own hands, or even to do so "in secret." These were to be constructed on the basis of accurate drawings, but by other people, in another place.[20] The model for the church of San Francesco in Rimini was built "judiciously and with extraordinary diligence in Florence" by Salvestro Fancelli, who was also in charge of the building works; the model for Sant'Andrea of Mantua was built by a certain Luca Fiorentino.[21]

4.3
Filippo Brunelleschi, wooden model of the lantern of the cathedral of Florence. Museo dell'Opera di Santa Maria del Fiore, Florence.

Even if these objects have not survived, we can easily imagine them by looking through Alberti's extraordinary *De re aedificatoria*. Alberti subdivided the *res aedificatoria* into *lineamenta* (contours) and *structura* (structure). The design, which by means of angles and straight lines orders the form of the construction, is clearly independent of the material used.[22] Like Vitruvius, Alberti makes no mention of the model in that part of his treatise dedicated to *lineamenta* (*De lineamentis, & eorum vi ac ratione*), but does so at the beginning of Book II, about the material (in "quo de materia agitur"). The design must be developed by means of sketches, drawings, and models, with the constant supervision of expert persons.[23] Profoundly aware of the moral aspect of building, Alberti's ethic increasingly reduces individualistic Gothic pride. The architect's commitment to his art seems on the contrary to acquire dignity of a collective sort thanks precisely to those experts. To surmount the difficulty of the task, he simply advises prolonged reflection. The research time seems to be the only remedy against the desire for new building (*libido aedificandi*) that leads the "inconsiderate" to demolish venerable old buildings (*vetusta aedificia*) and to waste money in "monstrous foundations for all the works" (*immania universi operas fundamenta*).[24] His model is an instrument of experimentation and reflection with which to ascertain the building's structural stability, its orientation, the layout of the main walls, and the adequacy of its roofing. It is used to try out the most likely solutions to each single problem and to make a precise calculation of the costs of the work. The sort of model Alberti describes is laconic, concise, and not in the least self-celebratory. Its simplicity is not a function of the unsaid, as in Brunelleschi, but is both ontological and deontological at the same time. Indeed, Alberti considers it unworthy of the architect to trick his patrons by presenting them with models that are rich in ornament and covered with *picturae lenociniis*:[25] if anything, the model should be "nudos et simplices," crafted from simple materials so that it is the architect's true conception that emerges, rather than the skill of the model maker. It is the painter's task to make the *prominentias ex tabulae … umbris et lineis et angulis comminutis*. The inclusion of shadow and foreshortening in the architect's drawing would only create ontologically defective images, and the conception of the design would lose precision, together with the clarity of its reasoning.[26]

Roughly ten years after Alberti's "most refined work," Filarete described to Piero de' Medici matters that were "somewhat thorny and difficult to understand."[27] The obscure passages of Vitruvius are illuminated not by Alberti's perfect Latin, but rather by his almost homely tone, which is no less engaging

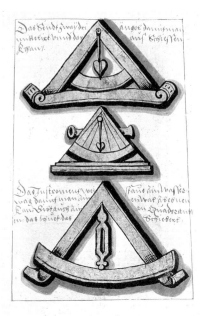

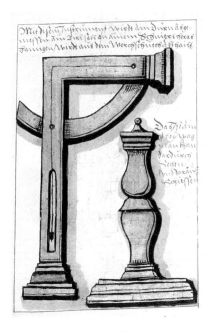

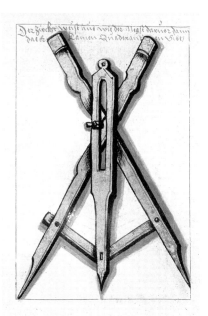

4.4–4.7
Franz Helm, *Kriegsbuch*, southern Germany,
c. 1550. Österreichische Nationalbibliothek,
Vienna. Codex 10895.

for that. If, for Alberti, the architectural project was a mental activity, drawings and sketches were nevertheless necessary steps toward the definition
of the *fabrica*. Filarete instead makes no specific reference to their use in his
planning stages. His design method goes beyond the mental dimension of
Alberti and opens out onto fantastic worlds of the imagination. The creative
process is described in the lively tones of a fourteenth-century novella: "He
who wishes to build something should engage an architect and together with
him generate it, and then the architect should give birth and then after he
has done this, the architect becomes the mother of the building." The design
phase follows naturally from the gestational phase: "just like a woman, who
carries it in her body for nine or seven months … in the same way the architect must for nine or seven months let his imagination run freely and think
and turn it [the building] over and over in his mind in many different ways."
Only after he has "thought about it and considered it under many aspects" will
he be able to select the best solution, and then he will make "a small model
of wood, measured and proportioned according to how the final product is
intended."[28]

4.8
Anonymous, mining works, Tyrol, 1556.
Österreichische Nationalbibliothek,
Vienna. *Schwazer Bergbuch*, Codex 10852.

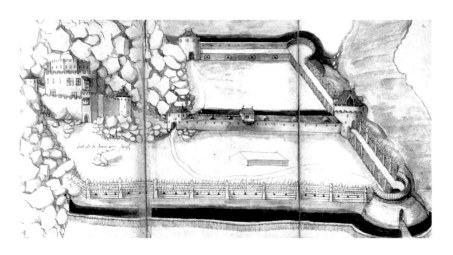

4.9
Anonymous, drawing of fortifications made
for the emperor Maximilian, Tyrol, 1510.
Österreichische Nationalbibliothek, Vienna.
Befestigungen in Tirol, Codex 2858.

4.10
Joseph Furttenbach the Younger, preparatory
drawing for the volume *Mechanische
Reisladen* (Ulm, 1644). Österreichische
Nationalbibliothek, Vienna. Codex 10918.

The final decision is thus wholly contained in the *disegno piccolo relevato di legname*, that is to say, a small wooden model. The *disegno lineato* is clearly intended as the *fondazione* or ground plan,[29] with all the attributes of the building and design specifications that Vitruvius entrusted to his *ichnographia*. Filarete himself provides an explanation of what this means: "I wish to design the ground plan on this panel and build the design in wood on top of it."[30] The design of the ground plan delimits and subdivides the various parts, but doesn't condition the vertical elements, which rise freely into Filarete's fantastic pinnacles; in this way he follows a common method that characterized all late fifteenth-century architectural design, which was often very close to, and indeed, more or less superimposed upon, the relief of the *vetusta aedificia*.

There is obviously more of the human than the humanistic in Filarete's beguiling talk of "mulling over" and "giving birth." But the corporeal quality that he gives to his imaginative description shifts the image of the model toward a less secret and theoretical dimension, allowing instead an original, two-way interaction with the drawing. The theoretical sequence seems to be turned on its head, with the model taking on the role of generator rather than generated. While on the one hand the model brings light to bear on the image of the building, which has been first conceived and then contemplated in the mind, on the other it also seems that the models themselves provided a strong impetus for the elaboration of Filarete's extraordinary elevations and section drawings.[31]

A similar impression is given by the drawings of fortresses by Francesco di Giorgio Martini. His oblique drawings seem to have been done by laying out models on the floor, then composing them by means of adding or subtracting lunettes, ramparts, and walls.[32] The renowned architectures of Leonardo also suggest the use of small-scale models that could be arranged at will.[33] But in his case the observer was a painter interested in stereotomy, not an engineer engaged in studying anthropomorphic solutions for fortresses that seemed fantastical but were in fact deadly serious.

The geometrical diagrams of Luca Pacioli, the perspective sections of Filarete, and the "X-ray" drawings of Leonardo for the dome cladding of Milan cathedral are experiments whose influence can be felt in the architectural model, now transformed into a prototype for study and the starting point for still more drawings and modifications.

The fortress builders of the Veneto made extraordinary use of this new potential, turning the model into a plastic memory of the dynamics of a siege. It was a possibility exploited to a far greater extent in Venice than in Florence, where erudite discussion gave little consideration to practical experience. So it comes as no surprise to find Vasari describing models in rather limited terms as the simple "work of carvers and builders,"[34] while Filippo Baldinucci, in summing up the ideas of Alberti, ventures no further than to recommend the use of wax models in order to accommodate more quickly and cheaply those changes demanded by clients.[35]

In the Veneto, the question is subjected to an altogether more searching and complex analysis. While the anti-Vitruvian Alvise Cornaro holds that the model is a necessity,[36] Daniele Barbaro only mentions it briefly in passing since it does not affect the canonical drawings.[37] But in his suggestion that the third type (scenography) be extended to include a section drawing (*profilo*), Barbaro ends by legitimizing, certainly unintentionally, those modifications to Vitruvius's *species* that are recommended in the treatises on fortifications in the second half of the sixteenth century: in this way, the texts by Girolamo Maggi and Jacomo Castriotto and by Buonaiuto Lorini, to cite the most famous, are without undue disquisition able to introduce the use of "soldierly perspective" and of section drawing.

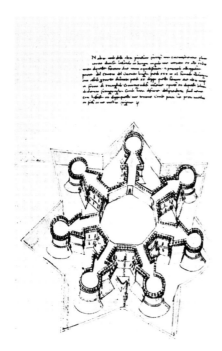

4.11
Francesco di Giorgio Martini, star-shaped fort, end of fifteenth century. Biblioteca Nazionale, Florence. Magliabechiano Codex II. I. 141, folio 62v.

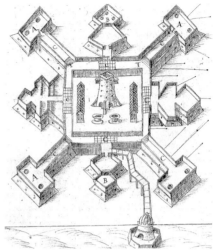
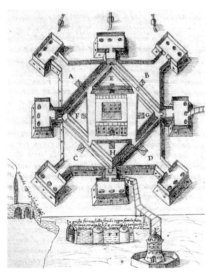

4.12–4.15
Giovan Battista Minio, plates from the
treatise *Il cavaliere* (Vicenza, c. 1550).
Österreichische Nationalbibliothek, Vienna.
Codex 10854.

4.16 (facing page)
House in the center of a fortress with lines
showing lookout views. Buonaiuto Lorini,
Fünff Bücher von Festung Bauwen (Frankfurt
am Main, 1607).

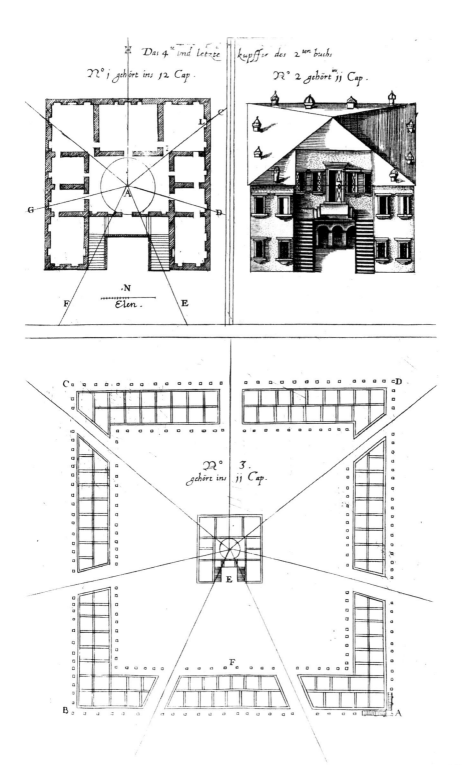

Das 4ᵗᵉ vnd letzte kupffer des 2ᵗᵉⁿ buchs

N° 1 gehört ins 12 Cap.

N° 2 gehört ins 11 Cap.

N° 3.
gehört ins 11 Cap.

.N
Elen.

The graphic experimentations of Italian architects and military engineers also spread rapidly in France, thanks to the residence there of Leonardo, Fra Giocondo, Serlio, and Castriotto.[38] The ideas of Alberti were decisive for Philibert de l'Orme, the greatest architect of the French Renaissance.[39] Many pages of his architectural treatise are dedicated to the Albertian concept of the model. In a polemical and passionate discussion, transcribed literally as he spoke, de l'Orme advises the gentleman client to trust only those who can display great ability in the construction of models. This, he hisses, is a prerogative only of those persons gifted with great competence and intelligence.[40] The references to Alberti's treatises are stated openly, and border on literal translation: he favors models that are simple and undecorated,[41] that effectively express the idea rather than show off manufacturing skill, and that are accurate enough to allow a calculation to be made of the quantities and costs of the materials. But the most interesting aspect of his impassioned description is the sequence in which he presents his plans. De l'Orme deems it necessary to show his client only plans and front elevations. Later he advises the construction of models in wood, paper, or stiff card.[42] In his opinion, no important work could be completed without first building large-scale models that permitted a view of the interiors, which were usually concealed in small-scale models. Models of this type were also necessary for testing hydraulic machines, which, while they might function on a small scale, were apt not to work when built at a large scale.[43] The qualitative changes that come about with a change in scale are rendered vividly by Vincenzo Scamozzi, who observed that "models are like small birds whose gender is difficult to discern because of their size; but when they are enlarged, we can see that they are eagles or crows."[44]

One of the most famous of de l'Orme's works, the *trompe* at the Château d'Anet, is described in the two books he dedicated in his treatise to the theory of cutting stone. We cannot say if his explanation of the drawing method (*trait* or *traicts*) is easier now than it was for his ignorant colleagues. Their drop in morale cannot have been too different from that of mathematicians when Descartes revealed the obviousness of the solutions contained in his revolutionary geometry. Fortunately for us, Robin Evans[45] has provided a lucid reconstruction of the *traicts* of the *trompe* at the Château d'Anet. In his opinion, the true form of the *trompe* could not have been defined if not by making recourse to a particular representational method, unknown to us, and probably derived from the *traicts*. The characteristics of the model described by de l'Orme seem to resolve the questions posed by Evans. The presentation of the project, as we have seen, excludes any recourse to the model. But a model is considered necessary for the actual building in order to show, on a large scale, the hidden parts of complex constructions like the *trompe*. The portrayal of its structure in its entirety and not by means of foreshortening was almost certainly resolved by means of the construction of accurate development boards. By means of this procedure, of little use in Italian architecture, which is basically trilithon, de l'Orme's construction model would have been created out of the complicated assemblage of concave and convex ashlars. These were probably made by folding the cardboard upon which the cuts defined in the *traict* had been performed. Thus the model was created out of an ideal kit, the instruction booklet for which was the very same geometrical construction of the *traict*. It would have been impossible to imagine the bizarre geometry of the Anet balustrade by the sole means of rotating and overturning. The stone-masons would have had no end of difficulty in understanding how the stones they were cutting would fit together to form a whole.

With the decline of the figure of the artist-scientist, a category to which de l'Orme in many ways belonged, theoretical knowledge became progressively extracted from practice and gathered together into specialized treatises. For those less cultured members of the profession, the model substituted other representational methods that required a profound knowledge of geometry. Pietro Cataneo suggests that the architect who does not have "knowledge of perspective" make "a model of wood or of wax, or even of clay, or stiff card, according to the quality and magnificence of the building."[46] It was an ideal shortcut for those men of arms who were forced to traverse the deadly geometries of ballistics on the battlefield. Indeed, it was at their request that a soldierly perspective was created, which would have a practical use, would be easy to use, and whose forms would not be dictated by actual measurements.[47] Oblique drawing and the model were in this sense equals. Just as the civilian model had become an object of experimentation, redesign, or in some instances an assembly diagram, in the same way the military model was enlarged to include the site, and so allow for the dynamics of war and permit control from a distance of siege actions as well as simultaneous comparison with alternative solutions.[48] In 1502, Basilio della Scola, who until then had served as a soldier and artilleryman, began what was to be a successful career as a military engineer with the presentation to Venice of a wooden model of a fortress that incorporated all of the latest French, Italian, and German innovations.[49] Orders relating to the execution of models are found throughout the whole of Venetian history;[50] drawings are mentioned rarely. The drawing

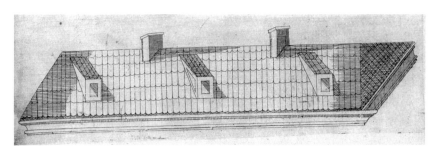

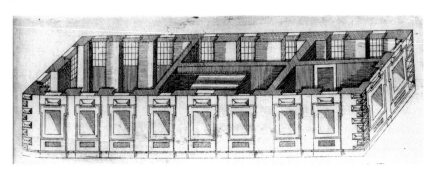

4.17
Exploded oblique projection of a civilian
house. From Abraham Leuthner, *Grünliche
Darstellung der fünf Säulen* ... (Prague,
end of seventeenth century).

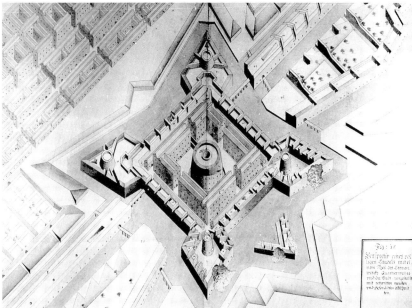

4.18
Colored wooden relief model of the
fortress of Belgrade, seventeenth century.
Heeresgeschichtliches Museum, Vienna.

4.19
Ernst Friedrich von Borgsdorff, *Die befestigte
Stütze eines Fürstenthumbs* (1686). Österreich-
ische Nationalbibliothek, Vienna. Codex 10811.

tells us more about the architect's intention or, more frequently, about the imperatives of the "chiefs of war," or the magistracy. A typical example of this is the order imparted in 1532 to Michele Sanmicheli for the execution of "a wooden model made to order and according to the design of his Excellency our Commander General."[51]

In responding to the needs of soldiers, engineers, and architects, the treatise writers of the second half of the sixteenth century, having distanced themselves from the civil tradition, show some impatience with the *res aedificatoria*. Alberti's *concinnitas* has little place in decisions about the placing of bastions, ravelins, and salients; nor can *utilitas* be made to conform to the pictorial illusionism of *perspectiva artificialis*. Representation by means of the converging lines of linear perspective will remain a cultural affectation maintained in some treatises, but only in order to enhance the graphic aspect of the text. There would be no sense in representing the dimensions of the perspectively foreshortened fortress. The observing eye belongs not to a harmless traveler in search of a beautiful view but to the fiery glare of the artillery. The only proportion that matters to this eye is the range of fire, for at the moment in which the projectile passes beyond the frame of appearances to shatter its target, all perspective is dissolved. The image of the fortress must now be composed in the deforming, parabolic perspective of ballistics. It is the projectile range that truly determines the distance between ramparts, that brings forward the counterscarps, raises the cavaliers, and shields the weak parts of the curtain. The pantographic advance and retreat of the artillery drags the fortress design along with the *guasto* (cleared field of fire). When the site has a complex topography, the model is the only representation capable of rendering the crowded geometry of the artillery fire raining in on all sides of the fortification. Even the urban forms within the fortress will be reshaped and cut out of these geometries without memory.

To men more familiar with the battlefield than with the drawing table, respect for Vitruvian conventions appears out of place, for what is at stake here is not beauty, but the survival of kingdoms and principalities. Opinion is thus bitterly divided in the numerous treatises on the subject and, from the second half of the sixteenth century onward, the question of fortifications gives rise to fierce argument: Gabriello Busca prefers the written word and direct tracing out on the ground over drawing or models.[52] Giovan Battista de' Zanchi scorns those who carry out only "the manual architecture of models" and who "are only sufficiently trained to design innumerable plans for fortresses."[53] Antonio Paolo Sarti is of the opinion that drawings are misleading

4.20
Daniel Specklin, *Architectura* (Strasbourg, 1599).

and that it is enough to communicate ideas verbally among experts.[54] Gian Giacomo Leonardi redrafts the role of the architect in almost humiliating terms: his duty is to represent the decision of the general by delivering it to him "in the form of drawings, and in several models that should be made first in wax or clay before being made out of wood, in order to give the General time to think, make alterations, enlarge, accommodate his own ideas, his own conclusions." For Leonardi, the architect is a synecdoche: "he may be called the hand, for his task is to execute that which is commanded by the eye and the mind of the Prince."[55] Ultimately, the model becomes the place in which practical experimentation and political expediency are contrasted and accumulate; it is a matrix that bears the imprint of the general's considerations and modifications, and upon which he has allowed his thoughts to range freely. The military chiefs and the *Provveditori* (superintendants) of the fortresses are in fact asked to "stamp" their opinion on the "appropriate relief models," cataloged and preserved since 1550 in a room of the Palazzo Ducale in Venice.[56] Beautifully executed drawings apparently failed to persuade anybody. Belluzzi, who, like any self-respecting Venetian, declined to consider fortifications to be architecture, declared his diffidence with regard to good drawing: "A Prince should never believe in drawings but have models made and then have the said models corrected *in situ* by men of war, leaving Architects and Doctors to one side."[57] Even the commander in chief Francesco Maria della Rovere was moved to observe to the unfortunate architect of the fortress of Senigallia that although "the drawing in itself is very pleasing," this did not mean that the solution was the right one.[58]

In Venice, the biggest publishing center for military treatises of the sixteenth century, the widespread use of the model thus found an ideological *raison d'être*. The general may not have known how to draw or make models, but he certainly knew how to make sure that the proposals were in line with his prince's thinking.[59]

By the end of the sixteenth century, military treatises concluded the debate on the model, crystallizing the model as a routine procedure. Francesco De Marchi, the author of the most complete treatise on fortifications of the sixteenth century, lists the steps as if they were a well-known tune: "drawings and models, then one proceeds to the building."[60] In the same way, although with slight differences, Aurelio De Pasino, Antoine De Ville, and Sarti suggest that the model be constructed as a preliminary to building. In the complex discussion on representational methods that drew to its conclusion at that time, the most relevant factor seems to have been the progressive assimi-

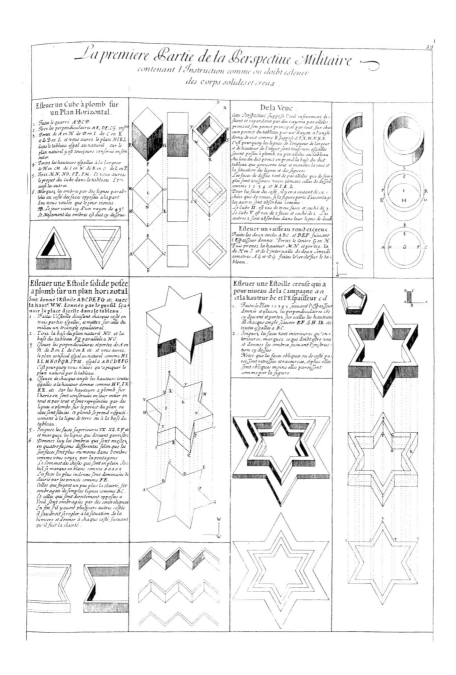

4.21
Théodoric Luders, *Traicté mathématique*
(Paris, 1680), plate 28.

lation of the model with *alla cavaliera* oblique drawing. It is significant that already, in the widely known treatise of Alain Manesson Mallet, an explanation of drawing in *prospettiva cavaliera* appears alongside a series of illustrations showing the construction of models in clay and plaster,[61] and that Giulio Troili, known as *il Paradosso* (the Paradox), used *prospettiva militare* for the construction of a model in cardboard.[62]

From 1668, as we know from Louvois's letter to Vauban regarding the plan of Ath, *plans-reliefs* were beginning to be carried out for French fortresses. Larger than Venetian prototypes, these models on a scale of 1:600 provided an exact description, not only of the fortress, but also of the type of vegetation, the buildings, canals, and rivers in the surrounding area. Usually they were built with the help of very precise maps and concurrently with the building of the fortress. These extraordinary facsimiles of the territory were far superior to any drawing, describing the topography in the manner of modern air reconnaisance.[63]

At the beginning of the eighteenth century, the model was considered the equivalent of parallel projection drawing, a practice that by this date had become widespread thanks to the numerous and lucidly written treatises of seventeenth-century Jesuits.[64] Louis Bretez unexpectedly confirms this in a text dedicated to the practical perspective of architecture. In a fine illustration at the end of his book, the author declares that, thanks to his cavalier perspective, "les ingénieurs éviteront la peine de faire des modèles," and landscape painters can work in their studios without having to journey to the site.[65] This was obviously not a discovery, but the fact that graphic description could be substituted for models reveals a renewed interest in its potential that would reach its peak in the *Programme* of Gaspard Monge's *Géométrie descriptive*.[66]

When the perspective views of the Galli-Bibiena had become known throughout Europe and the treatise of Padre Pozzo concluded the heroic phase of perspective studies, the architectural model seems to have been put temporarily to one side. In the eighteenth century, France was studded with fortresses built or renovated by the Scholastic approach of Vauban. Wars were now being conducted outside of national territory and the only things striking fortresses were the admiring glances of travelers. The exigencies of sight could therefore be considered once again. Jean Courtonne criticized military models because, "since the model is smaller than the work to be built, the eye is not at all in its rightful place and it easily discovers that which it would only imperfectly observe in the finished building."[67] Only perspective can give a proper view, from an established distance and a suitable height. Yet at the

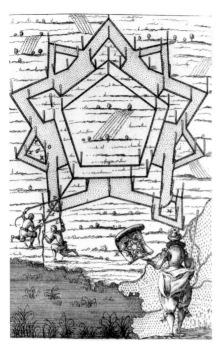

4.22
Drawing of the outline of a fortress on the ground. From Alain Manesson Mallet, *Les traveaux de Mars ou l'art de la guerre* (Paris, 1672).

4.23
C. Ielbema, plate of *Perspectief of teikenkonst* (Amsterdam, 1729). Universiteitsbibliotheek, Amsterdam.MS. II* A 32 a, II* A 32 b.

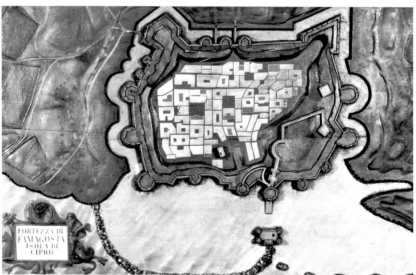

4.24
Anonymous, *Famagusta Fortress, Island of Cyprus ... 1571*, wooden model, 1548–1570. Museo Storico Navale, Venice. Inv. 1120.

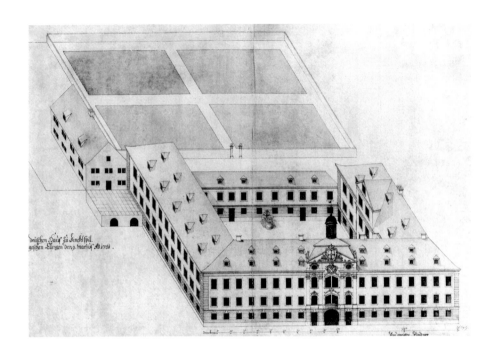

4.25
House of the Teutonic Order at Dinkelsbühl,
1761. Deutschordenszentralarchiv, Vienna.
File number 17.

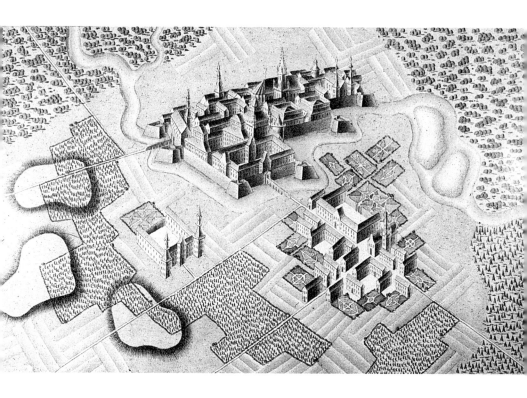

4.26
Louis Ange, *Plan d'une campagne avec une perspective cavalière*, France, eighteenth century.

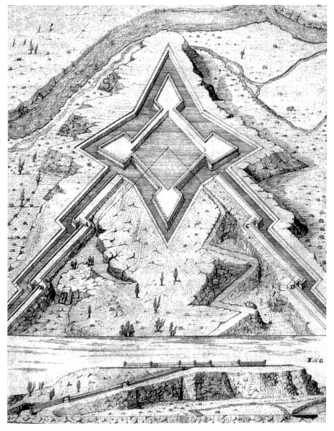

opening of the military college of Verona in 1759, the traditional diffidence toward design so characteristic of the Veneto made its appearance once again. Girolamo Francesco Cristiani, "Civil Engineer of the Serenissima,"[68] in his address to that very body, advanced theses opposed to those of Courtonne, observing that "already for some time the Mathematicians have been induced to prefer the use of Models over the use of drawings."[69] Drawings, Cristiani goes on, may perhaps be useful to those who cultivate the art of mathematics, but not to practitioners. The model has the advantage of being "an idea that is material, made of wood, of card, of clay or other," and since "the principal requisite of ideas is to look like objects," the model must be a replica of the thing and "correspond in everything and in every way to the things represented." In proposing a pedagogical meeting between idea, model, and thing, Cristiani was challenging two thousand years of philosophy with surprising temerity: "Models are the instruments most suited to augmenting ideas that are clear, well-explained, and long-lasting," since the greater "the number of images that are introduced to the imagination by means of our senses, the greater grows the strength of our mind."[70]

The revolutionary France of Monge was unable to export descriptive geometry to America. But somehow Cristiani's theories made the journey to the other side of the Atlantic, convincing American pragmatists to adopt those wood and card ideas that he so wholeheartedly recommended to the soldier cadets of Verona.

4.27
Alessandro Belleardi, plan for a ship with cannon, second half of seventeenth century. Österreichische Nationalbibliothek, Vienna. Codex 8175.

4.28
Giovanni Giacomo Enea di Conti Zoardi, plate from *Della fortificazione riformata*, second half of seventeenth century. Österreichische Nationalbibliothek, Vienna. Codices 10568–10569.

Notes

1. The *species dispositionis* (in Greek, *idéai*) are drawings carried out with ruler and compass that facilitate the transition from ideation to the actual building; they thus allow: (1) the various parts of the building to be traced directly on the ground (plan); (2) the vertical aspect (elevation) to be accurately shown; (3) an adjacent wall to be shown along with the elevation, receding in such a way as to give a view of both the interior and exterior (section?). All three types of drawings, which Vitruvius names respectively as *ichnographia*, *orthographia*, and *scaenographia*, are created "ex cogitatione et inventione"; that is, they are the expression of a *ratiocinatio* that resolves a given problem in either a known or a novel way. The Vitruvian term *scaenographia*, often interpreted as a perspectival view, is impossible to translate with any certainty. Daniele Barbaro understood *scaenographia* to be an analog of *sciagraphy* (from the Greek *skíagraphia*) and thus a section drawing (part elevation): "The way in which the section drawing is used induces me to interpret the term as sciagraphy and not scenography.... Others insist that it means model, but this does not fit with the argument in question, even if it is true that it gives clarity and certainty to the Architect's plan: there is also the fact that it does not accord with Vitruvius's definition of the model ... and I would further add that he had of necessity to treat the section drawing in his treatise." *I dieci libri dell'architettura tradotti e commentati da Mons. Daniele Barbaro eletto Patriarca d'Aquileia* (Venice: Francesco de' Franceschi Senese, Giovanni Chrieger Alemanno Compagni, 1567), 30–32. For an interesting analysis of perspective in the time of Vitruvius, cf. Jean H. Luce, "Géométrie de la perspective à l'époque de Vitruve," *Revue d'histoire des sciences* 1 (1953): 308–321. Studies of the use of the term *perspectiva* in classical times have drawn attention to the term's use in relation to a "frontal view measured from a single, fixed distance" as early as the Justinian era: Francesca Salvemini, "Analisi terminologica della voce volgare prospettiva attraverso le fonti. I secoli XII–XIII," *Storia dell'Arte* 52 (1984): 221–231. A succinct analysis of how the term *scaenographia* has been interpreted in the various editions of Vitruvius may be found in Maria Teresa Bartoli, "Orthographia, ichnographia, scaenographia," in Luigi Vagnetti, ed., *2000 anni di Vitruvio* (Florence, 1978), 197–208.

2. For a discussion of the artist's status in the classical world, cf. Ranuccio Bianchi Bandinelli, "L'artista nell' antichità classica," in *Archeologia e cultura* (Rome: Ricciardi,

1979), 45–62, and Margherita Guarducci, "Sull'artista nell'antichità classica," in Filippo Coarelli, ed., *Artisti e artigiani in Grecia* (Bari: Laterza, 1980), 87.

3. In this connection cf. also the recent discovery of drawings on a scale of 1:1 cut into the walls of the unfinished temple at Didyma, near Miletus. Cf. Lothar Haselberger, "The Construction Plans for the Temple of Apollo at Didyma," *Scientific American* 253 (1985): 114–122. With regard to contracts, the most famous is that drawn up between Philon and Euthydemos for the construction of the naval arsenal of Piraeus (340–330 BC), in which mention is made of a model. Cf. Spiro Kostof, "Architecture in the Ancient World: Egypt and Greece," in Kostof, ed., *The Architect* (New York: Oxford University Press, 1977), 3–27.

4. In a detailed inscription on the Thólos of Epidaurus (IG IV 2 103), we read that the architect Komodion was paid 50 Attic drachmas for a model of the astragal and the *kymation*, and 615 drachmas and one and a half obolos for the execution of the same ornament. Cf. Nikolaus Himmelmann, "La remunerazione dell'attività artistica nelle iscrizioni edilizie d'età classica," in Coarelli, *Artisti e artigiani in Grecia*, 146.

5. For Egypt, cf. the study of the scale model of a New Kingdom house (Paris, Louvre, n. E5357) by C. Desroches, "Un modèle de maison citadine du Nouvel Empire," *Revue d'Egyptologie* 3 (1938): 3–25. The most complete study of representations of ancient Egyptian architecture is still that of Alexander Badawy, *Le dessin architectural chez les anciens égyptiens* (Cairo: Imprimerie Nationale, 1948), which includes a discussion of models on 63, 73, 75 and 200–201; for a discussion of planning methods, see Badawy, *Ancient Egyptian Architectural Design: A Study of the Harmonic System* (Berkeley: University of California Press, 1965). The most famous examples of Egyptian models of houses are those of Meketra's house, now divided between the Metropolitan Museum of Art, New York, and the Egyptian Museum, Cairo. See H. E. Winlock, *Excavations at Deir el Bahri* (New York: Macmillan, 1942). Egyptian temples were planned according to type and the layouts were preserved inside the temple. Following a period of apprenticeship as a scribe, the Egyptian architect was awarded the title of "Master of Secret Things in the Temple." Senenmut, the famous chief architect to Queen Hatshepsut, proudly wrote: "I had access to all the writings of the Prophets; there was nothing I did not know of what happened in the beginning." James Henry Breasted,

4.29
Urn of Publius Volumnius. Volumnii sepulchre, Perugia.

4.30, 4.31
Theatrical stages, first century AD. Museo Romano, Rome.

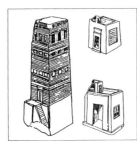

4.32
Models of houses from the Greco-Roman era. From Reginald Engelbach, "Four Models of Graeco-Roman Buildings," *Annales du Service des Antiquités de l'Égypte* 31: 130.

4.33
Model of an Egyptian house, New Kingdom. From Christiane Desroches, "Un modèle de maison citadine du Nouvel Empire," *Revue d'Egyptologie* 3 (1938), figure 11.

Ancient Records of Egypt, 5 vols. (Chicago:University of Chicago Press, 1906), 2:149, 353. A brief but interesting iconography of votive or funerary modelsis given in Bernard Rudofsky, *The Prodigious Builders*(New York: Harcourt Brace Jovanovich, 1977). For antique models in Italy, cf. R. A. Staccioli, *Modelli di edifici etrusco-italici. I modelli votivi* (Florence: Sansoni, 1968); Margarete Bieber, *The History of Greek and Roman Theater* (Princeton: Princeton University Press, 1939); D. S. Robertson, *Greek and Roman Architecture* (1929; Cambridge: Cambridge University Press, 1980). The most important Mesopotamian example is a relief of the eighth century BC discovered at Nimrud showing the scale model of a captured fortress being offered to Sargon II during a procession. Edith Porada, "Battle-ments in the Military Architecture and in the Symbolismof the Ancient Near East," in Douglas Fraser, Howard Hibbard, and Milton J. Lewine, eds., *Essays in the History of Architecture Presented to Rudolf Wittkower* (London: Phaidon, 1967), 1–12. For a discussion of the Roman *Pompa Triumphalis* (in which models of defeated fortresses and cities were paraded), cf. Joachim Marquardt, *Römische Staatsverwaltung* (Leipzig: S. Hirzel, 1881), 1:584.

6. This problem was discussed for the first time by Julius von Schlosser, "Beiträge zur Kunstgeschichte aus den Schriftquellen des frühen Mittelalters," in *Sitzungsberichte der philosophisch-historischen Classe der Kaiserlichen Akademie der Wissenschaften* 123 (1891): 37. The role of *neokóros* was bestowed by the Roman Senate and related to the building and consecration of a temple dedicated to the emperor. The Greek term *neokóros* means guardian or protector of the temple (Plato, *Laws* 6.759 and Xenophon, *Anabasis* 5.3.6); the Latin equivalent is *aedituus*, cf. August Pauly, *Real-Encyclopädie der classischen Alterthumswissenschaft* (Stuttgart: G. B. Metzier, 1848), s.v. For the depiction of the donor with model, cf. the in-depth study by Elizabeth Lipsmeyer, "The Donor and His Church Model in Medieval Art from Early Christian Times to the Late Romanesque Period," Ph.D. diss., 1981 (Ann Arbor: UMI Research Press, 1987), the source of much of the information contained in the present text. Coins depicting *neokóroi* are exclusive to Asia Minor, however, and to the city of Filipopolis in Thrace, and cease after the reign of Gallienus, toward the middle of the third century. Lipsmeyer, Ihm, Bloch, and Kocks are reluctant to posit a continuity between these depictions and those found in Christian basilicas. Cf. Christa Ihm, *Die Programme der christlichen Apsismalerei vom vierten Jahrhundert bis zur Mitte des achten Jahrhunderts* (Wiesbaden: Steiner, 1960);

Peter Bloch, "Zum Dedikationsbild im Lob des Kreuzes des Hrabanus Maurus," in Victor Heinrich Elbern, ed., *Das erste Jahrtausend: Kultur und Kunst im werdenden Abendland an Rhein und Ruhr*, 3 vols. (Düsseldorf: L. Schwann, 1962), 1:474; Dirk Kocks, "Die Stifterdarstellungen in der italienischen Malerei des 13–15 Jahrhunderts," inaugural dissertation (University of Cologne, 1971), 41. For a discussion of a possible iconographic continuity between these coins and the Christian tradition, cf. Behrendt Pick, "Die Templetragenden Gottheiten und die Darstellung der Neokorie auf den Münzen," *Jahreshefte des Österreichischen archäologischen Institutes* 7 (1904): 1–41; von Schlosser, "Beiträge zur Kunstgeschichte aus den Schriftquellen des frühen Mittelalters," 5 and 63; Otto Benndorf, "Antike Baumodelle," Jahreshefte des Österreichischen archäologischen Institutes 5 (1902): 178; and André Grabar, *L'empéreur dans l'art byzantin* (Paris: Belles Lettres, 1936), 154. It should be noted that when the theme reappeared in basilicas of the sixth century, its character had changed substantially from that of the Roman era. Then, it was used as witness of a conquest or with celebratory intent, now it was rather a symbol of *pietas*, a prayer of salvation and hope. It was in this form that the theme began its migration into the worlds of both Western and Eastern Christianity, and it did so in an astonishingly pervasive manner; Kocks has counted around a thousand examples in Italian painting alone.

7. The following is a translation of Du Colombier's note on the text in which the model is described as *opera exemplar*: "As far as the construction of the model is concerned, an *artifice* has to be found ... one of those people who go by the name of architect nowadays.... As for the *magistri operum*, the Masters of Works, they are executors or administrators of sorts. They play no part in the proceedings until the model has been completed." Pierre Du Colombier, *Les chantiers des cathédrales* (Paris: A. & J. Picard, 1973), 95.

8. A careful analysis of the fourteenth-century contract for Palazzo Sansedoni in Siena was carried out by Franklin Toker, "Gothic Architecture by Remote Control: An Illustrated Building Contract of 1340," *Art Bulletin* 1 (1985): 67–94. The document was first published by Annarosa Garzelli, "Un disegno di architettura civile del 1340," *Antichità viva* 12 (1973): 36–41. The wall measurements were calculated with reference to the *Trattati dell'abbaco* produced by the masters of the Florentine school, to which Paolo Toscanelli belonged. For a comparison between the geometric approach of

4.34
Domenico Fetti, *The Architect Antonio Maria Viani Presenting Margherita Gonzaga with the Model of the Church of Sant'Orsola*, early seventeenth century. Palazzo Ducale, Mantua.

northern Europe and the mathematical basis of the Italian tradition, see Diane Finiello Zervas, "The Trattato dell' Abbaco and Andrea Pisano's Design for the Florentine Baptistery Door," *Renaissance Quarterly* 28 (1975): 483–503.

9. Here we paraphrase the definition of the image formulated by Gregory the Great who, in a letter to the Bishop of Marseilles, expressed his disapproval both of the adoration of images as well as of their destruction, since "their purpose is to instruct the minds of the ignorant" (*Epistulae* 11.13).

10. Sangallo was paid 1,500 *scudi* for his 1:30 scale model, while a sum of 4,184 *scudi* was paid to Antonio Labacco for materials and construction. The sum paid to Komodion for his model, however, was equivalent to 1/12 of the cost of carrying out the work. The data relating to Sangallo's model are in Vincenzo Scamozzi, *L'idea dell'architettura universale* (1615; Venice: Girolamo Albrizzi, 1714), 51–52.

11. For Renaissance architectural drawing and the importance of orthographic projection, cf. Wolfgang Lotz, "Das Raumbild in der Architektur Zeichnung der italienische Renaissance," *Mitteilungen des Kunsthistorischen Institutes in Florenz* 7 (1956): 193–226. English translation, "The Rendering of the Interior in Architectural Drawings of Renaissance," in Lotz, *Studies in Italian Renaissance Architecture* (Cambridge: MIT Press, 1977), 1–65.

12. For a historical analysis of the figure of the architect, see Kostof, *The Architect*; John Harvey, *The Mediaeval Architect* (London: Wayland, 1972); Martin S. Briggs, *The Architect in History* (Oxford: Clarendon Press, 1927); cf. the chapter dedicated to the figure of the architect in Richard A. Goldthwaite, *The Building of Renaissance Florence: An Economic and Social History* (Baltimore: Johns Hopkins University Press, 1980). For the use of the term *architect*, see the now classic Nikolaus Pevsner, "The Term 'Architect' in the Middle Ages," *Speculum* 17 (1942): 549–562.

13. Ludwig H. Heydenreich, "Architekturmodell," in *Reallexikon zur deutschen Kunstgeschichte* (Stuttgart: A. Drunkenmüller, 1937), 1:918–940, with bibliography and predominantly German iconography; Benndorf, "Antike Baumodelle," 175ff; Arthur L. Frothingham, "Greek Architects," *Architectural Record* 23 (1908): 85ff; Martin S. Briggs, "Architectural Models," *Burlington Magazine* 54 (1929): 174–183 (part I), 245–252 (part II); Jacob Burckhardt, *Die Baukunst der Renaissance in Italien* (Basel: Schwabe, 1955), 80–83; an account of the minor role played by the model

compared to the plan is given in James S. Ackerman, "Architectural Practice in the Italian Renaissance," *Journal of the Society of Architectural Historians* 13 (1954): 3–11; Richard A. Goldthwaite, "The Building of the Strozzi Palace: The Construction Industry in Renaissance Florence," *Studies in Medieval and Renaissance History* 10 (1973): 99–194, see especially 191–194 for the smallcollection of documents dating from around 1490 ordering the construction of models: "modello della chasa" (1490); "modello delle facciate" (1489); "modello del piano della chasa" (1490) (model of the house, model of

4.35, 4.36
Alessandro Antonelli, wooden model of the dome of San Gaudenzio, c. 1840. Church of San Gaudenzio, Novara.

4.37
Giuseppe Segusini, wooden model of the bell tower of Canova's temple at Possagno, first half of nineteenth century. Giacinto Bernardi Collection, Onè di Fonte.

the facades, model of the layout of the house); Goldthwaite, *The Building of Renaissance Florence*. Bucher has suggested that small-scale models were used for reliquaries from the Carolingian period, and even more interesting is his suggestion that these small-scale models, executed by goldsmiths, might have provided the bridge to architecture: from 1400 these small commissions represented 25 percent of the work undertaken by northern architects, referred to significantly by Filarete as "goldsmiths": see François Bucher, "Micro-Architecture as the 'Idea' of Gothic Theory and Style," *Gesta* 15 (1974): 71–81. In the attribution to Giacomo da Campione of the facade of the Certosa di Pavia, depictions in fresco and stone of the models provided useful comparisons: Gianpiero Borlini, "The Façade of the Certosa di Pavia," *Art Bulletin* 3 (1963): 321–336; Anna Matteoli, "I modelli lignei del '500 e '600 per la facciata del Duomo di Firenze," *Commentari* 25 (1974): 73–110; Henry A. Millon, "A Note on Michelangelo's Façade for a Palace for Julius III in Rome: New Documents for the Model," *Burlington Magazine* 121 (1979): 770–777; Peter Gercke, ed., *Antike Bauten in Model und Zeichnung um 1800* (Kassel: Staatliche Kunstsammlungen, 1986), catalog of the exhibition at the Staatliche Kunstsammlungen Kassel of the cork models by Antonio Chichi; Paul-Henry Boerlin, "Die Stiftskirche St. Gallen," thesis (Basel, 1963), in which the eighteenth-century models by Gabriel Looser are discussed; "Maquette," *Rassegna* 32 (1987), especially the articles by Riccardo Pacciani, "I modelli lignei nella progettazione rinascimaentale," 7–19; Massimo Quaini, "Le forme della terra," 63–73; and Jacques Guillerme, "Il modello nella regola del discorso scientifico," 29–37. For a discussion of models of French fortifications, see Bruno Fortier, "Il museo dei Plans-Reliefs a Parigi. La pace delle Cittadelle," *Casabella* 533 (1987): 44–53. For Ottoman models, see Gulru Necipoglu-Kafadar, "Plans and Models in 15th and 16th-Century Ottoman Architectural Practice," *Journal of the Society of Architectural Historians* 45 (1986): 224–243.

14. Giorgio Vasari, *The Lives of the Most Excellent Painters, Sculptors, and Architects*, trans. Julia Conaway Bondanella and Peter Bondanella (Oxford: Oxford University Press, 1998), 119. Cf. the Brunelleschian models referred to in Carl Frey, ed., *Il libro di Antonio Billi* (Berlin: G. Grote, 1892), 31–37, and Antonio di Tuccio Manetti, *The Life of Brunelleschi*, ed. Howard Saalman (University Park: Pennsylvania State University Press, 1970).

15. "Noli cum multis participare inventiones tuas." Frank D. Prager and Gustina Scaglia, *Brunelleschi: Studies of His Technology and Inventions* (Cambridge: MIT Press, 1970), 144.

16. "La Vita di Brunelleschi," in Manetti, *The Life of Brunelleschi*, 117, rr. 1386–1389. This strategy of not making everything explicit is probably also why Brunelleschi's perspective panels have remained as mysterious to us as they were to his contemporaries. Manetti's description seems to omit much more than it explains, even leaving us in doubt as to the size of fifteenth-century lentils.

17. "For by his own doing, in making his things very beautiful, he would have laid himself open to much annoyance and regret, for it was not his intention to show everything." Ibid., rr. 1377–1384.

18. Ibid., r. 1396.

19. The model of Palazzo Strozzi executed in 1490 by Filippo d'Andrea after the designs of Giuliano da Sangallo is a good example of this. The Strozzi model is one of the few surviving architectural models of whose date we can be certain. Older prototypes, such as the papier-maché model for the church of Saint Maclou in Rouen or that of Brunelleschi for the Florentine cathedral, are today considered to be reconstructions from a later date. The model of Saint Maclou is preserved in the Musée Le Secq des Tournelles at Rouen and would seem to postdate the building of the church, which was under way between 1432 and 1512. Frothingham has theorized that it is the work of Jehanson Salvart, who in 1414 was paid 300 gold *scudi* for work pertaining to the church under construction. Cf. Arthur L. Frothingham, "Discovery of an Original Church Model by a Gothic Architect," *Architectural Record* 22 (1907): 111–116. Jean Lafond proposes a date between 1541 and 1611. Cf. Pierre Provoyeur, "Du labyrinthe au temple," in *Le temple* (Paris, 1982), 23. For the Brunelleschi model and the reconstruction of the building project for Santa Maria del Fiore, see the recent essay by Pacciani, "I modelli lignei nella progettazione rinascimaentale," and the convincing reconstruction of the dome made by Massimo Ricci, "Il segreto della Cupola di Santa Maria del Fiore," *Scienze* 7 (1987): 42–56. The model of Palazzo Strozzi was studied by Guido Pampaloni, *Palazzo Strozzi* (Rome, 1963). An example of the building of a large model for purely presentational purposes may be seen in *Codice Barberiniano* (f. 39v), which contains a reproduction *in pulito* of the drawing for the model of a palace that Ferdinando I, King of Naples, commissioned from

4.38–4.40
Filippo d'Andrea, wooden
model of Palazzo Strozzi
made to the design of
Giuliano da Sangallo, 1490.
Istituto del Rinascimento,
Florence. Palazzo Strozzi.

Sangallo through the mediation of Lorenzo the Magnificent. In December 1488 Giuliano da Sangallo accompanied the large model to Naples, and Vasari tells us that "it took much time to transport it there." Vasari, *The Lives*, 272.

20. The only known drawing by Alberti, identified by Howard Burns in the codex Ashburnham 1828 (App), fols. 56v–57r, is in the Biblioteca Medicea Laurenziana in Florence. It is a scale drawing executed with instruments *in pulito*. It may be supposed that this type of drawing was sent to the model makers. See Burns, "A Drawing by L. B. Alberti," *Architectural Design* 46 (1979): 45–56.

21. Vasari, *The Lives*.

22. "Neque habet lineamentum in se ut materia sequatur.... Et licebit integras formas praescribere animo, et mente, seclusa omni materia." *De re aedificatoria libri decem Leonis Baptista Alberti Florentini viri clarissimi, & Architecti nobilissimi, quibus omnem Architectandi rationem dilucida brevitate complexus est* ...(Strasbourg: M. Iacobus Cammerlander Moguntinus, 1541), f. 3r and v. ("Nor do lineaments have anything to do with material.... It is quite possible to project whole forms in the mind without any recourse to the material." Alberti, *On the Art of Building in Ten Books*, trans. Joseph Rykwert, Neil Leach, and Robert Tavernor [Cambridge: MIT Press, 1988], 7.)

23. "Modulis, exemplariisque factis asserula, seu quavis re universum opus." Ibid., f. 18r.

24. Ibid., f. 19r.

25. Ibid., f. 18r.

26. "Architectus spretis umbris prominentias ex fundamenti descriptione ponit, spacia vero, et figuras frontis cuiusque, et laterum alibi constantibus lineis atque veris angulis docet." Ibid., f. 18v. ("The architect rejects shading, but takes his projections from the ground plan and, without altering the lines and by maintaining the true angles, reveals the extent and shape of each elevation and side." Alberti, *On the Art of Building*, 34.)

27. When the Prince remarks, "I do not like these thorny questions," Filarete assures him that he will not use the technical language of Vitruvius but those expressions "in use today." Filarete, *Antonio Averlino detto il Filarete, Trattato di Architettura*, ed. Anna Maria Finoli and Liliana Grassi (Milan: Il Polifilo, 1972), 216.

28. Ibid., 40.

29. In the documents relating to the construction of the church and bell tower of Santa Maria del Fiore (see Cesare Guasti, *Santa Maria del Fiore*, Florence, 1887), we

often find expressions such as: "an example of the design in wood" (81); "of the design in wood" (82); "an example of a column" (96); "plaster and draw the example of the column and the capitals" (116); "*ad faciendum designum seu modellum ecclesiae*" (168); or, "carve out with chisels the model of the badia [abbey]" (103). A document of 19 November 1367 (207) is important for clarifying the relationship between the two terms: *che ogni altro disegnamento, sì di mattoni chome di legname e di charta, si deba disfare* (and that all other designs, whether of brick or wood or of paper, must be destroyed). The terms *disegnamento, disegno,* and *designo* (from the Latin, *designo*) thus signify the concept, or the intention, as expressed in line, or by means of an *exemplum* (in Latin, *modellum,* which in Italian becomes *esempro, asempro,* or *essenpro*). See Andreas Grote, *Studien zur Geschichte der opera di Santa Reparata zu Florenz im vierzehnten Jahrhundert* (Munich: Prestel, 1959), especially the chapter titled "Entwürfe, Vorlagen und Modelle," 113–119. Calepino gives the definition of *delineo* as "ex De et Lineo, quod a linea fieri certum est, significat designo et ruditer depingo," while *designare* is defined as "denotare, quasi per signa, demonstrare." See Ambrogio Calepino, *Ambrosii Calepini Dictionarium …* (Leiden, 1544), s.v. In France, *dessin,* the noun deriving from the verb *dessiner,* is rare in the seventeenth century, but we find it used in 1430 to mean the "plan of a building." See Walther von Wartburg, *Französisches etymologisches Wörterbuch* (Tübingen: Mohr, 1949), s.v. *Dessein,* the noun derived from the verb *desseigner,* is a variant of *dessiner* and means "tracer l'image d'un objet" (sixteenth and seventeenth centuries) and corresponds, until the end of the eighteenth century, to *dessin* in the sense of project, idea. The *Dictionnaire de l'Académie Française* (Paris, 1694) includes only *dessein*: "résolution de faire quelche chose, l'intention, prétention; dessein se prend aussi en peinture, plan d'un bastiment." For the terminology of models mentioned in fourteenth- and fifteenth-century artists' contracts, see Hannelore Glasser, *Artists' Contracts of Early Renaissance* (New York: Garland, 1977), especially 115–149.

30. Filarete, *Trattato di architettura,* 207. In order to construct medium-sized wooden models, Scamozzi advised making "small channels" on the base in correspondence with the interior and exterior of walls, in a sort of ichnographic "imprint." See Scamozzi, *L'idea dell'architectura universale,* 51–52.

4.41
Anonymous, papier-mâché model of the Church of Saint Maclou, Rouen, early fifteenth (?) century. Musée d'Art Normand, Rouen.

31. See especially f. 144r. His characteristic method of uniting plans and perspective elevations in highly imaginative renderings may be seen in fols. 87r and 119v. Filarete, *Trattato di architettura*, 11, plates 65, 89, and 108.

32. These observations came about during the course of a conversation with Howard Burns in the winter of 1987 at Harvard University. Pedretti has advanced the theory that the Tempio degli Angioli "was conceived in terms of a bird's-eye view of the cathedral." Leonardo must have seen that bird's-eye model when Verrocchio's sphere was placed in the tambour of Florence cathedral. See Carlo Pedretti, *Leonardo architetto* (Milan: Electa, 1981), 14. The same procedure, derived from Francesco di Giorgio Martini, of a variation on models seems to have been repeated much later, and in a much less elegant way, by Giovan Battista Minio, *Opera nuova intitolata il Cavaliere, nella quale minutissimamente si scuopre tutti i secreti et avisi mirabili, che il pratico et diligente Governatore di forteze, & Capitano d'esserciti deve havere, con tutta l'arte del Bombardiero, accresciuta di varij, & molti secretij* (Vicenza, c. 1550–1560). Vienna, Österreichische Nationalbibliothek, Cod. 10854. Giovan Battista Minio is named as mayor of Vicenza in 1556 in *Relazioni dei rettori di Terraferma, Vicenza*, vol. 2 (Milan: A. Giuffrè, 1976). Barbaro makes no mention of him. In 1557 there is a Girolamo Minio, son of "Giò Batta mayor of Vicenza in 1557 and in 1560 Captain of Treviso … Giovanni Minio, son of Lorenzo, died on the first of October 1560; buried in the church of Santa Lucia where his tomb may be seen with the inscription added by Andrea his brother." See Girolamo A. Cappellari, *Il Campidoglio Veneto* (Venice, Biblioteca Marciana, MS. III M–Q, 146–155). Book IV (79ff.) contains drawings of variously shaped fortresses, all drawn in military perspective (oblique parallel projection), with some parts tipped up with respect to the ground plane. Here, as in the famous Zichy Codex of Budapest, Francesco di Giorgio Martini's influence in the Veneto is very obvious. The treatise may also be linked to the fact that in 1551 Ferdinand I of Austria had begun to fortify Vienna. For a discussion of Martini's drawings, see F. Paolo Fiore, *Città e macchine del '400 nei disegni di Francesco di Giorgio Martini* (Florence: Leo S. Olschki, 1978). It should be noted that Martini used the word *model* only to indicate the module and sometimes the plinth, but never the actual architectural model.

33. Leonardo's use of parallel projection is more evident in his drawings of machines (Codex Hammer, fol. 6r), in the studies of structural strength applied to

stereotomy (Cod. Madrid I, fols. 142v and 143r), and in the more famous drawings of centrally planned buildings, which appear to be axonometric representations of models (Cod. Ashburnham, dis. 183, fols. 4r, 5v; ms. B, fols. 22r, 25v). See also the sketch of ramparts, which is a true military axonometry (Cod. Madrid II, fol. 93v), and the exploded view in oblique projection of a mechanism (Cod. Atlantico, fol. 8v–b). This combination of figurative techniques results in greater precision and integrity in the representation of both interior and exterior views of the project, testifying to a complex set of relationships with a dense interweave of mutual influence between Leonardo and Bramante on the one hand, and between Francesco di Giorgio Martini and Leonardo on the other. The meeting of the latter, in Pavia in 1490, is documented in the annotations to Martini's treatise (Cod. Laurenziano Ashburnham 361, made, according to Pedretti, between 1506 and 1507). Parallel projection is used in the stereometric figures of the *Divina proportione* for which Leonardo drew the beautiful polyhedrons that were the object of an essay by Marisa Dalai Emiliani, "Figure rinascimentali dei poliedri platonici. Qualche problema di storia e di autografia," in Pietro C. Marani, ed., *Fra Rinascimento manierismo e realtà* (Florence: Giunti Barbèra, 1984), 7–16. Pomponius Gauricus recommended the same procedure for small-sized objects. See *Gaurici Pomponii Napoletani, De sculptura ad Divum Herculem Ferrariae principem* (Florence: Junta, 1504); republished as Pomponius Gauricus, *De sculptura*, ed. André Chastel and Robert Klein (Geneva: Droz, 1969); the description of tracing in parallel projection is found on 190–193, in the chapter titled "De perspectiva." In numerous relief drawings of trabeations in the Codex Coner (London, Soane Museum), oblique parallel projection is used, with the receding plane set at 45 degrees. See Thomas Ashby, "Sixteenth-Century Drawings of Roman Buildings, attributed to Andreas Coner," *Papers of the British School at Rome* (Rome, 1904), 2:1–88. These drawings, dating from about 1515, have been attributed to Bernardino della Volpaia by Tilmann Buddensieg, "Bernardino della Volpaia und Giovanni Francesco da Sangallo: Der Autor des Codex Coner und seine Stellung im Sangallos Kreis," in *Römisches Jahrbuch für Kunstgeschichte* 15 (Tübingen: Wasmuth, 1975), 89ff. See also the group of drawings preserved at Casa Buonarroti showing the outline of architraves (2A, 3A, 4A9), perhaps copies carried out by Michelangelo's assistants on the basis of the Codex Coner, or from the prototype from which it derives (Ashby). See Charles De Tolnay, ed., *I disegni di Michelangelo nelle collezioni italiane* (Florence: Centro Di, 1975), 84–85, and Wolfgang Lotz, "Zu Michelangelos Kopien nach Codex Coner," in *Akten des XXI Internationalen Kongress für Kunstgeschichte* (Berlin, 1964), 12ff. For the model as object of redesign, see the important sheet 2v in the Cod. Icon Mon. (Munich, Bayerische Staatsbibliothek), which shows a graphic distortion in the transept, probably because the drawing was based on the model by Antonio da Sangallo the Younger. See Christoph Luitpold Frommel, Stefano Ray, and Manfredo Tafuri, eds., *Raffaello architetto* (Milan: Electa, 1984), 299–300 and 302 dis. 2.15.44e. Some interesting considerations on the analytic model established by Leonardo for his anatomical studies (such as representation by means of transparent layers) may be found in the monumental Kim H. Veltman with Kenneth D. Keele, *Linear Perspective and the Visual Dimensions of Science and Art* (Munich: Deutscher Kunstverlag, 1986), 211–218.

34. Vasari, *The Lives*. Note that the definition appears in the introduction dedicated to painting; where architecture is concerned, Vasari refers the reader to the treatises of Vitruvius and Alberti.

35. "The first and most important task in the making of the work is the model, since it is by means of trying out his ideas and altering them that the Artificer arrives at the most beautiful, most perfect solution. It is useful to architects in order to establish lengths, widths, heights and thicknesses, and the number, size, type and quality of all things, how they should be disposed so that the building will be perfect: and also to calculate which craftsmen must be employed, so that the expenditure may be worked out." Filippo Baldinucci, *Vocabolario toscano dell'arte del disegno* (Florence: Santi Franchi, 1681), s.v. In the inventory drawn up after Borromini's death, dated 3 August 1667, four models in red wax and three in wood are listed. See Paolo Portoghesi, *Borromini nella cultura europea* (Rome: Officina Edizioni, 1964), 387.

36. "The model ... is a mold in wood or in stiff card, of how the building should be, making it possible to see at a glance the ground plan and the elevation, and this is necessary for anyone wishing to build, because it allows him to see the finished work, its breadth and height." Alvise Cornaro, "Trattato di architettura," in Paola Barocchi, ed., *Scritti d'arte del Cinquecento* (Milan and Naples: R. Ricciardi, 1977), 3:3141.

37. Barbaro admits that its use makes "the architect's intention clearer and more certain." See note 1.

38. Briggs, *The Architect in History*, 203; Reginald Blomfield, *A History of French Architecture from the Reign of Charles VIII till the Death of Mazarin*, 2 vols. (London: G. Bell and Sons, 1911).

39. Philibert de l'Orme, *Architecture de Philibert de l'Orme, conseiller et aumosnier ordinaire du Roy, et Abbé de sainct Serge lez-Angers ...* (Rouen: David Ferrand, 1648), chapters X–XII, 21–24. The title of the first edition was *Le premier tome de l'architecture* (Paris: Fédéric Morel, 1567), republished in 1568, 1576, 1648, and 1894, with the addition of the *Nouvelles inventions pour bien bastir et à petits fraiz* (Paris: Fédéric Morel, 1561).

40. Philibert de l'Orme criticizes those *maîtres maçons* who proclaim themselves architects, as well as ignorant architects who, like *perroquets*, do not know what they are saying. In general his invective is aimed at more or less everybody involved in architecture, whom he angrily defines as "donneurs de portraicts & faiseurs de desseins ... tailleurs d'images." Ibid., fol. 21r.

41. "Simplement unis, et plustost imparfaicts que polis et mignons." Ibid., fol. 23r.

42. "Faire ses lignes pour dresser proprement un plan, et une montée faicte nettement avec toutes ses proportions et mesures, afin que le Seigneur l'entende. Puis dresser ses modelles qui seront de bois ou papier, ou de charte, ou d'autre maniere, ainsy qu'elle luy viendra à propos." Ibid., fol. 22r

43. Without being able to explain why, de l'Orme realizes that the functioning of kinematic chains changes according to scale. With regard to this, see the interesting discussion on the effectiveness of mechanical models in Bernard Palissy, *Discours admirables de la nature des eaux et fontaines ...* (Paris: chez Martin le Jeune, 1580). See Guillerme, "Il modello nella regola del discorso scientifico," 29.

44. Scamozzi, *L'idea dell'architettura universale*, 52.

45. Robin Evans, "La Trompe d'Anet," *Eidos* 2 (1988): 50–57. Frézier writes that a *trompe* "normally is a semi-conic vault that shows us its base." Amédée-François Frézier, *La théorie et la pratique de la coupe des pierre et des bois, pour la construction des voutes et des autres parties des bâstiments civils & militaires, ou Traité de stereotomie à l'usage de l'architecture* (Paris: Jombert, 1754).

46. Pietro Cataneo, *Dell'architettura libri VIII* ...(Venice: Aldo Manuzio, 1567), 175.

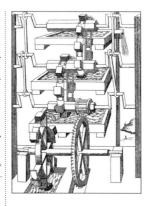

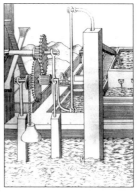

4.42, 4.43
Ottavio da Strada, plates from *Variae ac faciles molendina construendi inventiones* (Prague (?), c. 1600). Österreichische Nationalbibliothek, Vienna. Codex 10846.

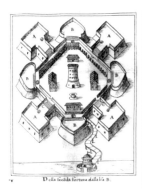

Della seconda fortezza dalla lt'a B.

47. See the chapter "Elements for a History of Axonometry" in this book.

48. A significant example is reported by Vasari in the case of the siege of Florence in 1529. During the night, Tribolo and an assistant secretly built an accurate relief model in cork, several meters wide, of the city and its fortifications. It was smuggled out of the besieged city in various pieces concealed inside bales of wool. This allowed the pope, aided by Baldassarre Peruzzi, to direct operations from a distance. Briggs, *The Architect in History*, 153. Although the relief was made in the style of a pictorial view, it was considered evidence of espionage. On this subject, see Goethe's recounting of the episode in his *Italian Journey*: on 14 September 1786 at Malcesine, the local authorities tore up the drawing he had made for his own pleasure of an abandoned castle. Johann Wolfgang von Goethe, *Viaggio in Italia* (Turin: Utet, 1965), 80. The same thing had happened one hundred years prior to the architect Joseph Furttenbach, who sketched fortifications on the journey from Savona to Antibes in 1619: he was stopped and served with a notice. See Margot Berthold, "Joseph Furtenbach von Leutkirch—Architekt und Ratsherr in Ulm (1591–1667)," *Zeitschrift für Geschichte und Kunst* 33 (1953): 160.

49. Bartolomeo Scola, *Di Basilio della Scola …* (Vicenza: Tipografia di S. Giuseppe e G. Rumor, 1888), 15–33; John R. Hale, *Renaissance Fortification* (London: Thames and Hudson, 1977), 35.

50. The models executed in Venice on the order of the Magistrati were usually in colored cardboard. The only retribution mentioned in the documents is that relative to the cost of cardboard and paint, while, as Donatella Calabi kindly pointed out to me, no recompense was paid for the planning or the idea. The construction of models must have been quite a long and costly process. In a meeting of 5 March 1514, Alessandro Leopardi promised a model for the Rialto market, which was only examined on 28 July. In a meeting of 26 August, a final decision was taken after reexamination of all three models, and in the end the choice was made "di tuor certo disegno havia fata quel proto dil sal" (Marin Sanudo, *Diarij* XVIII, coll. 401 and 470). See Raffaello Brenzoni, *Fra Giovanni Giocondo veronese. Verona 1435–Roma 1515* (Florence: Olschki, 1960), 40, 41, and 58. On the question of the Rialto bridge, see the definitive reconstruction of events in Donatella Calabi and Paolo Morachiello, *Rialto. Le fabbriche e il ponte* (Turin: Einaudi, 1987), 50–60.

4.44
Giovan Battista Minio,
plate from the manuscript
Il cavaliere (Vicenza, c.
1550). Österreichische
Nationalbibliothek,
Vienna. Codex 10854.

4.45
Leonardo da Vinci, two
centrally planned churches,
1517. Institut de France,
Paris. Manuscript B,
folio 17v.

51. The order came from Francesco Maria della Rovere, governor-general of Venice from 7 September 1523. See Ennio Concina, *La macchina territoriale* (Bari: Laterza, 1983), 20.

52. For Busca the design of the fortress consists basically of a relief made from the survey carried out *in situ*: "It is extremely difficult to decide on the design of a fortress, since they are not on level ground, and everything that cannot be rendered in drawing must be clarified in writing to clear up any doubts. In the case of those fortresses to be built on high rocks, I like first to stake them out, and once the fortress is established, to then make a plan from it … and when I am actually present on the site I make adjustments, bring the walls in here, out a little there, back again, and push them out once more … and having marked off all the angles, I get the design and reproduce it all in the drawing." Gabriello Busca, *Dell'architettura militare, libro primo* (1601) (Milan: G. Bordone and P. Martire Locarni, 1619), 92. Two more books were planned but never published.

53. Given that the layout of a fortress is very closely dependent on the unique topography of the site, it seems to him "useless to supply designs in this treatise." See Giovan Battista de' Zanchi, *Del modo di fortificare le città* (1554; Venice: P. Pietrasanta, 1558). The designs in the treatise are not by Zanchi, nor are those which appear in La Treille's French edition. The treatise was well received and Maggi, who was personally acquainted with Zanchi, described him admiringly as "a very ingenious man of great worth."

54. Sarti's diatribe against those who, though ignorant of the rules of war, wish to plan fortresses *more architectonico* (according to the layout of architectural drawings) continues: "I am happy to have dealings with soldiers who are experts in their field and veterans in the affairs of war, thus have I chosen (speaking for myself) to use a form of words that is suitable for such subjects; I have explained matters that concern them without recourse to illustrations or drawings; this is quite unlike the customary form of addressing beginners." Antonio Paolo Sarti, *L'archivio di diverse lettioni militari* (Venice: appresso E. Deuchino, 1630), 2, and *La reale et regolare fortificazione descritta in quesiti e risposte* (Venice: Evangelista Deuchino, 1630), 6.

55. Gian Giacomo Leonardi, *Libro delle fortificazioni de' nostri tempi* (transcription by Tommaso Scalesse), *Quaderni dell'Istituto di Storia dell'Architettura* 20–21 (1975): 60.

56. The *Provveditori* (superintendents) of the Ducal Palace were ordered to prepare "a room in the new attic

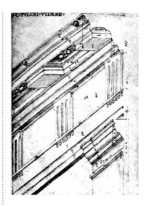

4.46
Bernardino della Volpaia, drawing of an architrave, c. 1515. Sir John Soane's Museum, London. Coner Codex, folio 78*r*.

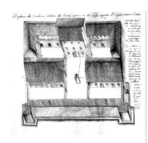

4.47
Paolo Artico of the Verona
Military College, Lazzaretto
di Castelnuovo di Albania,
1 September 1767. Archivio
di Stato, Venice. Provveditori
alla Sanità, b. 9, dis. 7.

for keeping models and drawings." See "Ordine ai Rettori sulle fortezze del 19 dicembre 1550," in Concina, *La macchina territoriale*, 184. The procedure by which fortification works were carried out was initiated by a ruling of the military chiefs and the *Provvedditori alle Fortezze* (instituted 24 September 1542, with jurisdiction over the *Stati da mar e da terra*), with an inspection of the site conducted on the "appropriate relief model," after which it was deliberated by the Collegio and the Senate which then transmitted the orders to the *Rettori* and *Provveditori* who had the task of assigning posts to the engineers.

57. "If you say to me again that a man draws well, I would reply that it is a good thing to stay indoors, for a man can draw anything he wishes on a piece of paper, and I too can do things on paper which will elicit much praise, but that can never be built, because drawing is misleading and can show things that are false." See Giovan Battista Belici (Belluzzi), *Nuova inventione di fabricar fortezze* … (Venice: R. Meietti, 1598), 88.

58. Francesco Maria della Rovere, *Discorsi*. See Concina, *La macchina territoriale*, 90.

59. In his *Libro delle fortificationi de' nostri tempi*, Leonardi lucidly enunciates a hierarchy in which *res militaris* seems to prevail over *res aedificatoria*: "To make a city, and fortify it, is the duty and concern of the commander in chief and the Prince … while the engineer's duty and concern is this: that having noted the idea, the opinion, the solution settled upon by the Prince, he will concern himself with making a design of it." Concina, *La macchina territoriale*, 48.

60. "It will be necessary to make drawings and models and show them off to people; and then go to hear everybody's opinion…. It will be as well not to begin building while one still has doubts, in case one is led into making mistakes, as I have seen some do; on the contrary, it is best to take a second look, and to be patient so that one can remedy any mistakes that one has incurred. He will be an architect of great merit who makes a building in such a way that others can neither add to it nor subtract, if not erroneously." See Francesco De Marchi, *Dell'architettura militare, libri tre, nelli quali si descrivono* … (Brescia: C. Presegni, 1599). His *Trattato delle fortificazioni* (Paris, Bibliothèque Nationale, Cod. 7743) was presented as a gift to Philip II in 1554.

61. Alain Manesson Mallet, *Les traveaux de Mars ou l'art de la guerre* (1672) (Paris: chez Denys Thierry, 1684), 1: 155 passim.

62. The receding edge is inclined by 25 degrees with respect to the horizontal line. The procedure is described: "If the said body is to be solid, then take two pieces of card, as we have said, or even two pieces of wood, which can be cut to size." See Giulio Troili da Spinlamberto detto il Paradosso, *Paradossi per pratticare la Prospettiva senza saperla, fiori, per facilitare l'intelligenza, frutti, per non operare alla cieca* (Bologna: G. Longhi, 1683), 3:30–31.

63. The oldest models of cities still extant today are those commissioned by the duke of Bavaria Albrecht v from Jakob Sandtner of Straubing between 1568 and 1574. They show the city of Burghausen (1574) and that of Landshut (1571) and are preserved in the Bayerisches Nationalmuseum of Munich. The model of Burghausen also includes the Salzach River, which forms the border of Bavaria and Austria. See *Dizionario enciclopedico italiano* (Rome, 1982), vol. 9, plate 269, and Hans Reuther, "Wesen und Wandel des Architekturmodells in Deutschland," *Daidalos* 2 (1981): 98–110. The Musée des Plans-Reliefs in the Hôtel des Invalides still possesses 37 models out of the 50 originally made. Many (those of Canada) were damaged after their transfer from the Louvre during the eighteenth century, and in 1815 the Prussians removed eighteen, which were of France's northeast border. The collection remained until 1870. Initially exhibited as marvels in the Grande Galerie du Louvre, they served to train young army officers who were admitted by a special concession of the king. In 1965 Jean Pierre Paquet used the old model of Besançon in order to elaborate the management plan of the city. See Michel Parent, *Vauban, un encyclopédiste avant la lettre* (Paris: Bereer Levrault, 1982), 128.

64. "Les fortifications se représentent ou par des desseins sur le papier ou par des modelles en bois, de plâtre ou de carton." See Leonhard C. Sturm, *Le véritable Vauban, se montrant au lieu du Faux Vauban* (The Hague: N. Wilt, 1708). The same was true in a civilian context for Paulus Decker, *Fürstlicher Baumeister oder Architectura Civilis wie ...* (Augsburg: Jeremias Wolff, 1711).

65. Louis Bretez, *La perspective pratique de l'archi-tecture* (Paris: Bretez and P. Miquelin, 1706). The same consideration is made by Fiedler a century and a half later: "By following the methods of descriptive Geometry he may substitute drawings for the models which are so much more costly." Wilhelm Fiedler, *Trattato di geometria descrittiva* (Florence: Le Monnier, 1874), 1.

4.48
Orthographic projection of Lazzaretto del Varignano, eighteenth century. Archivio di Stato, Venice. Provveditori alla Sanità, b. 11, dis. 25.

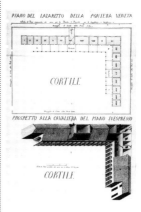

4.49
Antonio Ferro, sergeant-major of the engineers at Verona Military College, Lazzaretto di Pontebba Venta, *Prospetto alla cavaliera ...* , c. 1765. Archivio di Stato, Venice. Provveditori alla Sanità, b. 489, dis. 1.

66. The book was published without the *applica-tions* because Monge was engaged on a scientific mission with Napoleon's troops in Egypt. The *Programme* is writ-ten with a lofty sense of purpose: "Pour tirer la nation française de la dépendance ou elle a été jusqu'à present de l'industrie étrangère, il faut, premièrement, diriger l'éducation nationale vers la connaissance des objets qui exigent de l'exactitude, ce qui à été totalement négligé jusqu'à ce jour, et accoutumer les mains des nos artistes au maniement des instrumens des tous genres … c'est une langue nécessaire à l'homme de génie qui conçoit un projet … elle offre des exemples perpétuels du passage du connu à l'inconnu….Elle est non seulement propre à exercer les facultés intellectuelles d'un grand peuple, et à contribuer par là au perfectionnement de l'espèce humaine." Gaspard Monge, *Géométrie descriptive. Leçons données aux écoles normales. L'an 3 de la République par Gaspard Monge, de l'Institut national* (Paris: An VII [1798]), 1–2.

67. Jean Courtonne, *Traité de la perspective pratique avec des remarques sur l'architecture* (Paris: Jacques Vincent, 1725), 89–91.

68. Girolamo Francesco Cristiani, *Dell'utilità e della dilettazione de' modelli. Dissertazione* (Brescia: G. B. Bossini, 1765); *Della Media Armonica Proporzionale da applicarsi nell'architettura civile …* (Brescia: G. B. Bossini, 1767). Described by Cicognara as "greatest of mathemati-cians, and engineer" in *Catalogo ragionato dei libri d'arte e d'antichità posseduti dal Conte Cicognara* (Pisa: Capurro, 1821), n. 484, Cristiani also wrote *Trattato delle misure d'ogni genere, antiche, e moderne: con note letterarie, e fisico-matematiche, a giovamento di qualunque architetto* (Brescia: Bossini, 1760) and *Altra dissertazione per confutare le idee innate, letta in Brescia in un'Accademia letteraria* (Brescia: Bossini, 1766).

69. In a letter of 1759, the governor-general of Verona is required to pay a sum of money for the purchase of various materials and for *istromenti* (Venice, State Archive, *Senato Militar di Terra Ferma, filza* March 1759). See M. D. Anselmi, "Arsenale e territorio: l'organizzazione della viabilità del Settecento Veneto" (degree thesis, IUAV, Department of the History of Architecture, 1978–1979).

70. Here Cristiani seems to reiterate the ideas on the relationship between the senses and mental abstraction, which Diderot had expressed in his *Lettre sur les aveugles à l'usage de ceux qui voient* and taken up again in his *Pensées sur l'interprétation de la nature*: "As long as something exists only in the mind, it remains an opinion … it

becomes meaningful only when linked to things which are external to it. This linkage is achieved either by an uninterrupted series of experiments or through an un-interrupted line of reasoning, one end of which is rooted in observation and the other in experimentation.... Everything is dependent on proceeding from the senses to reflection, and from reflection back to the senses." Arthur M. Wilson, *Diderot* (New York: Oxford University Press, 1972). The teaching program for the Military College of Verona included linear orthography and eleva-tions (military or cavalier perspectives), as is evident from the designs of engineers trained there. Cristiani's enthu-siasm for models finds its echo in the teaching programs of the college, which, immediately after it was founded on 3 March 1759, began to include requests for models, among those for various other materials. A later and more sizeable request was made on 21 December 1771 (Venice, State Archive, *Senato Militar di Terra Ferma*, filza December, 1771). "Public assent was given to the suggestion of making a number of models in order to aid the pupils in their work and the *Savio* in question [Savio alla Scrittura or Minister of War] is ordered to get hold of a separate list of a whole group of models." Anselmi, *Arsenale e territorio*.

4.50
Alessandro Antonelli, detail of a wooden model for the dome of San Gaudenzio, c. 1840. Church of San Gaudenzio, Novara.

5.1
Filippo Brunelleschi, wooden model of
the dome and apse of the cathedral
of Florence. Museo dell'Opera di Santa
Maria del Fiore, Florence.

5

BRUNELLESCHI'S MODEL FOR THE DOME OF SANTA MARIA DEL FIORE AND THE GHERARDI DRAWING

It is almost impossible to precisely date the model of the cathedral of Florence kept in the Museo dell'Opera di Santa Maria del Fiore because, while the dome of the church was being built, models of all its component parts were ordered from various makers.[1] The historian Piero Sanpaolesi considers the surviving model to be "contemporary with the construction … one of the many which, for various reasons that were clear at the time but are unknown to us and almost impossible to discover, were made during the construction of the vault … and it lacks those features which would allow us to date it somewhere between 1420 and 1452."[2] However, the discrepancies between the model and the actual construction allow us to narrow the time period in which it was made. The only substantial reservation regards the octagonal drum and parts of the apse, which could have been executed earlier, in the late fourteenth century.

The model itself reproduced the irregularities actually present on the sides of the earlier constructed drum (the maximum difference between the width of the sides in the actual drum is approximately 60 centimeters). The corner pilasters of the drum are the same width from the base to the impost of the dome, yet we know from Antonio Manetti's biography that, after the death of Brunelleschi, his successor Antonio di Manetto Ciaccheri "reduced the width of the pilasters in the upper section"[3] when the marble facing was begun in 1465. Therefore, it may be safe to assume that the model was made prior to 1465, but this does not explain how it survived; usually, when substantial modifications were made, a new model was constructed and the old one destroyed. Giuseppe Marchini[4] hypothesizes that the model could be the one ordered from Ghiberti and Brunelleschi on 22 September 1429[5] to replace the one built near the campanile and demolished on 23 January 1431.[6] This thesis appears to be borne out by a request made of Brunelleschi on 17 June 1434 to "complete the model of the church and the great dome and its lantern"[7] after he had previously been asked for a model of the lantern on 30 October 1432. In another hypothesis[8] Marchini suggests that the dome is older, and is in fact the one mentioned by Giovanni di Gherardo Gherardi in 1425, when he says, "This form [the pointed fifth curvature] was decided on six years ago, and I made a wooden model." The oculi in the drum are not excessively splayed; in the actual drum, Manetti complained, this was "due to the incompetence of the *capimaestri* who later worked there and made the splays too wide on the outside of the oculi."[9] The splays in the model are less accentuated than those in the built oculi, and the diameter of the oculi is smaller than it ought to be. The balcony area (*ballatoio*) at the base of the dome, which in the model is "without ornamentation," as Brunelleschi intended, may correspond to the project of 1420. Wolfgang Braunfels also believes that the model is contemporary with the construction.[10]

5.2
Drum and dome of Santa Maria del Fiore,
Florence.

The Wooden Model of the Lantern of the Cathedral of Florence

The wooden model of the lantern, made of elm and walnut,[11] is in fairly good condition. It is composed of two parts made at different times. The base of the model, carved in two parts held together by two dovetail joints, represents the upper part of the dome, from which three external sail vaults have been removed to show all the ribs. In the upper part are modeled the octagonal oculus and the small rooms in the ring surrounding it; all of these parts are covered by the floor of the lantern above. The shape of the lantern is an irregular octagon; in each face windows are placed between fluted Corinthian pilasters, the capitals of which were made of *pastiglia* (gesso) and covered with wax. In the sides of the buttresses, which support the pilasters, there are rectangular openings topped with scallop-shell-shaped niches. Above the molded cornice, the fluted cone, consisting of a number of pieces of walnut, is surmounted by a globe and wooden cross. The number 1673 painted on the model almost certainly refers to the year when the model was painted off-white; this is still visible in an old Alinari photograph taken before the 1966 flood in Florence. On 27 June 1432 Brunelleschi was asked to produce a project for the ring of the lantern in two versions: one circular and the other octagonal.[12] On 12 August 1432 an order was placed for a model of the octagonal oculus to be placed at the crown of the dome;[13] on 25 June 1433 the width of the oculus was reduced from 10 *braccia* to 9⅔.[14] On 31 December 1436 the models presented in the competition for the lantern were examined:[15] these included models by Brunelleschi, Lorenzo Ghiberti, Antonio di Manetto Ciaccheri, Bruno di Ser Lapo Mazzei, and Domenico Stagnario. The jury, composed of "architects, painters, goldsmiths, and other intelligent citizens" ("Architectores, Pictores, Aurifices, et alios Cives intelligentes"), selected Brunelleschi's design as being the most robust and, at the same time, the lightest; moreover, it permitted better lighting and formed efficacious protection against the elements. Thus Brunelleschi was asked to "set aside all rancor" and carry out the modifications that had been requested: to incorporate the best features of the other models. The needs of the state overrode the interests of the individual and his pride: the end result had to be perfect.[16]

Vasari described Brunelleschi's model as being "superb," with the famous stairway in the form of a hollow tube that led up through one of the pilasters right to the base of the gilded bronze orb made by Andrea del Verrocchio in 1468.[17] In fact, this detail does not exist in the extant model, and the orb is made of wood, not gilded metal. The style in which the lantern is executed lacks the terseness that was the hallmark of Brunelleschi's work[18] and was recommended by his friend Alberti in *De re aedificatoria*.[19] It is quite possible

that Brunelleschi furnished Ciaccheri—who made the model to his specifications—with more detailed information and allowed the execution of additional
decorative features. The model may have been made by Brunelleschi or it may
be one of the models made for him by Ciaccheri in 1436. After Brunelleschi's
death in 1446 and a brief period under Michelozzo, Ciaccheri was appointed
capomaestro in 1452. The registers of the *Opera* do not state whether Ciaccheri
used Brunelleschi's model or made a new one for the completion of the lantern.
This writer is of the opinion, however, that Brunelleschi's model, which had
been restored on 30 December 1449, was in use until the work was completed.[20] The sculpted peapods and flowers on the volutes of the buttresses
added by Ciaccheri may be justified by the absence of any specific indications
in Brunelleschi's model. Regarding other details, the lack of information in
the model meant that work had to be suspended, as was the case with the
architraves of the doors in the buttresses: "Thus, the marble sculptures over
the architraves of the small doors, which are in the buttresses under the vine
ornaments, since they were not finished in the model, were not executed on
the lantern, because by then Filippo was no longer of this world."[21]

5.3
Lantern of Santa Maria del Fiore,
Florence.

5.4
Filippo Brunelleschi, wooden model of the
lantern of the cathedral of Florence. Museo
dell'Opera di Santa Maria del Fiore, Florence.

The lightning that repeatedly damaged the lantern until a lightning rod was installed in 1859[22] must certainly have convinced the administrators of the *Opera* (*provveditori*) that it was advisable to keep the original model. However, one of the most widely accepted theories is that the disastrous collapse in 1600, or on a later occasion, led to the construction of the present model.

Grand Duke Ferdinand I's letter would appear to support this hypothesis: "And when they [Bernardo Buontalenti, Gherardo Mechini, and Bronzino] cannot remember the old design of the damaged lantern" they go to all the Florentine architects to seek those who have "made the plans and drawings or model of the dome with the correct measurements."[23] But Ferdinand I wrote without having personally ascertained the extent of the damage or having checked if drawings and models were really available. He asked the architects of the *Opera* for a copy of the original, not an interpretation, "without making any modifications, whether they be great or small."[24] In reality the lightning had not damaged the lower part of the lantern, and part of the cone must still have been standing if Mechini was able to report, "for a large part of its height, its shape has not been affected."[25] If a new model had been made, it would certainly have been depicted in the engraving that Jacques Callot executed later than 1611, after a drawing by Matteo Rosselli; instead Ferdinand appears before a drawing and not a model.[26] Moreover, it should not be forgotten that in Bronzino's report to the grand duke, the architect does not propose the construction of a model but suggests that "all the old models of the building should be carefully examined to see what purpose they served."[27] For what would have been the point in making a model that faithfully represented the original if the restoration work was then carried out in quite a different way and contrary to the grand duke's orders? Too many details in the model differ from those in the present lantern: the pinnacles have two annulets in the model and three in the actual building; the capitals on the external pilasters are different, since there are four in the pilasters on the model and three in those on the building; there are four flutes on the tops of the actual buttresses, but in the model there are only two; lastly, the volutes in the model are more elegant and without the uninspired peapod and flower ornamentation designed by Michelozzo and Ciaccheri.[28] This decoration must have been remade exactly as it had been after the collapse of 1492, since Antonio da Sangallo the Younger drew it. On the other hand, Giovanni Battista da Sangallo, in his inaccurate sketch of the lantern, gives the impression of having corrected his hasty observation of the real volutes by reproducing those seen on the model.[29]

The model appears, therefore, to be the one made by Brunelleschi to which the sources refer,[30] with the upper part of the dome and the rooms in the ring planned in 1432 and the lantern designed for the competition in 1436. It is just possible that it might be the one made by Ciaccheri, without the stairway in the form of a hollow tube, but this was so similar to Brunelleschi's model that he said, "Make another copy of it, and that will be mine."[31]

In the lower part of the model may be seen a part of the dome with the thirty-eight steps on the extrados of the inner shell. It corresponds almost exactly to the part that was not yet vaulted in 1430—that is, to the point where the date 1430 was found at the level of the third corridor up from the drum.[32] That Brunelleschi designed this part is confirmed by three features: the absence of the brick arches that link the smaller ribs to the main ones, the positions of which were decided on the spot; the curved shape of the external wall of the ring, where the ribs are attached, which reflected the plan for a circular ring that was subsequently abandoned; the internal windows of the rooms in the ring, which are circular, and a proposal for three square openings on one side, as they were in fact built.[33]

Giovanni di Gherardo Gherardi Drawing with Critical Annotations

The parchment[34] prepared by Giovanni di Gherardo Gherardi of Prato, who substituted for Ghiberti from 1420 to 1426, is the only extant document containing drawings relating to the dome of Santa Maria del Fiore that is contemporary with its construction. It was published for the first time by Cesare Guasti in 1874 with an interpretative note by Nardini Despotti Mospignotti. The *pentimenti* in the drawing and the deletions in the text ("se" and "sest"), as well as comparison with Gherardi's signature,[35] confirm that this is the original document.

The parchment should be viewed with the irregular side and the inverted 90 at the bottom (the number is repeated on the verso). It bears three drawings and five groups of annotations. To these should be added a sketch of masonry (top left) and a disc of the sun (bottom right). From work records it may be deduced that the parchment was prepared in the last four months of 1425: on 1 July 1425, at the request of the *Opera*, Lorenzo Ghiberti's salary was suspended,[36] and on 15 February 1426 the registers of the *Opera* record payment to Giovanni da Prato "for his work and materials, having provided the *Opera* with the number of drawings and a clay model, which demonstrated how the necessary work should be carried out in the large dome."[37] The model has not survived, but one of the drawings is certainly the one being analyzed here.

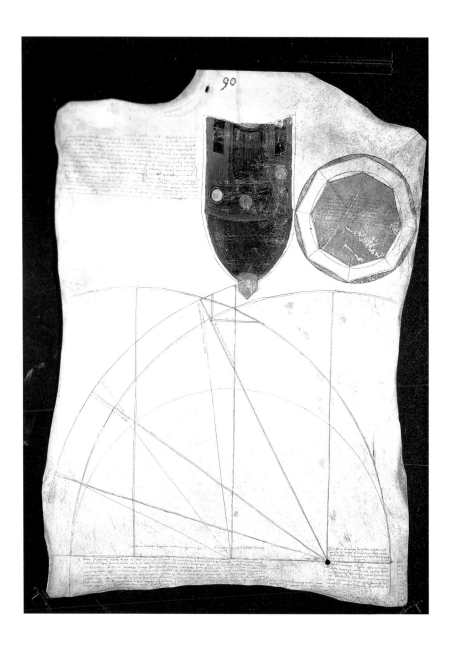

5.5
Giovanni di Gherardo Gherardi, drawing with
critical observations concerning the dome
of Santa Maria del Fiore. Archivio di Stato,
Florence. Inv. Mostra 158.

In 1425 less than a third of the dome had been constructed and doubts must certainly have arisen regarding the correctness of the calculations and building techniques. In accordance with medieval custom, a committee of experts was convened, which included Gherardi, the painter Giuliano d'Arrigo, called "Il Pesello," and the mathematician Giovanni di Bartolo dell'Abaco. The first two were substitute superintendents of the dome, while the third was an expert in "practical arithmetic" whose training had been in accordance with the mathematical tradition that linked Leonardo Fibonacci of Pisa to Paolo dell'Abaco (Paolo Dagomari) from Prato, founder of the school "opposite S. Trinita," which boasted nearly six thousand students.[38] Giovanni di Bartolo began to teach at the school in 1390, when he was nineteen years old; he also taught at the University of Florence, where Gherardi was responsible for "Dantean studies" from 1417 onward.[39]

Giovanni dell'Abaco, who also taught Paolo dal Pozzo Toscanelli, certainly played an important role in the measurement of the dome and the solution of the problems related to its construction;[40] as early as 30 June 1417 he was paid five gold florins for his mathematical and geometrical calculations "with regard to the construction of the large dome."[41] His first task may have been linked to the purchase of ropes for effecting measurements on 18 September 1416, the sheets for drawing on 28 April 1417,[42] and the making of a model that probably served to confirm the pointed fifth curvature ("curvatura a quinto di sesto acuto") before the public competition of 1418. Then on 1 April 1420 dell'Abaco received one florin,[43] and finally ten florins in 1425. This same year Ghiberti's authority seemed to wane. Having displayed uncertainty with regard to the technical problems of the construction, Ghiberti attempted to assert his theoretical point of view through Gherardi's opinions. In this report, the last one recorded in the registers of the *Opera*, Gherardi attacks Brunelleschi without referring to him except as "someone who invents irrational things." This epithet was immediately taken up by Giovanni Cavalcanti when he condemned Brunelleschi's project during the siege of Lucca in 1430: "Some of our inventors of fantasy, including Filippo di Ser Brunellesco ...with their false geometry."[44]

Gherardi's arguments begin with the question of the lighting and continue with the slope of the masonry courses (*ricaschi*). Our examination of the text will proceed in the same order. Next to the drawing of the crossing on the right there is a block of text divided into two parts. After the first six lines referring to the adjacent drawing the author begins his exposition thus: "I, Giovanni di Gherardo Gherardi ... having been requested to give my opinion regarding the building of the dome." He states, therefore, that he wishes to express his opinion on what has been done so far. He maintains that it is necessary to think about the lighting of the dome before continuing to build it "without windows or openings"; besides, in view of the distance between the oculi of the drum and the lantern, he says that the absence of openings makes the dome dark and gloomy.

In pleading his case, Gherardi draws on his studies of optics at Padua, under the guidance of the authoritative Biagio Pelacani da Parma, from 1384 to 1388. It was not by chance that Biagio appeared as "a universal philosopher and mathematician" in the unfinished *Paradiso degli Alberti*, together with Coluccio Salutati, the Paduan physician Marsilio di S. Sofia, and the humanist Francesco Landini.[45] Gherardi also includes in this group the Augustinian mathematician Grazia de' Castellani, author of a *De visu*,[46] which was certainly known to Brunelleschi as the theory of the "certified vision" of Biagio Pelacani.[47]

To describe the poor lighting in the dome, Gherardi draws the vertical section of the crossing in brown ink and shades it with indigo-black so as to stress the oculi in the drum and the circular shaft of light on the masonry. Three oculi are drawn in the drum: the side ones are shown as oval and the central one, colored with ocher and gold, is circular (with a diameter of 17 millimeters). When the drawing is studied under a Wood light, two circumferences inscribed with a compass (of diameter 12 millimeters) can be discerned at the sides of the central oculus, and an oval on the left. They are probably hypotheses for the projection of light, later discarded in order to avoid interference with the oculi in the drum and to stress the credibility of the thesis that the lighting is inadequate. Gherardi also depicts a gleam of light descending from the roughly sketched lantern, barely reaching the ring.

Biagio's optical theories are echoed by Gherardi's subsequent statements: "As common sense seems to suggest" and "as can be found in the treatise on mirrors and perspective," the light reflected on the wall would not be sufficient to illuminate the sixty *braccia* from the oculi to the lantern, even if the oculi in the drum were without windowpanes. In order to support his thesis he gives an example: the "oculi with windowpanes" constructed by the *capomaestro* Giovanni d'Ambrogio in Santa Reparata in 1415 were evidently insufficient to illuminate the interior of that church.[48] Gherardi's solution was to contrast with the proposals of the "ignorant and foolish" individuals who suggested that windows should be constructed in the vault. Gherardi pointed out that five years earlier he had prepared a drawing for the construction of twenty-four windows immediately above the cornice of the drum.[49] But we know that his proposal was never seriously taken into consideration. On 24 January, when Gherardi was about to retire to Prato after the suppression of his course at the University of Florence, Brunelleschi replied disdainfully: "Nothing has been said concerning the light because it is our firm belief that there will be enough light thanks to the eight oculi underneath: but even if it were seen that light was necessary after all, it could easily be obtained from the upper part next to the sides of the lantern."[50] In 1442 Paolo dal Pozzo Toscanelli put an end to the controversy by tersely asserting that the much-criticized panes of glass in the oculi of the drum were intended "to serve as ornament rather than for light."[51]

Now the parchment should be viewed the other way up. Gherardi's second criticism is more complex and regards the two remaining drawings: a plan of the octagonal drum colored red (top right) and a large section passing through the diameter of the octagonal drum (in the lower part). Under the latter drawing, which is essentially a diagram, is the explanatory text; this continues the previous one—"Once again I, the aforementioned Giovanni"—and concludes in the caption on the plan. The three blocks of text regard two different questions that are dealt with very briefly: they relate to the technique to control the geometry (*sesto*) of the sail vaults and the slope at which the courses of bricks should be laid (*ricaschi*).

Here Gherardi amplifies the seriousness of his accusations with the rhetorical invective typical of republican Florence. This is no longer merely the defense of an unsuccessful project, but rather the denunciation of Brunelleschi's "duplicity." Gherardi, who was ten years his rival's senior, states with studied solemnity that "on no account may the curvature that has been agreed upon be changed or reduced in size; this form was decided on six years ago, and a wooden model was made." This reminder is apparently superfluous, but it is immediately related to Brunelleschi's default with regard to the project of 16 April 1420: "The dome is vaulted according to the size of the pointed fifth at the angles on its inner side."[52] Possibly already established in the model of 1367, this curvature, as Gherardi writes, had been borrowed from the "form of S. Giovanni"—the neighboring baptistery. He also affirms that the acceptance of the pointed fifth curve for the dome was finalized by one of the many models that were specially built, probably the one made in 1418.[53]

Failure to respect the project agreed to under oath—"I swear to Almighty God … that this building will be constructed according to the model"—was a very serious act of negligence for an architect, *capomaestro*, or mason.[54] Aware of this, Gherardi predicts that Brunelleschi wants to build the remaining three-quarters of the dome—"the greater part"—with those "strange follies without any basis," which he had used so far. Because of this, he accuses Brunelleschi of having sought to "rashly damage and render hazardous" the whole building by laying the bricks at incorrect angles and changing the curvature (*sesto*) of the dome.

Gherardi's skilled rhetoric was intended to be interpreted at different levels. To the experts he is saying: "Note that up to now the curvature has been built with an incorrect center and not with its proper center, or rather centers, that is, from the cornice upward where the curve springs." To the *capimaestri* and masons he explains that this incorrect procedure is "due to ignorance and presumptuousness" on the part of those who have been entrusted with the direction of the work, and adds—evidently addressing the administrators of the *Opera*—"they have been handsomely paid for this." Thus, he is able to display both his intellectual capacity as a free citizen and his diligence as a substitute superintendent to the *nobiles viri* (noblemen) and the consuls of the Arte della Lana (the Wool Merchants' Guild): "I have written this so that if what I fear is only too likely to happen does occur"—in other words, that the building should be damaged and risk collapse—"then I would be excused because it would not be my fault." Having exhorted everyone involved to be prudent "in the name of the Lord, which I am sure you will," he reminds them that "the cathedral of Siena threatened to collapse" because credit had been given to "someone who invented things irrationally."

Here he is referring to the imprudent extension of the cathedral of Siena under the direction of Camaino di Crescenzino and the subsequent project by Lando di Pietro. The work, initially carried out in great haste and then without adequate skill, had caused subsidence of the columns and cracking in the dome and the arches below. The advice of Francesco Talenti, then *capomaestro* of Santa Maria del Fiore, and Benci di Cione had convinced the twelve governors of the Republic of Siena of the need to demolish the dangerous parts and stop work on the extension.[55] It was with skilled rhetoric that Gherardi associated Brunelleschi with the dangerous "follies" of the Sienese builders, contrasting this recklessness with the wisdom displayed hitherto by the Florentines responsible for Santa Maria del Fiore.

In order to give visible form to his accusation, Gherardi draws a diagrammatic section of the dome passing through the diameter of the octagonal drum (see figure 5.6, the first of five interpretive drawings). This is a drawing of considerable geometrical and structural significance in which nothing is superfluous or fortuitous. All the lines regarding the geometry of the pointed fifth curve, the pointed fourth curve, the lantern, and the inclination of the masonry courses to the center of the pointed fifth are drawn with double lines (red and brown). The half-circumference on the diameter of the base and the inclined masonry courses at its center are drawn with a single line. It is evident that the "correct" lines are the double ones. All the elevation lines have been constructed geometrically, while the base diameter is drawn arithmetically.

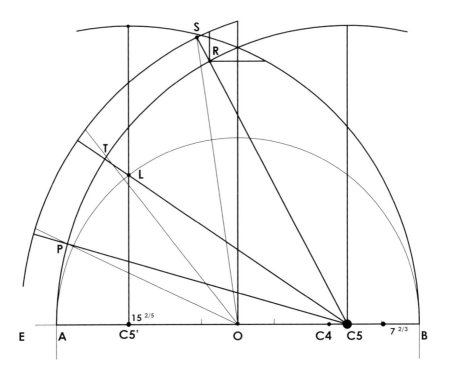

5.6
This diagrammatic drawing shows how Gherardi constructs the inner dome (a pointed fifth curve) based on two circles centered at C5 and C5'. These circles have a radius of ⅘ (C5A) relative to the inner diameter AB. The outer dome (a pointed fourth curve) is centered at C4 with a radius of C4E. C4 is positioned at ¾ of AB, and the measure at this point has been erased in the original, probably because C4E is a pointed fourth curve relative neither to the inner diameter nor to the outer diameter. In Gherardi's original diagram the double lines are drawn in red and brown. Here they are thickened into single lines.

On diameter AB the measurement "$15\frac{2}{3}$ *braccia*" is written at C_5' ($\frac{1}{5}$ of the diameter AB); halfway between C_5 and B the measurement "$7\frac{2}{3}$ *braccia*" is written. Gherardi then emphasizes the center of the pointed fifth curve (radius equal to C_5A), with a conspicuous hole on the right, where he writes: "This is the center of the pointed fifth curve and not of the round curve." Then, placing the point of the compass at C_5' with a spread of $15\frac{2}{3}$ *braccia* plus $7\frac{2}{3}$ *braccia* (thickness EA of the corner ribs), he intercepts the extension of the diameter AB at a point E located off the parchment. From this point springs the pointed fourth curve of the outer dome, which has its center at point C_4, located at $\frac{3}{4}$ of the inner diameter of the base AB. But instead of using a radius of C_4A ($\frac{3}{4}$ AB), which could have described the fourth pointed curve, Gherardi increases the spread of the compass to point E, at the extreme left point of the outer diameter. It is evident that although he is using two centers, according to medieval tradition, the segment C_4E has no significant relationship to the inner and outer diameters.

Above the center C_4 of the pointed fourth curve the measurements have been carefully erased. It is not known when this correction was made, but certainly Gherardi made a mistake here that may have weakened his argument. Evidently he had not realized that Brunelleschi was constructing the inner dome and the outer dome with two curves having different radii (C_5A and C_5E) but the same center at point C_5, this procedure being contrary to medieval practice.[56] In fact, since the thickness of the drum at the corners is $7\frac{2}{3}$ *braccia* (essentially half of $15\frac{2}{3}$), the external diameter of the drum is divisible into four parts measuring three times $7\frac{2}{3}$ each. Therefore, for Brunelleschi the center of the pointed fifth curve, calculated on the basis of the internal diameter, coincides with the center of the pointed fourth used for the external diameter (see figure 5.7 for diameter subdivisions by Gherardi and, below, by Brunelleschi).

Further examination of the original diagram (figure 5.6) shows that the three pairs of inclined masonry courses (*ricaschi*) converging two by two on three points of the corner rib (P, T, S) originate from the centers O and C_5.

The first pair of inclined masonry courses intersects at P, the height the dome had reached when Gherardi wrote his report in 1425 (under the level of the second passageway, at approximately 12 *braccia*). It should be noted that at this height the circumference (round-arch curve [*sesto del mezzo acuto*]) differs only slightly from the pointed fifth curve. It is likely that this difference was difficult to observe at the level of P, as was the difference between the inclinations of the two masonry courses; the objective difficulty of evaluating the situation no doubt favored this extraordinary attempt to put Brunelleschi's motives in doubt.

The second pair of inclined masonry courses, OT and C5T, are drawn near the left half of the pointed fifth curve. Here the difference in inclination is quite evident; the slope of the masonry courses to the center of the curve of the round arch O is a clear warning of the technical difficulties to be overcome when the bricks are laid. This second pair intersects the base circumference AB at point L, which appears to be crucial for verifying the pointed fifth curvature. Here the geometrical diagram ceases to be abstract. The drawing not only shows the geometrical line surrounding the structure, but might also represent a precise technical device used to verify the curvature in the angles. The third inclined masonry course, C5R of the pointed fifth curve, is drawn to determine geometrically the sloping sides SR of the ring (figure 5.7) and the oculus at the apex of the dome, which was planned to be 6 *braccia* high and 12 wide in the 1420 project; the latter figure was reduced to 10 *braccia* in August 1432 and to 9⅔ in June 1433.[57]

Observe now in figure 5.8 the segment that is perpendicular to the base at the pointed fifth center C5' on the left. The half-circumference radius C5'W intercepts this segment at point L, through which also passes the second masonry course slope (C5T). This point divides the radius C5'W into two equal parts, since the segment C5'L is the *mean proportional* of ⅕ and ⅘ of the base diameter AB.[58]

Now, instead of considering the half-circumference of the base as the outline of the round arch, we will regard it as its plan and complete it from a theoretical point of view. The prolongation of the lower half of the segment will meet the mirror image of the half-circumference of the base at a point M that is symmetrical to L. It is likely that the resulting figure could have been used to check the curvature at the corners of the drum, without needing to use the center of the pointed fifth curve C5', which is located in midair, 15⅖ *braccia* from the corners. The segment LM, divided into two parts by the center of the pointed fifth curve C5', is the base of the isosceles triangle with a height equal to ⅘ of the diameter and its vertex in the angle of the octagon. As it rotates upward from its base LM, the mobile vertex B of the triangle precisely verifies the pointed fifth curvature, while always remaining at right angles to the corner ribs (see figure 5.9) In practice it was sufficient to determine geometrically the point of intersection of this segment with the sides of the drum so as to locate the hooks on which the wires were fixed for measuring.[59] The hooks still in place above the architraves of the small doors (top internal gallery) may have served this purpose. The wires must have been those mentioned in a payment to Brunelleschi “for wire and rope purchased for measuring his model.”[60]

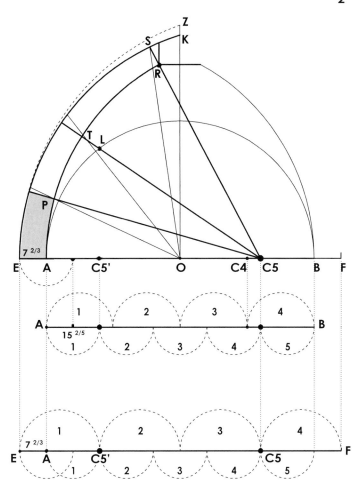

5.7

According to Gherardi and Brunelleschi, center C5 of the pointed fifth curve (intrados) has a radius equal to C5A (⅘ of AB). C5 is the only center that Brunelleschi used to trace the extrados in the pointed fourth curve ES (radius C5E) and the intrados in the pointed fifth curve AR (radius C5A). In C5P Gherardi shows the right inclination for the masonry layers (*ricaschi*), and the wrong inclination in PO. The same applies to C5T in contrast to TO, and to C5S in contrast to SO. In addition, C5S (*ricasco*) geometrically defines the ring of the dome. Below the dome, diagram AB shows the subdivision proposed by Gherardi; diagram EF shows Brunelleschi's subdivisions, based on the outer diameter. Gherardi's report was submitted in 1425 when construction of the dome had only reached 12 *braccia*, below point P. At that time the difference between the intrados of a round-arch curve (wrong) and that of the pointed fifth curve (correct) could have been very difficult to ascertain.

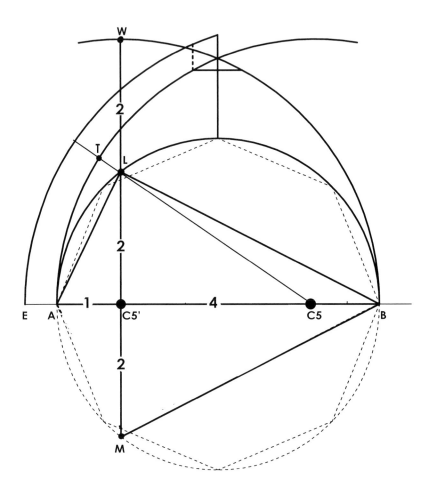

5.8
The half-circumference with diameter AB intercepts segment C5'W at point L, through which also passes the second masonry course slope (C5T). This point divides the radius C5'W into two equal parts, since the segment C5'L is the mean proportional of ⅕ and ⅘ of the base diameter AB. The segment LM (⅘ of the diameter), divided into two parts by the center of the pointed fifth curve C5', is the base of the isosceles triangle with a height equal to ⅘ of the diameter and its vertex in the angle of the octagon. As it rotates from its base ML, the mobile vertex B of the triangle precisely verifies the pointed fifth curvature along the corner rib.

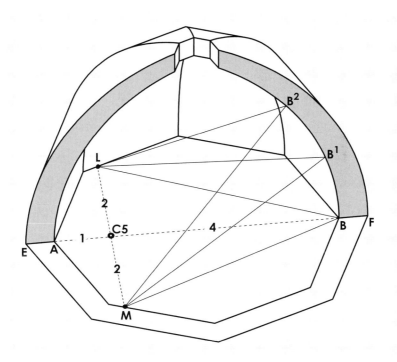

5.9
This hypothetical reconstruction shows how
the regularity of the pointed fifth curvature
was maintained throughout the entire curve,
up to the lantern.

We shall now return to the first part of Gherardi's accusation, written under the section of the dome: "Up to now, note that the curve has been built with an incorrect center and not with its proper center, or rather centers, that is, from the cornice upward where the curve springs." This assertion, placed under the center of the pointed fifth curve, seems to be reasonably clear. But not all the *nobiles viri* were well versed in geometry. Thus Gherardi directs our attention to the large hole on the right where he inscribes the following words: "This is the center of the pointed fifth curve and not of the round curve." Also wanting to show that the construction of the dome was erroneous, not only in the corner ribs but also in the sail vaults—where the curve has been moved horizontally into the cornice—he adds: "Thus you can see the grave error which has been committed by causing the curve to spring from the cornice," because there, too, "the construction is based on the round arch and not on the pointed fifth."

Gherardi then gives a more precise meaning of the expression "its proper center, or rather centers" compared to the incorrect center ("false center") in the text on the left, under the diameter: "Strangely, when establishing the center of the round arch, he indicates just one center, while each angle has one of its own, according to the model which is shown in this figure." Brunelleschi seems to be proceeding "strangely" because he uses a single center for the inclined masonry courses, when, according to Gherardi, he should use the two centers of the pointed fifth curve ("its proper centers"), which lie on the diameter of the octagon near the angles ("each angle has one of its own"). Since this reasoning is valid for all four of the diameters of the octagon, Gherardi proposes his figure as a "model" that can be repeated.

But a single section is not sufficient to allow the complexity of the criticism to be properly understood. Consequently, Gherardi completes his disquisition on the plan with a red border (figure 5.10). As it is the last drawing to be executed on the parchment, he uses all the space available between its edge and the section of the crossing. Rather than drawing the drum to scale, he is attempting to compare the diameter of the inner octagon to that of the section of the crossing on the right. Then, without the aid of a compass, he draws the circle freehand that circumscribes the inner octagon of the drum, and at this point he creates a small hole.

Now the parchment should be turned round once more. Above the exact center of the octagon, Gherardi writes: "Above the round arch. This is the center of the round arch and not the pointed fifth." In other words, unlike the drawing in the upper half of the parchment, the point underneath corresponds

Plan of the octagonal drum. Angle A, formed
by the position of the hole and the line AB,
corresponds to AOD in the section.

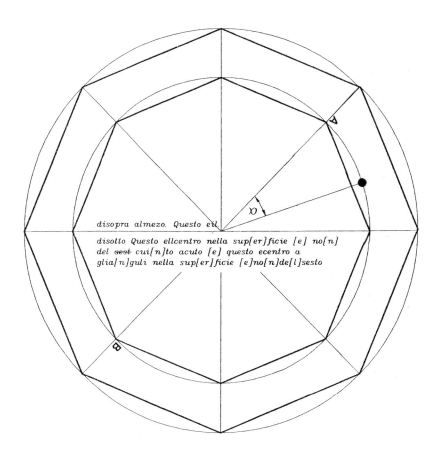

disopra almezo. Questo eil

disotto Questo ellcentro nella sup[er]ficie [e] no[n]
del ~sest~ cui[n]to acuto [e] questo ecentro a
glia[n]guli nella sup[er]ficie [e]no[n]de[l]sesto

to the center of the round arch and not to that of the pointed fifth curve. In this way he correlates the position of the round arch in the section and in the plan. Then, referring exclusively to the plan, he writes: "Under this is the center on the surface and not of the pointed fifth arch, and this is the center at the angles in the surface and not in the curve that extends upward. That is, unless the curve is a round one. See, therefore, what a terrible mistake is being made." In other words, the hole underneath is the center of the surface identified by the diameters of the octagon and not of the pointed fifth curve, and this corresponds to the intersection of the bisectors of the eight angles of the drum ("center at the angles") and it is not the center of the curve which "extends upward"; that is, unless the curve is round, as seems to be Brunelleschi's intention with the inclined masonry courses he uses. The circumference shown by one line, which appears in the plan circumscribing the inside octagon of the drum, corresponds to the half-circumference AB, seen in the section of figure 5.7. Both represent the same hemispherical dome, in plan and in section, in accordance with the practice of the ancient treatises on *Metrica*, such as Heron of Alexandria's codex.

It is evident, therefore, that Gherardi is accusing Brunelleschi of using a single "incorrect center" for the inclined masonry courses instead of using, two by two, the eight centers of the pointed fifth curves in the angles. And if Brunelleschi complies with the pointed fifth geometry in the corner ribs, but builds with the masonry courses inclined to the center of the round arch, Gherardi predicts that the dome will collapse. The considerable inclination to the center of the round arch in the upper part of the masonry courses would seem to suggest this. In reality, Gherardi knew perfectly well that, according to longstanding practice, the voussoirs of an arch had to converge on the center of its curve. Since he did not doubt that Brunelleschi was perfectly aware of this, he believed that the adoption of masonry courses inclined to the center of the round arch was not only a risky building practice, but also evidence of the architect's intention to "modify by reduction" the curvature that had already been decided. The document seems to have enumerated the sum total of Gherardi's criticisms, even if the difficulty of interpreting it might have admitted diametrically opposed readings.[61]

We have also seen how these figures contain geometrical features that the text does not explicate. It is likely either that they were taken for granted or that it was not thought expedient to divulge them. A further example is the hole on the circumference of the internal octagon on the red plan of the drum. It is not explicitly mentioned in the text for the simple reason that it is the mobile curve of the center of the rounded curve that is being discussed. In fact, it appears on the plan where the whole description refers to the "erroneous" rounded curve, just as in the section everything regards the "correct" pointed fifth curve. Therefore, the hole represents the "incorrect" curve (round curve) that "springs from the cornice"—between the corners of the octagon, the one that "goes up" *inside* the sail vaults, considering the circumference as the section (reversed) of the spherical dome. This may be confirmed by observing the plan without turning the parchment around, as would be necessary in order to read the text: the angle of elevation of the hole with regard to the diameter underneath is identical to that of the first inclined masonry course at the center of the round curve, with regard to the diameter of the base in the section. Here Gherardi, somewhat perfidiously, presents a problem that seems to be very complicated to describe in the drawing, but which must have been easy to resolve in practice.[62]

Under the drawing of the plan lurks Gherardi's insidious question: How can the pointed fifth curve be changed in the angles when the curve springs horizontally from the cornice? It is clear that, since the impost of the vault is octagonal, it was not possible to maintain the same radius in the sail vaults as in the corner ribs, whether the construction was a pointed fifth or a round arch. This was a problem with which Brunelleschi was familiar, and he knew he could solve it as the dome was being constructed. In fact, in the report of 1420, he cautiously limited himself to guaranteeing the pointed fifth curve in the angles and, certainly referring to the sail vaults, wrote that the work would proceed "in the way that is advised and decided by those masters who will build … because, while building, experience will teach us what we should do."[63] This "way" was difficult to represent in an intelligible drawing. This way of doing things without any explanation, so typical of Brunelleschi, may have convinced Ghiberti and Gherardi to pose this question with regard to the technical description, thereby causing difficulty for their rival. Contrary to his usual practice, in the reply of 1426 Brunelleschi was obliged to specify the technical procedure as well: the laying of the bricks in a catenary curve (*corda blanda*) between the corner ribs and with a herringbone pattern.

It is possible, however, that in his survey Gherardi identified a problematic aspect of the construction methods. He may not have realized that at the outset Brunelleschi was building with a single center of curvature in order to counteract the side thrusts more effectively. This means that the initial part, now buried in the masonry, was designed to be a sort of "chained" annular base supporting the entire dome, which evidently had to have the inclined masonry courses with a single center.[64] The change in the curvature under the second passageway, first observed by Eugenio Battisti, could mark the upper limit of the stone construction of the annular stylobate.[65] Piero Sanpaolesi and Herbert Siebenhüner have suggested that the first courses of wedge-shaped bricks were laid with their thinner ends facing toward a single center[66] and that their base course, therefore, related to the center of the octagon and not to the eight centers of the pointed fifth curves of the respective diameters.[67]

However, there can be no doubt that Brunelleschi was familiar with the principle that arches should be built with their masonry courses inclined toward the center of the curve, as his friend and admirer Leon Battista Alberti wrote twenty years later: "Throughout the arch it is necessary to arrange the blocks of stone in such a way that they face the center of this arch."[68]

In fact, the inadequacy of our knowledge of the real sequence of construction and the way the bricks were arranged inside the walls does not allow us to confirm or refute any of these hypotheses. However, even a rapid examination of the corner ribs is sufficient to reveal that the inclined courses of the bricks are nearly always at right angles to the pointed fifth curve, so that they cannot converge on the center of the round arch. After Gherardi's criticisms, the document of 1426 written by Brunelleschi insists on the need for the annular strengthening of the vault: "The bricks should be placed in rings … to allow a perfect ring which surrounds the dome outside so that this arch should be complete and not broken";[69] he also refers to the problem of centering, which serves to check the curvature of the corner ribs; and, lastly, he says that the bricks will be laid in a herringbone pattern with the use of the *gualandrino a tre corde*. Thus, steps should be taken to make the eight sail vaults of the dome structurally sound, and moreover, to ensure that the pointed fifth curve is respected. It is quite possible that the idea of setting up massive centering was proposed; this would have served to verify that the correct curvature was maintained. In the report of 1426, he clearly expressed impatience with the objections that had been raised, including those of Gherardi.

Brunelleschi puts an end to the question of centering by stating, somewhat irritably, that "it would be difficult to construct centering without scaffolding; in fact, centering was abandoned expressly to avoid having to use scaffolding."[70] However, it is likely that small-scale centering with a pointed fifth center was used during the construction; this would have been moved as the dome grew, its vertical position in the corners being determined by the aforementioned wire method. Connected to this mobile centering along the sail vaults was the *gualandrino a tre corde*, which ensured that the bricks in the webs were laid correctly on a curve corresponding to that of a slack rope.[71] Although historians have given free rein to their fantasies with regard to the nature of this instrument and the etymology of its name, it must have simply been a sort of *calandrino* or bevel square; this is defined by the 1990 edition of the Devoto and Oli *Dictionary of the Italian language* (published in Florence and hence with a Tuscan bias) as "a wooden square with adjustable wooden arms that fit together, used by carpenters and stonemasons."

It is not possible to conclude this analysis without mentioning that during the construction of the dome, or in the years immediately before this, Brunelleschi, in a manner of speaking, invented perspective. In fact, it is legitimate to ask whether perspective developed as part of the endeavor to apply the laws of optics to painting or whether it derived from the optical measurement of buildings—that is, from architectural surveying. Manetti wrote that when Donatello and Brunelleschi were surveying "almost all the buildings in Rome," they ascertained their heights by means of "strips of parchment … bearing the numerals used in the abacus."[72] This was in the first decade of the fifteenth century, when, as a result of the vogue for antiquities, the hunt for Greek codices by men of letters, intellectuals, and patricians was under way. But while Petrarch and Boccaccio had already collected the precious codices of classical literature and philosophy (including Vitruvius) for "hundreds of years" nobody had "built in the ancient manner."[73] Brunelleschi, however, had studied this technique for many years, and there is no doubt that it contained the basis for the invention of perspective. It is possible, therefore, that when measuring the heights and widths of Roman buildings with a graduated sight ("with the numerals used in the abacus"), Brunelleschi had understood how the apparent measurements varied in inverse proportion to the distance, and that, in fact, the "strips of parchment … bearing the numerals used in the abacus," by creating a plane at a fixed distance from the eye, stressed the perspective of the real dimension.

There are, therefore, valid grounds for believing that the method of one-point perspective drawing was born of the architectural survey—that is, of the problem of proportional measurement. Thus, the famous perspective panels would appear to be an amusing application of what Brunelleschi had invented, or rather rediscovered, during his surveys in Rome. It had yet to be discovered whether Brunelleschi used a perspective device to check the radius of the pointed fifth curve in the angles of the dome, which was supposed to remain constant; this operation could have been carried out very easily with the aid of a small T-square, since all the relevant measurements had been taken.

Notes

1. The wooden model of the dome (measuring 100 × 90 cm central part, 55 × 63 × 35 cm side parts) is kept in the Museo dell'Opera di Santa Maria del Fiore. It comprises parts of the apse and the block formed by the dome and drum, with a portion of the piers and arches underneath. Until the 1966 flood in Florence, these component parts were displayed separately on the Museo dell'Opera shelves; after this event they were restored by Otello Caprara (1967–1968) and reassembled, since it was noted that they were all to a scale of 1:50. On the whole, the model is in good repair, even though numerous cleaning and restoration operations have removed coloring and stuccowork. The dome is without the lantern; the drum underneath is supported by pointed arches and pierced by splayed oculi (external diameter, 11.2 cm; internal diameter, 6.2 cm) on each of the eight faces (36 cm). The springing line of the dome is enclosed by a wide strip, which indicates the overall dimensions of the external *ballatoio*, or gallery, that Brunelleschi and Ghiberti had provided for in 1420. The upper exedra is crowned by the same form, 5 cm in height, which is found at the base of the octagonal drum under the dome. The parts of the apse are composed of two exedrae, one above the other and semioctagonal in shape. The three frontal faces (32 × 25 cm) of the exedra at the base are separated by three blind round arches (span ca. 6.5 cm); in the center of the middle one is a splayed opening in the form of a pointed arch. The two faces adjacent to the masonry of the drum (32 × 17.5 cm) contain two blind round arches, also with a splayed opening in the form of a pointed arch; in the upper part the five faces of the smallest exedra (30 × 15.5 and 30 × 13 cm) have the same openings as those underneath, but they are inscribed in round arches and are separated by buttresses. The model has been published in the following: *Catalogo del Museo di S. Maria del Fiore* (Florence: G. Carnesecchi, 1891), 35, nos. 160 and 163; Giovanni Poggi, ed., *Catalogo del Museo dell'Opera del Duomo* (Florence: Tipografia Barbèra, 1904), 61, nos. 160 and 163; Piero Sanpaolesi, *La cupola di S. Maria del Fiore. Il progetto. La costruzione* (Rome: Istituto Poligrafico dello Stato, 1941), 11; Wolfgang Braunfels, "Drei Bemerkungen zur Geschichte und Konstruktion der Florentiner Domkuppel," *Mitteilungen des Kunsthistorischen Institutes in Florenz* (September 1965): 218; Giulia Brunetti, "Il museo dell'Opera di Santa Maria del Fiore," *Atti della Società Leonardo da Vinci* 3, no. 6 (1975): 22; Giuseppe Marchini,

"Il ballatoio della cupola di Santa Maria del Fiore," *Antichità viva* 16, no. 6 (1977): 39; Mario Fondelli, "Studio geometrico di un antico modello ligneo restaurato," in *Atti del convegno sul restauro delle opere d'arte* (Florence: Edizioni Polistampa, 1981), 179–182, fig. 2; Mattia Preti, *Museo dell'Opera del Duomo di Firenze* (Milan: Electa, 1981), 31, 33.

2. Sanpaolesi, *La cupola di S. Maria del Fiore*, 11.

3. Antonio Manetti, *Vita di Filippo Brunelleschi*, ed. Domenico De Robertis and Giuliano Tanturli (Milan: Mondadori, 1976), 115.

4. Giuseppe Marchini, "La cupola: medievale e no," in *Filippo Brunelleschi. La sua opera e il suo tempo*, Atti del Convegno internazionale di studi, October 1977 (Florence: Centro Di, 1980), 2:915–920.

5. Cesare Guasti, *La cupola di Santa Maria del Fiore, illustrata con i documenti di Archivio dell'Opera secolare* (Florence: Barbèra, Bianchi, 1857), doc. 61.

6. Ibid., doc. 68.

7. Ibid., doc. 70.

8. Ibid., doc. 250.

9. Manetti, *Vita di Filippo Brunelleschi*, 115.

10. Braunfels, "Drei Bemerkungen zur Geschichte und Konstruktion der Florentiner Domkuppel," 115.

11. The wooden model of the lantern originally included parts (capitals of the pilasters) in gesso and wax, now lost. Its maximum dimensions are 84 × 70 cm. The model has been published in: Giorgio Vasari, *Le vite de' più eccellenti pittori scultori ed architettori scritte da Giorgio Vasari pittore aretino*, vol. 2, with comments by Gaetano Milanesi (Florence: Sansoni, 1878–1885), 362, n. 2, and 363–364; Carl von Stegmann and Heinrich von Geymüller, *Die Architektur der Renaissance in Toscana, I, Filippo di Ser Brunellesco* (Munich: Bruckmann, 1885), 36; *Catalogo del Museo di S. Maria del Fiore*, 35, no. 164; Poggi, *Catalogo del Museo dell'Opera del Duomo*, 61, no. 164; Hans Folnesics, *Brunelleschi. Ein Beitrag zur Entwicklungsgeschichte der Frührenaissance Architectur* (Vienna: Schroll, 1915), 109; Martin S. Briggs, "Architectural Models—I," *Burlington Magazine* 54, no. 313 (1929): 180, fig. IIa; Ludwig H. Heydenreich, "Spätwerke Brunelleschis," *Jahrbuch der Preuszischen Kunstsammlungen* 52, no. 1 (1931): 21; Sanpaolesi, *La cupola di S. Maria del Fiore*, 11–12, fig. 1; Walter and Elizabeth Paatz, *Die Kirchen von Florenz*, vol. 3 (Frankfurt: Vittorio Klostermann, 1952), 462, no. 102; John Coolidge, "Recensione a Sanpaolesi," *Art Bulletin* 34(1952): 166; Piero Sanpaolesi, *Brunelleschi* (Milan: Club del Libro, 1956), 11–29; (1962), 70–71, 157; Eugenio

Luporini, *Brunelleschi: forma e ragione* (Milan: Edizioni di Comunità, 1964), 212, n. 156; Ferdinando Rossi, *Il bel San Giovanni, Santa Maria del Fiore, l'Opera del Duomo* (Florence: Arnauld, 1964), 96; Luisa Becherucci and Giulia Brunetti, *Il museo dell'Opera del Duomo di Firenze*, vol. 2 (Venice, 1968), 211–214, no. 1; Otello Caprara, "Il modello della lanterna di Santa Maria del Fiore," in *Catalogo della mostra di restauri a sculture e oggetti d'arte minore* (Florence, 1968), 28, n. 34; Carlo Lodovico Ragghianti, *Filippo Brunelleschi. Un uomo, un universo* (Florence: Vallecchi, 1977), 414, 419, fig. IX; Cornelius von Fabriczy, *Filippo Brunelleschi. La vita e le opere*, trans. A. M. Poma (1892; Florence: Uniedit, 1979), 128, n. 69; Howard Saalman, *Filippo Brunelleschi: The Cupola of Santa Maria del Fiore* (London: Zwemmer, 1980), 146, fig. 106; Eugenio Battisti, *Filippo Brunelleschi* (Milan: Electa, 1981), 257–259 and 383–384; Richard A. Goldthwaite, *La costruzione della Firenze rinascimentale* (Bologna: Il Mulino, 1984), 520; Riccardo Pacciani, "I modelli lignei nella progettazione rinascimentale," *Rassegna* 32 (1987): 13; Massimo Scolari, "L'idea di modello," *Eidos* 2 (1988): 17; Preti, *Museo dell' Opera del Duomo di Firenze*, 31–32.

12. Guasti, *La cupola di Santa Maria del Fiore*, doc. 247.

13. Ibid., doc. 248.

14. Ibid., doc. 251.

15. Ibid., doc. 273.

16. Piero Sanpaolesi, "La lanterna di S. Maria del Fiore e il modello ligneo," *Bollettino d'Arte* 41 (1956): 24–25.

17. Vasari, *Le vite de' più eccellenti pittori scultori*, 363–364.

18. Manetti, *Vita di Filippo Brunelleschi*, 116.

19. Leon Battista Alberti, *L'architettura* (*De re aedificatoria*, 1485), ed. Giovanni Orlandi and Paolo Portoghesi (Milan: Il Polifilo, 1989), 52.

20. Saalman, *Filippo Brunelleschi*, 287, no. 333.

21. Manetti, *Vita di Filippo Brunelleschi*, 117.

22. Ferdinando Rossi, "La lanterna della cupola di S. Maria del Fiore," *Bollettino d'Arte* 41 (1956): 130–132; Giuseppe Marchini, "Fulmini sulla cupola," *Antichità viva* 4 (1977): 22–25.

23. Guasti, *La cupola di Santa Maria del Fiore*, doc. 363.

24. Ibid.

25. Ibid., doc. 367.

26. Saalman, *Filippo Brunelleschi*, fig. 107.

27. Guasti, *La cupola di Santa Maria del Fiore*, doc. 368.

28. Ibid., docs. 307, 309.

29. Florence, Uffizi Department of Prints and Drawings, Uff. 1130A and Uff. 3913A, respectively.

30. Vasari, *Le vite de' più eccellenti pittori scultori ed architettori*, 363–364.

31. Manetti, *Vita di Filippo Brunelleschi*, 113.

32. Franca Falletti and Leonardo Paolini, "Una nuova data per la cupola del Brunelleschi," *Prospettiva* 11 (1977): 57–58.

33. See Sanpaolesi, "La lanterna di S. Maria del Fiore e il modello ligneo," 22, fig.17. Brunelleschi's paternity of the model of the lantern is not recognized by: Milanesi (G. Vasari, *Le vite de' più eccellenti pittori scultori ed architettori*, 362, n. 2, and 363–364); Stegmann and Geymüller, *Die architektur der Renaissance in Toscana*, 1:36; Fabriczy, *Filippo Brunelleschi. La vita e le opere*, 128, n. 69; Folnesics, *Brunelleschi*, 109; Heydenreich, "Spätwerke Brunelleschis," 21; Saalman, *Filippo Brunelleschi*, 146; Pacciani, "I modelli lignei nella progettazione rinascimentale," 13.

On the other hand, those in favor of attributing the model to Brunelleschi include: Poggi, *Catalogo del Museo dell'Opera del Duomo*, 61, n. 164; Sanpaolesi, *La cupola di S. Maria del Fiore*, 11–12; Sanpaolesi, "La lanterna di S. Maria del Fiore e il modello ligneo," 11–29; Sanpaolesi, *Brunelleschi*, 70–71, 157; Rossi, "La lanterna della cupola di S. Maria del Fiore," 130–132; Rossi, *Il bel San Giovanni, Santa Maria del Fiore, l'Opera del Duomo*, 96; Luporini, *Brunelleschi*, 212, n. 156; Caprara, "Il modello della lanterna di Santa Maria del Fiore," 28, n. 34; Goldthwaite, *La costruzione della Firenze rinascimentale*, 520. Eugenio Battisti believes that the lower part dates from the fifteenth century and the lantern from the sixteenth century. Battisti, *Filippo Brunelleschi*, 257–259, 383–384.

34. The parchment has irregular edges with drawings executed in brown and red ink; light traces of lead point and tempera with red pigment, yellow ocher with particles of pure gold, and dark indigo blue-black. The text, written with the same ink as the drawings, is in clear early Quattrocento handwriting with typical abbreviations and ligatures. Maximum dimensions: 64.4 × 48.7 cm (Florence, Archivio di Stato, inv. Mostra 158).

In order to make Gherardi's text more intelligible the terminology needs to be explained. The *sesto* is the spread of the compass, that is, the radius of the circumference; the latter may be subdivided into six parts starting from any point of it. The *centro di sesto* is the point at which the pivot arm of the compass is placed (*centro*), and the *sesto che va in alto* is the arm that describes the portion of the vault; *murare al sesto* means to vault with a given curve. The *sesto di mezzo acuto* is known today as the round arch and corresponds in the drawing to the half-circumference on the diameter of the base. In order to describe an arc with the form known as *quinto acuto* (pointed fifth), two centers must be used: the segment is subdivided into five equal parts, then with the compass spread at ⅘, the portions of the arc are described by placing the pivot arm in the first part and then in the fourth.

35. Giovanni da Prato, *Opere complete*, vol. 1, *Il Paradiso degli Alberti*, ed. F. Garilli (Palermo: Libreria Athena, 1976), app. I, III, IV.

36. Guasti, *La cupola di Santa Maria del Fiore*, doc. 74.

37. Ibid., doc. 60.; Howard Saalman, "Giovanni di Gherardo da Prato's Designs Concerning the Cupola of Santa Maria del Fiore in Florence," *Journal of the Society of Architectural Historians* 18, no. 1 (1959): 12.

38. Diane Finiello Zervas, "The *Trattato dell'Abbaco* and Andrea Pisano's Design for the Florentine Baptistery Door," *Renaissance Quarterly* 28 (1975): 485.

39. Gino Arrighi, "Le scienze esatte al tempo di Brunelleschi," in *Filippo Brunelleschi. La sua opera e il suo tempo*, 1:93–103.

40. Marvin Trachtenberg, "Howard Saalman, *Filippo Brunelleschi: The Cupola of Santa Maria del Fiore*," *Journal of the Society of Architectural Historians* 43 (1983): 296.

41. Guasti, *La cupola di Santa Maria del Fiore*, doc. 23.

42. Saalman, *Filippo Brunelleschi*, 148, nos. 40 and 44.

43. Guasti, *La cupola di Santa Maria del Fiore*, doc. 46.

44. Giovanni Cavalcanti, *Istorie fiorentine*, ed. F. Polidori (Florence, 1938). Compare Eugenio Garin, *La cultura filosofica del rinascimento italiano* (Florence: Sansoni, 1979), 328; Carlo Frey, *Il codice Magliabechiano* (Berlin, 1892), 65.

45. Giovanni da Prato, *Opere complete*, 1:164.

46. Arrighi, "Le scienze esatte al tempo di Brunelleschi," 95–96.

47. Graziella Federici Vescovini, *Filosofia, scienza e astrologia nel Trecento Europeo. Biagio Pelacani Parmense* (Padua: Il Poligrafo, 1992), 47–49.

48. Cesare Guasti, *Santa Maria del Fiore. La costruzione della cupola e del campanile, secondo i documenti tratti dall'Archivio dell'Opera secolare e da quello di stato* (Florence: M. Ricci, 1887), doc. 474.

49. Guasti, *La cupola di Santa Maria del Fiore*, doc. 46.

50. Ibid., doc. 75.

51. Ibid., doc. 202.

52. Alfred Doren, "Zum Bau der Florentiner Domkuppel," *Repertorium für Kunstwissenschaft* 21 (1898): 249–262; Frank D. Prager and Gustina Scaglia, *Brunelleschi: Studies of His Technology and Inventions* (Cambridge: MIT Press, 1970), 139–140.

53. Guasti, *La cupola di Santa Maria del Fiore*, doc. 22.

54. Guasti, *Santa Maria del Fiore, la costruzione della chiesa e del campanile*, doc. 480.

55. Vittorio Lusini, *Il Duomo di Siena* (Siena, 1911), 154–187.

56. Roland Bechmann, *Villard de Honnecourt* (Paris: Picard, 1991), 216.

57. Saalman, *Filippo Brunelleschi*, 138.

58. Euclid, *Elements* 6.13.

59. Braunfels, "Drei Bemerkungen zur Geschichte und Konstruktion der Florentiner Domkuppel," 204, fig. 4, and 215, fig. 5; Corrado Verga, *Il dispositivo Brunelleschi 1420* (Crema: Tip. Donarini e Locatelli, 1978), 44, fig. 14.

60. Guasti, *La cupola di Santa Maria del Fiore*, doc. 47.

61. Massimo Ricci, *L'accusa di Giovanni di Gherardo Gherardi a Filippo Brunelleschi. Spiegazione integrale della pergamena, dei disegni e relativi contenuti tecnici* (Florence: Salimbeni, 1987); Ricci, "Il segreto della cupola di Santa Maria del Fiore," *Le Scienze* (July 1987): 54–55.

62. Ibid.

63. Guasti, *La cupola di Santa Maria del Fiore*, doc. 51.

64. Roland Mainstone, "Brunelleschi's Dome," *Architectural Review* (September 1977): 161; Verga, *Il dispositivo Brunelleschi 1420*, 14; Paolo Alberto Rossi, *Le cupole del Brunelleschi. Capire per conservare* (Bologna: Calderini, 1982), 15; Trachtenberg, "Howard Saalman," 294.

65. Battisti, *Filippo Brunelleschi*, 144, fig. 144.

66. Aristide Nardini Despotti Mospignotti, "Un disegno di Giovanni di Gherardo da Prato. Appendice," in *Belle Arti. Opuscoli descrittivi e biografici* (Florence, 1874), 123–128.

67. Sanpaolesi, *La cupola di Santa Maria del Fiore*, 28; Herbert Siebenhüner, "Brunellesco und die Florentiner Domkuppel," *Mitteilungen des Kunsthistorischen Institutes in Florenz* 5 (1940): 434.

68. Alberti, *L'architettura*, 127.

69. Guasti, *La cupola di Santa Maria del Fiore*, doc. 75.

70. Ibid.

71. Andrea Chiarugi and Demore Quilghini, "Tracciamento della cupola del Brunelleschi. Muratori e geometria," *Critica d'arte* 3 (1984): 42–43, figs. 5 and 6.

72. Manetti, *Vita di Filippo Brunelleschi*, 67–68.

73. Ibid.

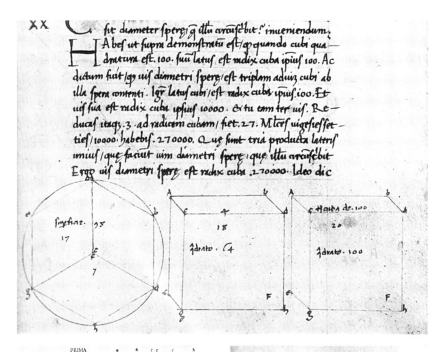

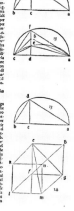

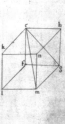

6.1
Piero della Francesca, *Libellus de quinque corporibus regolaribus*, 1490. Biblioteca Apostolica Vaticana, Rome. Urb. Latin codex 632, folio 30r.

6.2
Luca Pacioli, *Divina proportione* (Venice, 1509), page 9.

6.3
Luca Pacioli, *Divina proportione*. Biblioteca Ambrosiana, Milan. MS. 170 sup., folio XXXIr.

6

DEMONSTRATION FIGURES

Two methods of representation are used in Luca Pacioli's treatise *Divina proportione*, printed in Venice by Paganino de' Paganini in 1509: the solids drawn by his friend Leonardo da Vinci are presented in a pictorial, perspectival fashion, while in the margins of the text there are diagrams. These different approaches seem fully justified given the presentational nature of Leonardo's solids and the demonstrative character of the figures in the margins. Among the latter is a cusp-shaped, or almond-shaped, ellipse that on first sight seems to be either an error or a rough approximation. For the history of mathematics, the circumstances are no doubt irrelevant, but for the scholar of representational methods, this figure raises a number of questions. First, why, in a context in which more sophisticated graphic solutions were available, has the ellipse been drawn in such an unusual way? Leonardo was one of the principal innovators of representational methods between the end of the fifteenth and beginning of the sixteenth centuries. In his drawing of the corner solution adopted by Bramante for Palazzo Caprini in Rome, for example, he used both vertical and conical projection;[1] the same ability is shown in the "transparent" drawings of the drum of the Milan cathedral,[2] which show similarities with the "X-ray" method Leonardo used in his anatomical studies. For this reason, and given Leonardo's obvious ability to draw the ellipse freehand, it is not immediately comprehensible why Pacioli should have represented the base of the cuspidate cone that appears in the margin of his text in this way.

The second question regards the diagrammatic character of those drawings. Pacioli has often been accused of a lack of scientific accuracy in his argumentation, and undoubtedly there are many passages in his works that encourage such a criticism. Should we therefore impute the simplifications and graphical errors of his texts to this supposed tendency to "approximate?" Or should we see these figures as evidence of a different and older knowledge? And if the second hypothesis is correct, how old is this knowledge and what is its origin?

daremo el ⅓ cioe la sua terza parte :e quel tan
to a ponto fia la quantita corporale de la detta
pyramide :e ma t falla .Verbi gratia . Sia la pyra
mide rotonda . abc . de la quale la basa fia el cer
chio . bc . el cui diametro e 7 . El suo axe : a d . ql
sia . 10 . Dico che prima se quadri la basa :como
de sopra :in la colonna rotonda fo facto . pero :
che commo se disto de le colonne :e de le pyrami
di fienno le medesime basi :e le medesime altezze
Haremo per la superficie de la basa . 38 4/7 : qual
multiplicato per l'axe . a d . cioe per . 10 . fara 385 .
per la capacita de tutta la sua colonna . Ora de
questo dico che se prenda el ⅓ :che sen . 128 ⅓ .
e questo fia la quantita de detta pyramide . El
perche e da notare per la precisione adueta :
che nelle rotonde :a numero consegano re s
pondere secondo la proportione :fin hora tro
uata fra l diametro :e la circumferentia . E pero :
quella de sopra detta fra .11 . e 14 q . le quali co
mo in quel luogo se disse non sonno con pre
cisione :ma pocouatia :per Archimede troua
ta . M . non resta quello che disto habiamo
che la pyramide rotonda in quantita non sia

6.4
Luca Pacioli, *Divina proportione*. Biblioteca
Ambrosiana, Milan. MS. 170 sup., folio
LXXVIIv.

6.5
Leonardo da Vinci, studies of Palazzo
Caprini in Rome. *Codex on the
Flight of Birds*, cover page. Biblioteca
Reale, Turin.

Let us begin by analyzing the character of the diagrammatic sketch of the cube, a classic figure in Euclidean and Heronian treatises on stereometry.

In Piero della Francesca's *Libellus* there are two figures of great interest: an unusual orthogonal projection (today called isometric orthogonal axonometry) of a cube in a hexagon, and two parallel projections that might appear at first sight to be oblique projections.[3] The projection of the cube in a hexagon appears here for the first time in a Renaissance treatise, although it is present in Greek mosaic work and as symbol of the nimbus in the Christian art of the West.[4] This figure presents the germ of an orthogonal axonometry that will be unveiled three centuries later in William Farish's paper "On Isometrical Perspective." Piero's oblique cube is drawn in such a way as to illustrate its measurements, not as a geometrical demonstration. The numerical indications placed near the edges correct the viewer's perception of the measurements: in fact, the cube is perspectivally foreshortened in a rather approximate manner. Ten years later, Piero's pupil and friend Pacioli drew his figure of a cube inscribed within a sphere, and did so in a way that showed the nature of representation had changed substantially. Pacioli's drawing[5] for his *Divina proportione* follows the Euclidean construction procedure *more geometrico*, but the transparent shape that results is, paradoxically, ambiguous to the point of confusion, in that the line CF is erroneously continued to the point where it meets LM.[6]

In an interesting study of Platonic polyhedrons,[7] it has been suggested that Leonardo may have modified Piero's cubes for Pacioli's transcription. However, on closer inspection it is evident that this was not a transcription because the graphic procedures are very different. Piero uses a perspectival procedure and his graphic rendering is corporeal (his cubes are not transparent), while Pacioli uses a diagrammatic method, and the constituent elements of the cube are drawn in such a way as to be consistent with the procedure of reasoning and demonstrating, not with indicating appearance. Pacioli describes the procedure for constructing a cube inscribed within a sphere. He makes continual reference to Euclid's *Elements*, which he was studying at that time and which he would later publish in Venice, erroneously citing the author's name as "Euclide Megarense."[8] His proximity to Leonardo during the two years when they were both employed in Milan at the court of Duke Ludovico Sforza "il Moro," to whom Pacioli dedicated a manuscript copy of his *Divina proportione* in 1498,[9] meant he had the opportunity to collaborate extensively with the older artist. At that time, however, Leonardo's competence in Euclidean geometry seems to have been rather uncertain. We know from his notes

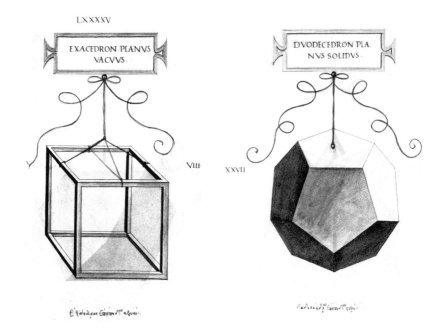

LXXXXV

EXACEDRON PLANVS
VACVVS·

DVODECEDRON PLA.
NVS SOLIDVS·

VIII

XXVII

6.6–6.8
Leonardo da Vinci, Platonic solids drawn
for Luca Pacioli's *Divina proportione* (Venice,
1509). Biblioteca Ambrosiana, Milan. MS.
170 sup., folios LXXXXVr, CIIIIv, CXVIIIIv.

COLVMNA ROTVNDA.
SOLIDA

XLII

that his study of the *Elements*, conducted under the guidance of his friend Pacioli, had been interrupted after the first books. But quite apart from this fact, it is noticeable that Leonardo's famous polyhedrons, which we know only through the replicas carried out by copyists, are rendered perspectivally and appear in a separate "anthology" at the end of *Pars prima*. They seem to have been drawn from wooden models that Leonardo, as Marisa Dalai Emiliani has perceptively suggested, might have hung in his studio, using string knotted in such a way as to pass through the center of gravity. Furthermore, in confronting one of the classic problems of Greek geometry, Leonardo executed what is an improbable duplication of the cube in a perspectival sketch.[10] The figures in the margins of the text of *Divina proportione* seem instead to have been taken down *viva voce*, directly from Pacioli, and they address the eye of the intellect rather than that of the body; they belong more to the homogeneous space of geometrical operations rather than to the psycho-physiological space inhabited by Leonardo's polyhedrons. It is no accident that the edges of the cube, which should be hidden, like in Piero's and Leonardo's versions, are instead here visible, producing that phenomenon of instable perception known to those familiar with wire frame forms rendered in isometric axonometry.[11] In order to counter doubts about possible optical ambiguities in the oblique faces and to guarantee the geometrical cohesion of the figure, Pacioli dedicates several lines of text to assure his readers that the receding faces of the cube are square, and that the obtuse and acute angles in reality represent right angles. In his discussion of the graphic construction of the octahedron, Pacioli reinforces his point with expressions that would certainly have irritated Euclid, such as "piercing and penetrating the said square."[12]

Pacioli does not include any actual demonstrations; by resolving the Euclidean theorems like problems, he gives his treatise an applicatory character. But to give credit to Pacioli and his "leonardesque" assistant, it must be admitted that in the figure of the cube, with its faces receding by about 45 degrees, not only is the parallelism of the sides maintained in both the manuscript and printed versions, but all of the angles of the cube are "isometric" as well, in conformity with the procedural indications contained in the text. If the result seems today like a cavalier axonometry, this should not lead us to conclude that Pacioli's aim was to represent the cube's three-dimensionality, or that he obtained the figure as the result of a true parallel projection. There is not sufficient proof to make such a statement: Pacioli provides no explanation as to how the perpendicular lines should be drawn from the vertices of the base square from which he starts. Following the example of no less a person than

Euclid, he says only that they should be drawn "going upward." And it is this practical nature of the operation that leads us to think that the figure has been obtained by drawing two perpendicular lines from the vertices of the square's diagonals. After this, Pacioli may well have rotated the diagonal plane onto a geometral plane in an operation that was typical of classical Greece and used by both Archimedes and Apollonius.[13]

If this was indeed his method, then it was simply an artifice, used without explanation, for suggesting spatial coherence, while at the same time making barely any reference to the illusionistic nature of the diagram. This kind of representation is quite different from the search for solidity and corporeality that so preoccupied perspective-dominated fifteenth-century artistic tradition. It belongs to an earlier, perhaps a Greek or a late antique mathematical-geometrical tradition.

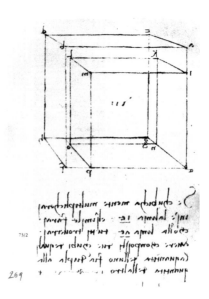

6.9
Leonardo da Vinci, wrong duplication of a cube. Biblioteca Ambrosiana, Milan. Codex Atlanticus, folio 58r.

The nature and legitimacy of this type of geometrical figure may be seen if we briefly consider the mathematical-geometrical component of Greek philosophy. In his commentary on the first book of Euclid's *Elements*, Proclus says that it is necessary to detach ourselves from the tangible world and be able to see all things without dimensions and parts. Mathematical reasoning shows things that appear difficult to understand "to be evident, trustworthy, and undisputable simply by means of images."[14] That there existed in Plato an implicit recognition of the knowledge value offered by the geometrical figure is evident from numerous passages. The concern of all Platonic thought with the question of copying and of appearances seems to find respite in those fragile line illustrations devoid of solidity and of parts, that is, the point and the line. In the laboriously achieved rarefaction of their perceptible connotations, these elements offer the security of an intelligible procedure. In the dialog of *Theaetetus*, the interlocutor's bewilderment is compared to the confusion generated by illusionistic representation, the so-called art of appearances which is so clearly described and condemned in the *Sophist* dialog.[15] Pure geometrical figures are, however, acceptable, for they solicit reminiscence and allow what already exists in the soul to emerge from it. Even for the Neoplatonist Proclus, the problem of abstract objects that are stripped of all sensible reality is keenly felt: "For the circle [in our understanding] is one, yet geometry speaks of many circles, setting them forth individually and studying the identical features in all of them; and that circle [in our understanding] is indivisible, yet the circle in geometry is divisible"; thus the circle in the sensible world "is infected with the straight line,"[16] with radius, diameter, secant, and tangent.

Knowledge that is a product of reasoning must make reference to demonstrations that use perceptible figures; however, in order to accede to pure knowledge it will be necessary to renounce these figures. Euclid's primary elements are characterized by precisely this adimensionality in figures that are immutable and without genesis: "the point is partless," the line is "extension without thickness," and the surface has only width and length, but no other attribute. But the point, like all figures, cannot be part of geometry without appearing and, as a result, becoming ontologically defective. Only Plotinus will succeed in overcoming the gnoseological aporia of figures by transforming them into passageways devoid of truth, but necessary in order to achieve greater understanding.

The diagram is, by definition, dimensionless and not visible in real space; that is, it cannot be deduced from real space. Because of this characteristic,

Aristotle stated that only diagrams and sketches were acceptable for the illustration of scientific texts, and that sometimes they could substitute for the theorem itself. This latter significant passage is in *Metaphysics*, where the philosopher asks: "Why is the sum of the internal angles of a triangle equal to two right angles?"[17] Aristotle makes use of Euclid's demonstration of Proposition 32 of Book I, deducing that "the angles that are formed on a straight line around a single point are equal to two right angles."[18] Up to this point, there is nothing unusual. But the statement that follows is of great interest: "If we had drawn a line parallel to the face, the answer would have been evident to anyone as soon as he saw the figure."[19] Here Aristotle underlines the importance of diagrams and auxiliary constructions as essential to scientific discovery, since they make it possible to show connections in an instantaneous demonstration. In classical Greek thought, diagrams are valued as demonstration figures, even though they can only communicate by being perceptibly traced on the drawing plane. In mathematical papyri,[20] geometrical figures are drawn as bodiless, transparent entities, exactly as they appear in Pacioli's *Divina proportione*. The Vatican codex provides clearly drawn "wire frame" stereometric representations, with numbered references to the text, especially where the difficult books XI–XIII of Euclid's *Elements* are concerned.

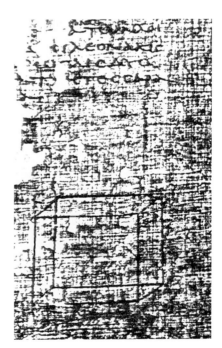

6.10
Commentary on *Theaetetus*, papyrus from first century BC. Hermann Diels, *Antike Technik* (Osnabrück, 1965).

In medieval translations of Euclid, Pacioli would have been able to see an antique mode of representation as well as figures of Platonic solids that were clearer and more sophisticated than modern representations. Figures such as these, coming straight from the heart of Greek geometry, showed the elements that made up the construction of solids, not their visual appearance; according to this method, the drawing was faithfully taken down from the geometer's description (*viva voce*) of the construction of the stereometric figure.[21]

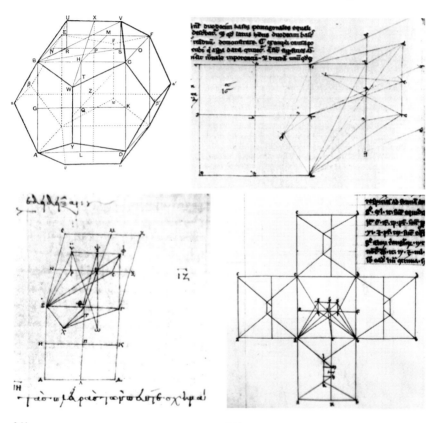

6.11
The cube within the dodecahedron. Euclid, *The Thirteen Books of the Elements*, trans. Thomas L. Heath (New York, 1956), 3:499.

6.13
Euclid, *Elements*, ninth-century manuscript. Biblioteca Apostolica Vaticana, Rome. Cod. vat. gr. 190, folio 213v.

6.12
The cube within the dodecahedron, Euclid's *Elements*, translated from the Arabic by Gherardo da Cremona, fourteenth century. Biblioteca Apostolica Vaticana, Rome. Reg. lat. 1268, folio 133r.

6.14
Adelard of Bath, Latin translation of Euclid's *Elements*, thirteenth century, XIII, page 130. Biblioteca Nazionale Marciana, Venice. Lat. Z. 332 (=1647), folio 222v.

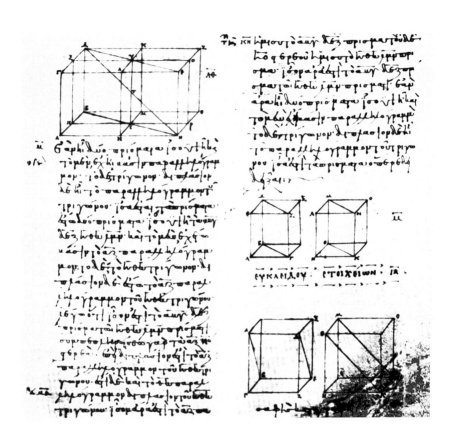

Euclid, *Elements*, XIII, 17, ninth-century
manuscript. Biblioteca Apostolica Vaticana,
Rome. Codex vat. gr. 190, folio 213v.

If it is true that Pacioli's figures were derived from the classical tradition of diagrams, can we surmise that the same was true for the cuspidate ellipse? In Pacioli's manuscript text, the cone and the truncated cone both have an almond-shaped ellipse, except where the column is drawn in vertical oblique parallel projection.[22] Leonardo is always very punctilious in his drawings of the ellipse and it seems improbable that, if he effectively collaborated on the drawing of Pacioli's cube, he did not also do so in the case of the oblique representation of the cone. In the case of the printed edition, a possible explanation might be that the engravers had difficulty executing curved lines on the wooden block with the gouge, or that there was no direct supervision on the part of the author. But Pacioli was certainly present in Venice in 1508, at the exact time the woodcuts were in preparation.[23] Furthermore, where the manuscript copy is concerned, such an explanation seems even less plausible for obvious reasons, unless, paradoxically, the two extant manuscripts were copied from the printed edition.

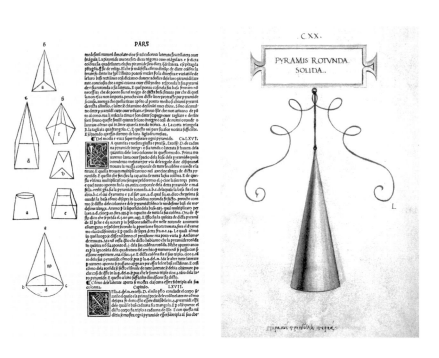

6.16
Luca Pacioli, *Divina proportione* (Venice, 1509), folio 20v.

6.17
Luca Pacioli, *Divina proportione*. Biblioteca Ambrosiana, Milan. MS. 170 sup., folio CXXr.

Clearly, it was not simply a question of oversight on the part of the copyist or even of a technical shortcut on the part of the engraver. One reasonable hypothesis for the cuspidate form might be that it was the result of a search for precision. In fact, if the base had been represented by a circle, the two tangents drawn from a finite point (the vertex) would not touch its diameter.[24] Instead, reducing the base circle to its cuspidate form has the interesting advantage of clearly showing the points of intersection of the base circle with the diameter, and of enabling the two tangents to be conducted with precision from the vertex. If this consideration is correct, the character of this diagram immediately recalls the procedural protocols of the Arab tradition of astronomy and pneumatics, and, by natural affiliation, the graphic art of pre-Ptolemaic Greek astronomy. This would provide a clue as to the classical origin of the stereometric representational methods used between the end of the fifteenth century and the beginning of the sixteenth. An approach that took gnomonics and astronomy into account might allow a renewed enquiry into the Vitruvian definition of *ad circini centrum*, as well as into the astronomical terminology used by Leon Battista Alberti in his explanation of perspective construction.

But in order to confirm this hypothesis it is necessary to establish whether there were similar and earlier representations of the ellipse in the geometrical, cosmographical, and mechanical disciplines.

The ellipse is one of the few figures that has been correctly drawn since the fourth and third centuries BC in the wheels of carriages or in shields, although Pappos of Alexandria observes that "it is not easy to draw a conic section on a flat surface. However, the geometers of old managed it admirably by using instruments made for exactly that purpose."[25] Indeed, Euclid cites the ellipse as one of the classic optical illusions produced by the wheels of carriages.[26] In accordance with an earlier optical and pictorial tradition, and in a context that was undoubtedly associated with illusionistic representation, Ptolemy recommends that the circle not be drawn as an oval, projected according to the "third method"[27] with a cuspidate end, so as not to give the impression of an interruption.[28] This unexpected recommendation may be explained by the attempt to unite the diagrammatic rigor of classical mathematical description with the exigencies of illusionistic representation. These requirements are clearly visible in the very definition of Ptolemy's *Geography*:[29] an imitation (*mimesis*) of the known world by means of drawing. The coincidence of the eye with the center of projection as a control factor of the projected image may also be seen from the indications Ptolemy himself provides about how to color distant and near circles. The necessities of mathematical rigor and pictographic description seem to alternate with each other in *Geography*.[30] In a context in which the attempt is made to create anew the spatial coherence of geographic representation by conciliating mathematical rigor with vision, Ptolemy's recommendation shows just how familiar the form of the cuspidate ellipse was in mathematical circles as early as the second half of the fourth century BC.

The astronomer and mathematician Autolycus of Pitane, a contemporary of Aristotle and Euclid, uses a cuspidate ellipse to represent the position of the ecliptic in relation to the horizon (circumference), upon which it should be possible to accurately predict the rising and setting of a star.[31] Mathematical astronomy clearly ranked the exigencies of thought above those of sight, so the visual appearance of the ecliptic took second place in relation to the precise determination of points.[32]

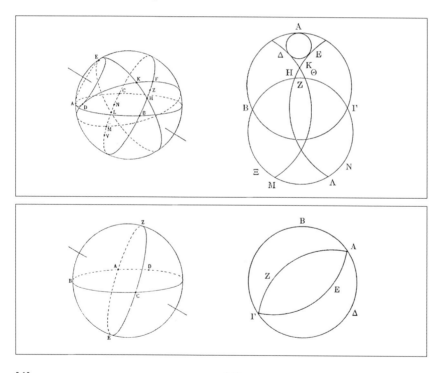

6.18
Autolycus of Pitane, *Levers et couchers héliaques*, I, 10, in *La sphère en mouvement; Levers et couchers héliaques; Testimonia*, ed. Germaine Aujac (Paris, 1979), page 92.

6.19
Autolycus of Pitane, *Levers et couchers héliaques*, I, 6, in *La sphère en mouvement; Levers et couchers héliaques; Testimonia*, ed. Germaine Aujac (Paris, 1979), page 84.

Clindorus est figura quadrata
habens superius semicirculū i soliuū
conon est figura que ab amplo
in angustum finit sicut orogonii;
Pyramis est figura que in moꝺū
ignis ab amplo in acutū consurgit
ignēenim apuꝺ grecos phyrin
appellatur.
Sicut aut infra decem omnis
est numerus ita intra unum
hunc circulum omnium figu
tarum concluditur ambitus.

Teneatur in soliꝺū rece. colin
drus ē figura que ceꝺracce. heebent
superius semicir culum rca
Conon figura quae ab amplo
in angustum finit · sicut orthogo
mum recc. Piramis ē figura
que in moꝺū ignis ab amplo enim
in acutū consurgit · ignis apuꝺ grēc
pirinꝺꝭ rca. Sicut hic omni
bꝰ infra. x. ꝑenī numerus rca;
In hunc cir culum omnꝭū figu
rærū concluditur ambitus:

6.20
Isidore of Seville, "chilindrus," *Etymologies*,
twelfth-century manuscript. British Library,
London. Additional Codex 15603, folio 32r.

6.22
Heron, *Metrics*, from a twelfth- or thirteenth-
century manuscript. Topkapi Library, Istanbul.
Cod. Cost. Pal. Vet. 1, II, folio 95r.

6.21
Isidore of Seville, "cylindrus est figura
quadrata, habens superior semicirculum,"
Etymologies III, xii (seventh century).
British Library, London. Cod. Harl. 2686,
folio 36r.

It could now be hypothesized that the form of the almond-shaped ellipse derives from antique astronomy and that its presence in Pacioli's text is neither accidental nor due to lack of drawing skill.[33] After all, for the whole of the medieval period, and before classic Greek texts were brought back to the West through the Arabs, geometric figures presented synthetic representations that had nothing to do with "seeing." In the section dealing with geometry in the *Etymologies* of Isidore of Seville, the cylinder is represented by a square surmounted by a semiellipse, while the text contains the following explanation: "cylindrus est figura quadrata, habens superior semicirculum."[34] This singular definition-representation of the cylinder shows a graphic notation that is rarely used, and is substituted, in thirteenth-century versions of the *Elements*, by the circle. But here too thought prevails over sight. It is here, hesitating between the cuspidate figure, which derives from ancient Greco-Arabic astronomy, and the circle, nearer to medieval Latin tradition,[35] that Pacioli is to be found.

We now return to Italy, having deepened our understanding of the unique representational methods used in Pacioli's treatise by the evidence of classical authors. Five years before Pacioli's treatise was published, Pomponius Gauricus described in his *De sculptura* the procedure for drawing a parallel-epiped rectangle (representing a book) that was perfectly consonant with the rules of appearances: "Starting from the four uppermost corners, we draw parallel lines either a short way upward or a short way downward, according to preference... you will immediately see that [the book] tends to lean to one side. Is not the shape we saw before, changed thus, similar to what we see with our eyes?"[36] Gauricus shows how it is possible, in the case of small objects, to create the illusion of depth without a perspectival construction. This perspectiveless procedure, which he calls "parallel mode" (*paralleli modo*), though not derived from considerations of primary geometry, appears to have its roots in a representational method that was widespread in the fifteenth century, both in practice and in drawings of machines. What is singular about finding it here is not so much that it presents a novelty but that it is described for the first time in a text that is totally devoid of illustrations, even though the subject is perspective.

Stereometric illustrations would remain associated, except in rare cases, with this type of oblique drawing.[37] This is the thread that binds Piero, Pacioli, Leonardo, and Gauricus, and also runs through Cesariano's extraordinary 1521 edition of Vitruvius, dedicated to Leo x, the same pope to whom Raphael would dedicate his famous letter on the survey of the ancient monuments of

Rome. While Raphael declared the necessity of "the systematic separation of plans, elevations and sections,"[38] it was also the case that during the 1520s, especially in Roman circles, there was a tendency to unite the different views and contaminate the perspectival method, as demonstrated in Baldassarre Peruzzi's famous drawing for St. Peter's.[39] Outside the Roman sphere of influence and in the technical engineering context, Cesariano favored a more archaic representation: the "bird's-eye" view, as it is often inappropriately defined.[40] In reality, the Codex Coner drawings of Falconetto and, later, those of Palladio may be related to an ancient representational method that transcribes what is measured, rather than what is seen.

Among the illustrations, certainly in the work of Cesariano himself,[41] there is much use of oblique drawing, which characteristically "shows both sides without foreshortening," together with the "divergent" perspective style found in fifteenth-century representations of *machinatio*. They are used to render foundations, wall structures, and in the classic figure of a cube[42] drawn with its sides subdivided into six units; on either side of the cube is a die, a figure that also appears in Fabio Calvo's[43] translation of Vitruvius. Cesariano's cube is transparent, and the receding side is inclined at the same angle as Pacioli's figure, although it differs from the latter in that it is not isometric. Here, for the first time, Cesariano introduces notches along the edges of his cube to indicate measurement.[44] In his *Institutiones geometricae*, Albrecht Dürer[45] represents the figure of the cube in parallel projection, constructing it in exactly the same way as does Pacioli. The procedure is translated into the illustration by drawing the perpendiculars from the base square, as had been suggested by Gaurico. To see dimension and geometry coexist in the oblique figure of the cube, we must wait for a singular geometer like Oronce Finé and his *De geometria pratica*. Pacioli's "plagiarism" of Piero's *Libellus*, written immediately before the painter's death in 1492, is repeated by Finé, who was as skillful in paralogism as he was in the production of pirated editions.[46] In his *De geometria pratica*, published in 1544, Pacioli's figure reappears, in an identical position and with its receding side at an identical angle of about 45 degrees. Finé may have copied it during his stay in Milan as an engineer at the court of Francis I.

Finé's cube maintains Pacioli's rigorous parallelism in the receding sides and in their isometry, but it is significant that the five feet mentioned in the text are marked by notches on the edges of the cube drawn an identical distance apart. Finé's cube has all of the elements of correct cavalier axonometry: the plane parallel to the square is maintained in orthogonal projection; the

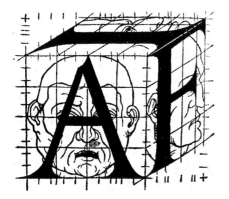

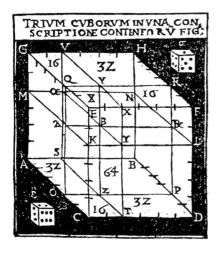

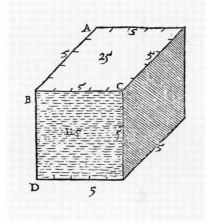

6.23
Geoffroy Tory, oblique drawing of a cube.
Geoffroy Tory, *Champfleury* (Paris, 1529).

6.24
Cesare Cesariano, *De architectura* (Como, 1521), V, LXXII.

6.25
The cube in oblique drawing. Oronce Finé, *De geometria pratica* (Strasbourg, 1544), page 105.

oblique sides are at the required 45 degrees to the horizontal line; what are now called reduction coefficients are shown on the axes forming the classic trihedral trirectangle. All of the elements seem to be in place for representing an object in parallel projection and with correct measurements, but this is not so. Too many conceptual elements are still missing for the formulation of an axonometric space. The idea of the infinite as an auxiliary in the search for the plastic properties of space would not be introduced until Girard Desargues. After all, the idea of axes, which had already been advanced by Nicole Oresme, would only be proposed by Descartes in his coordinate system more than two centuries later, and Descartes's axes were not even orthogonal to each other.

Notes

1. *Codice sul volo degli uccelli*, cover (Turin, Biblioteca Reale, MS. Varia 95). See Jean Guillaume, "Leonardo and Architecture," in Paolo Galluzzi, ed., *Leonardo da Vinci: Engineer and Architect* (Montreal: Musée des Beaux-Arts, 1987), 250–251 and plate 274, 255–256 and plate 288. To the left of this drawing are some variations on Palazzo Caprini, and next to them the only complete drawing of the palace planned by Leonardo between 1506 and 1507 in Milan for Charles d'Amboise. See also Jean Paul Richter, *The Notebooks of Leonardo da Vinci*, 2 vols. (New York: Dover, 1970), 2:66–67.

2. Studies for the lantern of the Milan cathedral (c. 1487–1488; Milan, Biblioteca Ambrosiana, Codice Atlantico, fol. 850r/310r-b, fol. 851r/310v-b). See Carlo Pedretti, *Leonardo architetto* (Milan: Electa, 1981), 36–38; Guillaume, "Leonardo and Architecture," 212, figs. 206 and 207.

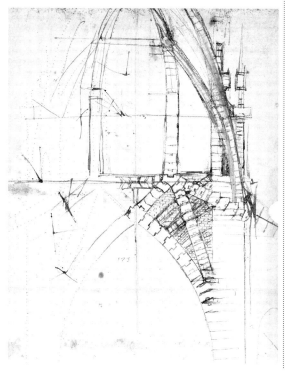

6.26
Leonardo da Vinci, dome of the Milan cathedral. Biblioteca Ambrosiana, Milan. Codex Atlanticus, folios 310v to b.

3. In the oblique drawing, the receding side diminishes by about one-third. See Piero della Francesca, *Libellus de quinque corporibus regolaribus* (1490; Rome, Biblioteca Apostolica Vaticana, Cod. Urbinate Lat 632, fol. 30r). The drawings are reproduced in Marisa Dalai Emiliani, "Figure rinascimentali dei poliedri platonici. Qualche problema di storia e di autografia," in *Fra Rina-scimento manierismo e realtà* (Florence: Barbera, 1984), 7–16, fig. 2. For an analytical overview of the *Libellus*, see Margaret Daly Davis, *Piero della Francesca's Mathematical Treatises* (Ravenna: Longo, 1977), 44–63.

4. Cf. the panel portraying "Hope" by Andrea Pisano on the door of the Florentine baptistery. For the figure with the square nimbus, usually adopted when the person is living, and the nimbus in *forma ovi*, see Gerhart B. Ladner, *Images and Ideas in the Middle Ages*, 2 vols. (Rome: Edizioni di Storia e Letteratura, 1983), 1:115–170 and 2:1012–1020; André Grabar, *Le vie della creazione nell'iconografia cristiana. Antichità e Medioevo* (Milan: Jaca Book, 1983), 255. For the church of St. Demetrius in Thessaloniki, in which there is an unusual arrangement of the saint and the faithful donors portrayed side by side, cf. André Grabar, *La peinture byzantine* (Geneva: Skira, 1953), 50–51. The projection of the cube into a hexagon, earlier published by Cousin (see note 23 of the chapter "Elements for a History of Axonometry"), is repeated by François d'Aguilon, *Opticorum libri sex ac Mathematicis utiles…* (Antwerp: ex Officina Plantiniana, widow and son of J. Moretus, 1613), prop. LXIII, 557.

5. Luca Pacioli, *Divina Proportione. Opera a tutti gli ingegni perspicaci e curiosi necessaria ove ciascuno studioso di Philosophia Prospectiva Pictura Sculptura: Architectura: Musica: e altre Mathematice: suavissima: sottile: e admirabile doctrina consequira: e delectarassi: con varie questione de secretissima scientia* (Venice: Paganino de' Paganini, 1509), I, XX–VII, 9. In this oblique parallel projection of the transparent cube, all of the edges of the figure are shown, resulting in a visually ambiguous image in which the eye perceives two different versions. The switches in perception of the axonometric drawing of the transparent cube were noted by Necker in 1832 in relation to representations in oblique parallel projection of crystals (clinographic projection). The phenomenon made popular by Schroder's scale was used in order to explain how "seeing the figure of a cube in two ways" implies the ability to perceive relationships between the parts of a whole (Ludwig Wittgenstein, *Tractatus Logico-philosophicus* and *Notebooks 1914–1916*). For the

phenomenon of image inversion, see Fred Attneave, "Multistability in Perception," *Scientific American* (1971): 225, 62–71.

6. This error does not, however, appear in the manuscript copy Luca Pacioli presented to Giangaleazzo Sanseverino, which contains only the first part of the printed version (1492; Milan, Biblioteca Ambrosiana, MS. 170 sup., fol. XXXIr).

7. Dalai Emiliani, "Figure rinascimentali dei poliedri platonici."

8. Carlo Maccagni has observed how one of the first printed books to include figures in the form of "geometric sketches" was the *editio princeps* of Euclid published in Venice by the typographer Erhard Radolt in 1482, with a translation from Arabic and commentary by Campano da Novara. See Carlo Maccagni, "Le scienze nello studio di Padova e nel Veneto," in Girolamo Arnaldi and Manlio Pastore Stocchi, eds., *Storia della cultura veneta. Dal primo Quattrocento al Concilio di Trento* (Vicenza, 1981), 3/III, 157.

9. A copy is now preserved in the library of the University of Geneva. The copy made for Soderini has been lost, while the one made for Sanseverino is preserved in the Biblioteca Ambrosiana in Milan; see note 6.

10. See *Codex Atlanticus*, fols. 218v and 58r. Marinoni has demonstrated how Leonardo, probably with the encouragement of Pacioli, only began to study Euclid's *Elements* between 1496 and 1504, when he was fifty years old. Augusto Marinoni, "The Writer," in Ladislao Reti, ed., *The Unknown Leonardo* (London: Hutchinson, 1974), 73.

11. On this subject, see also the *Euclide Megarensis* (Venice: Paganini, 1509), fol. 127v, which uses the same woodcut.

12. Luca Pacioli, *Divina proportione* (Milan, Biblioteca Ambrosiana, MS. 170 sup., fol. XXIIv).

13. *Conics* by Apollonius of Perga was translated by Giovanni Battista Memo and only published in 1537 in Venice by the printer Bernardino Bindone. The codex was brought to Venice from Constantinople around 1427 by Francesco Filelfo who, together with Bessarion and Giorgio Valla, gathered together an important corpus of scientific manuscripts. Those of Bessarion would later constitute the central nucleus of the Biblioteca Marciana of Venice, while those of Valla are today preserved in the Biblioteca Estense of Modena. See Maccagni, "Le scienze nello studio di Padova e nel Veneto," 154.

14. Proclus, *Commento al I libro degli Elementi di Euclide*, ed. Maria Timpanaro Cardini (Pisa: Giardini, 1978), 41. The manuscript was in the possession of Giorgio Valla,

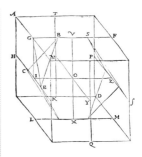

6.27
François de Foix, comte de Candale, *Euclidis Megarensis mathematici clarissimi elementa* (Paris, 1588).

who taught at the school of San Marco in Venice. His translation into Greek (Munich, Bayerische Staatliche Bibliothek, Cod. Lat. 6) was first published in 1533, in Basel, while a Latin translation by the Venetian Francesco Barozzi was published in Padua in 1560. See Maccagni, "Le scienze nello studio di Padova e nel Vento," 155.

15. *Theaetetus* 208e. Turolla risks the word *perspective* in his translation: "It is as if we were standing before a painting in perspective." Plato, *I dialoghi*, ed. Enrico Turolla (Milan, 1964), 2:730. Minio-Paluello has a more cautious approach with "painted scene": "like one who approaches a painted scene, and does not understand it entirely." Plato, *Opere complete*, ed. Lorenzo Minio-Paluello (Bari, 1979), 2:177.

16. Proclus, *Commento al I libro degli Elementi di Euclide*, 42–43.

17. Aristotle, *Metaphysics* 9.9.1051a.

18. See Euclid, *The Thirteen Books of the Elements*, trans. Thomas L. Heath (New York: Dover, 1956), 316–322.

19. Aristotle, *Metaphysics* 9.9.1051a.

20. An illustration of the two transparent cubes is contained in a Greek papyrus of the first century BC of a commentary on the *Theaetetus*, reproduced in Hermann Diels, *Antike Technik*, vol. 2 (Osnabrück: Zeller, 1965). An analogous figure is found in a copy of Euclid's *Elements* (ninth century; Rome, Biblioteca Apostolica Vaticana, MS. vat. gr. 190); cf. John E. Murdoch, *Antiquity and the Middle Ages* (New York: Scribner, 1984), 124–125.

6.28
Witelo, *Perspectiva libri X* (Nuremberg, 1535), page 92.

6.29
Heron, *Metrics*, from an eleventh- or twelfth-century manuscript. Topkapi Library, Istanbul. Cod. Cost. Pal. Vet. I, II, folio 93v.

6.30
Mathematical papyrus, first century BC. Österreichische Nationalbibliothek, Vienna. Pap. gr. 19996.

In the copy of the *Codex Costantinopolitanus Palatiis Veteris* I (twelfth century; Istanbul, Topkapi Sarayi), which was discovered in 1896, Heron's *Metrica* reproduces the drawing of two "wire frame" pyramid trunks (fol. 56r), which are very similar to those of the Vienna papyrus (first half of the first century BC, Vienna, Österreichische Nationalbibliotek, Papyrus. Gr. Vindob. 19996) and to the truncated pyramid in the papyrus in Moscow (1950 BC; Moscow, Museum of Fine Art, MMP 14 col. 29).

21. See the figure of the icosahedron and dodecahedron in Murdoch, *Antiquity and the Middle Ages*, 129–131.

22. Milan, Biblioteca Ambrosiana, MS. 170 sup., fol. LXXIIV.

23. On 11 August 1508, Pacioli held an introductory lecture to Book V of Euclid's *Elements* in the Venetian church of S. Bartolomeo.

24. If the vanishing point is that of the eye, then "when a cone with a circular base is viewed, then what is seen of it is less than half" (*Optics* I, XXXI). See Giuseppe Ovio, *L'Ottica di Euclide* (Milan, 1918), 143.

25. *Pappi Alexandrini Collectionis* … , ed. F. Hultsch (Berlin, 1876), 1:54. See Paul Lawrence Rose, "Renaissance Italian Methods of Drawing the Ellipse and Related Curves," *Physis* 4 (1970): 374.

26. "Carriage wheels sometimes appear circular, sometimes elongated" (*Optics* I, XL). See Ovio, *L'Ottica d'Euclide*, 164.ff.

27. Stereographic projection is described by Ptolemy in his *Planisphaerium* for determining the time of sunrise using only plane trigonometry. Claudius Ptolemaeus, *Planisphaerium*, in *Opera*, ed. J. L. Heiberg (Leipzig, 1907), 2:225–259. The third method, called *stereographic*, was first defined by François d'Aguilon: "quod universam corporis objecti profunditatem et peripheriam ipsam unico prospectu explanet" (*Opticorum libri sex*, Antwerp, 1613, 573). The same construction is used for the astrolabe, an instrument that allows celestial phenomena to be observed by means of the rotation of a series of circles above a disc (equatorial plane) on which the celestial sphere is projected from the South Pole. This results in a series of concentric circles, with one eccentric representing the ecliptic. According to Otto Neugebauer, "The theory of the solar meridians is perhaps at the origin of one of the classic problems of Greek mathematics, that is, the trisection of the angle." Otto Neugebauer, *Le scienze esatte nell'Antichità* (Milan: Feltrinelli, 1974), 220 and 265.

28. Otto Neugebauer, "Ptolemy's Geography: Book VII, Chapters 6 and 7," *Isis* 50 (1959): 24. The passage

6.31
Jacopo de' Barbari, *Portrait of Luca Pacioli*. Museo Nazionale di Capodimonte, Naples.

from Ptolemy is also cited by Samuel Edgerton in a different context, but one that is very important for understanding one of the possible sources for Brunelleschi's perspective experiment: Samuel Y. Edgerton, "Florentine Interest in Ptolemaic Cartography as Background for Renaissance Painting, Architecture, and the Discovery of America," *Journal of the Society of Architectural Historians* 33 (1974): 285, n. 46. In this essay, Edgerton states that the first two methods illustrated by Ptolemy are not projections from one viewing point but a mathematical method for showing the true distances (north latitudes) as closely as possible, with a defective latitudinal subdivision; in order to correct such a defect Toscanelli was induced to make a rough calculation on the map provided to Columbus for his famous voyage. But Ptolemy's third method is, according to Edgerton, the "direct ancestor of Renaissance linear perspective." Neugebauer is not so convinced of the precision of this third type of projection: it does not appear in the tables accompanying the surviving manuscript editions. In reality, Ptolemy provides two mathematical rules for constructing a grid system representing longitudinal and latitudinal circles as constants. The resultant drawings are not images of a sphere seen from one particular viewpoint. The only construction that we could call perspectival is found in Book VII (chapter 6). The projection point is situated in such way that no part of the ecumene is hidden. Portrayed thus, the globe is not perspectival but a structure that is very similar to the second type of projection. See Edgerton, "Florentine Interest in Ptolemaic Cartography," 275–292. A controversial interpretation of Ptolemy's text is found in Jean-Gabriel Lemoine, "Brunelleschi et Ptolémée," *Gazette des Beaux Arts* 51 (1958): 281–296. According to Neugebauer it is more of an "illustration" than a map in the true sense. Indeed, it is the only one that appears "incoherent and of absolutely no utility, anticipating Medieval taste." See Neugebauer, *Le scienze esatte nell'Antichità*, 262.

29. See Morris R. Cohen and I. E. Drabkin, *A Source Book in Greek Science* (New York: McGraw-Hill, 1948), 162–179. In the present text, we have adopted Girolamo Ruscelli's translation in the edition corrected by Giovanni Malombra and printed by G. Zilietti in Venice in 1574. See Aldo Mieli, *Manuale di storia della scienza. Antichità* (Rome: Casa editrice Leonardo da Vinci, 1925), 401–406. The plates are taken from Claudius Ptolemaeus, *Cosmographia*, trans. Jacopus Angelus (Ulm, 1486).

30. According to Polaschek, Ptolemy had "regional" maps made only for his first edition. At the end of Book

VIII, and in as many as eight manuscripts, the authorship of the plates is claimed by a painter: "I, Agathos Daimon, an artist [technician] from Alexandria, drew the map in the *Geography* of Ptolemy." See Erich Polaschek, "Ptolemy's Geography in a New Light," *Imago Mundi* 14 (1959): 17–37. However, Fischer, who edited the famous Vatican edition of Ptolemy (thirteenth century, Rome, Biblioteca Apostolica Vaticana, Cod. Urb. Gr. 82), believes that there is no evidence to support the statement that the plates of the manuscript collected together in the late Byzantine era were derived directly from those of Ptolemy. See *Claudii Ptolemaei Geographiae Codex Urbinas graecus* 82, ed. Joseph Fischer, 3 vols. and an atlas (Leiden and Leipzig, 1932). In particular see the *tomus prodromus*, 192–208, for the first editions of the Greek and Latin codices and their identification. For a study that sets the work of Ptolemy in a geo-topographical context that is not purely mathematical or astronomical, see O. A. W. Dilke, *Greek and Roman Maps* (London: Thames and Hudson, 1985), 75–80, 161–164, 198–201; Numa Broc, *La géographie de la Renaissance (1420–1620)* (Paris: Bibliothèque Nationale, 1980).

31. Autolycus wrote his work in the years 333–323 BC, at a time when many thinkers were engaged in the search for a solution to the problem posed by Plato: to find hypotheses to support the circular motion of the planets, which were believed, despite the obvious irregularity of their movements, to be regular and uniform. Autolycus's answer was the homocentric sphere, a solution adopted by Aristotle together with the spherical model presented by Eudoxus. Autolycus used geometrical procedures and a Euclidean method of demonstration. Of the forty-four known manuscripts, the oldest dates from the nineteenth century (Rome, Biblioteca Apostolica Vaticana Cod. Vat. gr. 204 [A]). The text is presented by the curators with a modern "perspective" figure and with the original redrawn (on the right), which, according to Otto Neugebauer, is not very different from the fourth-century version. See Autolycus of Pitane, *La sphère en mouvement; Levers et couchers héliaques; Testimonia*, ed. Germaine Aujac with Jean-Pierre Brunet and Robert Nadal (Paris: Belles Lettres, 1979). See also Joseph Mogenet, "Autolicus de Pitane: histoire du texte suivie de l'édition critique des traités *De la sphère en mouvement* et *Des levers et couchers*," *Recueil de Travaux d'Histoire et de Philologie* 37 (1950); O. Schmidt, "Some Critical Remarks about Autolicus's *On Rising and Settings*," in *Den 11te Skandinaviske Matematikerkongress, Trondheim (22–25 August 1949)* (Oslo, 1952), 202–209.

6.32

Autolycus of Pitane, *La sphère en mouvement; Levers et couchers héliaques; Testimonia*, ed. Germaine Aujac (Paris, 1979), page 66.

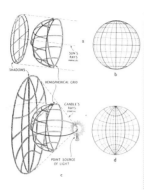

6.33
Cartographic projections: orthographic and stereographic. Peter Jeffrey Booker, *A History of Engineering Drawing* (London, 1963).

32. Naturally, this is a hypothesis, which is also elaborated by Peter Jeffrey Booker, in which the cuspidate form is derived from primary geometry: that is, from the projection of a hemisphere, constructed of meridians and parallels, from a point on the equator or from an exterior point (a candle in the first case, the sun in the second). This procedure was probably well known. The technique underlying the construction of the meridians, familiar since the seventh century, was part of astronomical practice. The ancient world does seem to have had a certain familiarity with projective phenomena, if what Pliny tells us is true: that the projected shadow is at the origin of classical figuration itself (*Naturalis historia* 35.5), and that the same term, *skiagraphia* (shadow painting) links astronomical and pictorial traditions to the perspective studies of Agatharchus of Samos, mentioned by Vitruvius. See Peter Jeffrey Booker, *A History of Engineering Drawing* (London: Chatto and Windus, 1963), 4.

33. See the Byzantine codices of machines, the Islamic codices such as the *Automata* by al-Jazari (1206; Istanbul, Topkapi Sarayi, n. A3472) and the Ottoman manuscript *Shah-nama*, which shows a large armillary sphere with almond-shaped circles (sixteenth century; Istanbul, University Library, F. 1404, fol. 56v). In the West there are numerous examples, such as the frontispiece of the *Suma de geographia* (1519) by Martin Fernandez de Enciso, in the works of Oronce Finé, and in the *Gnomonica* by Benedetti, among other examples.

34. Isidore of Seville, *Etymologies* (London, British Library, Cod. Harl. 2686, fol. 36r). See Murdoch, *Antiquity and the Middle Ages*, 126, §119.

35. There is an interesting comparison to be made between the cylinder in Boethius's version of the *Etymologies*, the ninth-century Greek manuscript of the *Elements*, the *Elements* of Adelard of Bath in the two versions of the thirteenth and fourteenth centuries in which the cuspidate ellipse, more common in Arab astronomical codices, prevails. Murdoch, *Antiquity and the Middle Ages*, 128, §120. It seems evident that the square surmounted by a semicircle, typical of Isidore and of Boethius, pertains more to writing than to geometry, and that it is not possible to conduct geometrical operations of any kind on it.

36. *Gaurici Pomponii Napoletani, De sculptura ad Divum Herculem Ferrariae principem* (Florence, 1504). The description of the drawing in parallel projection reads as follows: "Esto hic liber ... Esto uti apparet in pluteo rectus, recta etenim primo esse omnia oportebit, quae-

cumque in aliam erunt status racionem transitura Sic, ducantur de omnibus quattuor angulis in longum paralleli linae, paulo et sursius et dehorsius ut libuerit, age Sic, Singuli autem et heic anguli suis contineantur lineis Sic, viderit ut iam resupinarit Spectetur idem et a tergo in hunc modum, Altitudo hec, ipsaque latitudo, non enim dum. Sic apparuerint, quicquam de iis comminuitur, erit huiusmodi, aequabilis autem hec superior paginarum planicies, productis paululum ab latitudine lineis in rursum, Sic, item et hec inferior ad eandam racionem status, Sic, Nonne praesentata nobis species videtur?" This is given further detailed explanation with the example of the book of the *Odyssey*: "Sic ducantur de singulis angulis in longum, eondem ut diximus *paralleli modo*. Sic, Suis mox unusquiusque descriptus finiatur lineis. Sic, quam prope eadem oculis, in hanc alteram commutata ninc est forma illa prior." See Pomponius Gauricus, *De sculptura*, ed. André Chastel and Robert Klein (Geneva: Droz, 1969), 191–193, chapter titled *De perspectiva*, §V.

37. See the treatise by Santbech for the calculation of the depth of cylinder or quadrangular cavities: Daniel Santbech, *Problematum astronomicorum et geometricorum sectiones septem, in quibus* … (Basel, 1561), 185. See also the treatise by Digges, where in book III, on stereometry, *oblique drawing* is used for the cube, the pyramid on a square base, and the cylinder. All of the figures are drawn "wire frame." Cf. Thomas Digges, *A Geometrical Practical Treatize named Pantometria, divided in three Books. Longimetria, Planimetria and Stereometria* (London, 1591), 82.

38. See Wolfgang Lotz, *Studi sull'architettura italiana del Rinascimento* (Milan: Electa, 1989), 18. Lotz's study clearly and precisely illustrates how the representational methods of architecture changed around 1520. The method of drawing trabeation, typical of a fifteenth-century prototype and destined to be used again by Falconetto, is considered by Lotz to be "a cavalier perspective," which he erroneously refers to as the "bird's-eye method." See also note 33 of the chapter "The Idea of Model."

39. Florence, Gabinetto Disegno e Stampe degli Uffizi, 2A.

40. See note 33 of the chapter "The Idea of Model."

41. In the *Oratio*, which forms a premise to the text, Aloisio Pirovano writes, "I have made drawings for many excellent painters, and for engravers by no means mediocre I have similarly cut out the figurations using *circino*, compass and a ruler." But this must refer to a reedition with illustrations based on originals made by Cesariano

6.34
Depiction of a cylinder in
a twelfth-century version
of Euclid. Bayerische
Staatsbibliothek, Munich.
Latin codex 23511, folio 24r.

6.35
Euclid, *Elements*, XII,
Proposition 15, ninth-century
manuscript. Biblioteca
Apostolica Vaticana, Rome.
MS. vat. gr. 190, folio 227r.

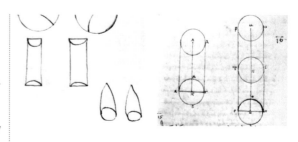

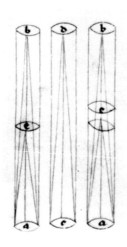

6.36
Euclid, *Elements*, XII,
Proposition 14, Campano
da Novara's version.
Cylinders with circular
bases, fourteenth century.
British Library, London.
Ar 84, folio 94r.

6.37
Adelard of Bath, Latin
translation of Euclid's
Elements, thirteenth century.
Bodleian Library, Oxford.
Auctarium Manuscript,
F.5.28, folio 4r.

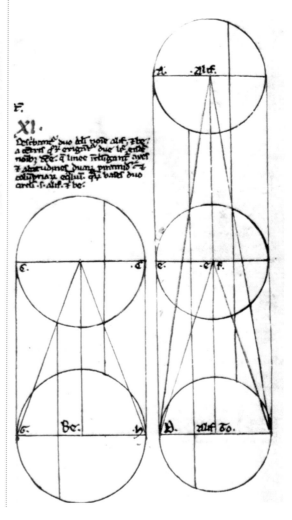

for his treatise. *De architectura translato commentato et affigurato da Cesare Cesariano* (Como, 1521); anastatic edition, ed. Arnaldo Bruschi, Adriano Carugo, and Francesco Paolo Fiore (Milan: Edizioni il Polifilo, 1981).

42. Ibid., V, fol. LXXIIr. Villalpando provides an interesting example of a cube in cavalier perspective with the scale (depth) halved, in the manner of cabinet drawing, though dating from a later period. *Encyclopaedia Britannica* (London, 1958), s.v., 636. See Juan Bautista Villalpando in *Ezechielem explanationes et apparatus urbis ac templi ...* (Rome, 1596–1604), III, 294.

43. Vitruvius, *De architectura* (Munich, Bayerische Staatsbibliothek, Cod. It. 37 abc, fols. 57v and 58v). See *Vitruvio e Raffaello. Il "De architectura" di Vitruvio nella tradizione inedita di Fabio Calvo ravennate*, ed. Vincenzo Fontana and Paolo Morachiello (Rome, 1975), plate 5.

44. See the woodcut by Geoffroy Tory (*Champfleury*, Paris, 1529), which reproduces that of Cesariano, but with letters drawn on the sides and, on the front receding side, superimposed upon the figure of a man drawn frontally and in profile. See *Effetto Arcimboldo* (Milan: Bompiani, 1987), 42.

45. "Primum igitur accipe quadratum a.b.b.a. quod paulante fecimus, & eleva illud rectissime tantum quanta latitudo ipsius est, fieris cubus aequilaterus & ac aequiangulus." *Albertus Durerus nurembergensis pictor huius aetatis celeberrimus, versus è Germanica lingua in Latinam, Pictoribus, Fabris aerariis ac lignariis, Lapicidis, Statuariis, & universis demum qui circino, gnomone, libella, aut alioqui certa mensura opera sua examinant propè necessarius, adeò exacte Quatuor his suarum Institutionum geometricarum libris, linea, superficies & solida corpora tractavit, ad hibitis designationibus ad eam rem accomodatissimis* (Paris, 1532), 1:3. In his depiction of the cochlea, Dürer uses projectively united orthogonal multiviews in a manner similar to that used by Piero della Francesca. On the latter, some interesting observations have been made in Robin Evans, *The Projective Cast: Architecture and Its Three Geometries* (Cambridge: MIT Press, 1995), 147, 162. The same system is used by Dürer in his depictions of the ellipse, the parabola, and the hyperbole. In Book III, on page 113, a solar clock is reproduced in oblique parallel projection with an inclination of 50 degrees (see the same inclination in Louis Bretez, *La perspective practique de l'architecture ...*, Paris, 1706). See also the wire frame figure of the cube (fig. 5) and of the solar clock (fig. 25), in *Underweisung der Messung...* (Nuremberg, 1525).

46. Maurolico was a harsh critic of the work of Oronce Finé: he accused him of ineptitude, false reasoning, and of attributing his own errors to Archimedes. See Paul Lawrence Rose, *The Italian Renaissance of Mathematics* (Geneva: Droz, 1975), 171. Oronce Finé (Orontius Finaeus, or Fineus) published his *Arithmetica* in 1519, and in 1525 he produced the first map of France. He translated the encyclopedia of the German Gregorius Reisch (*Aepitoma omnis philosophaie. Alias Margarita philosophica tractans de omni genere scibili*, Strasbourg, 1504), a popular work that was widely read at the beginning of the sixteenth century. Francis I took him to Piedmont and entrusted him with the task of designing fortifications for Milan. He also acted in an advisory capacity at the siege of Pavia. In Paris, he held private lessons in mathematics, attracting many students, until he was finally rewarded with the chair in mathematics at the Collège Royal (1530 or 1532), a position he held until his death. While he was still teaching at the Collège, Pedro Nuñez of Portugal published a detailed list of all the errors made by Finé in his writings, and a similar list was published by his pupil Jean Borel after Finè's death. See *De erratis Orontii Finaei, qui putavit inter duas datas lineas binas medias proportionales sub continua proportione invenisse, circulum quadrasse, cubum duplicasse, multangulum quodcunque rectilineum in circulo describendi artem tradidisse et longitudinis locorum differentias aliter quam per eclipse lunares, etiam dato quovis tempore, manifestas fecisse, Petrii Nounii Liber unus* (Coimbre, 1546); Jean Borrel (Johannes Buteo), *De quadratura Circuli, ubi multorum quadraturae confutantur* (Lyon, 1559) and *Io. Buteonis confutatio quadraturae circuli ab Orontio Fineo factae, in Io. Buteonis delphinatici opera geometrica, quorum tituli sequuntur* … (Lyon, 1554), 42–50. In the scientific field, fierce criticism was a common occurrence: the argument between Nicholas of Cusa and Toscanelli concerning the squaring of the circle was interrupted by Regiomontano, who called Cusa a "geometra ridiculus." See the letter of 1471 to Christian Roder of Erfurt, in Rose, *The Italian Renaissance of Mathematics*, 30. Finé was also the editor of two pirated editions of the famous work by Jean Pèlerin Viator, *De artificiali perspectiva* (Toul, 1505): one published in Strasbourg in 1512 and the other in Basel in 1535.

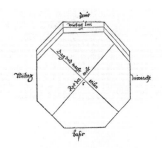

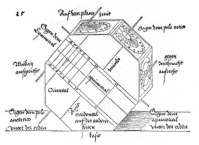

6.38
Solar clock. Albrecht Dürer,
Underweisung der Messung
... (Nuremberg, 1525),
figure 25.

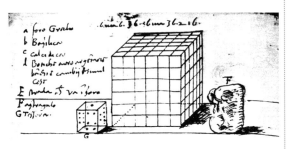

6.39
Copyist of Fabio Calvo,
drawing of a die and
a cube. Bayerische
Staatsbibliothek, Munich.
Italian codex 37abc,
folio 58v.

6.40
"Wire frame" cube. Albrecht
Dürer, *Underweisung der
Messung* ... (Nuremberg,
1525), folio 5.

S On nun von der leng vñ breyte/das ist die ebne ein wenig geredt ist/was sie sey/ So will ich
nun sagen was die leng vnd breytte mit sambt der dicke sey/das sind die Corpora/auß der
selben will ich etliche antzeygen vnnd leren/wie sie gemacht mügen werden/Erstlich nun
die vorgemacht gesirt ebne.a.b.b.a.vnd für gerad mit vbersich/ als hoch als breyt sie ist/so
wirdt ein recht gesirter würffel darauß/von gleichen seyten/von gleiche ebnen/vñ von gleichen winck
len/Darnach nym die vorgemacht rund ebne/vnd reis aus dem mittel puncten.a.g erad hynauß biß
ans endt der runden/da seß ein.c.also das.c.a.b.ein gerade lini sey/vnnd seß auff die ein seiten auser
halb der runden ebne ein.d.auff die andern seyten.e.Aber.c.a.b.sey die art/daran mus dise ebne vmge=
went werde vom.d.biß zum.e.so reist diser runder ryß/ein gantz runde kugel/die von aussen allenthal
ben gleich weyt zü jrem mittel puncten.a.hat/ Doch mus im vmb wenden die art in den punckt.c.b.
stett bleiben/also hastu zwey volkomne Corpora/Aber kein volkumner Corpus ist/das allenthalbē glei
cher ist dann ein kugel/Dise zwey Corpora hab ich auff geryssen.

Eyn gesirt Corpus oder würffel/   Eyn runde kugel oder sper/

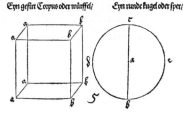

A iij

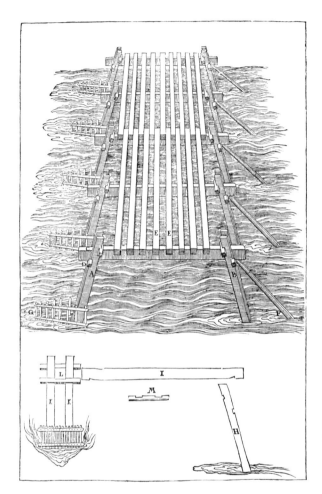

7.1
Andrea Palladio, Caesar's bridge over the
Rhine. *The Four Books of Architecture*,
III (Venice, 1570), page 13v.

7.2
Coin with effigy of Demetrius Poliorcetes,
third century BC.

7

MACHINATIONS

"As far as general security is concerned, an engineer can contribute as much as the commander of an army and decide the fate of whole nations … but you, Callicles, disparage him and his art … and wouldn't give your daughter to his son, nor would you take one of his daughters for your wife."[1] With this speech, Plato demonstrated that the figure of the technician (*mechanikós*) was not held in high regard in classical times. He was considered an untrustworthy individual because of his artisanal status (*demiurgós*) and because he belonged to a world outside the *pólis*, his usual place of work being the journey. He was a foreigner (*xénos*) of unknown origin and unknown destination. But because his work was constructing machines and buildings, he was necessary to the community, and he was therefore accepted by it, even though his skill appeared to be the work of magic and people were suspicious of it.

Julius Caesar's bridge over the Rhine was, in the eyes of the barbarians who witnessed its building, another act of magic, although Caesar played down this aspect in his *De bello gallico*. It was built with the intention of eliciting surprise and awe in the local population, and it was destroyed after a quick expedition. The barbarians were struck by the speed of its construction, in the same way that the inhabitants of Rhodes had been struck by the beauty of the *helépolis*, or siege tower, of Demetrius I "Poliorcetes," as it advanced toward the city wall to destroy them. The deviser of the bridge, praised by Caesar and cursed by the Germanic tribes, was regarded with a mixture of admiration and fear. Vitruvius's clever idea to reinforce the bridge with a strength equal to that of the surge of water flowing beneath it continues to astonish architects even today. Yet he, too, was a man of *téchne*, and perhaps would not have escaped Plato's disapprobation of the technician (*mechanopoiós*).

All machinery, wrote Vitruvius, is a "true and faithful imitation of nature."[2] This "imitation" was, however, subject to errors that could exponentially increase the cost of public buildings and theatrical machines.[3] In order to avoid such damage to the public purse, Vitruvius believed an explanation of the *principia machinarum* was in order. His audience was made up of engineers, the rhetoricians who brought the *principia* to bear on the world of matter and know-how. In Book x of his *De architectura*, alongside the *exempla* in which the protagonists are siege engines, the chief engineer of Caesar's army drew up a series of precise definitions and sharp distinctions, which provide an outline of the technical knowledge of the Hellenistic and Roman worlds.

Most importantly, as was the case with all public works, the cost of the machine had to be ethical, fair, and containable,[4] and furthermore, it had to be justified in terms of social value. In fact, the machine did facilitate the dragging and lifting of weights; it was an ingenious artifice without which nothing could be moved without superhuman effort. Vitruvius, with something of the inflexible spirit of Cato,[5] was at pains to remind his reader of this quality of utility. In order to carry out this liberating function, the machine was endowed with a continuous circular motion, which dramatically increased the hoisting power of the arms. The Greeks called this principle *baroulkón* (crane). Stationary machines with an upward motion (mobile towers, flying bridges) were termed *akrobatikón*. Mechanisms driven by air pressure, which caused them to emit sounds, were called *pneumatikón*. For the first it was necessary to be competent *in agendo cum prudentia*; the second called for a spirit of daring, *non arte sed audacia gloriatur*; the pneumatic machine instead necessitated scientific refinement, those *elegantes artes* that seemed, to the technically and military-minded Vitruvius, somewhat alien.[6]

Next, a distinction was made between machine (*machina*) and instrument (*organum*). The former (ballistae and presses) required the strength of many workmen, the latter (rotation and gears) required the skill of only one. These mechanical contrivances, requiring strength on the one hand and skill on the other, both derived from a single fundamental principle of nature: the Earth's rotatory motion, the Lucretian *machina mundi*. By imitating the laws of the very *machina* that guaranteed light and the seasons, man perfected "the contrivances which are so serviceable in our life. Some things, with a view to greater convenience, they worked out by means of machines and their revolutions, other by means of engines, and so, whatever they found to be useful for investigations for the arts, and for established practices, they took care, step by step, to improve on scientific principles."[7] A proper reliance on experience meant that laws could be extracted from the great reserve of nature, which contains them all. The *mechanicus* rediscovered them gradually and applied them to his own works. His *téchne* was not creation but simply skilled description. Like the painter, the *mechanicus* was not to invent anything. His task was simply to discover that which already existed in nature, and this is why only the best practitioners were recognized by the classical world as possessing *sophía*: wisdom in doing.

The machines described by Vitruvius at the beginning of Book x are not, however, simple mills or lathes, but "machines which are of necessity built when temples and public buildings are under construction."[8] The first description is of what might be termed a mounting block for a crane for use in construction, along with various combinations of pulleys that would permit different traction solutions.[9] Vitruvius's method of presentation presupposes that his reader will need to use a crane, an expectation that facilitates the passage from reading to representation and thus to comprehension. One by one, the more complex points are discussed simply and clearly, and in a descriptive process that is like the opposite of an exploded diagram, in that it starts from the outside in, there is an account of how the mobile parts are joined to the fixed parts of the machine. The reader builds up a picture of "a combination of timbers fastened together, chiefly efficacious in moving great weights."[10]

Hoisting *machinationes* are based on two distinct and heterogeneous principles in which "as the powers and nature of the motion are different, so they generate two effects, one direct, which the Greeks call *eutheia*, the other circular, which they call *kykloté*; but it must be confessed that neither rectilinear without circular motion, nor, on the other hand, circular without rectilinear motion can be of much assistance in raising weights."[11] So how are these contrivances "which we rarely come across" portrayed?

De architectura has come down to us without illustrations. Given the complicated nature of the machines it describes, we might have expected it to contain numerous images. Instead, the only figure explicitly mentioned in Book x is the water screw, which, being spiral in shape, is therefore a "correct and faithful imitation of nature."[12] Are the illustrations to Book x missing or were they never part of the work?[13] As Pierre Gros has observed, Vitruvius seems not to have considered illustrations to be very important, referring to them variously as *forma*, *schema*, *diagramma*, *exemplar*. They occur only six times, toward the end of the book, with a further three in the footnotes.[14] The absence of illustrations in Book x might be explained by the fact that the machines described were already familiar to *technites*, therefore a classificatory description was enough to refresh their memory. Or, more simply, illustrations are omitted because the written description is so effective as to make them superfluous, as in the very precise descriptions contained in al-Jazari's *Pneumatica*, written twelve centuries later.[15]

But even if he underestimated the effectiveness of illustrations, Vitruvius was aware that the reader might have difficulty with the description of the hydraulic organ, for he states he has tried "with all due effort" to explain "an obscure argument" with clarity, and what is more, he has done so in a written text. Since "this is neither a simple system, nor one that is immediately comprehensible for those without a certain familiarity with the subject,"[16] he advises his reader to acquire a "direct knowledge of this mechanism." Only in this way will it be possible to understand how "all the elements are disposed with precision and in an ingenious manner."

From this it is clear that Vitruvius knew his text fell short of illuminating the complex stratification of mechanisms and of movements, which orthogonal drawings and overall views (*adumbratio*) would only further confuse. Vitruvius theorized that true knowledge was possible only in the presence of a model. The model (*parádeigma*) allowed a unified vision of each separate part of a contrivance, showing how each related to the other with an immediacy that was out of the reach of a paratactical written description.[17] Machines and instruments were the realm of the *mechanicus* rather than of the *architectus* who directed their use. In alluding to certain *machinationes*, Vitruvius's aim was to extol the *sophía* of the architect rather than the *téchne* of the mechanic, to show off the learning of those with knowledge of the principles, rather than the technical know-how of those who handled materials. With the same "virile" display of indifference affected by Cicero when listing the artworks stolen by Verres in Sicily,[18] Vitruvius mentions astonishing "singing blackbirds" and "small figurines that drink and even move." This is a moment of pure rhetoric, allowing Vitruvius to distance himself from similar trivial applications of mechanical skill and bring the discussion rapidly back to focus on the principles and ethics of Cato's concept of *utilitas*;[19] for those who are curious about these *elegantes* mechanical toys—notes Vitruvius—there are always Ctesibius's booklets. Yet clearly, for Vitruvius the *architectus* is also a *scriptor*. The ability to write is the most significant intellectual distinguishing mark between the *technítes* and the man who coordinates their work; he is a *rhetor* who directs with his words the actions of those who actually carry out the work.

In this debate between knowing and doing, the determining factor is not just having to use machines, but actually having foreknowledge of them. Whether the text was being read or listened to, it had to relate the conditions of constructability in the here and now, because soldiers had to build the machines with whatever materials were available on the spot. An illustration would have given visibility to the constructional gesture, but it would have

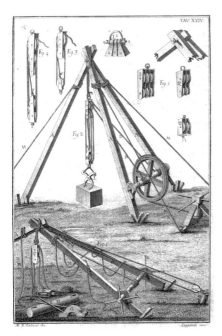

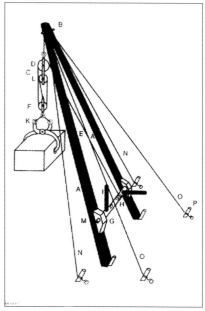

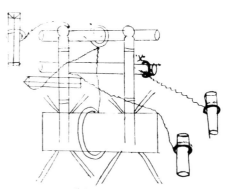

7.3
Berardo Galiani, *L'architettura di Marco Vitruvio Pollione* (Siena, 1790), plate XXIV.

7.4
Reconstruction of Vitruvius's hoist with trestle and winch. Philippe Fleury, *La mécanique de Vitruve* (Caen, 1993), figure 13.

7.5
Heron, *Mechanics*, winch and hoist. Universiteitsbibliotheek, Leiden. Cod. or. 51, page 61.

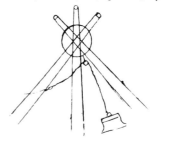

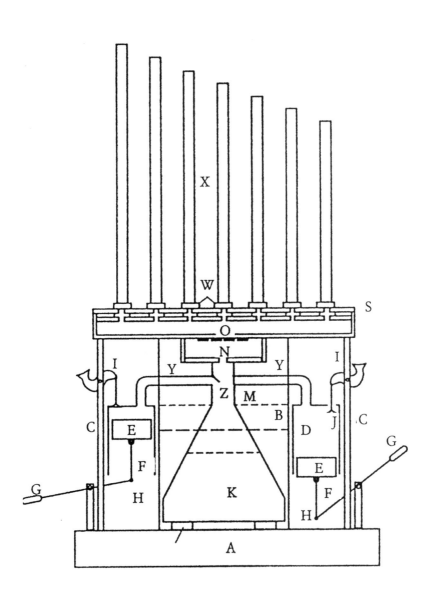

7.6
Reconstruction of Vitruvius's hydraulic organ.
Vitruvius, *De architectura*, ed. Pierre Gros
(Turin, 1997), page 1388.

weakened the modular principle; that is to say, the flexibility of type was favored over the rigidity of the model. The machine thus remained "an organized assemblage of diverse parts," even if Vitruvius could not conceal the lack of a general theory as to its function and the concept of force; it is an actual bodily object and not, as might have been preferred by a Greco-Alexandrian mechanic, a *schema*.

One of the characteristics of Book x, derived from Aristotelian rhetoric, is its visual liveliness, or *enárgheia*.[20] Thanks to this vivid description and to the precise account of the sequence of acts to be carried out, the machine materializes before the reader's eyes with each part tangibly animated. Despite Vitruvius's continual reference to principles as a means of ennobling his text, what captivates the reader is the seesaw motion as "the traction rope is carried over the sheave at the top, then let fall and passed round a sheave in a pulley below. Then it is brought back to the lower sheave of the upper pulley, and so it goes down to the lower pulley, where it is blocked through an eyebolt. The other end of the rope is brought back and down between the legs of the machine."[21] Then, strong hands see to it that "to the bottom of the lower block are fastened by pincers made of iron, whose jaws are brought to bear upon the stones, which have holes bored in them." When the causal relationship has been explained, the effect is described: "When one end of the rope is fastened to the winch, and the latter is turned round by working the handspikes, the rope winds round the windlass, gets taut, and thus raises the load to the proper height."[22]

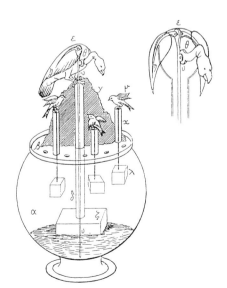

7.7
Philo of Byzantium, vessel with hydraulic mechanism, reconstruction. Bernard Carra de Vaux, *Le livre des appareils pneumatiques et des machines hydrauliques par Philon de Byzance* (Paris, 1902), page 157.

In this extraordinary sequence of frames that unfolds before the eyes of the reader, it is as if an invisible hand were guiding the ropes in their backward and forward motion. The pulling movement of this hand links the dislocated parts of the machine with the muscular memory acquired in repetitive actions. In this we can see the systematic intention inherited by Vitruvius from Greek tradition, and of which he wants to be a part:[23] to show that it is possible to impose order on the chaos of human actions, to provide men with machines and instruments that free them from the bestial nature of hard labor, to shift man's actions from the shadow of error and from the uncertain experimentation of practice without principles. So each time the stage is set for war, the text is able to offer a procedural protocol to the reality of military forces and to the conformation of the battlefield. But just as the text of Greek tragedy was subject to change and innovation, in the same way, the text of the *machinatio* made reference to the most up-to-date technical procedures, entrusting them to the memory of experience, which in turn would consign them to an altogether new text, with "the gradual institution of a science."[24]

The central argument of Book x deals with war and the devices designed for defense and self-preservation. Vitruvius writes as if the act of conquest, far from being a matter of violent attack, were an untroubled process quite devoid of danger. The machines that served this purpose were scorpions, catapults, and ballistae. These were common weapons known to all, but their construction posed complex problems of calibration, involving the relationship between projectile, rope length, and the wooden structure. First, Vitruvius described the various parts of which they were composed and the "basic modular relationships" governing the size of components and the calculation of ballistic performances: "The measurements of catapults and scorpions depend on the length of the arrow that the instrument is to throw, a ninth part of whose length is assigned for the sizes of the holes [*modulo*] in the capitals through which the rope is twisted, that retain the arms of the weapon."[25] The results of the calculation could then be applied proportionately to all parts of the machine: the construction was realized "according to numerical relationships" and "proceeded by means of additions and subtractions," with case-by-case adjustments.

For the construction of ballistae, Vitruvius supplied a table of proportional guidelines noting not linear dimensions but the weight of the projectiles to be thrown. Here too, the specialist's knowledge was deemed a necessity: "hence the rules will only be understood by those who are acquainted with arithmetical numbers and their progression."[26] But in war time there is "no time for calculations," and in order that "those who are not masters of geometry may be prepared against delay on the occasions of war" Vitruvius has taken the opportunity to state "the results of my own experience as well as what I have learnt from the masters": "how in Greece the loads to be weighed are related to the *moduli*."[27] Once the *modulo* has been defined, the sizes of the various elements may be derived from it.

Clearly, Vitruvius as a soldier is not reciting magic spells here, and in the same way the testimonies of Heron of Alexandria, Philo of Byzantium, and Athenaeus Mechanicus were not fairy tales. Theirs are texts that speak only to those who must use them, to experts who understand the difficult language of *téchne*. And as further proof of this, Vitruvius writes that it is useless to give a description of the most simple contrivances since soldiers are well aware of how to construct them for themselves.[28] But in the case of more complex machines the technical language is incomprehensible for those who are not practitioners. It is a language that seems to stumble and uses meaningless terms (*barbarízousa*),[29] especially when compared to the expressive means of a person that has received a classical education (*paidéia*). It is the language of Hephaestus, a god in whom none had faith, yet it was to him that Thetis turned when she begged him to fashion the mighty shield for Achilles, described by Homer in an extended *ékphrasis*.[30]

Ending the chapter on machines, Vitruvius stresses the importance of tactical intelligence in countering the Daedalus-like qualities of the *machinationes* designed for sieges. This proud donning of the mantle of intellectual responsibility would be recalled in the sixteenth century when the blind brutality of artillery fire prompted anxious debate about strength as opposed to reason.

"The city is like a great house and a house in its turn like a small city."[31] With a risky disregard for dimension, Leon Battista Alberti used this image to launch a very humanist challenge: conceiving a big machine as a small body, fashioned in the image of God. Polykleitos's canon[32] being lost, Christian humanism regarded the small human frame as an ideal model for governing the proportions of buildings and machines. Man's perfectly proportioned body had been quantified numerically by Albrecht Dürer, rendered unusable in the steeply foreshortened bodies of the Florentine Michelangelo, but seems instead to be in perfect harmony with the structure of Albertian machines, which "may be considered on a level with inanimate bodies that have exceptionally strong hands."[33] These hands may be used to save time in producing effects and strength in producing causes. Thanks to its multiplication of energies, the machine shortens the action time and increases thinking time.

7.8
Anonymous, lightning-strike ballista.
De rebus bellicis, 1436. Bodleian Library,
Oxford. Cod. oxo. can. class. lat. misc.
378, 18, 16–20.

7.9
Ballistae. *Iusti Lipsi Poliorceticon
sive De machinis, tormentis, telis,
Libri quinque* (Antwerp, 1596),
page 148.

7.10
Anonymous, four-wheeled ballista.
De rebus bellicis, 1436. Bodleian Library,
Oxford. Cod. oxo. can. class. lat. misc.
378, 7, 1–2.

7.11
Ballista, 113 AD. Trajan's column, Rome.

7.12
Mobile ballista. Drawing after Trajan's column, Rome.

7.13
Reconstruction of Vitruvius's ballista. Vitruvius, *De l'architecture*, ed. Louis Callebat and Philippe Fleury (Paris, 1986), page 222.

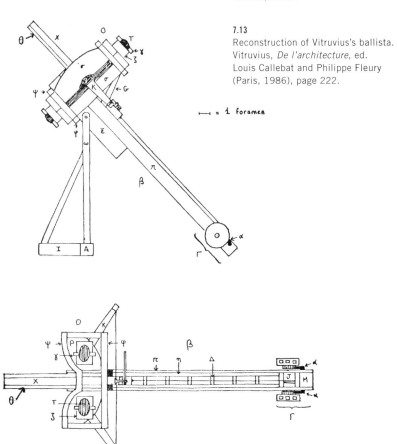

Alberti's text, like that of Vitruvius, is not accompanied by illustrations.[34] To find out why, we need to look at the manuscripts that inspired Vitruvius and that were responsible for transmitting the Greek-Hellenistic iconography of the *machinatio* to the West.

In the Middle Ages there existed a tradition of *machinatio* that had been preserved from classical times. There was a similar continuity of representational method, the antiquity of which conferred scientific authority to the texts.[35] Numerous works of a technical nature were brought to the West by Arab scholars working at the school of Toledo and in Sicily,[36] thus providing a bridge between Hellenistic tradition and medieval European tradition. Roger II summoned many Arab mechanics to his court in Sicily, and the Hohenstaufen kings who succeeded him extended this interest by collecting manuscripts that would later form part of the Vatican Library, frequented by the likes of Nicholas of Cusa, Bessarion, Toscanelli, Alberti, and Pacioli.[37]

Among these technical works, the most famous is perhaps al-Jazari's *Book of Knowledge of Ingenious Mechanical Devices* (*Automata*).[38] Even if direct knowledge of this manuscript in the West had not yet been documented, it certainly served as a model for other works that were known to Latin culture.[39] Al-Jazari's work presents consistent analogies with texts in the Hellenistic-Alexandrian tradition of Philo and Heron of Alexandria. Indeed, Kurt Weitzmann described one of Heron's illustrations as a "bird's-eye view."[40] In reality, it is not a bird's-eye view, but an oblique drawing that does not attempt to show the object in space.[41] The author of a later critical edition of the work, Carra de Vaux, found the original illustrations to be so defective that he had them redrawn.[42] But it is precisely the analytical character of the drawings, their deformed and anti-perspectival appearance, that confirms their direct provenance from the Greek tradition of technical drawing. Weitzmann maintained that in the Arabic translation of Heron's text made by Qusta ibn Luqa, the drawing style continued to be inspired by the Greek model, and that the same was true for the later Byzantine and Arabic copies, where the illustrators had obviously "kept strictly to showing such information as was absolutely necessary, without any concession to aesthetics."

In Donald Routledge Hill's study of al-Jazari's work,[43] which shows far greater sensitivity to representational problems than Carra de Vaux demonstrated, he notes that even in the absence of measurements and of a precise orientation, the effectiveness of the figures is increased by the presence of captions, which refer, by means of letters, to the corresponding parts of the figures. This may be seen particularly in the first category (*prima categoria*), where there is an oblique drawing of the mechanism of a clock in which the two pulleys are represented as true circles, whereas the circular gear mechanisms, shown horizontally, are generally represented as spindle- or almond-shaped.[44]

Few of the machines used in medieval building sites are known and little is understood about how they were built. However, it is possible to get an idea of how they were represented by analyzing the corpus of Gothic drawings and some small notebooks such as that of the master builder Mathes Roriczer, which was printed in Regensberg on 28 June 1486. Beginning with the solemn premise that "all art is matter, form, and measure" the *caputmagister* demonstrates how to duplicate a square and how to calculate the elevation from the ground plan.[45] In fact, Plato had already dealt with this problem in his *Meno*, and it was taken up again by Vitruvius in *De architectura* and again in Cesariano's beautiful edition of Vitruvius. The procedure for the duplication of squares seems to have become customary by the time Villard de Honnecourt[46] produced his model book in the first half of the thirteenth century, the golden age of the Gothic.

After Spain's expulsion of the Moors, hundreds of translations of the mathematical works left by the Muslims in Spain were added to those brought from Constantinople in 1204, following the crusade of the Franks. Villard's *Portfolio*, which was created in this context, allows us to verify the state of architectural and machine representation in the thirteenth century. Villard's work is more scientific in its approach than its appearance—thickly inscribed letters on calfskin—would suggest, and it shows characteristics that recall the diagrammatic drawing of ancient Greece. But that is not all. Its representational method is curiously close to that of the manuscripts of Philo of Byzantium and of Heron of Alexandria, as well as to the later and better-known Vitruvius.[47] This is significant because the two earlier works were responsible for the transmission of the Greco-Hellenistic *machinatio* to the West. Some of the machines in the *Portfolio* clearly confirm this hypothesis, although during Villard's time, machines had not yet been classified into a few types of mechanism.[48] Not until the abstractions of Guidobaldo del Monte[49] in the second half of the sixteenth century would machines be rationally grouped according to the five classic mechanisms of Greek tradition, which were well known to Arab scientists. In the thirteenth century machines were bodies that could hammer, lift, grind, drill, and kill. They creaked and labored like the breathless monster Hephaestus. So what is it that makes their representations so interesting? It is enough to open Villard's *Portfolio* and observe two: a *trabucco*,[50] which was a catapult

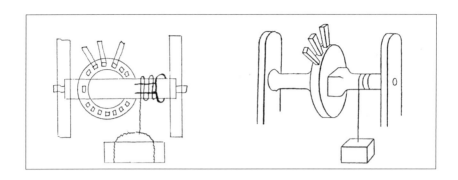

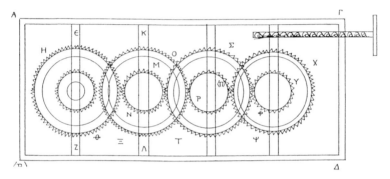

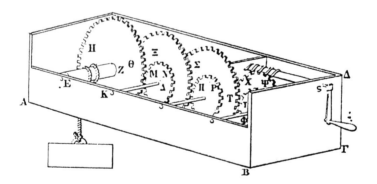

7.14
Design for a winch from the Arabic original, and perspectival reconstruction. Heron of Alexandria, *Les mécaniques*, Arabic text by Qusta ibn Luqa, trans. Bernard Carra de Vaux (Paris, 1988), pages 241 and 116.

7.15
Heron, *baroulkós,* from *Dioptra.* Bibliothèque Nationale, Paris. Mynas Codex, folio 82r. Below, reconstruction by Ludwig Nix.

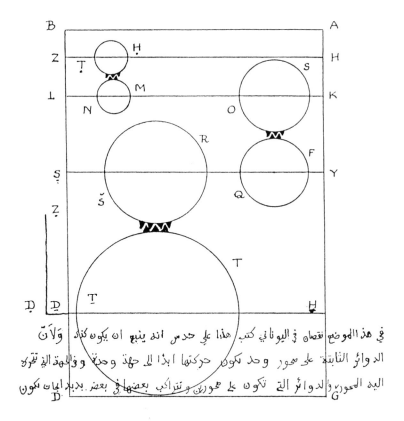

وفي هذا الموضع نقصان في اليوناني، كتب، هذا على حدس، أنه ينبغي أن يكون كذلك. ولأن الدوائر النابتة على محور، وحد تكون حركتها ابدا الى جهة وحدة، والجهة التي تقوى اليه المحور، والدوائر التي تكون على محورين وتتراكب بعضها في بعض، بدبرانات تكون

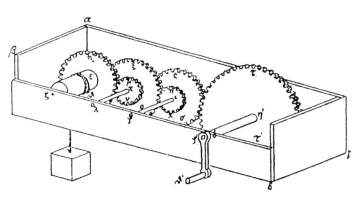

7.16
Heron, *baroulkós,* from *Mechanics.*
Universiteitsbibliotheek, Leiden.
Cod. or. 51. Below, reconstruction by
Ludwig Nix.

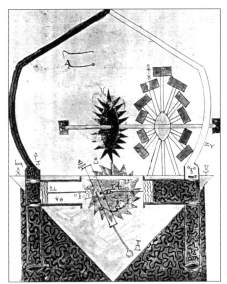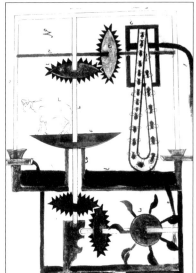

7.17, 7.18
Ibn al-Razzaz al-Jazari, pump and machine
for lifting water, 1354. Bodleian Library,
Oxford. MS. Graves. From *The Book of
Knowledge of Ingenious Mechanical Devices*,
ed. Donald R. Hill (Dordrecht and Boston,
1974), pages 189 and 183.

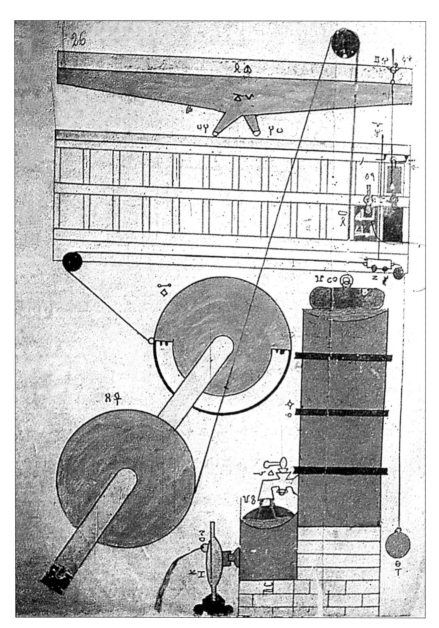

7.19
Ibn al-Razzaz al-Jazari, water-driven clock,
1354. Bodleian Library, Oxford. MS. Graves
27. *The Book of Knowledge of Ingenious
Mechanical Devices*, ed. Donald R. Hill
(Dordrecht and Boston, 1974), page 31.

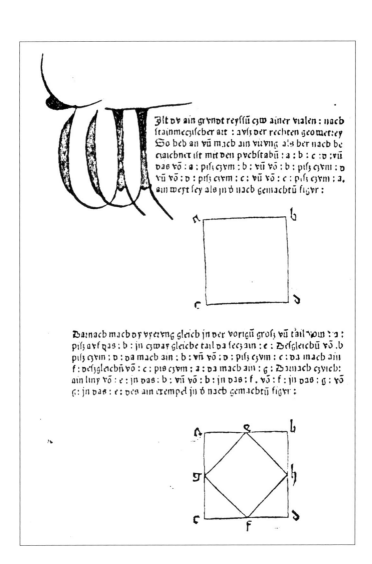

Jlt dr ain grvnot reyfffu cyw ainer vialen : nacb
fraynmecyifcber art : avfs der rechten geometrey
So beb an vu macb ain vurvng als ber nacb be
cyaicbnet ift mit den pvcbftabu : a : b : c : d :vu
das vo : a ; pifs cyvm : b ; vu vo : b : pifs cyvm : d
vu vo : d : pifs cyvm : c ; vu vo : c : pifs cyvm : a,
ain weft fey als jn d nacb gemacbtu figvr :

Darnacb macb dy vyeyvng gleicb jn der vorigu grofs vu tail vow : a :
pifs avf das : b : jn cyway gleicbe tail da feczain : c : Defgleicbu vo .b
pifs cyvm : d : da macb ain : b : vu vo : d : pifs cyvm : c : da macb ain
f : defsgleicbu vo : c : pia cyvm : a : da macb ain : g : Darnacb cyvicb:
ain liny vo : e : jn das : b : vu vo : b : jn das : f . vo : f : jn das : g : vo
g: jn das : e: des ain cxempel jn d nacb gemacbtu figvr :

7.20

Mathes Roriczer, *Von der Fialen*
Gerechtigkeit (Regensburg, 1486).

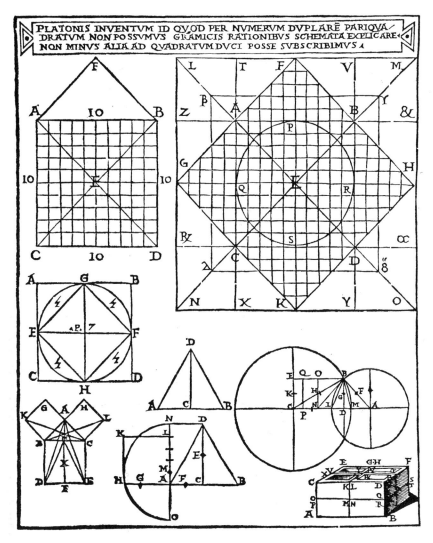

7.21
Cesare Cesariano, *De architectura* (Como, 1521), IX, 144.

7.22
Villard de Honnecourt, subdivision of a rectangle, thirteenth century, from *Album*. Bibliothèque Nationale, Paris. French manuscript 19093, folio 20v.

for throwing large stones, and a hydraulic saw. The first has a structure that is disconcerting, but only because, as one discovers upon reading the text, the page showing the elevation is missing. The remaining drawing is exceptional in its demonstrative brevity. It would appear that all the components of the basic structure of the catapult are in place and that they relate functionally to each other, but without an elevation it is difficult to imagine how the machine might work. For a reader unfamiliar with this machine, the drawing is useless, and it fascinates him precisely because he can see something he cannot fully understand. This helps us to understand the meaning of the omission in the technical drawing. A *mechanicus* was not obliged to draw everything in order to show how a device worked. He noted only what was *different* about a device compared to one that was already known. He would frequently enlarge certain parts of the machine without any regard for the proportional relationships with the rest. The result was an image of how something worked, formed only in the mind of the *mechanicus*, who knew how the moving parts related to each other. Villard's *Portfolio* is, in some sense, like an illustrated synopsis; unlike Vitruvius, he entrusted the understanding of how a machine worked solely to figurative representation.

The second drawing, of a hydraulic saw, can be associated with the devices of al-Jazari or with the schemata of Greco-Alexandrian poliorcetics. Despite naturalistic elements such as the knotty appearance of the branches, the annotative method of the antique mechanic is here perfectly reproduced. What counts is that the elements responsible for transforming rotary motion into alternating rectilinear movement by means of an elementary escapement are visible to the observer. Like that of the *mechanicus*, Villard's main preoccupation was with making visible each separate piece of the machine, and he arrayed them in such a way that they touch at those points where the eye expects to glimpse a transmission of energy, right where the teeth of the gears transmit power by means of the movement of the lever.

The methods by which machines are represented sometimes coincide with the objectives of naturalism and sometimes not: no allowance is made for the presence of an observer in space, and because all action originates in the mechanism's interior, often there is no indication of top and bottom, back and front. There is a free use of certain juxtapositions and superimpositions, forming a sort of technical notation that makes sense only to specialists. Geometrically, the object is considered solely in terms of its measurements, and not according to the geometry of various viewpoints that examine the object from the exterior and from a distance. This is what distinguishes a painting

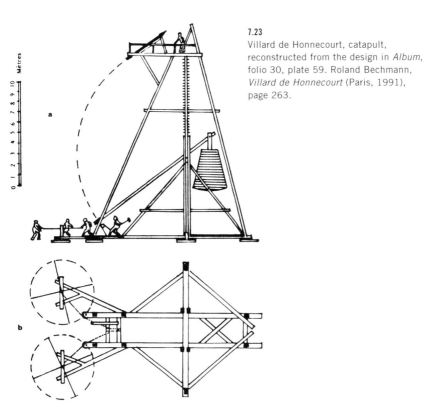

7.23
Villard de Honnecourt, catapult, reconstructed from the design in *Album*, folio 30, plate 59. Roland Bechmann, *Villard de Honnecourt* (Paris, 1991), page 263.

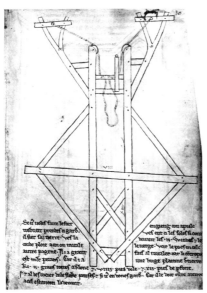

7.24
Villard de Honnecourt, catapult ground plan, thirteenth century, from *Album*. Bibliothèque Nationale, Paris. French manuscript 19093, folio 30.

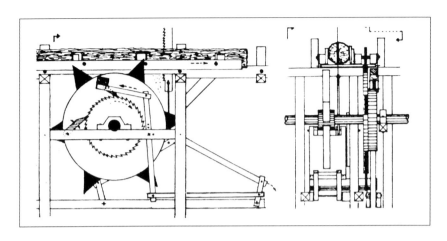

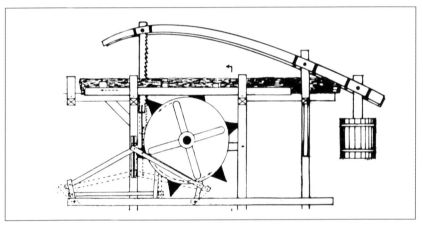

7.25, 7.26
Villard de Honnecourt, device for sawing tree trunks, reconstructed from *Album*, folio 22v. Roland Bechmann, *Villard de Honnecourt* (Paris, 1991), pages 282–283.

7.27
Villard de Honnecourt, device for sawing tree trunks, thirteenth century, from *Album*. Bibliothèque Nationale, Paris. French manuscript 19093, folio 22v.

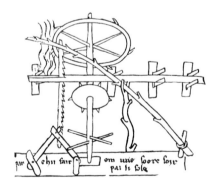

from an architectural drawing and from the drawing of a machine. The problem with drawing machines consists not so much in *what* has to appear in space, but in how to *diagram its operation*, how to illustrate the convergence of forces on the intersections. What is important is to demonstrate the kinematic credibility of the whole and show how it works; neither imperative has anything to do with representing the object in space.

The object's space, within which the machine functions, must abandon the comfortable, convergent vision of Greek illusionism. The language of the machine is like an abridged text, made up of lines that indicate, but do not separate or conjugate; together they create a series of superimpositions that defy the logic of anyone who is unfamiliar with what lies behind the dentated ovals of the wheelwork.

The princes of Italy dreamed of being able to deploy powerful ballistae, scorpions, catapults, chariots armed with blades, towers with bridges and battering rams, and all manner of ingenious machines that would terrorize their enemies and win the admiration of their allies. Parallel to the rediscovery and annotated translation of the great classics of ancient Greece was the reemergence, during the second half of the fourteenth and the whole of the fifteenth century, of Greco-Byzantine poliorcetics. These medieval repertories were studied, investigated and redrawn by physicians, technicians, and architects. In 1328, when Philip VI of Valois was organizing a crusade, Guido da Vigevano prepared a treatise for him on war machines that could be taken apart and put back together again. His proposals included rotating assault towers, bridges on floating barrels, propeller-driven vessels, and so on. The whole repertoire was founded on the principle of *akrobatikón*.[51] The treatise is divided into thirteen chapters, each of which describes a machine. Various representational methods are used: rotated and upside-down views as well as oblique drawings show the layout of kinematic linkages and reveal the true dimensions of hidden sides. The assault tank mounted on two wheels, which can be lifted by means of a winch system, seems to be an improvement on the *helépolis* attributed to Posidonius[52] by Biton.

Almost all of these fourteenth century manuscripts consistently show two representational types. In the Conrad Kyeser manuscript in Göttingen,[53] the catapult is represented with an oblique drawing, while the brake- (or wind-) driven system lift (or descending lift) is shown in a mix of orthogonal and vertical oblique drawings. The rotating elements are presented in orthogonal projection and turned 90 degrees with respect to the supporting structure. In each case, the kinematic linkages are made visible and the workings rendered

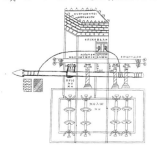

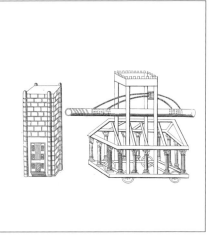

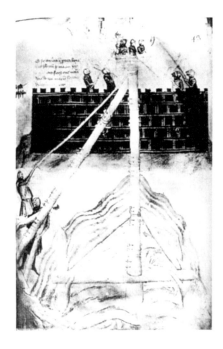

7.28
Athenaeus Mechanicus, mobile testudo, tenth-century manuscript. Bibliothèque Nationale, Paris. Cod. par. suppl.gr. 607, folio 23r. Reconstruction (right) of Athenaeus's wheeled testudo, from Carle Wescher, *Poliorcétique des grecs* (Paris, 1867), page 26.

7.29
Guido da Vigevano, *Texaurus regis Franciae*, 1335. Bibliothèque Nationale, Paris. Latin manuscript 11015.

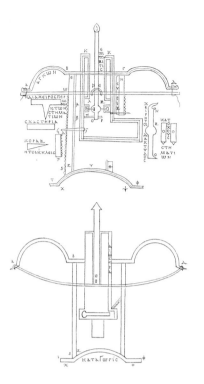

7.30
Crossbow or "belly shooter." Heron, *Belopoeica*, as redrawn in Carle Wescher, *Poliorcétique des grecs* (Paris, 1867), page 80.

7.31
Crossbow or "belly shooter." Biblioteca Apostolica Vaticana, Rome. Cod. gr. 1164, folio 110v.

7.32
Mobile battering ram, palace of Ashurnasirpal II at Kalakh, ninth century BC. British Museum, London.

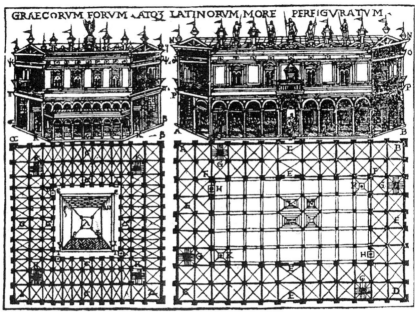

GRÆCORVM FORVM ATQ3 LATINORVM MORE PERFIGVRATVM

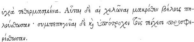

ἱερὰ πεθερμασμένα. Αὗται δὲ αἱ χελῶναι μακρόθεν βέλεσι πη-
λούσθωσαν· συμπεπηγυίαι δὲ κỳ ὑποτρόχοι ῖς τείχεσι προσφε-
ρέσθωσαν.

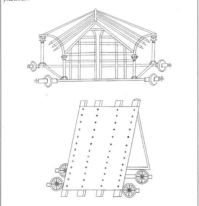

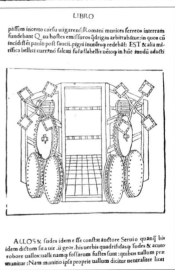

LIBRO

paſſim incerto cuirſu uagarent:Romani murices ferreos interram
fundebant Q̃ ua hoſtes emiſſuros q̃drigas arbitrabâtur:in quos cũ
incidiſt et paulo poſt ſaucii.pigri inutilesq̃ redebãt: EST & alia mi-
rifica bellici cure̅no falcati foꝛa flabellis ueioꝗ in hũc modũ adacti

ALLOS & ſudes idem e ſſe conſtat auctore Seruio quãꝗ bis
idem dictum ſit a uir .ii geor .his uerbis quadrifidasꝗ ſudes & acuto
robore uallos:ualli namꝗ foſſarum ſuſtes ſunt :quibus uallum præ
munitur :Nam munitio ipſa proprie uallum dicitur neutraliter licet

7.33
Cesare Cesariano, *De architectura*
(Como, 1521), V, 82r.

7.34
Apollodorus, *Poliorcetica*, tenth century.
Bibliothèque Nationale, Paris. Cod. par.
suppl. gr. 607, folio 59r.

7.35
Roberto Valturio, *De re militari*
(Verona, 1472).

explicit. In those parts drawn in orthogonal projection, the shadows cast by the object are utilized without any indication as to the location of the light source.[54] The flat representational method, in which the wheels are tipped with respect to the axles, was typical of late Roman and Byzantine models and its use was maintained for the whole of the early medieval period. In the early sixteenth century, the engineer Cesariano used it unhesitatingly in his edition of Vitruvius in order to show the elevation and perspectival sections at once.

In the second half of the fourteenth century, technological achievements underwent a considerable reevaluation. As far as siege machines were concerned, the main players continued to be trebuchets, ballistae, catapults and crossbows, and armored towers armed with rams' heads like the one represented in the bas-reliefs of Kalakh,[55] which date from the ninth century BC. Everything has already been perfected and now it is simply a case of repeating the gestures of the great men of the past, of mastering their technical secrets by means of illustrated manuscripts, and of reading Vegetius, Polybius, and Frontinus. The images of this period offer very little in the way of planning elements; the innovations are not so much to be found in the mechanical contrivances themselves as in the way they are deployed or used alongside already familiar mechanisms.

At the beginning of the fifteenth century,[56] the influence of perspective studies made itself felt in the field of machine representation. Brunelleschi transformed medieval fantasies into ponderous devices that lifted, squeezed, and sliced. The entire range of fourteenth-century representational methods, such as the simultaneous display of two parallel sides, or showing a mechanism's box with divergent sides, took its place alongside the organizing principle of perspective. Even though the machine continued to exist in its own functional space, the system of perspective that was spreading rapidly through the workshops of painters caught up with the machine and showed it off to the eyes of patrons. Fontana, Taccola, Valturio, and, above all others, Francesco di Giorgio Martini would reunite the rotated view with the viewpoints of their princely patrons who looked upon such costly *machinationes* with admiration and desire.

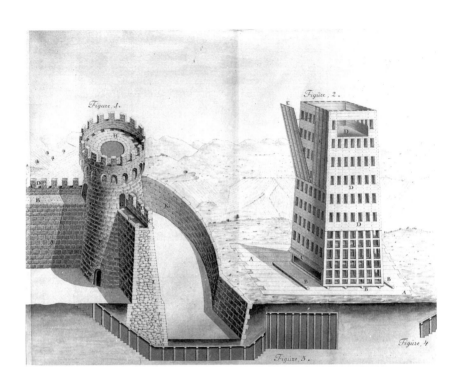

7.36
Studies for Archduke Joseph. *Lehrbuch
des Festungskrieges* (Vienna, 1760).
Österreichische Nationalbibliothek,
Vienna. Handschriften, Cod. S.n. 12002.

Notes

1. Plato, *Gorgias* 512c.

2. Vitruvius, *De architectura* 10.6.2.

3. At the beginning of Book X, Vitruvius expresses the wish that the same laws would apply in Rome as in Ephesus, where architects were made to pay the difference in cost if their works exceeded the original estimate by more than a quarter. *De architectura* 10.*praef*.1–3.

4. Vitruvius had already expressed his disapproval of the excessive costs of painted decorations. His objection to the decadence of painting, which he considered uselessly expensive and bizarre, was made in the form of a list of the pictorial genres that were to be found in painted imitations in Greek buildings between 50 and 40 BC. *De architectura* 7.5.

5. "Sine quibus nulla res potest esse non impedita [without which nothing can be unattended with difficulties]." Vitruvius, *De architectura* 10.1.3.

6. Vitruvius, *De architectura*, ed. Pierre Gros, trans. Antonio Corso and Elisa Romano (Turin: Einaudi, 1997), 2:1367, n. 20.

7. Vitruvius, *De architectura* 10.1.4.

8. Ibid., 10.1.2

9. On the representation of machines for lifting, see Philippe Fleury, *La mécanique de Vitruve* (Caen: Université de Caen, 1993), figs. 13–15. See also Giangiacomo Martines, "Macchine da cantiere per il sollevamento dei pesi nell'Antichità, nel Medioevo, nei secoli XV and XVI," *Annali di Architettura* 10–11 (2000): 261–275.

10. Vitruvius, *De architectura* 10.1.1.

11. Ibid., 10.3.1.

12. Ibid., 10.6.2. The text makes explicit reference to this figure, "in extremo libro eius forma descripta est in ipso tempore." To form a right angle with a rope divided by 13 knots, Vitruvius uses a triangle with catheti of 3 and 4 units and a hypotenuse of 5, according to a method already used by the Egyptians a few thousand years before Pythagoras (*De architectura* 9.*praef*.6). This method allowed a module to be fixed and to place the Archimedes's screw with the correct inclination along the hypotenuse. The physician Giuseppe Ceredi (*Tre discorsi sopra il modo di alzar acque da' luoghi bassi*, Parma: Seth Viotti, 1567) published a short work on Archimedes's screws in which, for the first time in a printed text, the ratio for the scale drawing was provided. See Carlo Maccagni, "Il disegno di macchine dal Medioevo al Rinascimento," in *Disegni di macchine* (Pordenone, 1987), 19.

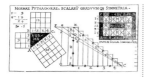

7.37
Cesare Cesariano,
De architectura (Como, 1521), IX, 145r.

7.38
Archimedes's screw. Agostino Ramelli, *Le diverse e artificiose machine ...* (Paris, 1588).

13. Renaissance editions of this book aroused the interest of illustrators, anticipating the fashion for *Theatri machinarum*, which only lessened toward the end of the sixteenth century when the art of mechanics took on a modern scientific dimension, along with perspective, stereotomy, cartography, etc. The enigmatic mention of the marvelous hydraulic machines pioneered by Ctesibius and Heron inspired numerous sixteenth-century publications on pneumatics, engendering a taste for mechanical marvels that was shared by princes, scientists, and scholars from the end of the sixteenth century. Along with the publication of classics of Greco-Alexandrian mechanics (*Artificiosi et curiosi moti spirituali d'Herrone*, trans. Giovan Battista Aleotti [Ferrara, 1598], and *Automati di Herone*, trans. Bernardino Baldi [Venice, 1589]), the inventories of machines built by technicians began to be published, such as Jacques Besson, *Theatrum instrumentorum et machinarum ...* (Lyon: apud Barth. Vicentium, 1578); Agostino Ramelli, *Le diverse ed artificiose machine composte in lingua italiana, e francese* (Paris: in casa dell'Autore, 1588). Vittorio Zonca, *Novo teatro di machine et edificii* (Padua: appresso Pietro Bertelli, 1607); Giovanni Branca, *Le machine* (Rome: Iacomo Mascardi, 1629); Georg Andreas Böckler, *Theatrum machinarum novum* (Cologne: publ. Paulus Furtsten, print. by Christoff Gerhard, 1662). See also the series of "theaters" published in Leipzig by Jacob Leupold: *Theatrum machinarum hydraulicarum* (1724), *Theatrum machinaria generale* (1724), *Theatrum machinarium hydrotechnicarum* (1725), *Theatrum pontificale* (1726), *Theatrum arithmetico geometricum* (1727), *Theatrum machinarum molarium* (1735), and numerous others, see Maccagni, "Il disegno di macchine dal Medioevo al Rinascimento," 16–17.

14. Pierre Gros, "Vitruvio e il suo tempo," in Vitruvius, *De architectura*, ed. Gros, 1:lx and 102, n. 294.

15. See the chapter "Demonstration Figures" in this book.

16. Vitruvius, *De architectura* 10.8.6.

17. See the chapter "The Idea of Model" in this book.

18. See Cicero's famous oration against Verres's depredations while governor of Sicily between 73 and 71 BC. Cicero, who referred to Verres scornfully as "graeculus," feigned indifference toward works of art for which the "Greeks nourish an incredible passion ... things for which we do not in the least care" (*In Gaium Verrem actionis* 4.127, 134). These were the years in which artworks from all around the Mediterranean were beginning to arrive in

Rome and the first collections were being established. It was, as Pliny would later write, "the end of wooden and terra-cotta statues in the temples of Rome, replaced by imported works of art" (*Naturalis historia* 34.34).

19. After mentioning Ctesibius's machine for pumping water (a bronze, two-cylinder pump), Vitruvius lets it be understood that he doesn't find pneumatic machines particularly useful because their sole aim is "pleasure and entertainment." However, those interested "may satisfy their curiosity by consulting directly the writings of the said Ctesibius" (*De architectura* 10.7.5). On the relationship between medicine and pneumatics, see the interesting theory of a correlation between Herophilus of Chalcedon's studies of the cardiac pump and Ctesibius's design for a two-cylinder pump, which works by means of a valve that is very similar to that of the heart. See Luigi Russo, *La rivoluzione dimenticata. Il pensiero scientifico greco e la scienza moderna* (Milan: Feltrinelli, 2001), 165.

20. Aristotle was aware of the power of images. In his *Rhetoric*, he recommends beginning an oration or a story with the description of a painting in an attempt to transfer to words something of the immediacy of the image. He defines visual evidence as *enárgheia*, laying things "before the eyes" (*Rhetoric* 1411b), and as *kinesis*, movement, as opposed to *ékphrasis*, the simple description of objects

21. Vitruvius, *De architectura* 10.2.1.

22. Ibid., 10.2.2.

23. Admiration for the culture of Archytas and Democritus induced him to state: "The discoveries of these men constitute a lasting service to mankind, not only to correct the morals of mankind, but also for the public good." He compared this with "the glory of the athletes [which] soon declines together with their bodies: so that they do not bring lasting good to mankind … as do instead men of science with their thinking" (Vitruvius, *De architectura* 9.*praef.*15).

24. Ibid., 10.1.4.

25. Ibid., 10.10.1.

26. Ibid., 10.11.1.

27. Ibid., 10.11.2.

28. Ibid., 10.16.1.

29. Lucian maintains that the *téchne* can only speak a stuttering language (*barbarízousa*) and compares him unfavorably with those familiar with the *paidéia*, the education based on the study of rhetoric and literature, which in antiquity was considered incomparably superior (*Vision* 8). "You may turn out a Phidias or a Polykleitos,

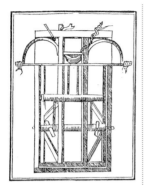

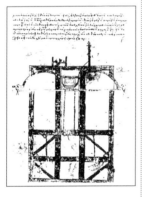

7.39
Top and middle: Ballista
according to Fra Giocondo
(1511) and comparison with
that of Biton. Bibliothèque
Nationale, Paris. Cod.
parisinus gr. 2442, folio 63v.
Bottom: Similar illustration
in Biblioteca Apostolica
Vaticana, Rome. Cod. vat. gr.
1164, folio 102v.3.

to be sure, and create a number of wonderful works; but even so, though your art will be generally commended, no sensible observer will be found to wish himself like you; whatever your real qualities, you will always rank as a common craftsman who makes his living with his hands…. Socrates himself was educated in Statuary, but no sooner could he discern the better part, than he deserted her and enlisted with me" (*Vision* 9 and 12).

30. In the *Iliad*, Hephaestus is a giant who, despite his powerful shoulders and hairy chest, limps along on spindly legs: "With that he heaved up from the anvil block—his immense hulk hobbling along but his shrunken legs moving nimbly. He swung the bellows aside and off the fires, gathered the tools he'd used to weld the cauldrons and packed them all in a sturdy silver strongbox. Then he sponged off his brow and both burly arms, his massive neck and shaggy chest, pulled on a shirt and, grasping a heavy staff, Hephaestus left his forge and hobbled on. Handmaids ran to attend their master, all cast in gold but a match for living, breathing girls. Intelligence filled their hearts, voice and strength their frames, from the deathless gods they've learned their works of hand. They rushed to support their lord as he went bustling on and, lurching nearer to Thetis, took his polished seat, reached over to clutch her hand and spoke her name" (*Iliad* 18.410–423). Thetis begs him to fashion new armor for Achilles and he consents, forging with apparent ease the mighty shield that, according to some scholars, represented a complex cosmological and cartographical encapsulation of the world.

31. Leon Battista Alberti, *L'architettura*, ed. Giovanni Orlandi (Milan: Polifilo, 1966), 1:64.

32. Plutarch attributes to Polykleitos an artistic approach of rigorous precision: "The most difficult part of a work is when the clay is under the fingernail … perfection is achieved by means of much measuring and by attention to the smallest details" (Plutarch, *Quaestiones conviviales* 636c).

33. "May be considered on a level with inanimate bodies that have exceptionally powerful hands which, in order to move weights, behave exactly as each one of us … with … bending in the same way as we bend our limbs and our nerves, in leaning, in pushing, pulling, and carrying weight" (Alberti, *L'architettura* 1:496).

34. The only drawing that can be attributed, with any certainty, to Alberti was identified by Howard Burns. See the chapter "The Idea of Model," n. 20, in this book.

35. Pier Nicola Pagliara has shown how Fra Giocondo used late antique poliorcetic manuscripts for the illustrations in his edition of Vitruvius. See Pagliara, "Una fonte di illustrazioni del Vitruvio di Fra Giocondo," *Ricerche di Storia dell'Arte* 6 (1977): 113–120.

36. Ranuccio Bianchi Bandinelli, *Hellenistic-Byzantine Miniatures of the Iliad (Ilias Ambrosiana)* (Olten: Graf, 1955), and "Virgilius Vaticanus 3225 e 'Ilias Ambrosiana.' Continuità ellenistica nella pittura di età medio e tardo antica," in *Archeologia e cultura* (Milan: R. Riccardi, 1961).

37. Paul Lawrence Rose, *The Italian Renaissance of Mathematics* (Geneva: Droz, 1975), 39.

38. *The Book of Knowledge of Ingenious Mechanical Devices by Ibn al-Razzaz al-Jazari*, trans. and with notes by Donald R. Hill (Boston: Reidel, 1974). The translation was based on the manuscript with the most complete and best-preserved set of illustrations (Oxford, Bodleian Library, MS. Graves 27). Two further copies of the Graves manuscript are preserved in Leiden (Universiteitbibliotheek, n. 117) and in Dublin (Chester-Beatty Library, MS. 4187).

39. In his introduction, al-Jazari (Abū al'Iz ibn Ismā'īl ibn al-Razāz al-Jaẓari, 1136–1206) supplies an interesting description of his methodology of work: "I found that some of the earlier scholars and sages had made devices and had described what they had made. They had not considered them completely nor had they followed the correct path for all of them, for every [part] of constructional knowledge was not verified in practice, and so wavered between the true and the false. So I assembled the division that they had separated and put forth branches from roots where they had been correct, and devised specimens which worked splendidly, lit internally and externally" (al-Jazari, *The Book of Knowledge*, 16).

40. Kurt Weitzmann, "The Greek Sources of Islamic Scientific Illustrations," in Clayton G. Miles, ed., *Archaeologica Orientalia in Memoriam Ernst Hertzfeld* (New York: J. J. Augustin, 1952), plate XXXIII, fig. 1. Only one eleventh-century manuscript copy remains of Heron of Alexandria's *Belopoiká* (Rome, Biblioteca Apostolica Vaticana, Cod. Gr. 1164). Among Heron's various treatises is also a *Mechanica*, of which a few fragments are extant. The Greek version is lost but an Arabic translation survives, made by Costa ben Luqa (Qusta ibn Luqa) between 862 and 866, and on which the French edition is based. See Bernard Carra de Vaux, *Héron d'Alexandria. Les mécaniques ou l'élévateur des corps lourds* (Paris: Belles Lettres,

7.40
Iusti Lipsi Poliorceticon sive De machinis, tormentis, telis, Libri quinque (Antwerp, 1596), page 162.

1988). The Leiden copy, which is the most complete, was copied in 1445 (Library of Leiden, Cod. 51 Gol). An anonymous text dating from the end of the eighth century, the *Archimede* shows not the machines in their entirety, but only sketches of some details, drawn with ruler and compass; each part is precisely named. The description is very short and lacks the clarity of al-Jazari. See al-Jazari, *The Book of Knowledge*, 10. Hill reveals that, compared to those of ben Musa (813–833), the machines of Philo and Heron made conical valves and were generally much more complex. The drawings of ben Musa are executed with a single stroke and usually also show the machine's interior (exploded view); measurements and details are not supplied and the explanatory text is never longer than a page. See al-Jazari, *The Book of Knowledge*, 9.

41. "At the same time the object is reduced to a two-dimensional plane, and this is typical of similar construction drawings in all poliorcetic treatises." Weitzmann, "The Greek Sources of Islamic Scientific Illustrations," 246.

42. This opinion was shared by the authors of the German edition, who used the same redrafted drawings. Ludwig Nix and Wilhelm Schmidt, *Herons von Alexandria Mechanik und Katoptrik* (Leipzig: Teubner, 1900).

43. For a contrary opinion, see Hill's observations on al-Jazari's treatise, judged by Needham to be clumsy. See al-Jazari, *The Book of Knowledge*, 279–280; Joseph Needham, "The Prenatal History of the Steam Engine," *Transactions of the Newcomen Society* 35 (1900): 57.

7.41
Pneumatica. Biblioteca Nazionale Marciana, Venice. Cod. Gr. Z. 516 (=904), folio 171r.

44. For the spindle or almond-shaped form of a circle, see the Greco-Latin version of Euclid's *Optics*: "Si in eondem plano in quo est oculus, circuli periferia ponatur, ea circuli periferia recta linea apparet" (*Liber de visu*, prop. 23). See Wilfred R. Theisen, *The Mediaeval Tradition of Euclid's Optics* (Ann Arbor: University Microfilms International, 1972), 77. In the translation from Arabic to Latin of the *Optics* of Ptolemy, edited by Admiral Eugenius of Sicily in the twelfth century, there is an explanation of an optical phenomenon that might be related to the perception of the circle in the egg shaped form: "Rursus res quae similes est disco, cum velocitate movetur circa aliquem diametrorum suorum, apparet illi qui eam aspicit lateraliter, et non a parte diametri, circa qui volvitur, habere figuram ovi." See *L'Ottica di Claudio Tolomeo da Eugenio Ammiraglio di Sicilia—Scrittore del Secolo XII. Ridotta in latino sovra la traduzione araba di un testo Greco imperfetto ...* , ed. Gilberto Govi (Turin: Stamperia reale della ditta G. B. Paravia e C. di I. Vigliardi, 1885), 41–42. Ptolemy's *Optics* was known to Roger Bacon, who cited it in many of his works.

45. The statutes of the city of Regensburg, approved by Emperor Maximilian in 1498, imposed total secrecy on the master builders regarding the secrets of their profession. See Pierre Du Colombier, *Les chantiers des cathédrales* (Paris, 1973), 52. However, it is clear from the booklet by Mathes Roriczer (*Von der Fialen Gerechtigkeit*, Regensberg, 1486), published with the consent of the bishop of Eichstätt, Wilhelm von Reichenau, that such secrecy was no longer adhered to, and had not been for a long time. On folio 3r he writes: "If you want to trace the outline of a spire according to the Steinmetz method of plane geometry, begin by making a square described here as follows with the letters a: b: c: d." He goes on with the description of an *ad quadratum* construction, which was already to be found in the well-known *Meno* by Plato and in the numerous copies of Vitruvius that were circulating in the Middle Ages (Plato, *Meno* 82b–85b; Vitruvius, *De architectura* 9. praef. 4–5). See Mathes Roriczer, *Il libretto delle proporzioni delle guglie*, ed. Franco Cardini, n.p. and n.d.; Matthäus Roriczer, *Das Büchlein von der Fialen Gerechtigkeit. Geometria Deutsch*, ed. Ferdinand Geldner (Hürttgenwald, 1998).

46. It is worth recalling here that calculations of the same type were being made as early as about 1800 BC in the plains of Mesopotamia. See John E. Murdoch, *Album of Science: Antiquity and Middle Ages* (New York: Scribner, 1984), 115. Villard, in a drawing on folio 20v, proposes

7.42
Illustration of a press contained in the manuscript of Heron's *Mechanics*. British Museum, London. Additional manuscript 23390. Below, reconstruction by Ludwig Nix.

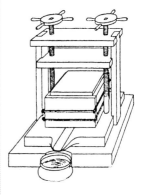

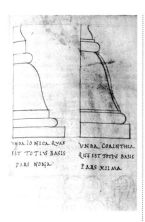

VNDA IO NICA QVAE
EST TOTIVS BASIS
PARS NONA

VNDA CORINTHIA
QVE EST TOTIVS BASIS
PARS XIIMA

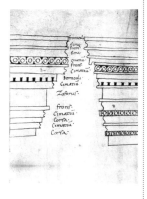

7.43, 7.44
Vitruvius, *De architectura*,
tenth-century copy.
Bibliothèque municipale,
Sélestat. Manuscript 1153,
folios 36 and 37.

dividing the square into two equal squares, a solution known to the author from the text of Vitruvius. The caption accompanying the drawing, written after Villard's death, reads: "[P]ar chu partis om une pirre que les II moitié sont queres" (in this way a stone may be divided so that the two halves are square). See Jean-Baptiste Antoine Lassus, *Album de Villard de Honnecourt*, with notes of J. Darcel (Paris, 1858). In the drawing for the facade of the cathedral of Strasbourg (c. 1275, Strasbourg, Musée de l'Opera, known as project B), the geometrical construction is based on a rigorous respect for proportions. The architect would present his plan without including measurements or architectural details; in some cases the plan was the architect's original creation, such as the one Villard de Honnecourt presented, together with Pierre de Corbie, in his *Portfolio*. The plan was frequently an imitation, but with the addition sometimes of more or less personal adaptations, as may be seen from the sketches that Villard made of the cathedral of Rheims before he began to work on Notre Dame de Cambrai. The facade could not be designed before the ground plan was decided because the architects derived it proportionally *ad quadratum* and *ad triangulum* from the church's ground plan. For a detailed study of Villard's *Portfolio*, see Roland Bechmann, *Villard de Honnecourt. La pensée technique au XIII siècle et sa communication* (Paris: Picard, 1991). This same procedure seems to have been central to the planning process in antiquity as well. A clue to this comes from Constantinople, after the earthquake of 557 destroyed part of Hagia Sophia. We learn that "Isidore the younger [grandson of Isidore of Miletus] and the other architects, upon examination of the earlier plan, and from the parts of the building still standing, could understand the structure of the parts that had fallen down." Agathias Scholasticus, "Storie. V," in Umberto Albini and Enrico V. Maltese, eds., *Bisanzio nella sua letteratura* (Milan: Garzanti, 1984), 140. As far as ancient Egypt is concerned, the planning procedure was closely linked to the sphere of the sacred and began with the ground plan, one side of which was measured in order to determine the other: "My perfection [Kheperkara, son of Ra, Sesostris] will be recorded thus in his temple: my name is the pyramid, my monument is the lake: these excellent monuments procure eternal life. The king whose works are remembered does not die." The king then addresses the royal treasurer who is his executor: "Your time is the moment of action, it is as long and as wide as you desire.... Order the workers to carry out what you have decided … then the chief ritualist, the scribe of the divine book, tightened the string and laid it on the ground. It was built in the same way as this temple." See *The Foundation of the Temple of Heliopolis*, a copy in hieratic on a leather scroll dating from the period of Amenhotep III (c. 1405–1367 BC, Berlin, Aegyptisches Museum und Papyrussammlung, P 30929); measurements were taken by means of a piece of string with 13 knots, the intervals of which corresponded to a cubit of seven spans (equivalent to 52.5 cm), which the Egyptians used also as a simple way of establishing a right angle. Senenmut, the architect of Deir el-Bahri, is often represented in block statues holding this rolled string in his hands.

47. In the thirteenth century Vincent of Beauvais lists the text of Vitruvius as present in his *Biblioteca mundi*. Petrarch mentions it in the margins of his copy of Virgil, and the book also figures among the sources of Boccaccio. The oldest known copy dates from the ninth century and contains drawings that are contemporary (Sélestat, Bibliothèque Municipale, MS. 1153bis). Around thirty copies circulated during the medieval period.

48. Heron of Alexandria's *Mechanics* lists five simple machines from the Greek mechanical tradition, which was well known to the Arabs: the winch or windlass, the lever, the double-sheave block or hoist and several pulleys (*polyspaston*), the wedge, and the screw. See Carra de Vaux, *Héron d'Alexandrie*, 115–121.

49. See Guidobaldo del Monte, *Mechanicorum liber* (Pesaro: Concordia, 1577); It. trans. *Le mechaniche tradotte in volgare da F. Pigafetta. Nelle quali contiene la vera dottrina di tutti gli strumenti principali da mover pesi grandissimi con picciola forza* (Venice, 1581).

50. See the trebuchet (*trabocco*) catapult shown in the fresco of *Guidoriccio da Fogliano* by Simone Martini (1328) in the Palazzo Pubblico, Siena.

51. The only ancient copy of Guido da Vigevano's manuscript is in the Bibliothèque Nationale in Paris. A later copy is in Turin in the Biblioteca Nazionale, MS. Lat. 11015.

52. The manuscript in Leyden (Universiteitbibliotheek, MS. Voss. Gr. 189, fol. 19r) is similar to that in the Vatican, which dates from around the eleventh century (Rome, Biblioteca Apostolica Vaticana, MS. Vat. Gr. 1164). See *Age of Spirituality* (New York: Metropolitan Museum, 1979), 213. The Carthaginians were the first to use the assault tower, or *helépolis*, in the siege of Selinunte.

53. See Conrad Kyeser, *Bellifortis*, ed. Götz Quarg (Düsseldorf: V.D.I. Verlag, 1967). See also Richard Neher, *Der anonymus de rebus bellicis, Inaugural-Dissertation .... von Richard Neher* (Tübingen: J. J. Heckenhauer, 1911), a study of the machines present in the *Notitia Dignitatum*. For a comparison between Taccola's machines and those contained in the *Notitia Dignitatum*, see Marcelin Berthelot, "Pour l'histoire des arts mécaniques et de l'artillerie vers la fin du Moyen Age," *Annales de Chimie et de Physique* 6, no. 24 (1891): 433–521.

54. Franz Maria Feldhaus, *Die Technik der Antike und des Mittelalters* (Potsdam: Athenaion, 1931), 340.

55. In a neo-Assyrian relief from Kalakh dating from the Ashurnasirpal II era (883–859 BC), an armored chariot is shown demolishing a tower with a battering ram. The chariot probably has an internal balancing mechanism; it is mounted on six wheels and is surmounted by a tower with three windows and a semispherical top in which the observers would have sat. Another relief from the same series shows all of the activities regarding the siege of a fortress. It is executed in orthogonal projection with the city represented symbolically on a much smaller scale than the armored chariot. Good reproductions of the reliefs can be found in Pierre Ducrey, *Guerre et guerriers dans la Grèce antique* (Paris: Office du Livre-Payot, 1985), 171 and 173; Eva Strommenger and Max Hirmer, *Cinq millénaires d'art mésopotamien* (Paris: Flammarion, 1964), plate 205.

56. For an interesting excursus on Renaissance engineers, see Paolo Galluzzi, *Gli ingegneri del Rinascimento da Brunelleschi a Leonardo da Vinci* (Florence: Giunti, 1996).

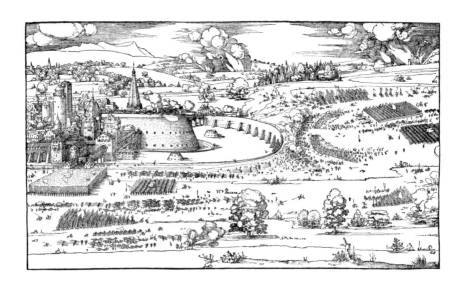

8.1
Albrecht Dürer, *Etliche Underricht, zu*
Befestigung der Stett, Schloss und Flecken
(Nuremberg, 1527).

8

SOLDIERLY PERSPECTIVE

"While I sing, Oh Lord our Savior / I see all Italy burning, set aflame / by these valorous French who have come / to lay waste I know not where."[1] Thus sang Captain Matteo Boiardo shortly before his death on 19 December 1494. Charles VIII had just invaded Italy with powerful artillery.[2] In September, before landing his troops, the Duke of Orléans assaulted Genoa with cannons, causing widespread panic when the city walls were destroyed and depriving the soldiers of their noble task of defending the population. Facing the lack of tactical intelligence, which made the weapons all the more terrifying, the city surrendered. Of course, the use of cannons in the battlefield was not new, but their adoption in attacking a city constituted an innovation in the art of war. The high medieval walls with their battlements and corbels were designed so that projectiles rained down on the enemy,[3] but these walls were no match for the French cannons.

It was no longer possible to solve the problem of defense by building walled structures, however high, and joining them together. Medieval fortification, which had remained faithful to the muscular structures of Hellenistic-Byzantine poliorcetics, now began to undergo a rapid and very expensive metamorphosis. Walls were modified in such a way as to make them thicker and lower so that they were able to resist cannon fire more effectively. Ancient towers, which had already been lowered during the second half of the fifteenth century, were replaced by bastions, the rounded forms of which had changed the appearance of fortresses at the beginning of the sixteenth century. Almost all the new projects abandoned multiple-level constructions, while cannons were positioned on *cavaliers*[4] (high platforms situated on top of the walls), or pulled back within the depths of the walls. French artillery radically changed the idea of warfare; wherever the French pointed their cannons, fortress construction was undertaken with greater rationality and precision. The task of the *guerriers mathématiques*[5] was to establish the distances between bastions and ravelins in order to pound the curtain broadside and shower it with

te.a e d.dal transito, ouer moto naturale.d b. ey dal ponto.a.il p onto
d.sia protratta la linea.a d c.hor dico che il ponto.d. è il piu lontan efs
fetto dal ponto.a.che far possa il detto corpo.b.sopra la linea. a d c. os
uer sopra quel piano doue è sita la detta linea, a d c. cosi conditione

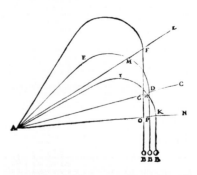

tamente eleuato.Perche se la detta possanza.a.a.traesse il medemo cors
po.b.piu elleuatamente sopra a l'orizonte ,quel faria il suo effetto di
moto naturale sopra la medema linea.a d c. come appar in la linea os
uer transito.a f g.m ponto.g.il qual eff. tto.g.dico che saria piu propin

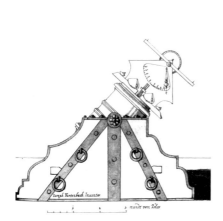

8.2
Joseph Furttenbach, *Halinitro-Pyrobolia*,
drawing. Österreichische Nationalbibliothek,
Vienna. Handschriften, Codex 10885.

8.3
Niccolò Tartaglia, *Quesiti et inventioni
diverse* (Venice, 1566).

fire. Vitruvius had recommended that "towers should be set at intervals not exceeding the range of an arrow";[6] sixteen centuries later, the calculation was updated to take into account the range of artillery fire.

In order to keep the besiegers' cannons at a distance, more complex building structures were studied, ditches were widened, and glacis enlarged. Geometric planning now determined how fortifications were built, imposing order upon the various parts of the fortress according to forms the proportions and sizes of which corresponded among themselves. Mathematician Niccolò Tartaglia's studies of the trajectories of projectiles were instrumental in curtailing architects' freedom, first by bringing about a geometrical modification of the outer walls of bastions and then by completely changing the way they were built.[7] Toward the first half of the sixteenth century, the debate about whether to continue thickening the walls or to shield them concluded in favor of the latter solution. For Tartaglia it was evident that "man's ingeniousness may be seen in the form of his walls, and not in the material, that is to say, in the thickness of them."[8]

After the decision was made to build a fortress, the question arose of which building tradition should inspire the project. The Prince had to decide whether to entrust his plans to Vitruvian tradition or to update them according to experience and the principles of the art of war. The factoring in of violence with civil planning was not so straightforward for those who had always followed the Vitruvian *venustas* imperative. Increasingly, the unlikely combination of medieval *machinatio* and Vitruvian philology came to be seen as an antiquarian blazon the sole purpose of which was to fulfill the dreams of princes, as in contraptions like the eagle-topped carriages that, three centuries later, Voltaire dared to propose to Richelieu and to Empress Catherine II.[9]

In the theater of modern warfare a more experimental and dramatic military dynamic took the place of consolidated defensive schemes and the knightly conduct of Orlando.[10] War was no longer "a noble and unanimous impulse of souls bent on glory," as Fabrizio del Dongo still dreamt three centuries later at the Battle of Waterloo.[11] Death came from afar, and with hissing speed. Invisible to the defenders, the fiery mouths of cannons snatched their victims away in a puff of smoke; there wasn't even time to look your enemy in the eye before dying. The scene was dominated by the figure of the bombardier who, from the heights of his deafening empiricism, demanded that Tartaglia "investigate speculatively the order and proportion of the shots."[12] The fortress became a Vitruvian *machina* in the true sense of the term, in which the cannons (*organa*) were modulated on the basis of the size of projec-

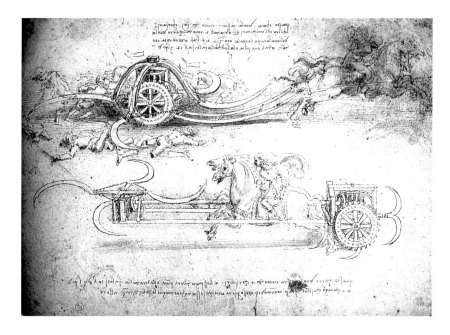

8.4
Leonardo da Vinci, chariot with scythe.
Biblioteca Reale, Turin.

8.5
Roberto Valturio, *De re militari*
(Verona, 1472).

tile they shot and the distance they had to cover.[13] The military engineers who presided over the design and execution of the new defense works were now asked to make their representations correspond with the geometrical power of the new firearms.

The astonishing penetrative capacity of the new steel projectiles was another factor that called for fresh ideas regarding building materials. The Italians, who above all loved beauty in architecture, obstinately studied the deflection angles of stone, as may be seen in the diamond-faceted Fortezza da Basso in Florence; northern fortress builders, on the other hand, proceeded unhesitatingly to build lower and thicker walls in more yielding materials. The "scorched earth" area (*guasto*) in front of curtain walls was shored up by the demolition of houses and churches, and no aesthetic questions were raised regarding the form of the city that this "device" controls and protects.

The production of treatises on fortifications, which had proceeded apace during the second half of the sixteenth century, now came into conflict with a type of architectural practice that recognized competence solely in the mastery of actual building skills and seemed not to contemplate the possibility of establishing a theory. None of the treatises on fortification venture beyond the almost immediate application of their proposals, while any technique acquired by experience is inscribed almost directly onto the built forms, without passing through the written word.[14] As Vitruvius had already asserted in the closing pages of his treatise, no machine can defeat tactical genius and the *architectorum sollertia*;[15] this meant an even greater range of overlapping competencies, and new *sollertiae* were expected of fortress builders: they had to be experts in weaponry, in administration, geometry, and architectural design. Nobody thought of inserting beauty as one of the prime exigencies of building; other components became a priority in planning, and it was left to the best solution to define beauty, just as in mathematics the best solution is always the most elegant.

When Buonaiuto Lorini, the pupil of Francesco Maria della Rovere, claimed that "experience allows us to recognize the errors of science, for the plan is never so perfect as the site,"[16] he was simply acknowledging that the asymmetrical elements of the site, which would reverberate in the fortress as deformities, constituted yet another element to be taken into account during the design process. Site and building interacted as never before. Representation came to terms with this novelty, penetrating the terrain in order to show underground workings[17] with large-scale, highly precise sections of fortified places: sections that bear a singular resemblance to the anatomical drawings of Leonardo or the sections of mines drawn by Georgius Agricola.[18]

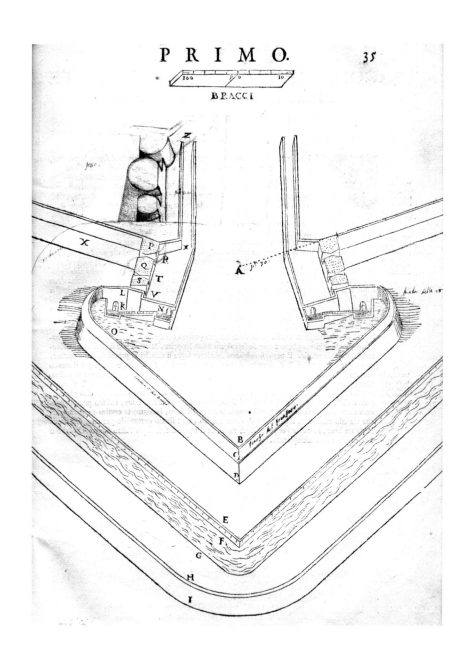

8.6
Buonaiuto Lorini, *Delle fortificazioni* (Venice, 1597), page 35.

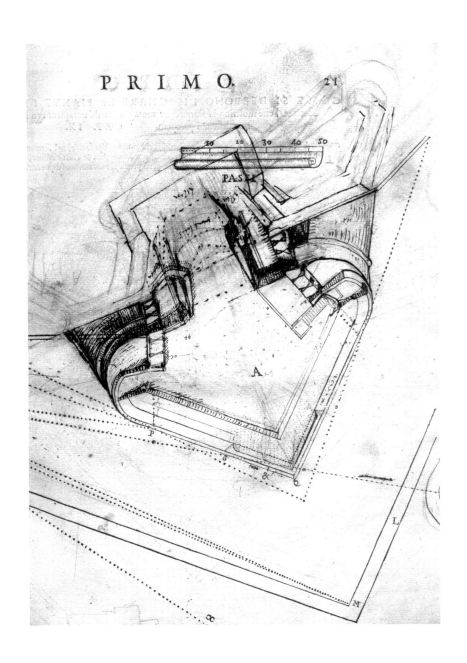

8.7
Buonaiuto Lorini, *Delle fortificazioni* (Venice, 1597), page 21.

Villa architecture had colonized its surroundings with the neat geometrical layout of gardens. Now nature's disharmonies acted like a second nature with a military *raison d'être* defining the contours of the defensive organism in an unprecedented way. The clear space in front of the curtain wall is incorporated in fortress design in order to disturb ballistic alignments and control the enemy's approach. Architects conceived an aesthetically pleasing and productive topography for the civilian landscapes of their villa-palaces. Now, with the advent of the fortress, the landscape became a pitted wasteland enveloped in dangerous, uneven and unexpected topography: the bucolic park was swept aside to make way for the ravaged area of the *guasto*.

Adaptation to the new conditions of war became a *conditio sine qua non*. For architects, this involved renouncing beauty per se in favor of the best possible adjustment to utility. For bombardiers, it meant acquiring drawing ability and proficiency in geometry and mathematics; for engineers trained in the fifteenth-century tradition, it meant learning how to organize and direct complex building sites with precision and economy.

Thus, the fortress builder progressively abandoned Vitruvius. Numerous specialists now began to cluster around the fortress: mathematicians such as Galileo; politicians such as Machiavelli;[19] architects such as Sangallo, Alghisi, Michele Sanmicheli; military engineers like Castriotto, Lorini, Giangirolamo Sanmicheli; bombardiers and soldiers such as Della Valle[20] and Capobianco.[21] There were also noblemen with a passion for war, clergymen as well as literary figures such as Maggi. Among this mixed array we also find doctors[22] who invented instruments for land surveying,[23] painter-spies who depicted the enemy's fortresses,[24] and adventurers who kept up-to-date lists of the most famous fortresses.[25]

After centuries of scholastic abstraction there was a return to direct observation and experimental verification. Anatomy, mechanics, architecture, astronomy, pyrotechnics, hydraulics, and pneumatics began to search in the real world for proof of the figures that had been passed down through ancient manuscripts to the era of Christopher Columbus. While sixteenth-century anatomical studies entered their post-Galenic phase with the dissection of the human body, the body of the building was subjected to a similar sectioning by the penetrating gaze of Leonardo. The most sophisticated descriptive techniques were subjected to scrutiny on the operating table of sixteenth-century representation. When it came to costly enterprises like designing fortresses, what mattered most was to make a rapid and accurate exposition of the basic criteria.[26] Like other sciences, the new science of fortification building had to

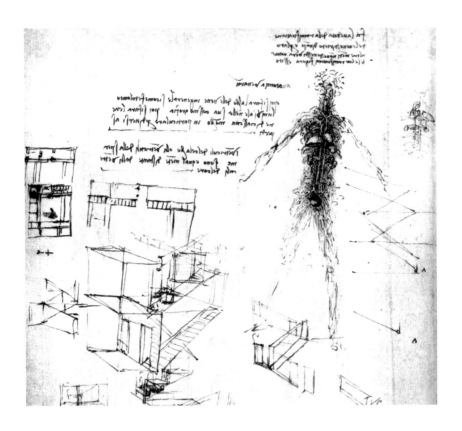

8.8
Leonardo da Vinci, stairs and the circulatory
system. Royal Library, Windsor Castle.
RL 12592r.

select its own method of representation and it did so by shifting to the inter-section between the new discipline of ballistics and that of military practice. The context within which this reconfiguration arose was a difficult one, par-ticularly with regard to the progressive abandonment of perspective repre-sentation. The sixteenth-century building site had evolved in such a way that a rapidly widening rift had appeared between the actual construction work and how its procedures were represented graphically. This had resulted in a separation between "the adaptation and diffusion of graphic techniques."[27] While architects remained faithful to Vitruvian definitions of *orthographia*, *ichnographia*, and *scaenographia*, and Raphael had his own reservations about perspective,[28] bombardiers and engineers tended instead to favor simpler and more synthetic procedures that enabled a more immediate description of the geometries of military action.

The measurement of a length must run parallel to the outline of which it is the graphic transcription: where a building has parallel lines, these can-not be rendered as converging lines in either the plan or the elevation of the building. On the battlefield, what sense would there be in drawing a fortress in perspective, which is the "sketching of the front and of retracting sides and the correspondence of all the lines to the center of the circumference"?[29] Everything that the medieval craftsman had been reticent to show in his model or drawing now had to be made explicit: the slightest discrepancy between the plan and the construction might leave many heads unprotected, with the consequent loss of the fortress. Unlike the procedure followed in civil architecture, in which the plan and elevations were prepared separately, in fortification design the two were planned together in order to facilitate rapid comparisons that would indicate the parts most likely to be hit by artillery fire.[30] The single viewpoint might have been of use to a landscape artist, but not to an artilleryman.

Slowly, the different disciplines entered into competition, incorporated and transformed one another. When a new professional conformation became unsatisfying, the spiral of adaptation began over again, with new roles being defined or preexisting ones transformed and completed. This process of assimilating diverse and contradictory military forms within a branch of the arts took some time.[31] Ennio Concina has shown how, as early as the first quarter of the sixteenth century in Venice, it had become necessary to clarify the difference between a *proto* and a soldier, or between an "engineer and a person expert in military matters."[32] In the preamble to a decree of 12 December 1526, it was emphasized that "the service of an expert engineer was needed for the many buildings erected for the fortification of the lands and the localities."[33] It was also clear, however, that the person in overall charge was the captain-general, whereas the engineer or the architect had only to carry out his orders.[34] In this way, the contrast between architect and engineer became, in the end, a problem of secondary importance.

In this chain of command, *res militare* seemed to prevail over *res aedificatoria*; although the services of an architect were often required for the "design" of the fortification, a clear distinction starts to be made between his activity and that of the engineers who directed the works.[35] The building of a fortress conditioned the work of everybody involved according to a rationale that was external to each of their separate disciplines. It was the rationale of the prince who gave shape to his political design with his mind's eye: "The mind's eye sees more fully into general things that the corporeal eye is able to see of details."[36]

Toward the end of the sixteenth century, the experimental phase ended and the discussion of theory in relation to practice was resolved by uniting the various qualities necessary in the same person. In order to "perfect a fortress, he who designs it should be a soldier whose experience of war has taught him good planning, while the captain should be a good master builder."[37] Should it be impossible to find the two qualities united in the same person, Belluzzi's advice was, "First, go to war. Then in peacetime, try to learn the true principles of Mathematics and of Architecture by the continual practice of drawing."[38]

In insisting on the importance of drawing, Belluzzi also suggests a representational method: "perspective which is useful to practice."[39] This type of representation was the opposite of that used by the painter for the simple reason that "the single viewpoint is of no use when it is necessary to show everything." A year before, Lorini had published his famous treatise in which he called this graphic procedure *prospettiva più comune*: "drawing the lines so that they fall perpendicularly in such a way that *even if they continued to infinity they would still be parallel to each other* … and in this way, a wall will be formed whose height will be perceived from diverse viewpoints, that is, from the inside and the outside, as if it were a real building in the country-side."[40] It was a procedure that had nothing in common with another simple projective idea, which would shortly be expressed by François d'Aguilon in his *Opticorum libri sex*.[41] His preferred representational method, which he called "perspective which is useful to practice" or "more common perspective," may be considered to have derived naturally from the older oblique drawing. Thus it was that Belluzzi and Lorini brought to a close a phase of graphic experimentalism that had endured, in a military context, for almost half a century. Before them, erudite men of letters such as Girolamo Maggi da Anghiari and the engineer and soldier Jacomo Castriotto had published an unusual treatise[42] in which the perspectival method was openly criticized and compared unfavorably to soldierly perspective.[43] This method, which reached its highpoint with Perret at the beginning of the seventeenth century, opened the long chapter of cavalier perspective. But the exclusion of vast portions of the battlefield from the design would lead to these perspectives being progressively abandoned in favor of plans and side elevations. Later, chromatic information[44] was added, and the introduction of spot elevations at the beginning of the nineteenth century led to the definitive abandonment of cavalier perspective. Oblique drawing, which Pomponius Gauricus termed *paralleli modo*, brought the "measured" illustrations found in treatises of architecture (Cesare Cesariano) and of practical geometry (Oronce Finé) in the first half of the sixteenth century closer to antique manuscript illustrations, upon which the scientific texts of the Renaissance were based. And indeed, sixteenth-century scholars were accustomed to seeing the parallel projection method as the more habitual method used for the illustrations in manuscripts about *machinatio*, practical geometry, clocks, pneumatics, and poliorcetics. In a certain sense, the continuing use of that method must have been perceived as a guarantee of their antique origins and thus of their authoritative quality. This almost certainly accounts for Fra Giocondo's decision to retain "the original mode of presentation" in his edition of Vitruvius, thus ensuring its philological correctness.[45]

Measured outlines, like footprints, have no point of view. Their size depends directly on the size of the thing they represent and they reflect its proportions through direct contact. Thus we find parallelism maintained in drawings of small areas of measured trabeations[46] and in the design of fortresses. In those operations involving accurate measurement, foreshortened representations are abandoned in favor of a tactile experience in which the hand ascertains the parallelism of the object and transcribes it in the survey drawing. It seems almost as if the representation is "deboned" and flattened out into the geometric plan, removing any trace of Lucretius's *obscurum coni acumen*. Leon Battista Alberti noted precisely this distinction between the painter's drawing and architectural drawing, in which "the architect rejects shading but takes his projections from the ground plan, and without altering the lines and by maintaining the true angles, reveals the extent and shape of each elevation and side—he is one who desires his work to be judged not by deceptive appearances but according to certain calculated standards."[47]

8.9
Joseph Furttenbach the Elder, *Mannhafter Kunstspiegel* (Ulm, 1662). Österreichische Nationalbibliothek, Vienna. Handschriften, Codex 10848.

But this was not the only reason for the adoption and diffusion of oblique drawing. In medieval poliorcetics, the object of the campaign, the fortress, was rarely shown on the same sheet of paper as the siege machine, the real protagonist of the campaign: what was shown was the space in which the machine functioned.[48] Now that the campaign was carried out from a distance, along certain given trajectories, the fortress itself became a kind of siege machine and was represented as such, according to the method typical of late antique *machinatio*.[49] This type of representation, defined as oblique drawing, was customary in Greco-Byzantine treatises, as well as in later Arab ones. And even if the antiquity of those machines was impossible to demonstrate, the method by which they were represented is certainly ancient. Grappling with the problem of dating medieval inventions, Marc Bloch wrote: "a millwheel … a plough, a horseshoe, a rustic wool-winder; none of these things have a style," so that we are unable to "establish the date of their invention."[50] Function does not have a style, but the way it is represented does, even if, frequently, bas-reliefs and miniatures are allocated new functions yet are produced by antique methods in order to bestow upon them the authority of an earlier era.

Notes

1. "Mentre che io canto, o Iddio redentore, / vedo la Italia tutta a fiama e a foco / per questi Galli, che con gran valore / vengono per disertar non so che loco." Matteo Boiardo, *Orlando innamorato*, ed. Aldo Scaglione (Turin: UTET, 1963), II, 625 (3, IX, 26).

2. The Christian West had already witnessed the power of cannon fire in 1453 when it pounded the walls of Constantinople, bringing about the fall of the city and the end of the reign of Constantine XI, the last of the Palaeologi. The French artillery that arrived in Italy on 2 September 1494 was proportional to an army of 40,000 men. In his *Storia d'Italia* (I, 9 and 11), Guicciardini counted 40,000 men, 36 large caliber guns, 104 culverins, 200 light falconets and 1,200 heavy harquebuses. On Charles VIII's artillery, see Piero Pieri, *Il Rinascimento e la crisi militare italiana* (Turin, 1952), 332, n. 1.

3. In the eleventh century, Cecaumenos advised building a second wall behind the outer wall of the city in case the enemy erected an embankment in front of the city. Two centuries later, Georgius Pachimeres recounted that the towers "were heightened by three cubits and the walls were also heightened, in proportion to the towers." See also the extraordinary description of the fall of Thessaloniki (1185) in the account given by Eustace of Thessaloniki, in which the enemy are described as "devourers of the wall": their "diggers, having completed their work, retreated to the tents of their comrades, while the supporting posts of the small tunnel were set on fire so that the wall began to weaken…. Thus when that infernal abyss opened up beneath us, it dragged us into mortal chaos." Umberto Albini and Enrico V. Maltese, eds., *Bisanzio nella sua letteratura* (Milan: Garzanti, 1984), 426–427, 617–620, 717.

8.10
Leonhard Beck (1480–1542), *The Battle of Padua*, woodcut, detail. Private collection.

4. The term *prospettiva alla cavaliera*, or simply *cava-liera* (cavalier perspective), derives from military termi-nology and is used to indicate the view obtained from an elevated position. "Cavaliers were and still are built in order to dominate the landscape and to engage the enemy from a greater distance, placed halfway along the curtain walls between the ramparts," in Carlo Theti (or Tetti), *Di-scorsi delle fortificazioni ove diffusamente si dimostra quali debbano essere i siti delle fortezze, le forme, i recinti, fossi, baloardi, castelli et altre cose a loro appartenenti con le figure di esse ora di nuovo da lui medesimo ricorrette, et ampliate del secondo libro* (Venice: Bolognino Zaltieri, 1575), I, x, 40. In one of his discourses on the fortifications of Candia (1537), Francesco Maria della Rovere speaks of the posi-tion in which the enemy finds himself on the counter-scarp: "quasi cavaliero a me" (almost below me). Ennio Concina, "*Discorsi militari, Istruttioni per la fortificazione*: La fortificazione della città," in *La macchina territoriale* (Bari: Laterza, 1983), 88. Lanteri suggests that the cavalier be placed "at the corners of the fortification." Giacomo Lanteri, *Due libri di M. Giacomo Lanteri del modo di fare le fortificazioni* (Venice: F. Marcolini, 1559), 19. Busca defines cavaliers as "buildings that stand out from the walls as a man seated on a horse overlooks those who are on foot." Gabriello Busca, *Dell'architettura militare, libro primo* (Milan: Girolamo Bordone & Pietro Martire Locarni, 1601), 157. For Bachot, "les cavaliers sont terasses eslevées sur le rampar, qui surpassent autant les autres ouvrages, qu'un Cavalier fait un homme de pied." Ambroise Bachot, *Le Gouvernail d'Ambroise Bachot capitaine ingenieur du Roy. Le quel conduira le curieux de Geometrie en perspective dedans l'architecture des fortifications, machines de guerre & plusieurs autres particularitez y contenues* (Melun: Bruneval, 1598), 29. The first time the term *prospettiva cavaliera* appears in a printed text is, as far as we know, in Manesson Mallet: "Ce chapitre prescript les regles qu'il faut observer pour representer les Plans dessignez sur le Papier, avec quelque Elevation; ce qu'on appelle ordinairement *perspective à la cavaliere*…. J'explique maintenant les moyens de leur donner quelque elevation; cela se fait, soit par l'usage des simples lignes qui son perpendiculaires ou paralleles entr'elle ce qu'on appelle Perspective cavaliere, soit en determinant un point de veuë … selon les regles de la perspective vulgaire." And as far as ordinary perspec-tive is concerned, he says that, "Cette maniere est fort embarassante … qui a ses Regles et Maximes particulieres, le plus souvent inconnuës a ceux qui suivent le Metier de

la guerre." Alain Manesson Mallet, *Les traveaux de Mars ou l'art de la guerre* (Amsterdam, 1672), 97, 155.

5. Bachot, *Le Gouvernail*, 3. Bachot was in charge of the fortifications of Melun in 1596. The *Dictionnaire de biographie française* cites only his son Jérôme (1588–1635), son-in-law of Charles Errard senior, who succeeded him as administrator of the fortifications in Brittany. Michel Prévost and Roman d'Amat, eds., *Dictionnaire de biographie française*, vol. 4 (Paris: Letouzey et Ané, 1956), 1091. The younger Bachot executed the drawing entitled "Vue cavalière dudict fort A, comme l'a commandé Monseigneur, le 18 juin 1625" in the collection of Benjamin Fillon. Among the many drawings he appropriated by signing them as the work of "Ambrosius Bachotus parisiensis inventor," is "l'art de notre perspective," which consists of "montrer en desseing ce que nostre oeil peut naturellement recognoistre" (plate 71). Naturally, this was a *military* parallel projection, a technique quite widespread by this date. An interesting insertion in the copy consulted is in plate 76: "Exemple d'une maniere universelle du S.G.D.L.... pour la coupe des pierres" (Paris, Bibliothèque Nationale, Rés. v. 411). This is clearly the method invented by Girard Desargues. The presence of this plate indicates that the collection was still being assembled at least until 1636–1640. In fact, Desargues's perspective method had been developed in 1636 and was published in only fifty copies in 1639 under the title *Brouillon projet*. Under the same title, Desargues published an essay on stereotomy, to which this plate refers.

6. Marcus Vitruvius Pollio, *Architettura*, ed. Silvio Ferri (Milan: Rizzoli, 2002), 125.

7. Niccolò Tartaglia, *Nova scientia* (Venice: Nicolò de Bascarini, 1550). In Book III, 23, there is an illustration of an instrument for calculating the trajectory of projectiles. Tartaglia was the first to scientifically establish laws of ballistics based on Euclidean geometry and the theory of *impetus* (the transition between motionlessness and violent movement). He demonstrated that cannons could reach their maximum range if the barrel was elevated 45 degrees to the horizon, and determined that the same target could be hit by firing at two different elevations whose angles were complementary. In Germany his ideas were emulated by Ryff, who wrote the first German book on modern fortification after that of Dürer. In the section of the book dedicated to ballistics, Ryff admitted his debt to Tartaglia. Walther Hermann Ryff [Gualterius Rivius], *Der furnembsten ... der Architectur*

Aurum probatur igni, ingenium uero Mathematicis.

8.11
The instruments of the
arts. Walther Hermann Ryff
(Gualterius Rivius),
*Der furnembsten notwen-
digsten der gantzen
Architectur …*(Nuremberg,
1547).

angehörigen mathematischen und mechanischen Künst (Nuremberg: G. H. Rivium, 1547), 4:1–52. See also Albrecht Dürer, *Etliche Underricht, zu Befestigung der Stett Schloss, und Flecken* (Nuremberg: gedruckt nach der gepurt Christi, 1527); Latin translation in *Alberti Dureri pictoris et architecti praestantissimi de urbibus, arcibus, castellisque condendis, ac muniendis rationes aliquot, praesenti bellorum necessitati accomodatissimae: nunc recens e lingua Germanica in Latinam traductae* (Paris, 1535).

8.   Niccolò Tartaglia, *Quesiti et inventioni diverse* (Venice: Venturino Ruffinelli, 1546), 140.

9.   Somewhat tardily, Destrées stated in 1563 that artillery had rendered every one of Vegetius's siege machines useless. As confirmation of his audacious theory, Destrées hit upon the idea of making a list of all the cities in France that had been conquered by French artillery fire. J. Destrées, *Discours des villes* (Paris: 1563). For Voltaire's proposal, see Anonymous, *Le cose della guerra*, introduction by Andrea Giardina (Milan: Mondadori, 1989), X–XI. For medieval *machinatio*, see Francesco Paolo Fiore, *Città e macchine del '400 nei disegni di Francesco di Giorgio Martini* (Florence: Olschki, 1978). For fourteenth- and fifteenth-century treatises: the treatise on war machines by Guido da Vigevano (Turin, Biblioteca Nazionale, MS. Lat. 11015, c.1328); Taccola [Mariano di Jacopo], *De ingeniis* (1427–1433) and *De machinis* (1441–1449), which contain illustrations of all the machines described in Vegetius's *Epitoma* and Frontino's *Stratagemmata*; Roberto Valturio, *De re militari libri XII* (Verona: Johannes de Verona, 1472), written for Sigismondo Malatesta, and printed with woodcuts by Matteo de' Pasti. Valturio's work is divided into twelve books, and is more important for its language than for the illustrations; Giovanni Fontana, *Bellicorum instrumentorum liber* (Munich, Bayerische Staatsbibliothek, Cod. Icon. 242, 1420–1450), in Eugenio Battisti and Giuseppina Saccaro Battisti, *Le macchine cifrate di Giovanni Fontana* (Milan: Arcadia, 1984). Fontana, who was familiar with the works of Heron, Philo, and Al-Kindi, also corresponded with Biagio Pelacani da Parma. The drawings in the *Nova compositio horologii* (Bologna, Biblioteca Universitaria, MS. 2705, 1418) show a combination of conical and cylindrical representations, most of which show the space enclosing the gears. In figure 19 the parallelism of the vertical lines corresponding to the horizontal diameter is deliberately distorted in order to show as much as possible of the interior, which tends to disappear beyond the point of the diameter. See Bertrand Gille, *Les ingénieurs de la Renaissance* (Paris, 1964), and Marcelin

Berthelot, "Sur le traité *De rebus bellicis*," *Journal des Savants* (March 1900): 171–177. Francesco di Giorgio Martini was the first to return to the study of war machines in Vitruvius's *De architectura*. Fiore, *Città e macchine*, 28–29. In his search for correspondences between the treatises of Taccola, Valturio, and Martini, Fiore has noted similarities between the drawings of the *Raccolta*, those of Harley's *Codicetto*, and the miniatures contained in *Notitia Dignitatum* and *De rebus bellicis*, a Byzantine *corpus* that has come down to us through a Carolingian copy. Berthelot suggests a comparison between Taccola's machines and those contained in the *Notitia Dignitatum*. Marcelin Berthelot, "Pour l'histoire des arts mécaniques et de l'artillerie vers la fin du Moyen Age," *Annales de chimie et Physique* 24, no. 6 (1891): 433–521.

10. Ariosto's invective against the arquebus, spoken through the voice of Orlando, fell on deaf ears: "O Maledetto, o abominoso ordigno, / che fabricato nel tartareo fondo / fosti per man di Belzebù maligno / che ruinar per te disegnò il mondo" (Oh wicked and abominable weapon, / fashioned in deepest Tartary, / by the evil Belzebeeb's hand, / to lay waste to the world) and "ch'al fulmine assimiglia in ogni effetto" (the effect of which is like that of a thunderbolt). Orlando hurls it into the depths of the sea with the accusation: "mai cavalier per te essere ardito, / né quanto il buono val, mai più si vanti il rio per te valere" (you have destroyed military glory, and dishonored the profession of arms; valor and martial skill are now discredited, so that often the miscreant will appear a better man than the valiant). Ariosto lists the effects of cannon fire in a tone of indignance: "che 'l ferro spezza, e i marmi apre e ruina, / e ovunque passa si fa dar strada" (it splits steel, and smashes stone to pieces, wherever it goes nothing can resist it). Ludovico Ariosto, *Orlando Furioso*, ed. Lanfranco Caretti (Torino: Einaudi, 1971), 22. English translation by Guido Waldman (Oxford: Oxford University Press, 1998).

11. In the midst of the Battle of Waterloo, Fabrizio del Dongo watches "a piece of tilled land that was being ploughed up in a singular fashion." The effect was due to silent cannon balls falling so that the soil "was flying about in little black lumps, three or four feet into the air." Stendhal, *La Certosa di Parma*, trans. Camillo Sbarbaro (Turin: Einaudi, 1976), 49.

12. Alessandro Biral and Paolo Morachiello, *Immagini dell'ingegnere tra Quattro e Settecento* (Milan: Franco Angeli, 1985), 32.

13. On the idea of the basic unit or module determining the construction of catapults and scorpions in classical artillery, see the relationship between the opening through which the rope to be twisted is wrapped, representing the unit, and the machine as a whole. See Vitruvius, *De architectura*, ed. Pierre Gros, trans. Antonio Corso and Elisa Romano (Turin: Einaudi, 1997), 2:1392, n. 161.

14. Zanchi observed that, "after the invention of artillery," nobody had discovered a new way to fortify towns that was not based on the writings of antique authors. The few men that had "served for long years in the military" and who, "having undergone numerous trials, have come to several very well-founded conclusions, and there being naturally very few of them, and these few being reluctant to express their opinion, either because they had only a soldier's training and knew nothing of military doctrine and held it in disdain and ignored it, and all the more easily because, as far as I know, there was no notable and true principle that had been established for those who wanted to make rules on the matter of building, so it was made all the more difficult." Giovan Battista de' Zanchi, *Del modo di fortificare le città* (Venice: Francesco Marcolini, 1556). It is known that many military works were lost because they were never printed, due to security concerns or to lack of interest in military theory. The isolated case of Charles V's *mestre de campe* is emblematic: Castaldo dictated his observations to Centorio degli Hortensi and the latter turned these into a work of military theory. Ascanio Centorio degli Hortensi, *I Discorsi di guerra divisi in cinque libri* (Venice: Gabriel Giolito de' Ferrari, 1558; further editions 1559, 1560, 1562, 1566). For a translation of Zanchi's work into French, see François de La Treille, *Manière de fortifier villes, chasteaux et faire autres liex fortz, mise en françoys par ...* (Lyon: Guillaume Rouillé, 1556). On page 72, he is critical of the amount of time required by the perspective procedure ("et encore que la premiere soit longue"). Among the necessities he lists is "perspective ... pour considerer et scavoir la distance and hauteur ... la manuelle Architecture des modelles, pour faire apparoir a chascun l'idee de son entendement ... mais la moins necessaire." La Treille claims that many people are capable of making models, but not of carrying out calculations.

15. "The techniques of defense thus require that one equips oneself not only with machines but above all with tactical plans [*maxime consilia sunt comparanda*]. ... Cities were able to resist besiegers not with the help of machines but rather thanks to the intelligence of archi-

tects." Vitruvius, anticipating the current of thought that was opposed to treatises, writes that "regarding defense systems, they should not be illustrated in a treatise, for the enemy certainly do not arrange their siege systems according to what we have written, and on the other hand, it often happens that their siege engines are destroyed by chance anyway without the help of machines, thanks to a fast-acting and ingenious tactical ability." He cites as an example the siege of Rhodes in which the *helépolis* built by Demetrius I Poliorcetes, 125 feet high, was captured by means of a cunning strategy whereby the colossal machine became stuck in the mud in front of the walls. See Vitruvius, *De architectura* 10.16.2 and 10.16.8; Vegetius, *Epitoma rei militaris* 20.1–4. On the problem of models whose scale is misleading when they are translated into actual constructions, see Vincenzo Scamozzi, *L'idea dell'architettura universale* (1615; Venice, 1714), 52. For the oblique drawing of *helépolis*, which Biton says was carried out by Poseidon for Alexander the Great, see Leiden Universiteitsbibliotheek, Cod. Voss. Gr. 189, fol. 19r, and an eleventh-century *Strategikon*, Rome, Biblioteca Apostolica Vaticana, Cod. Vat. Gr. 1164. On the characteristics of men as instruments of war, Joseph Boillot lists the eye, the ears, the mouth, the tongue, and finally the pen and the sword. See Joseph Boillot, *Modelles artifices de feu et divers instrumens de guerre avec les moyens de s'en prevaloir. Pour assieger, battre, surprendre toutes places. Utile et necessaire a tous ceux qui font profession des armes* (Chaumont-en-Bassigny: Q. Mareschal, 1598), 3, 7.

16. "L'esperientia fa riconoscere li errori della scientia, non esendo il disegno cosi giusto come è il sito." See the letter to Giulio Savorgnan on the modifications of Castello di Brescia, in Antonio Manno, "Buonaiuto Lorini e la scienza delle fortificazioni," *Architettura Archivi* 2, no. 2 (1984): 34–50. Christoval de Rojas also stressed the importance of the site. In addition to mathematics and arithmetic, the "soldado o ingeniero" should be able to "reconocer bien el puesto donde se ha de hazer la fortaleza, o Castillo." And this can only be learned through the experience of war. Christoval de Rojas, *Teórica y practica de fortificación* (Madrid: Sanchez, 1598). Gabriello Busca observed that "it is very difficult to establish the design of a fortress that is not on level ground: where the drawing cannot show it adequately one must compensate with writing and, by means of these notes, clarify those things that are in doubt. In the case of fortresses on mountaintops, I like to first establish where the fortress is to be built, and then make the plans from it. And on the place

8.12
Biton, *helépolis*, seventeenth-century manuscript.
Universiteitsbibliotheek, Leiden. Cod. voss. gr. folio 189, folio 19r.

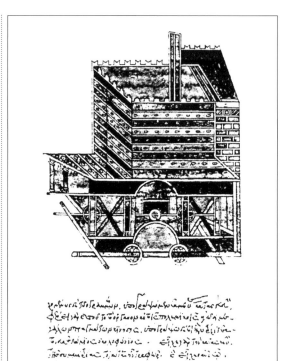

8.13
Biton, *helépolis*, eleventh-century manuscript.
Bibliothèque Nationale, Paris. Cod. par. suppl. Cod. voss. gr. folio 607, folio 29r.

itself I make it smaller, then bigger, push the walls outward … and having marked all the corners, I extrapolate the plan and adjust the drawing to make it coherent" (Busca, *Dell'architettura militare*, 92).

17. Gian Battista Della Valle, *Vallo, libro co[n]tinente appertinentie ad Capitanii per retenere,et fortificare una città co[n] bastioni, con nuovi artificij de fuoco aggio[n]ti, come nella tavola appare, et di diverse sorte polvere, et de espugnare una città* … (Venice: Gregorio de Gregori, 1524). Della Valle was the first to indicate a way of building tunnels in mines leading to the blast hole, known as *tomba*. Its military applications ensured that thirteen editions were published in forty-three years. The first edition, printed in Naples in 1521, was influenced by the tradition of Kyeser. In order to find out where the enemy was tunneling, Vitruvius advised amplifying the blows of the enemies' picks by listening to the sound they made through bronze vessels suspended from the walls, just as Tryphon of Alexandria had done when defending Apollonia. See Vitruvius, *De architettura* 10.16.10.

18. See Georgius Agricola, *De re metallica libri XII* (Basel: Froben, 1556). Drawings of building and roads in cross-section may be seen in MS. B, fols. 36r, 37r (Paris, Bibliothèque Nationale). See also Luigi Firpo, "Leonardo as Urban Planner," in *Leonardo da Vinci: Engineer and Architect* (Montreal: Montreal Museum of Fine Arts, 1987), 299, figs. 356–357.

19. Niccolò Machiavelli, *Sette libri dell'arte della guerra* (Florence: Filippo Giunta, 1521). The text's thesis seems to have been met with considerable success judging from the numerous editions: Florence 1541, Venice 1541, n.p. 1550, Florence 1558, London 1562, Venice 1587, Amsterdam 1610, Amsterdam 1679, Florence 1782 and 1796, Milan 1805, Karlsruhe 1833, Capolago 1843.

20. The copy preserved in Paris has a manuscript attached dated 18 December 1540 which on page 47v shows a figure with diverging sides, characteristic of fifteenth-century *machinatio*, and present also in Valturio (*De re militari* [Christianum Wechelum: Paris 1534]) and Cesariano (*De architettura* [Como: Viruvius Pilio, 1521], v, LXXXIIr). See Della Valle, *Vallo: Libro co[n]tinente appertinentie ad Capitanii* … (Paris, Bibliothèque Nationale, Rés. v. 2283).

21. Alessandro Capobianco, *Breve ragionamento sopra la fortificazione moderna e delle imperfettioni delle antiche, scoperte a' giorni nostri* (Venice, 1598).

22. The classical disciplines making up the *quadrivium* (mathematics, geometry, music, astronomy-astrology)

8.14

Georgius Agricola, *De re metallica* (Basel, 1556).

did not constitute autonomous schools in the medieval *universitas studiorum*. Classical tradition united the study of Mathematics with music and mechanical applications; medicine entered the *quadrivium* as if it had been derived from astrology and went on to form the central nucleus of a school in its own right. It is therefore not surprising to find the practice of medicine linked with the practice of astronomy and astrology, and thus also to instruments for measuring angles and distances. In his *Etymologiarum*, Isidore of Seville had explicitly included medicine among the liberal arts, and the medicine-astrology link would last for the whole of the sixteenth century. See Carlo Maccagni, "Le scienze nello studio di Padova e nel Veneto," in Girolamo Arnaldi and Manlio Pastore Stocchi, eds., *Storia della cultura veneta. Dal Primo Quattrocento al Concilio di Trento* (Vicenza: Neri Pozza, 1981), 136ff. Giovanni Dondi was a physician and came from a medical family, as did Guido da Vigevano (*Texaurus*, 1335), Conrad Kyeser (*Bellifortis*, 1405), Giovanni Fontana (*Bellicorum instrumentorum liber*, 1420–1450), Georgius Agricola (*De re metallica*), and Giuseppe Ceredi, *Tre discorsi sopra il modo di alzar acque da' luoghi bassi* (Parma: Seth Viotti, 1567).

23. Bartolomeo Crescenzio, *Proteo militar di Bartolomeo Romano, diviso in tre libri. Nel primo si descrive la Fabrica di detto Proteo e in esso nuovo Istrumento tutti gli altri istrumenti di matematica che imaginar si possano. Nel secondo e terzo si tratta dell'uso di detto Istrumento, nel quale si formano tutte le figure di geometria e gli strumenti di prospettiva, pittura, scoltura e d'architettura. Si insegna ancora l'arte del navigare, quelle del guerreggiare etc.* (Naples: Gio. Iacomo Carlino e Antonio Pace, 1595). The text is republished in part by Latino Orsini, *Trattato del Radio Latino con li commentarij del Rev. Padre Egnatio Danti* (Rome: Marc'Antonio Moretti & Iacomo Brianzi, 1586). However, the text has more applications and the plates are superior. Along with the *Radio Latino*, it cites the *Stativo*, the *Cursore del Pellettario*, and the *Squadra di Tartaglia*. The *proteo militare* could be used not only to find out the position of a ship, but also to describe the provinces, make images, form columns and capital letters, and served as an "instrument for prospectors of battles of every sort." On page 104, a circular fortress is described with a sort of central perspective, the viewpoint of which is perpendicular to the center of the plan. It is interesting to compare the beautiful spherical plan of Vienna during the Turkish siege, drawn by the Belgian H. Schmidts Geldriensis, with the destruction of the Löbelbastei (Vienna, Hofkammer

Archiv, Mi). See also the compasses in the form of daggers preserved in the Museo di Storia della Scienza in Florence (inv. 2515), attributed to Benvenuto della Volpaia (Maria Luisa Righini Bonelli, ed., *Il Museo della Storia della Scienza di Firenze* [Milan, 1976]), and another mathematical dagger (Ulrich Schütte, *Architekt und ingenieur. Baumeister in Krieg und Frieden*, exh. cat. [Wolfenbüttel: Herzog August Bibliothek, 1984], 338, cat. N. 259). For descriptions of other instruments, see for example: the cartridge case in Tartaglia, *Quesiti et inventioni*, 64–69; the holometer in Abel Fullone, *Descrittione et uso dell'Holometro. Per saper misurare tutte le cose, che si possono vedere coll'occhio così in lunghezza, et larghezza; come in altezza, et profondità* (Venice: Giordano Zilietti, 1564); the astronomical quadrant in Valentin Engelhart, *Quadrans Planispherii nobilissimum instrumentum, cuiis usu atque tractione variae tam Astronomicae quam Geographicae expediuntur & explicantur observationes, è quibus maior pars Astronomiae & tota fere' extruitur Geographia* (Wittenberg, 1559), c. Ai; the cosmolabe in Jacques Besson, *Le Cosmolabe, ou Instrument universel concernant toutes observations qui se peuvent faire par les sciences matematiques, tant en ciel, en la terre, comme en le mer, de l'invention de M. J. Besson* (Paris: Ph. G. De Rouille, 1567–1569); the Euclidean compass in Jacques Besson, *Description and Use of the Euclidean Compass* (Paris, 1571); the new military compass in Tetti [Theti], *Discorsi delle fortificazioni del Sig. C.T.*, 107; various instruments in Jacques Besson, *Theater des instruments mathematiques et mecaniques* (1578) (Lyon: Bartélémy Vincent, 1579), plates 1, 2, 4, 5–6; astronomical shafts in Antonio Lupicini, *Discorsi sopra la fabbrica e uso delle nuove verghe astronomiche* (Florence: appresso Giorgio Marescotti, 1582), 1; an instrument for measuring distance in Alessandro Capobianco, *Corona e palma militare di artiglieria nella quale si tratta dell'inventione di esso ... nuovo strumento per misurare distanze* (Venice: Bariletti,1598), 52; a compass and "la barque," an instrument for measuring distances, in Bachot, *Le Gouvernail* 2: plates 46–48; a spirit level with compass in Leonhardt Zubler, *Fabrica et usus instrumenti chorographici. quo mira facilitate describuntur Regione et singulae partes earum, veluti Montes, Urbes, Castella, Pagi, Propugnacula, et similia. Additae sunt Praeter duo instrumenta homogenea ...* (Basel: Casparo Wasero, 1607); various measuring instruments in Johann Faulhaber, *Mathematici Tractatuis duo nuper germanice editi, Joannis Faulhaberi, Ulmae arithmetici ingegnosissimi continentes, prior, noval geometricas opticas aliquot singularium instrumentorum inventiones, posterior usum intrumenti cuiusdam belgae de novo excogitatum, dimetiendis et describendis rebus aptum, et nostratum et exterorum magnatum et ducum, philomathematicorum gratia sermone latino versi per Ioannem Remellinum* (Frankfurt: sumptibus Antoni Hummen, excudebat Ioannes Bringer, 1610), 36, 39, 43; the instrument used by Lencker to draw the perspective of bodies in Johann Faulhaber, *Ingenieur. Schul in ein Compendium gebracht. Mit angechenckten Kunst Quaestionen* (Nuremberg: in Verlegung Wolffgang Endters, 1637), 39; the *radio latino*, the *viatorium*, and a pace counter in Ledinus Hulsius, *Vierdter Tractat der Mechanischen Instrumenten Levini Hulsii Grundtliche Beschreibung des Diensthafften und Nussbaren Instruments Viatorii oder …* (Frankfurt: Wolffgang Richetern inverlegung der Authorn, 1615); Benjamin Bramer, *Kurzer Berichtigung: eines Schreg oder winckel Instruments …* (Marburg: Egenolf, 1615); the Theodolite, the Circumferentor, the Peractor, and the Decimall in Aaron Rathborne, *The Surveyor in Foure bookes by Aaron Rathborne* (London: Stansby for Burre, 1616), 121; an instrument for land surveying and measuring heights in Johann Lörer, *Novum Instrumentum geometricum …* (Zurich: Hardmeyer, 1616); the pantograph in Christoph Scheiner S. J., *Pantographice seu Ars delineandi res quaslibet per parallelogrammum lineare seu cavum, mechanicum, mobile … prior Epipedographicen sive planorum, posterior Stereographicen, seu solidorem aspectabilium vivam imitationem atque proiectionem edocet* (Rome: Ludovico Grignani, 1631), 12, 29, 32, 95, 99.

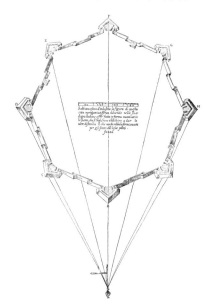

8.15
Bartolomeo Romano, *Proteo militare* (Naples, 1595).

24. The representations of cities and of sieges belong, as Pliny reminds us, to an ancient Roman tradition: "Lucius Hostilius Mancinus, who was the first to invade Carthage, had paintings hung in the Forum that reproduced the site of the city and the various phases of the assault." Pliny the Elder, *Naturalis historia* 35.23. In Mantegna's *Triumphs of Caesar*, which is based on classical sources (Suetonius, Plutarch, and Appian), both the *simulacra* and the *signa* of the defeated cities are represented. Mantegna may have consulted the copy of Biondo in the Gonzaga library: Flavio Biondo, *Triumphantis Romae libros* (Mantua: P. A. de' Micheli, 1473). Cf. Andrew Martindale, *The Triumphs of Caesar by Mantegna in the Collection of Her Majesty the Queen at Hampton Court* (London: Harvey Miller Publishers, 1979).

25. Giulio Ballino, *De disegni delle più illustri città e fortezze del mondo parte I; la quale ne contiene cinquanta: con una breve historia delle origini et accidenti loro, secondo l'ordine de'tempi* (Venice: Bolognini Zalterii Typis, 1569). This was a collection of views of fortified cities, some of which are dated 1566, engraved by D. Zen[v]oi. See also the summary by Girolamo Portignani, *Prospettiva di fortificazione dell'ingegnere et capitano G. Port. fiorentino. Nella quale rimirando ciascheduno professore esperto dell'Arte della Militia potrà in un subito come in uno specchio vedere tutto quello quasi che altrove alla lunga et del fabricare et del Defendere et dell'espugnare Fortezze, letto o in campagna in fatto, praticato havessi. Fatica utile e dilettevole non solo a tutti quelli che fanno professione di qualsivoglia modo di Soldato, ma ancora a qualunque altra persona o del Disegno o delle matematiche et in parte delle Prospettiva si dilettassero* (n.d., n.p). His effigy at the age of fifty-one appears in the frontispiece, executed by Augustinis Parisinus Baptista Negro Pontes Bononiae, and is dated 13 November 1591 when he was fifty-one years old. However, Marini and Cockle bring the date forward to 1648. See also the 161 methods of fortification by Francesco De Marchi, *Della architettura militare libri tre* (Brescia: Comino Presegni, 1597), reprinted in Brescia (1599 and 1600), in Bologna (1720), and in Rome (1815).

26. Lorini advised making the drawing on squared paper (one square = one pace) so that a precise calculation could be made of the amount of earth to be moved and the subsequent costs. Buonaiuto Lorini, *Delle fortificazioni* (Venice: Francesco Rampazetto, 1609), 28.

27. Yves Deforge, *Le graphisme technique son histoire et son enseignement* (Seyssel: Champ Villan, 1981), 51.

28. Raphael to Pope Leo X, letter on the Rome survey, in Paola Barocchi, ed., *Scritti d'arte del Cinquecento*, vol. 3 (Milan and Naples: Ricciardi, 1977), 2980.

29. "Item scaenographia est frontis et laterum abscendentium adumbratio ad circinique centrum omnium linearum responses" (Vitruvius, *De architectura* 1.2.2).

30. In his *Livre de portraicture* (Paris, 1571) Jean Cousin uses the orthogonal projection method already adopted by Piero della Francesca in his *De prospectiva pingendi*, written between 1472 and 1475, although it remained in manuscript until 1899. Relating figures by projection, as Piero della Francesca did, works for simple objects but is very difficult for complex ones. For this reason, the military studied objects only in terms of their actual measurements and did not use a viewpoint. Not until the eighteenth century was projection used again for plans and elevations, in the work of Frézier, but even he did not consider coordination between the two to be of any theoretical or practical use. See Amédée-François Frézier, *La théorie et la pratique de la coupe des pierres et des bois, ou trait de stéréotomie à l'usage de l'architecture*, vol. 1 (Strasbourg: chez Jean Daniel Doulksseker le fils; Paris: L. H. Guerin l'aine, 1737), 272.

31. See Kim Veltman, *Military Surveying and Topography: The Practical Dimension of Renaissance Linear Perspective* (Lisbon: Junta de Investigações Cientificas do Ultramar, 1979). For the first half of the sixteenth century, an architect's status depended solely on his skills in carpentry, metalworking, painting, and sculpture. Architects rarely came from families of elevated social standing and, in the absence of schools or of institutionalized apprenticeship systems, they achieved what authority they had through their ability to draw and make models. The Theodosian code invited architects and artisans to acquire skills and to pass them on to their sons. Spiro Kostof, "The Architect in the Middle Ages, East and West," in Kostof, ed., *The Architect* (New York: Oxford University Press, 1977), 69. For a history of the status of the architect during the Renaissance, see the chapter "The Idea of Model" in this book.

32. For stonework, what was required was a "good *proto* [superintendent of the fabric of St. Mark's in Venice] who knows his tasks, and not bombardiers and soldiers, for their skills in this are of no use" (Concina, *La macchina territoriale*, 10).

33. Ibid., 13.

34. Sigismondo de Fantis was employed as engineer of the fortifications and was expected to "carry out the

orders of our generals." The same order was given on 29 September 1531 in relation to Sanmicheli who, as engineer, was to assist the General in "carrying out what was needed" (ibid., 31).

35. This means there was an increasing demand for specialization in the planning of fortresses, a phenomenon that has already been noted by the second half of the sixteenth century. Horst de la Croix, "Military Architecture and Radial City Plan," *Art Bulletin* 42 (1960): 273–274. See the contrasting opinion of Simon Pepper and Nicholas Adams, *Firearms and Fortifications* (Chicago: University of Chicago Press, 1986), 178, who maintain that the transition from architect to military specialist was slower. Hale observed that in *Le imprese illustri* by Girolamo Ruscelli only two military architects figure—Zanchi and Lanteri—and no "civil" architect does; Francesco Tensini became a knight and Francesco Paciotto was invested with the knighthood of Philip II, given the title "Engineer General of Flanders." He ended his career as Count of Forte Fabbri at Urbino, after having served as architect general to the Duke of Savoy. See John R. Hale, *Renaissance Fortification* (London: Thames and Hudson, 1977), 25. The English were a case apart. Along with Richard Lee, John Rogers was the preferred military architect of Henry VIII. He began as a medieval master mason and ended his career as military engineer and surveyor of works at Calais, after 1550. This was the same title (engineer general of the fortresses) that Castriotto was awarded by the French in 1558 when, after the rapid conquest of Calais by the Duke of Guise, he was given the task of arming the city and completing its defenses. When Rogers was called to Hull Castle in 1541 he made four drawings, three plans and an oblique drawing. Plate D published by Shelby is described as a "bird's-eye view": it did not conform in all its details to the three plans and a close analysis shows it to be a readaptation of the first plan. See Lon R. Shelby, *John Rogers: Tudor Military Engineer* (New York: Oxford University Press, 1967). In reality, this plate is not a bird's-eye view at all, but a parallel *alla cavaliera* drawing. Rogers's oblique drawing presented to the king included measurements and all the drawings are done on a uniform scale. The time was ripe for elaborating a graphic procedure that was easy, fast, and trustworthy. The element of measurability of the three orthogonal angles is confirmation that even in the distant lands of Henry VIII, oblique drawing would soon demand that the axes be measurable. Indeed, perhaps it was no coincidence that isometrical

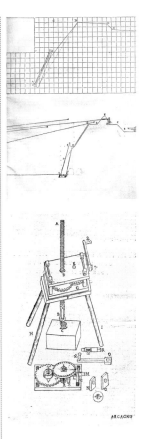

8.16
Buonaiuto Lorini, *Delle fortificazioni* (Venice, 1597), page 31.

8.17
Buonaiuto Lorini, *Delle fortificazioni* (Venice, 1597), page 188.

8.18
Buonaiuto Lorini, *Delle fortificazioni* (Venice, 1597), page 130.

8.19
Johann Caspar Bagnato, Commandery of Meinraw of the Teutonic Order, 1740. Deutschen Ordens Zentralarchiv, Vienna. Bildsmlg, lade 21.

drawing was invented by Farish and developed in England of all places.

In France, architects and city authorities were in charge of fortifications, while siege operations were directed by engineers. Antoine-Marie Augoyat, *Aperçu historique sur les fortifications, les ingénieurs, et sur le Corps du génie en France* (Paris: Tanera, 1860). The nature of their tasks was clarified during the reign of Henri IV and the first partial plans begin to appear together with topographical representations in *cavalier perspective*. From siege warfare engineers begin to turn their attention to the problem of fortification, with the title "ingénieurs des camps et armies et des villes ou provinces," but also as "ingénieurs ordinaires du Roi." Their lives were often put at excessive risk during sieges, which is why their role changed from "preneur de ville" to "fortificateur." The profession underwent considerable transformations; from weapons, cannon, and mine specialist, the role became that of architect and builder. But the engineer was still expected to be present on the battlefield: a 1703 print of the siege of Brissac shows Vauban mounted on a horse indicating the line of a trench with a stick. During the reign of Henri IV, Sully, the superintendent of finance, was also declared superintendent of fortifications. He commanded "ingénieurs, géographes controleurs et trésoriers." Only in 1645 was the role of "Intendants de fortifications" created for Michel de Tellier, Secretary of State for War. After the death of Mazarin the old division between fortress architects and military personnel with special responsibility for sieges was reproduced in the ministerial division of finance (Colbert) and war (Louvois); each possessed separate corps of military engineers. Those under Colbert were architects and inspectors of work; those commanded by Louvois were infantrymen. Curiously, the introduction of scientific map-making of mountainous country began with the abandonment of the high viewpoint of the battlefield, which, by producing cavalier projections of the mountains, had concealed large sections of territory. Augoyat considered the topographical work of Beaulieu "ingénieur et géographe ordinaire du Roi" (1679) to be unreliable for military topography since "ses plans appartiennent plutôt à la perspective cavalière qu'à la topographie militaire." Colonel Berthaut, *Les ingénieurs géographes militaires 1624–1831* (Paris: Imprimerie du Service géographique, 1902), 1ff. See also Chevalier de Beaulieu, *Les glorieuses conquistes de Loüis le Grand*, 3 vols. (Paris, 1667, Vienna, Kriegsarchiv, G Ia220 alfa, G Ia

3-11 alfa, G Ia 290-2 alfa). The French engineers almost always used a descriptive system without conventional triangulations and signs (introduced and imposed by Frederick of Prussia who geometrized cartography). Plans were pictorial and made use of cavalier perspective. The Ecole du Génie à Mézières was founded in 1748, but only in 1776 was its organization complete and the title of the diploma it conferred finalized as "ingénieurs pour les camps et armées." See Dupain de Montesson, *Art de lever les plans* (Paris: C. A. Jombert, 1763).

36. Tartaglia, *Quesiti et inventioni*, quesito VIII, 69r. According to Martini, this is "the mind's eye" that should belong to "the governor and rector of the city." Francesco di Giorgio Martini, *Trattati di architettura ingegneria, e arte militare*, vol. 1, ed. Corrado Maltese (Milan: Il Polifilo, 1967), 31, 3.

37. Giovan Battista Belici (Belluzzi), *Nuova inventione di fabricar fortezze di varie forme, in qualunque sito di piano, di monte, in acqua, con diversi disegni ed un trattato del modo,*

8.20
John Rogers, *Hull Manor*, pl. D, 1538. British Museum, London. Cott. mss. Aug. I. II. 13.

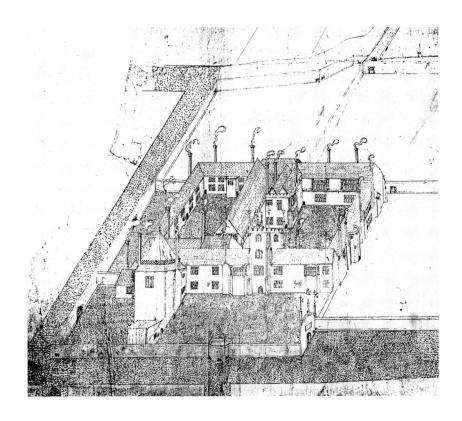

8.21–8.24
Antoine De Ville,
*Les fortifications
du chevalier A*
(Lyon, 1629).

*che sia da osservare in esse con le sue misure, ed ordini di levar
le piante tanto in fortezze reali, quanto non reali, con un discorso infine intorno al presidiare e a guardare esse fortezze e
quanto fa bisogno per il loro mantenimento* (Venice: Tommaso Baglioni, 1593), 3.

38. Ibid., chap. 2, "Dell ordine di levar le Piante."

39. Ibid.

40. Lorini, *Delle fortificazioni*, 33–34, n. 14 (emphasis
added). Lorini says that it is not necessary for those soldiers "whom I presume to address … to have a perfect
understanding of this science of *disegno*, but just enough
in order not to be ignorant of it." Naturally there were
those who, like Belluzzi, disdained *disegno*: "*Disegno* mis-
leads and can show things that are false … a Prince should
never believe in *disegno*." Belluzzi, *Nuova invenzione di
fabbricare fortezze di varie forme*, chap. 2. Or there are
those like Errard de Bar-le-Duc, who advises engineers:
"Qu'il ne consente jamais a un desseign, car l'honneur
qui on peut prouvenir n'est point grand et le deshonneur
est un monstre." Jean Errard de Bar-le-Duc, *La fortification demonstrée et reduicte en art par feu J.E. de B.l.D.* (Paris,
1620), 27. For Lorini, however, *disegno* was important. He
did not hesitate to call Charles V and Cosimo de' Medici
"grandi disegnatori" (great masters of drawing). One of his
preoccupations was that traditional perspective drawing could conceal certain parts, while the procedure that
he describes avoids this fault. The possibility of seeing
inside is an invention claimed as his own by Jacques Perret in his beautiful illustrations in *perspective militaire*:
"La perspective de dedans des batiments n'a encore este
faicte par aucun, que je sache, comme est icy en toutes les
figures suivantes." Jacques Perret, *Des fortifications et artifices, architecture et perspective de Jacques Perret gentilhomme
savoysien* (Paris, circa 1601). Bibliothèque Nationale de
France V. 424.

41. The design of the cube projected in a hexagon had
been published by Cousin, who treated it as a construction
auxiliary to perspective: "Le plan géométral du cube dressé
sur la pointe fait un exagone ainsi que voyez icy." Jean
Cousin, *Le livre de perspective* (Paris: Jean Le Royer, 1560),
cc. Pij and Pij. Aguilonius, whose book was illustrated
by Rubens, carried out the operation in a less empiric
context: "Cubus visu per opposites angulos transmisso,
proijcitur in Hexagono e tribus aequalibus similisbusque
Rhonbis conflatum," an operation carried out in a projective geometry context. In his *Propositio LXIII* he explained:
"Quid est Proiectio … Proiectio est rei solidae in planum

transcriptio," and in his *De re orthographice* he says that it "primo proiectionis genere ex infinita oculi distantia." François d'Aguilon, *Opticorum libri sex* (Antwerp: Plantin, 1613), 493, 503, 557. For Aguilonius's relationship with Rubens, see Julius S. Held, "Rubens and Aguilonius: New Points of Contact," *Art Bulletin*, no. 61 (1979): 257–264.

42. Girolamo Maggi and Jacomo Castriotto, *Della fortificazione delle Città. Libri III* (1559) (Venice: Camillo Borgominiero al segno di S. Giorgio, 1584). Jacomo Castriotto (Jacopo Fusti da Urbino) held the office of superintendent of the fortresses of Henri II of France. He wrote the treatise in Calais in 1558 and died there on 15 May 1564. Girolamo Maggi da Anghiari, philosopher and scientist, published the treatise after Castriotto's death. In 1571, Maggi was taken prisoner of the Turks at Famagusta and, after attempting to escape, was recaptured and strangled by the soldiers of Mehmet Pasha on 27 March 1572, in the house of the ambassador of the Holy Roman Empire. For a detailed reconstruction of the fates of these two authors and their role in the posthumous creation of the book, see Giorgio E. Ferrari, "Le edizioni venete di architettura militare del Maggi e Castriotto," in *L'architettura militare veneta del Cinquecento* (Milan: Electa, 1988), 179–194. In the same year the treatise of Girolamo Cataneo was published. Cataneo made use of oblique drawing, but when he had to represent an action taking place in a larger space, he tended to use linear perspective, in acknowledgment of the limits of the *alla cavaliera* viewpoint. Girolamo Cataneo, *Opera nuova di fortificare, offendere et difendere et far gli alloggiamenti campali secondo l'uso della Guerra ...* (Brescia: Gio. Battista Bazola, 1564). Treatises sometimes show perspective views instead of cavalier projections, especially in the case of important cities or those with a consolidated iconography, such as Jerusalem. Ballino, *De disegni delle più illustri città e fortezze del mundo parte 1*, 38, 45 (plan of Jerusalem), 47.

43. See *La prospettiva militare* in the first chapter of this book, "Elements for a History of Axonometry." Jacques Androuet du Cerceau showed how the builders used flat plans (*assiette*), rather than foreshortened plans. The former, known also as orthogonal plans, are typical of the architectural profession and are taken from life, respecting the measurements point by point, and "the builders follow them closely." Builders do not use perspective, not so much because of the consequent difficulty of measuring things accurately, but because "it would be too difficult to work them out." Jacques Androuet du Cerceau, *Leçons de perspective positive* (Paris: Mamert Patisson, 1576), fols. 3r ff.

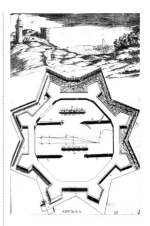

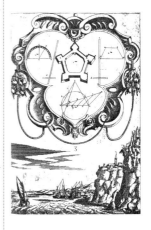

44. Father Natale Masucci, the famous Jesuit architect from Messina, was the author of a "vue cavalière de Trapani" and was probably involved in drawing up plans for the Trapani Jesuit College. In the drawing sent to Rome, he explained that "the parts shaded in purple … are already built; those parts colored in yellow are yet to be built." In the College of Ravenna, instead, we find "the red parts are those parts of the building already completed, while those shown in turquoise are not yet built." Jean Vallery-Radot, *Le recueil de plans de la Compagnie de Jésus conservé à la Bibliothèque Nationale de Paris* (Rome and Paris: Institutum historicum S. J. and Picard, 1960), 29, 39. A century later, an anonymous text provided the following indications: for the plan of a square, the buildings are to be outlined in crimson, with the space between the two lines shaded in light crimson fading into the external contour of the fortress. In a perspective drawing, if the work is to be built of stone, the rows of ashlars must be marked in China ink, "n'oubliant point d'exprimer les fuyantes par affoiblissement des teintes." The text advises using crimson for the facades, and indigo mixed with bistre for the perspective drawings: "Quand c'est quelque vieille mesure, on fait un coloris qu'en exprime la bizarrerie, tantôt avec de la gomme goutte et de l'indigue et tantôt avec de l'indigue clair, ombrant de bistre et d'indigue mettez un peu de vermillon et on lave de même y melant un peu du verd d'iris." Anonymous, *L'art de dessiner et de laver L'Architecture militaire et civile* (Paris, 1697). See also Anonymous, *L'art de dessiner proprement les plans, profiles, elevations, géométrales et perspectives, soit d'architecture Militaire ou Civile* (Paris, 1697).

45. See Pier Nicola Pagliara, "Una fonte di illustrazioni del Vitruvio di fra Giocondo," *Ricerche di Storia dell'Arte* 6 (1977): 113–120.

46. The numerous drawings of trabeations in the Codex Coner and those carried out by Palladio may represent a generic drawing type, intended to compensate for the inadequacy of the perspective view in rendering the relief decorations of antique marbles. Visual foreshortening cannot be accommodated in measurements since "the architect is unable to gauge the correct measurement from a foreshortened line; in order to do this, he must take all the measurements as they actually are, and represent them as parallel lines, not as lines that seem like something they are not." Raphael to Pope Leo X, letter, in Barocchi, *Scritti d'arte del Cinquecento*, 2981. The trabeations executed in oblique drawing that were circulating between the end of the fifteenth century and the begin-

ning of the sixteenth seem to belong to a class of templates (*modani*) made of cardboard or metal sheets, the outline of which the stonemason transferred onto the side of the block to be sculpted. It is not difficult to imagine those oblique drawings being copied from the sections of antique Roman trabeations scattered on the ground; these drawings were often grafted directly onto the building project, becoming an integral part of them. In a certain sense, it might be said that they belong to the Platonic category of the "copy," because "a likeness of anything is made by producing a copy which is executed according to the proportions of the original, similar in length and breadth and depth" (Plato, *Sophist* 235d). Renaissance drawings of trabeations in oblique drawing seem to derive from a single prototype, perhaps from a lost Vitruvian manuscript like that of Sélestat (tenth century), which reproduced several molds and trabeations in orthogonal projection. See Pierre Gros, "Vitruvio e il suo tempo," in Vitruvius, *De architectura*, ed. Gros, vol. 1, p. lx, n. 171. For the illustrations in the Vitruvius codex (Sélestat, Bibliothèque Municipale, MS. 1153 bis, fols. 36 and 37) see Salvatore Settis, ed., *Memoria dell'antico nell'arte italiana*, vol. 1, *L'uso dei classici* (Turin: Einaudi, 1984), figs. 65–68.

47. Leon Battista Alberti, *On the Art of Building in Ten Books*, trans. Joseph Rykwert, Neil Leach, and Robert Tavernor (Cambridge: MIT Press, 1991), 34.

8.25
Street decorations for the triumphal entry of Charles IV. Bibliothèque Nationale, Paris. Rés. Ib 33297, plate 37.

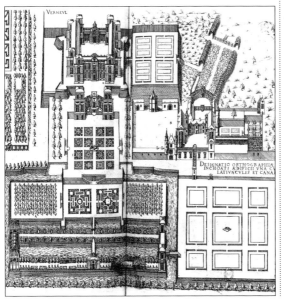

8.26
Verneuil Castle. Jacques Androuet du Cerceau, *Le premier volume des plus excellents Bastiments de France* (Paris, 1576).

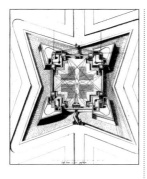

8.27
Hans von Schille, *Festung*
(Antwerp, 1580).

8.28
Benedetto Molli, Jesuit
houses in Montepulciano,
c. 1630. Bibliothèque
Nationale, Paris. Est.
t. 14 (n. 13).

48. This preoccupation, which sacrificed appearances in favor of the intelligibility of the plan of attack, is still visible at the beginning of the eighteenth century in the plans presented to the Académie Royale des Sciences and, for the same reasons, in the Privilegien Archiv (Patent Office) in Vienna and later in the Patent Offices all round the world. In the *Avertissement* to the first volume of his text, Gallon writes: "Dans quelques Machines, j'ai été oblige de m'écarter des regles de la Perspective; parce qu'en le suivant j'aurois caché certaines parties essentielles à l'intelligence de Dessein, et j'ai cru qu'il valoi mieux éviter cet inconvenient que l'autre." Jean Gaffin Gallon, *Machines et inventions approuvées par l'Académie Royales des sciences depuis son établissement jusqu'à present; avec leur description. Dessinées et publiées du consentement de l'Académie* (Paris: par M. Gallon, 1735–1777), 111.

49. See Pagliara, *Una fonte di illustrazioni*, 113–120. For the period before this, Berthelot suggests a comparison between the machines of Taccola and those contained in the *Notitia Dignitatum*. Berthelot, *Pour l'histoire des arts méchaniques et de l'artillerie*, 433–452). See also the study of the machines in R. Neher, "Der anonymus de rebus bellicis," *Notitia Dignitatum* (Tübingen: Kommissionverlag von J. J. Heckenhauer, 1911). The late antique representational type is found in many repertories of siege machines: in Lorenzo Ghiberti, Roberto Valturio, Conrad Kyeser, etc.

50. Marc Bloch, *Lavoro e tecnica nel Medioevo* (1959; Bari, 1984), 206.

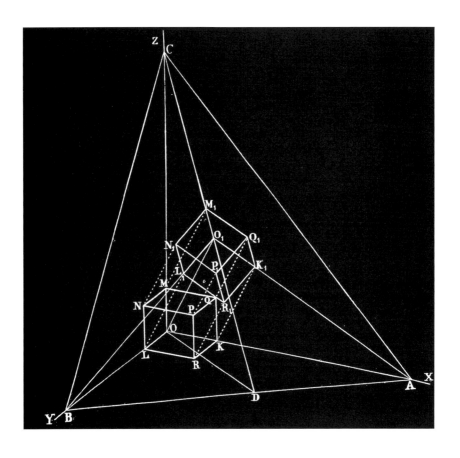

9.1
Julius Weisbach, "Theorie der
axonometrischen Projectionmethode,"
Der Civilingenieur, n.s. 2 (1856).

9

DRAWING IN *PARALLELI MODO*

The terminology we have used until now is not derived from modern geo-metrical manuals. For example, instead of the term *parallel perspective* used by Panofsky,[1] we have used expressions contained in sixteenth-century texts, such as Pomponius Gauricus's *paralleli modo*, or that have been reformulated in such a way as not to be temporally or methodologically incongruent. The definition of oblique drawing is used to refer to a graphic representation similar to that which is obtained from an oblique parallel projection of the figure, projected together with the three axes x, y, and z: the same graphic representation that will be known, after its nineteenth-century codification, as oblique monometric, diametric, or trimetric axonometry.

An example of classic procedural protocol can be seen in the oblique drawing of a cube, the wire frame figure found in ancient mathematical papyri and used again by Luca Pacioli in his *Divina proportione*. To evoke an object in space, a square is drawn, and from each of the four corners a diagonal line is traced that must be the same length as the sides of the square. These diagonal lines must be parallel to each other and orthogonal to a diagonal on the base square. The lines must be imagined to run perpendicularly from the drawing surface, but to make them visible the object must be rotated, otherwise their projection would appear on the drawing paper as a dot. Naturally, in mathe-matical manuscripts, the receding sides are not always inclined at 45 degrees and they are not always of the same length as a side of the base square. This has more to do with the problems inherent in freehand drawing than with the theory; although the resultant drawing is an approximation, this is always corrected by the accompanying text that describes the figure as a "cube." In a context of perspectival representation, the smaller the object is, the more effective this method of representing its three-dimensionality. Gauricus[2] explained that when the angle at which the object is viewed is reduced with respect to our optical cone, the resultant representations in *paralleli modo* are perfectly acceptable, as may be seen in fifteenth- and sixteenth-century portraits of people holding a book in their hands.

Today, parallel projection is usually studied as a particular kind of conical projection to be used when the center of projection (formerly the viewpoint) is at infinity. Gino Loria, author of an important work on descriptive geometry,[3] uses terminology deriving from projective geometry, which is to be found in all manuals of descriptive geometry: "Just as orthogonal projection is a particular type of parallel projection, so parallel projection is a particular type of central projection." From a projective point of view, Loria's definition cannot be faulted, but for the scholar of representational methods, it is not very meaningful.[4] In fact, oblique drawing precedes not only the codification of fifteenth-century linear perspective but also Pompeian pseudo-perspective, as is evident in Apulian vases of the fourth century BC.

Clearly, the history of representational methods cannot be recounted by following some imaginary line that takes us from two-dimensional representation to an illusionistic one in a sort of virtuous progress finally culminating in Renaissance linear perspective. A better understanding may be gained by studying the cultural priorities and techniques that in each epoch became the convention.[5] Remember, for example, that in the classical era and during the Renaissance the viewpoint at infinity made little sense. Guidobaldo del Monte wondered "under what circumstances can it happen that something should be a perspective projection with the point of view placed at an infinite distance?"[6] In fact, no image could be produced by cutting the visual pyramid with the picture plane, since no view, according to Proposition 8 of Euclid's *Optics*, may be supposed to be infinite. All the artists of late antiquity seem to have been aware of this. They also understood that the use of parallel projection is not so much the restitution of a view perceived by the eyes of the body, but—as Plotinus suggests—of an image that is seen by the inner eye, which annuls the distance between the thing and the observer in a process of identification.[7] It is not, therefore, so much a case of seeing as of comprehending and understanding. In his *De prospectiva pingendi*, Piero della Francesca definitively separated optics (*perspectiva*) from conic representation (*prospectiva*). However, in French and English treatises, a representation of the three dimensions of an object is defined as a *perspective*. Consequently, a term that is associated with optics (*perspicere*, to see through) is used inappropriately to denote the graphic representation of a three-dimensional object by means of parallel projection. Giulio Troili falls into the same trap, defining *prospettiva militare* as the "manner of representing in drawing the ground plan of fortresses."[8]

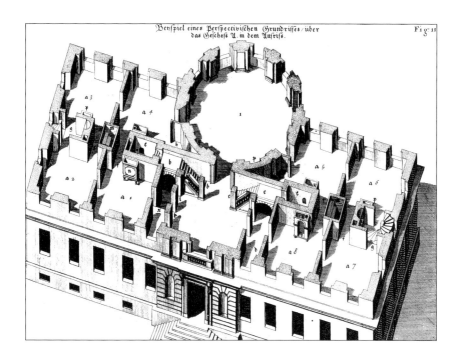

9.2
Leonhard Christoph Sturm, *Ausführliche
Anleitung zu der gantzen Civil Baukunst* ...
(Wolfenbüttel and Amsterdam, 1699),
figure II.

Thus, for the whole of the nineteenth century, oblique drawing continued to be defined as *perspective*,[9] if not *prospettiva*.[10] For Nicolas Breithof, *perspective cavalière* was a special sort of *perspective rapide*, and he showed how this method permitted orthogonal projections to be rapidly measured, adding to the illusionistic characteristics of linear perspective: "Elle donne des desseins qui font image et sur lesquels on peut mesurer."[11] This "drawing that became an image," and that could also be measured, had already been termed *perspective cavalière* by Théodore Olivier, although he noted that in this type of perspective, "the rules of art are never scrupulously observed [les règles de l'art ne sont pas scrupuleusement observées]."[12] The same improper use of the term *prospettiva cavaliera* appears in the books of Joseph-Alphonse Adhémar, Edgardo Ciani, and Domenico Regis.[13] Finally, the term was used correctly in the title of a book by Giulio Stabilini: *Sui sistemi di projezione assonometrica parallela*,[14] notwithstanding the disorienting tautology.

In the first half of the nineteenth century there was a need for greater specificity in the definitions of orthogonal parallel projection. In 1839, Guido Schreiber[15] criticized the use of the term *isometrical perspective*, adopted by William Farish and later taken up by the architect Joseph Jopling,[16] by observing that the drawing is not in reality a perspective drawing but an orthogonal parallel projection. While Farish spoke of an isometrical perspective, Thomas Sopwith, fifteen years later, defined this more correctly as isometrical drawing;[17] in 1869 William Johnson compared it once again to the French *perspective*, describing an isometrical projection as opposed to "true or exact perspective."[18]

In comparing the new method of *prospettiva parallela* with the traditional *prospettiva concorrente*, Giovanni Codazza did little to elucidate the terms of the problem. In particular, he supposed that "the eye of the observer is placed at an infinite distance on the continuation of one of the diagonals of the cube," and thus made the discovery (!) that a cube projected in this way is a regular hexagon. "The fundamental spirit of the method thus consists in this: that all the lines parallel to the three principal axes are represented in the same scale, and all the angles enclosed in them are represented by angles of 60 degrees, or by their supplementary angles."[19]

The correct term, *axonometrie*, was finally coined by Martin Herrmann Meyer and C. Th. Meyer in their treatise *Lehrbuch der axonometrischen Projektionslehre* (1855–1863), which bears the heading *Lehrbuch der Axonometrie*, incorporating the very idea of measurability along the axes. Oblique axonometric projection was given a general formulation in 1853 with Pohlke's theorem.[20] Pohlke was also responsible for clarifying the terms *prospettiva a volo d'uccello*,

Abraham Leuthner, *Grünliche Darstellung
der fünf Säulen* ... (Prague, after 1677),
plate XXXVII.

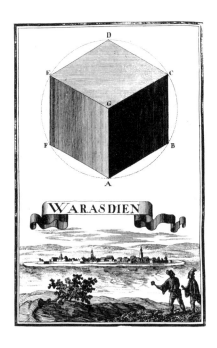

9.4
Abraham Leuthner, *Grünliche Darstellung der fünf Säulen ...* (Prague, after 1677), plate XXXVIII.

9.5
Antoni Ernst Burckhard von Birckenstein, *Ertz-Hertzogliche Handgriffe deß Zirckels und Lineals oder ...* (Augsburg, 1698).

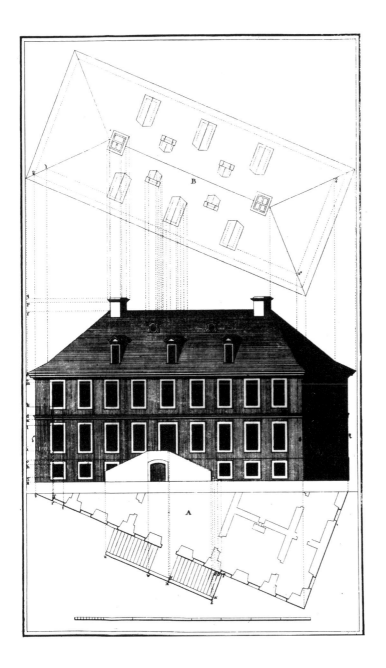

9.6
Johann Friedrich von Penther,
Bau-Kunst (Augsburg, 1745),
plate LIX.

prospettiva cavaliera, and *prospettiva militare*, which were simply historical definitions of oblique projections.[21] But despite the considerable effort expended in clarifying the terminology, it is still possible to find, in a chapter dedicated to parallel projection in an otherwise very lucid Russian text from the second half of the twentieth century, axonometry once again being described as a perspective: "La perspective axonométrique parallèle (cylindrique) consiste en principe à rapporter l'objet à un certain sistème de coordonnées et à le projeter par des projetentes parallèles sur un plan avec son système de coordonnées."[22] Even today in texts dealing with the history of art and of architecture, the terminology used to define the different methods and types of pictorial representation is left to the imagination of each single scholar, and only tempered by the good sense of readers who use their eyes to look at the illustrations.

Notes

1. Erwin Panofsky, *Perspective as Symbolic Form*, trans. Christopher S. Wood (Cambridge: MIT Press, 1991), 106, n. 24.

2. See note 36 of chapter 6, "Demonstration Figures."

3. Gino Loria, *Storia della geometria descrittiva* (Milan: Ulrico Hoepli, 1921).

4. On the problem of constituting this as a topic of academic study in schools of architecture, see Massimo Scolari, "La questione del disegno," *Casabella* 486 (1982): 38–39. See also Scolari, "Che il disegno sia centro nelle scuole di architettura," *XY* 10 (1989): 57–64.

5. On the concepts of realism and convention, see Nelson Goodman, *Languages of Art: An Approach to a Theory of Symbols* (Indianapolis: Bobbs-Merrill, 1976), 3–43. See also Goodman, *Ways of Worldmaking* (Indianapolis: Hackett, 1978).

6. Guidobaldo del Monte, *Planisphaeriorum universalium Theorica* (Pisa: apud Ieronimum Concordiam, 1579), 57.

7. Plotinus, *Enneads* v, 8, 10, 35–40. The idea of self-identification was taken up again in the modern age by the Plotinian philosopher Henri Bergson, who explains that there are two profoundly different ways of knowing something: "La première implique qu'on tourne autour de cette chose; la seconde, qu'on entre en elle." Henri Bergson, *Oeuvres* (Paris: Presses Universitaires de France, 1963), 1393. The citation appears in Vincenzo Cilento, *Saggi su Plotino* (Milan: Mursia, 1973), 277.

8. Troili explains his motive for using this method of representation: "To gratify those who would like to obtain or propose a geometric plan of his possessions, the elevations of houses, palaces, lands, etc., and furthermore, if he wishes drawings of military barracks, cavalry, or infantry and other military buildings, without upsetting the order and the measure and without disregarding the regulations or any rules of military perspective, in order to not create confusion when it is proposed to lay these geometrical plans of buildings on top of the elevations. And if the manner of proceeding is unknown, these shall be taught by me in the same way as they were taught to me at the Fortress of Urbano by the most illustrious signor Giovanni Battista Albici, keeper of the said fortress, as he, in his turn, had been taught in Flanders. And to this I will add the examples which follow, since I have had plentiful occasion to communicate them to several noble foreigners who came of their own volition to ask me about it (foreigners who were themselves experts in military architecture), showing me the plans and measurements

for a royal battery or a redoubt, and its outlines in such a way that I could design its elevation. I, finding myself unable to carry out such a task, judged it best to treat of such matters presently, and having gathered everything that one might desire to know about them from modern authors, I set about the work using the measurements that were already known." He also noted that in some quarters, the term *military perspective* was deemed incorrect, even though its use had become common: "The correct term is elevation." The procedure he describes is to start from the plan and trace from each of its corners "the hidden perpendiculars of all those parts according to the scale with which the plan has been measured, until the elevation is complete." It is interesting to find this reference to scale where drawings in military perspective are concerned. In the *Prattica XXIV* (taken from Guarini) there is a comparison of a Dutch rampart in side elevation, civil perspective (from two different points of view), and military perspective. He recommends that in the case of military perspective (rotated through 25 degrees), "the line of the country must not be parallel to the others, which are horizontal." This drawing may be used, according to Troili, as a basis from which to construct a cardboard model: "if this shape is desired in solid form, take two pieces of card, as we have said, or more properly, two pieces of wood in order to make the outlines." Giulio Troili da Spinlamberto [il Paradosso], *Paradossi per pratticare la Prospettiva senza saperla, fiori per facilitare l'intelligenza, frutti, per non operare alla cieca* (1672; Bologna: Langhi, 1683), III, 30–31.

9. Orthogonal axonometry is generally considered to have originated in the paper given by William Farish to the Philosophical Society of Cambridge on 15 November 1819. Farish wrote: "There is no difficulty in giving an almost perfectly correct representation of any object adapted to this perspective, to which the artist has access if he has a very simple knowledge of its principles and a little practice." Farish (1756–1837) was Jacksonian Professor of Physics at Cambridge. William Farish, "On Isometrical Perspective," *Transactions of the Cambridge Philosophical Society* 1 (1820). Despite the relative availability in Europe of Joseph Gwilt's *Encyclopedia of Architecture* (London: Longmans Green, 1872) written in 1842, no mention is made of isometric drawing. This is yet another example of the world of architecture's indifference or hostility toward a method that owed its origin to the technical world of engineering, at least until the time of Auguste Choisy. It was no accident that Choisy was both an engineer and a professor of architecture at the École des Ponts et

Chaussées. The 1,700 engravings by Sulpis, wrote Choisy in the *Notes* to his work, were carried out "en projection axonométrique, système qui a la clarté de la perspective et se prête à des mesures immédiates. Le lecteur a sous les yeux, à la fois, le plan, l'extérieur de l'édifice, sa coupe et ses dispositions intérieures." Auguste Choisy, *Histoire de l'architecture* (Paris: Edouard Rouveyre, 1899). At the beginning of the twentieth century, Guadet favored *dessin géométral* above all others, explaining that, for him, it was "le dessin exact, on peut dire le dessin par excellence," the foremost quality of which was its "exactitude absolue." In fact, some of the illustrations are in isometric orthogonal axonometry, such as in the construction details of the walls or the vaults, where Choisy is explicitly cited. Julien Guadet, *Eléments et théorie de l'architecture, cours professée a l'Ecole Nationale et Spéciale des Beaux Arts*, vol. 1 (Paris: Librairie de la Construction Moderne, 1909), 34, fig. on 227, 540. Gaudet was Inspector General of the Bâtiments Civils, and from 1894, he taught "Théorie de l'Architecture" at the École des Beaux-Arts of Paris.

10. Heineken uses the word *prospective* instead of the more common *perspective*. Paul Heineken, *Lucidum Prospectivae Speculum, Das ist eine heller Spiegel del Perspective* (Augsburg: Heirs of Jeremiah Wolff, 1727).

11. Nicolas Breithof, *Traité de perspective cavalière* (Paris: Gauthier-Villars, 1881).

12. Théodore Olivier, *Applications de la géométrie descriptive aux ombres, à la perspective, à la gnomonique et aux engranages* (Paris: Carilian-Goeury et V. Dalmont, 1847), 26. The author references the *Traité des ombres dans le dessein géométral* (1775–1870), used at the Royal Engineering School in Mézières. See Loria, *Storia della geometria descrittiva*, 96.

13. Joseph-Alphonse Adhémar, *Traité des ombres: théorie des teintes des points brillants et de la perspective cavalière* (Paris: Armand Colin et Cie éditeurs, 1874–1875); Edgardo Ciani, *La prospettiva cavaliera a quarantacinque gradi. Con undici tavole* (Milan: Hoepli, 1903); Domenico Regis, "Sulla prospettiva parallela," *Atti dell'Accademia di Torino* 35 (1902–1903): 314–329.

14. Giulio Stabilini, *Sui sistemi di projezione assonometrica parallela* (Bologna: Emiliano, 1910).

15. Guido Schreiber, *Geometrische Portfolio, Blätter über darstellende Geometrie und ihre Anwedungen* (Karlsruhe, 1843), 79, 116.

16. Joseph Jopling, *The Practice of Isometrical Perspective* (London: M. Taylor, 1842). Eight years previously Sopwith's

9.7
Oblique axonometric view
of silk winder, copyright by
I. Matti di Canzo, Como,
1832. Technische Universität
Privilegien Archiv, Vienna.
S. 26, folio 2938, 1842.

9.7
Oblique axonometric view
of silk winder, copyright by
I. Matti di Canzo, Como,
1832. Technische Universität
Privilegien Archiv, Vienna.
S. 26, folio 2938, 1842.

book had been published, in which this type of representation had been given a practical graphic character, very
unlike the scientific approach of the Germans. Thomas
Sopwith, *A treatise on isometrical Drawing as applicable
to geological and mining plans, picturesque delineation of
Ornamental grounds, perspective views and working plans
of buildings and machinery, and to general purpose of Civil
engineering; with details of improved methods of preserving
plans and records of subterranean operation in mining dis-
tricts* (London: John Weale, 1834). Gauss had elaborated
the basic theorems of orthogonal axonometry in a series
of lectures held at the University of Göttingen in 1831. The
contribution of Quintino Sella, *Sui principii geometrici del
disegno e specialmente dell'axonometrico* (Milan: O. Salvi,
1861) was very significant because it used only the theory
of similitude of figures. A mineral engineer, and later a
minister, Quintino Sella promoted the first expedition to
climb the Italian side of the Matterhorn in competition
with the English climber Edward Whimper. His brother
Vittorio is considered the most important mountain
photographer of the nineteenth century.

17. Sopwith, *A Treatise on Isometrical Drawing*. Sopwith
was a member of the Institute of Civil Engineers and
author of essays on mines ("Geological sections of
mines," "Account of mining district"). Farish gave his
judgment in the frontispiece: "Isometrical perspective
is preferable to common perspective on many accounts;
it is much easier and simpler in its principles; it is also
incomparably more easy and accurate in its application.

The information given by isometrical drawings is much more definite and precise than obtained by usual methods, and better fitted to direct a workman in execution." Sopwith also published *A set of projecting and parallel rulers* with the description of a series of instruments for isometric orthogonal axonometric drawing.

18. William C. E. Johnson, *The practical Draftsman's book of industrial Design ... founded upon the "Nouveau cours raisonné de dessin industriel" of MM. Armengaud Ainé, Armengaud Jeune and Amouroux, civil engineers* (London: Longman, 1869). The representational method is correctly defined as isometrical projection or, incorrectly, as "isometrical perspective as it is sometimes termed." See fig. 43. Also shown are the geometrical rules for obtaining actual measurements from isometric projection.

19. Giovanni Codazza, *Sopra un metodo di prospettiva pel disegno di macchine. Nota di geometria descrittiva* (Como: C. A. Ostinelli, 1842), 16, 23.

20. The general theory of axonometry formulated by Karl Pohlke (1853) enables a definition of the relationship between the reduction coefficients (s, t, u) and the angle of projection on the plane v: $s^2 + t^2 + u^2 = 2 + \cot^2 v$. The reduction factors along the three Cartesian axes are proportional respectively to the segments that represent the axonometric axes, which are perpendicular to each other. If the direction of projection on the plane is $v = 90°$, the axonometry is orthogonal and the sum of the squares of the reduction factor is equal to 2. This projection may even be considered as a particular type of orthogonal projection in which the plane of projection is placed in such a way that a solid rectangle projected on it shows three sides. In orthogonal axonometry, each axonometric unit is always less than the unit, and the angles formed by the lines x, y, and z cannot be arbitrarily assigned, nor can the axonometric units. In the case of isometric orthogonal axonometry, $s = t = u$, $2 = 3s^2$, and $s = 0.82$; the dimensions are therefore reduced by 18%. The UNI rules state that the dimensions cannot be reduced, so the image is enlarged by 1.22 times. In the case of a dimetric orthogonal axonometry, $s = u$, $t = 0.5s$, the reduction is by 0.47 and in fact the figure is enlarged by 1.06. In all the cases where the reductions that orthogonal axonometric projection bestows on the drawing sheet are not accounted for, it is more appropriate to speak of isometric drawing rather than isometric projection.

When v differs by 90°, this is oblique axonometry and the axonometric units may be greater, smaller, or equal to one, and the elements may be assigned arbitrarily.

When the projection plane is parallel to a plane of the coordinates, the axes of those coordinates are projected in actual size and their reduction ratio is equal to one, while the third will differ and according to the different angles v. If we assume that the angle v is formed by the direction of the projection with the plane equal to $45°$, we would have an *isometric oblique*, in which the reduction relationships are equal and the cotangent of v is equal to one ($\cot g\, v = 1$). This is called *military* or *cavalier* oblique axonometry, according to whether it is the plan or the elevation of the building that is placed parallel to the projection plane.

21. Karl Wilhelm Pohlke, *Darstellende Geometrie*, 2 vols. (Berlin: Gaertner, 1860–1876). Pohlke's theorem is expounded in part one (chap. VI, 101–117) under the title *Die Schiefe Projection*. The demonstration of the theorem is also published here, with the solution elaborated by Hermann Kinkelin, professor of the Basle Gewerbeschule.

22. N. Krylov, P. Lobandievski, and S. Maine, *Géométrie descriptive* (Moscow: Éditions Mir, 1971), 208.

10.1
Qiu Ying, *Morning at Han Palace*, section of
a horizontal scroll, c. 1510–1551. Taichung,
Palace Museum.

10

THE JESUIT PERSPECTIVE IN CHINA

By the end of the sixteenth century, Renaissance perspective had become established in the West as the most realistic system of representation. Having lost all symbolic significance, it had become a convention in artistic practice and had begun to be studied with a sort of antiquarian fascination by mathematicians. The studies carried out by Simon Stevin, Guidobaldo del Monte, François d'Aguilon, Girard Desargues, and Jean Dubreuil contributed to its definitive codification as an analytical-geometrical method, with Jean-Victor Poncelet's projective geometry completing the process at the beginning of the nineteenth century.

But just as linear perspective reached the apex of its acceptance as a convention, suddenly Jesuit missionaries exported it to China as a vehicle of Christian iconography. Matteo Ricci, the founder of the China mission in 1583, brought late sixteenth-century European perspective oil paintings with him. It was the first time that Western anthropocentric representations had appeared on the boundless horizon of Chinese art. Chinese painting made use of a consolidated method of oblique parallel projection and was organized into precise genres, obeying rigid descriptive rules. Balletic calligraphy and evanescent watercolor effects reiterated the philosophical and lyrical character of art. The representation was not a transcription of direct observation of the real but of what the inner eye was capable of grasping. The use of parallel orthogonal perspective abolished the primacy of the viewpoint and there were no depth cues, such as vanishing points or converging lines, only the contrivances of aerial perspective shrouding distances in mysterious vapors.

It is not surprising that this technique of painting struck the Jesuits as weak, while the Chinese found Western paintings to be "violent" and "devoid of any artistry." "The Chinese," wrote Ricci to his superior, "do not know how to paint in oils, nor do they shade the things that they paint, with the result that all their paintings are dull and totally devoid of life."[1]

At the end of 1610, after twenty years of petitioning, Ricci was finally admitted to the presence of the Emperor and presented him with three oil paintings. The Son of Heaven's reaction exceeded the Jesuit's expectations: after having exclaimed, "This is the living God," the Emperor venerated the marvelous image with "incense and perfumes." But he was so perturbed by the appearance of these gifts that he kept only the painting of Baby Jesus, dispatching the other two (*Salus Populi Romani* and *The Virgin between Jesus and John the Baptist*) to the Emperor Mother, who, perturbed in her turn, deposited them forthwith in the imperial treasury.[2]

During his long wait for admittance to the capital city, Ricci had the opportunity to witness the extraordinary reaction of the Chinese to strongly shadowed perspectival representation. Painting played an important role in the subtle and complex workings of the Jesuit missionary strategy, along with lenses, robots, hydraulic machines, and astronomical knowledge. *Captatio benevolentiae* comprised not only behaving in a humble and respectful manner toward the culture and language of the host people (something often omitted by Franciscans and Dominicans), but also the skillful intertwining of faith and wonderment.

However, the new perspective vehicle contained one insuperable contradiction. The religious images appeared to the Emperor's eyes solely as technical marvels, and as such were accorded an almost religious respect. The evangelical message was ignored since, for the Chinese, the manner of representation was not realistic.

In order to make those images more convincing and theologically more effective, it was necessary to familiarize the Chinese with the rules that governed perspective. Thus, alongside an obstinate and often futile evangelical activity, the Jesuits also embarked upon a program of scientific acculturation. In 1606, Ricci had his pupil Xu Guangqi translate the first six books of Euclid's *Elements*, an indispensable premise for perspectival construction.[3] The translation "was a very wondrous thing, showing with great clarity a manner of proof and demonstration, the like of which has never again been seen."[4] Euclidean geometry was a complete novelty for Chinese culture. Although deductive reasoning comparable to that of the Greeks may be found in the ancient Mohist Canons of the fourth century BC, the geometrical cognitions of the Chinese, from the Han Period onward, were limited to practical formulae for the approximate calculation of surfaces and volumes. As far as optics was concerned, as Joseph Needham writes, the theory of the emission of visual rays has always been extraneous to Chinese theory.[5] Euclid's error, which had permitted the

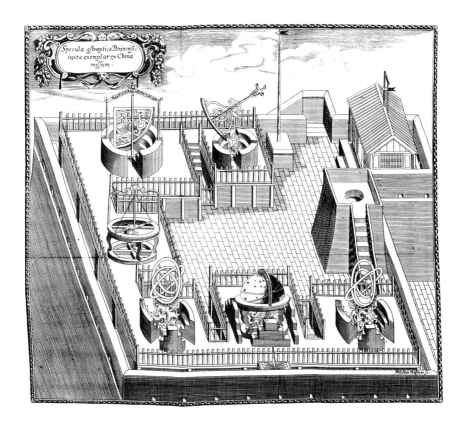

10.2
Ferdinand Verbiest, *Astronomia Europea sub
Imperatore tartaro sinico Cám Hy Apellato ex
Umbra in Lucem revocata* (Beijing, 1688).

formulation of Western perspective, was thus not known in China. Even the definition of *plane*, already present in the Mohist Canons, carried no optical or geometrical implications, since a plane is a surface that never reaches its sides.

But given the Chinese disinclination for generalist laws and theorizing, tangible demonstrations were necessary in order to convince them that perspective was the right way to see and therefore to represent: in short, the right way to think. Sight and thought had to converge in harmony toward that magical point where the parallel lines met and where the Western painting tradition placed the image and the idea of the divine infinite. Nineteen years after Ricci's death, the Jesuit Francesco Sambiaso published a book on perspective titled *Risposte alle questioni sul sonno e sulla pittura* (Replies to questions on sleep and on painting),[6] and later Father Buglio presented the Emperor with three paintings that exemplified the rules of perspective.[7] On this count, the astronomer Father Ferdinand Verbiest, who had been elevated to the grade of Mandarin and who was the director of the Astronomical Tribunal of Beijing, wrote: "Perspectiva lucidissimus suis oculis prima omnium oculos Imperatoris in se convertit…. Vix credi potest quantum haec ars omnium rapuit oculos non solum pekinensium."[8]

But if the victory of European astronomy was total and was accepted by the Chinese for practical reasons as the best method for ordering those rites that objectified their relationship with the heavens, the Emperor, and his subjects, the same did not happen with painting. Perspective was certainly "marvelous," but that did not make it better than traditional methods of painting, and the Chinese understood that its seduction concealed a "conversion" that had not been asked for and that conflicted with the attributes of the Emperor, who was both mother and father of his subjects. Resistance to perspective was thus very tenacious, and although they made use of it, even those painters who had converted to Christianity remained substantially bound to traditional Chinese painting. The attempts to acquaint the Chinese with the rules of perspective continued, however. In 1729, the greatest painter who worked in China, Giuseppe Castiglione, arranged for the translation and publication of the fundamental work of his teacher Andrea Pozzo.[9] Though this attempt was met with little success, Castiglione was, along with Verbiest, one of the seven Jesuits elevated to the status of Mandarin between 1581 and 1681, and therefore he played a role of some prestige at the imperial court. In the end it was the rigidity of the Confucian China of the Mandarins and literati, seduced by science and by the dignity of Ricci's life at the end of the Ming Dynasty, as well as by Castiglione afterward, that managed to colonize the colonialists.

10.3
Giuseppe Castiglione, *Kazakh People Present
Tribute Horses*, eighteenth century, detail.
Paris, Musée Guimet.

10.4
The Visitation of St. Elizabeth. Geronimo Nadal, *Adnotationes et meditationes in Evangilia* (Antwerp, 1595).

10.5
The same scene "in Chinese style" in Giovanni da Rocha, *Metodo del Rosario*, 1620.

CORONATVR SPINIS IESVS.   122
Matt xxvij. Mar xv loan xix.   xcv

A. IESVS ab atrio in aulam Prætorij
    crudelissime cæsus trahitur
B. Recesserat Pilatus in cubiculum, &
    quid vellet fieri, significauerat
C. IESVS veste pariter ac pelle acro-
    issime exutus, purpurea clamide
    per ludibrium induitur

D. Sedere iubetur in scamno; Capiti
    corona e spinis imponitur; arundo
    pro sceptro datur.
E. Acerbissime accusant, illudunt, feriunt arun-
    dine, consalutant Regem Iudæorum.
F. Virgo Mater foris cum suis omnia
    ex intermuncijs cognoscit.

10.6
Jesus crowned by thorns. Geronimo Nadal,
Adnotationes et meditationes in Evangilia
(Antwerp, 1595).

10.7
The same scene "in Chinese style"
in Giovanni da Rocha, *Metodo del
Rosario*, 1620.

In his *History of Wordless Poetry*, dedicated to the painting of the Ming Dynasty (1368–1644), Jiang Shaoshu writes: "Li Madou [Matteo Ricci] brought with him an image of the Lord of the Heavens according to the Western countries: it is a woman carrying a child in her arms ... the figures have a majesty and elegance that is quite beyond the abilities of Chinese painters." The admiration of the Chinese for the technical aspects of this achievement was on a level with their indifference to its religious significance. It was precisely in order to get around this contradiction that Jesuit policy almost completely gave up its attempt to impose perspectival methods of representation. Putting into practice the maxim "act as a Roman among the Romans and as a Greek among the Greeks," the Jesuits were "Chinese with the Chinese," assuming Chinese names, clothes, and customs. And little by little, they brought Christian iconography into the scope of Chinese methods of representation. When, around 1620, Giovanni da Rocha's *Method for Praying the Rosary* was published, Geronimo Nadal's illustrations, which had been prepared to accompany the text, were redrawn according to the Chinese method of oblique drawing.[10] A century later, Castiglione himself ended by painting in parallel perspective.

For Chinese culture, parallel projection was a sort of symbolic form, profoundly rooted in a pictorial experience that knew almost no interruption until the recent past. Changing the way of seeing, and therefore of representing, meant changing the mode of thinking, which was a futile exercise as long as it was conceived in terms of a conversion from the outside. Additionally, the attempt to institute a single viewpoint contradicted the very roots of Chinese thought, in which man is not the measure of all things. Rather, according to the Taoist conception, it is nature that expresses itself through the artist. And if it was accepted that perspectival representation was closer in appearance to vision, as early as the ninth century Sou Che had written: "He who judges painting according to the concept of resemblance shows the understanding of a child."

The same concept of realism, in a naturalistic sense, never found particular fortune in Chinese painting. In a text by Shen Kuo of 1080, the "realistic" attempts of the painter Li Cheng (907–960) are criticized for their depiction of things "from below." Shen Kuo writes, "That is all wrong. In general the proper way of painting a landscape is to see the small from the viewpoint of the large (*i ta kuan hsiao*), just as one looks at artificial mountains in gardens (as one walks about)."[11] This angle of totality is not just an aerial view, but also oblique parallel projection: cavalier viewpoint.

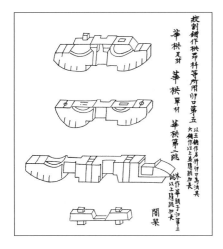

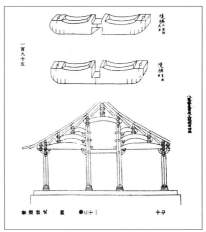

10.8
Li Jie, *Yingzao Fashi* (Method of
architecture), c. 1103, 1821 edition.

10.9
Li Jie, *Yingzao Fashi* (Method of
architecture), c. 1103, 1821 edition.

10.10
Warship reproduced in the 1510 edition
of *Wujing Zongyao* (Collection of the most
important military techniques), c. 1044.

庶殷丕作圖

SON DE PLAISANCE DE L'EMPEREUR
DE LA CHINE

Maison de plaisance de l'empereur de la Chine, Paris, Bibliothèque Nationale, Rès A. 117, Hd 89, plate twelve. Note the simultaneous presence of oblique drawing (right side) and perspectival rendition (left side).

It is true that oblique projection was incapable of rendering depth, since its geometrical nature meant that it could not cope with diminutions or convergences. But Chinese artists had made recourse to expedients that were able to give the impression of "distancing." Long before Leonardo introduced it into Western painting, Chinese landscape painters were able practitioners of aerial or atmospheric perspective. The painter-scholar Guo Xi (tenth century) was the first to codify ways of representing the third dimension in landscape painting. His text distinguished three types of distances: high distance (*gao-yuan*) was customarily used in vertical format works, in which a series of towering mountain ranges, each constituting a horizon in itself, is seen from below looking upward; deep distance composition (*shen-yuan*), the most commonly used, with the spectator placed at a high vantage point looking down; and level distance (*ping-yuan*), in which the scenery stretches away broadly and the spectator has an uninterrupted view into infinity.[12]

One of the most serious errors in painting was failing to distinguish between near and far. Generally, when distance could not be rendered atmospherically, the problem was resolved by placing an object, its size not necessarily diminished, in the highest part of the composition.

The Jesuit painters not only had to take such codifications into account, but also the question of the disposition of objects within scenes, which, while relatively free in Western painting, was governed by very precise rules in China. These regulations are exhaustively described in the famous *Mustard Seed Garden Manual of Painting*, published for the first time in 1679 by the Wang brothers.[13] This work exhorted the artist not to paint water without showing the spring, not to paint landscape without a wild region, a road without both an entrance and an exit, a stone without two sides, a tree with less than four branches, and so forth. Compared to such levels of exactitude, which the court painters and literati carried out with a high degree of naturalness, the advice contained in Federico Borromeo's *De pictura*[14] must have seemed to the Jesuit painters to be hopelessly bland, and yet painfully restrictive of their artistic activity.

For all these reasons, perspective construction and its resultant deformations appeared to Chinese eyes to be false and devoid of artistry. They perceived heavily shadowed areas as dark blotches that disfigured the compositional harmony. Sir John Barrow quotes the Emperor himself as passing a very telling judgment on Western perspective: "On enquiry, I found that Cast[i]glione was a missionary of great repute at court, where he executed a number of paintings, but was expressly directed by the Emperor to paint all his subjects after the Chinese manner, and not like those of Europe, with broad masses of shade and the distant objects scarcely visible, observing, as one of the missionaries told me, that the imperfections of the eye afforded no reason why the objects of nature should also be copied as imperfect. This idea of the Emperor accords with a remark made by one of his ministers, who came to see the portrait of His Britannic Majesty, and said 'that it was great pity it should have been spoiled by the dirt upon the face,' pointing, at the same time, to the broad shade of the nose."[15]

With this peremptory and disarming statement, the attempt to introduce perspective to China reached its end. With the dissolution of the Society of Jesus in 1773, the China mission was also abandoned, leaving space for missions of a more commercial nature.

Notes

1. *Opere storiche del P. Matteo Ricci, S.I.*, ed. P. Pietro Tacchi Venturi, S.I. (Macerata: Tip. F. Giorgetti, 1911–1913), 1:16.

2. Ibid., 1:366.

3. Xu Guangqi (Paolo Siu) was a Mandarin and disciple of Matteo Ricci. They translated together the six books taken from Cristoforo Clavio, *Euclidis Posteriores libri sex a X ad XV. Acc. XVI. de solidorum regularium comparatione Omnes perspectionis demonstrationibus, accur. scholijs ill.* (Rome: Avvaltus, 1574). The volume, titled *Jihe Yuanben* (Elementary geometry book), had great diffusion. However, because this perception of geometry was totally alien to the Chinese, Xu Guangqi was obliged to explain in his preface the characteristic way of Western thinking: "Rules in the West are different from ours…. Rules in the East that are the same as in the West are all right, those different from those in the West are all wrong…. Therefore, though The Ten Mathematical Classics are lost, this is not a pity, for they were nothing but worn-out shoes." Instructions for approaching the matter were also given: "Four things in this book are not necessary; it is not necessary to doubt, to assume new conjectures, to put to the test, to modify. In addition four things in this book are impossible. It is impossible to remove any particular passage, to refute it, to shorten it, or to place it before that which precedes it, or vice versa." Two copies were sent by Ricci to Rome in 1608, now kept in the Biblioteca Apostolica Vaticana. *Elements*, the complete Euclid book, was translated only in 1857.

4. Ricci, *Opere storiche*, 2:359.

5. See the chapter on perspective in Joseph Needham with Wang Ling and Lu Guizhen, *Science and Civilization in China* (Cambridge: Cambridge University Press, 1971), vol. 4, part III, 111–119.

6. Ibid., 4, III, 111. Francesco Sambias[o] (1582–1649), *Risposte alle questioni sul sonno e sulla pittura* (Replies to questions on sleep and on painting). See also Berthold Laufer, "Christian Art in China," in Rudolf Lange and Alfred Forke, eds., *Ostasiatischen Studien* (Berlin: Kommisionverlag von Georg Reimer, 1910), 104.

7. Jean-Baptiste Du Halde, *Description géographique, historique, chronologique, politique et physique de l'Empire de la Chine et de la Tartarie chinoise …* (Paris: P. G. Le Mercier, 1735), 3:269.

8. Ferdinand Verbiest, *Astronomia Europea sub Imperatore tartaro sinico Cám Hy* [Kangxi] *Apellato ex Umbra in Lucem*

revocata (Dillingen: Joannis Caspari Bencard, bibliopolae academici, 1687), cap. xx, 78. It is remarkable that in the list of Jesuits' books published in China, the Sambiasi book *Risposte alle questioni sul sonno e sulla pittura* is quoted as *De pictura*.

9. Andrea Pozzo, *Perspectiva pictorum et architectorum* (Rome: Komarek, 1693–1700).

10. In 1595 a compendium was published by Geronimo Nadal, *Adnotationes et meditationes in Evangelia quae in sacrosancto Missae sacrificio toto anno leguntur; cum Evangeliorum concordantia historiae integritati sufficienti* (Antwerp: Martin Nutius, 1593). Fourteen of these illustrations in "Chinese style" were engraved in *Method for Praying the Rosary* (*Song nianzhu guicheng*, 1620), by Giovanni da Rocha.

11. Needham, *Science and Civilization in China*, 115.

12. François Cheng, *Mille anni di pittura cinese* (Milan: Rizzoli, 1981).

13. See the modern edition of *The Mustard Seed Garden Manual of Painting*, facsimile of the 1887–1888 Shanghai edition, with texts translated by Mai-Mai Sze (Princeton: Princeton University Press, 1978).

14. Federico Borromeo, *De pictura sacra*, ed. C. Castiglioni with a preface by G. Nicodemi (Sora: Camastro, 1932).

15. Barrow writes here about the famous Milanese court painter Giuseppe Castiglione, S.J. (1688–1766). John Barrow, *Travels in China* (London: T. Cadell and W. Davies, 1804), 119. See also Cécile and Michel Buerdeley, *Giuseppe Castiglione: A Jesuit Painter at the Court of the Chinese Emperors* (London: Lund Humphries, 1972). Many of his works were destroyed; the remains can be found in the Taiwan Museum.

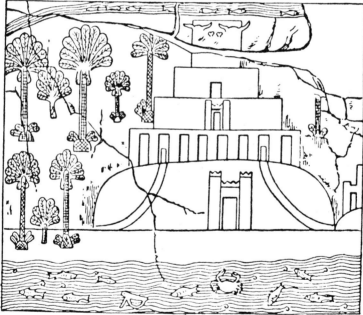

11.1
Pieter Bruegel the Elder, *The Tower of Babel*,
c. 1563, detail. Rotterdam, Boymans-van
Beuningen Museum.

11.2
Representation of a ziggurat on an
Assyrian relief, Ninevah, seventh century.
In André Parrot, "La Tour de Babel,"
Cahiers d'archéologie biblique (1953).

11

THE TOWER OF BABEL: FORM AND REPRESENTATION

To date, thirty-five Towers of Babel have been discovered in the ancient region of Sennaar, later known as Mesopotamia, but only one of them is the source of all of the legends and iconographies that are part of Western culture. While it may not have been the first, or the prototype of all subsequent towers, the Babylon tower became lodged in people's memory as an archetype. According to Assyro-Babylonian religion, the Etemenanki, the tower erected by Nabopolassar and Nebuchadnezzar, represented the doorway to heaven.[1] Like the other ziggurats constructed by "the people who came from the Eastern mountains,"[2] it was an artificial symbol of the imperturbable summit where mankind could approach the gods or invoke their descent. It represented the limit of human possibility, the reestablishment of the shattered primordial axis, a hand raised toward heaven and not against it, while according to the spies that Moses sent south of Canaan, towers were an expression of Oriental hyperbole: upon their return the men recounted that in those lands the cities were large and fortified "up to the sky."[3] It was natural that those constructions, erected by an idolatrous people who had enslaved the Jews, could not appear other than as a symbol of arrogance and oppression.

In the book of Genesis, man's freedom of action to "build ourselves a city and a tower with its top in the heavens" is identified as arrogance. The sacrilegious project is interrupted by the "confusion of tongues" (*confusio linguarum*) and the scattering of the peoples who, as a result, are no longer able to understand each other. This divine punishment accelerated the definitive diversification of languages that had begun after the Flood. Indeed, it had been with the descendants of Noah's sons Shem, Ham, and Japheth that "the whole earth was peopled."[4]

The question of dogmatism gave rise to a prolific literature after the texts of the Library of Ashurbanipal began to be published toward the end of the nineteenth century. During a famous conference in 1902, Friedrich Delitzsch[5] declared that the Old Testament was not only a revelatory text but also had derived many of its stories from Sumero-Babylonian texts. Traditional theology struck back in indignation. The dispute that arose between experts in Assyriology and the custodians of dogma has become less controversial over the course of time.[6] The scientific truth of archaeological research is today as incontrovertible as the dogmatism that led to Giordano Bruno's burning at the stake and to Galileo's abjuration. Recognition of the continuity of the stories, of what the Russian formalists would call *theme migration*, and reorganizing them as an ecumenical, universal human experience, is a form of authentic religiosity. The fact that recent studies have shown there are more than sixty stories of a universal flood from around the world does not gainsay either the story of Noah[7] or the earlier version contained in the *Epic of Gilgamesh*, which, it must be said, have many points in common. A period of nearly a thousand years separates history from revelation, and in that time the truth is not so much dispersed as diversified in terms of its ideological use.[8]

In the history of the pictorial representation of the tower, Cornelis Anthonisz and Hans Holbein were the first to give it a circular form, and with a few exceptions this would remain the norm until Assyriologists came up with a square reconstruction. The Renaissance predilection for the rounded temple form was undoubtedly responsible for consolidating this type, dominant between 1550 and 1650, the period in which the tower is most frequently depicted in European painting.

It is quite possible that the perspectival representation of the Renaissance, in which the summit disappeared "almost into infinity," suggested the transition from the parallel-walled medieval tower to the conical form, which became, in the sixteenth century, the most *realistic* mode of representation. In the earliest images of the subject, found in illuminated manuscripts and mosaics and executed in oblique and orthogonal projection, that "fist raised to the heavens" challenging divine infinity was reduced to a presumptuous intention without hyperbolic imagery. The towers were not much higher than the builders who were busying themselves with their construction, but the task of completing their sinful work was supposedly infinite. When perspective introduces the vanishing point, then the crime becomes flagrant. The summit that touches the clouds, spiraling upward to reach the unreachable, is halted by the Confusion of Tongues and by ruin. It is perhaps no accident that this sequence of mechanical attempts to reach divine infinity began assuming particular importance from the beginning of the sixteenth century. As a result of Luther's reforms and the Counter-Reformation, the theme of punishment seems to have been concentrated in representations of this biblical subject.

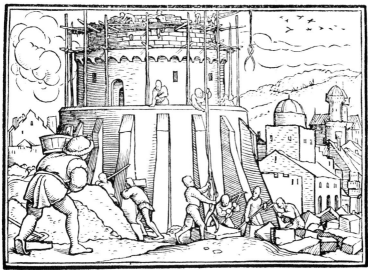

11.3
Cornelis Anthonisz
(after 1499–1553), etching.

11.4
Hans Holbein the Younger
(1497–1543), woodcut.

In addition, the Confusion of Tongues assumed a deeper significance for Luther, for its linguistic diversification underlined even more powerfully the rift with the Church of Rome:[9] it was the beginning of the national language, of the spread of *teutsch* through the diffusion of the *Volksbücher*.

The theme of human pride and corruption, given such sharp rendition in the biblical story, is now used against Rome-Babylon, *caput scelerum*, and also against heresy. It is significant that in 1619, the Lutheran Johann Valentin Andreae published a short text against the linguistic babel of the Rosicrucian movement, proposing a Christian reorientation.[10]

For Andreae, the *Turris Babel* continued to be a symbol of divine anathema, although the Dutch painters, who by this date had made the theme their own, depicted the tower as if it were a real architecture and placed it in a local or exotic landscape. After all, the travelers who had been visiting the places associated with the tower for two thousand years had made no contribution to defining either its physical appearance, which was impossible because no trace remained, or its precise location: biblical allegory made up for any figurative uncertainty.

In reality, this eighth wonder of the world had disappeared from the West's sight right at the beginning of the Christian era. The passage of time had reduced it to ruins and, like Babylon, it had been pillaged for the extensive building that had taken place all around it: "Because of the wrath of the Lord it shall not be inhabited, but shall be wholly desolate."[11]

In the twelfth century, Rabbi Benjamin of Tudela observed that the tower of "Bélus had been destroyed by fire from the heavens."[12] But neither he nor his fellow travelers, including Pietro della Valle in 1616 and Father Superior Vincenzo Maria of St. Catherine of Siena in 1657, actually laid eyes on the ruins of the tower.

The tower withdrew from the eyes of men, escaping all attempts at discovery. During an expedition carried out under the patronage of Frederick v of Denmark between 1761 and 1767, Carsten Niebuhr believed he caught sight of it, but in reality what he had seen were the ruins of Birs Nimrud; a description of these same ruins was written between 1780 and 1800 by Joseph de Beauchamp, vicar general in Baghdad.

In 1781, the archaeologist and numismatist Domenico Sestini complained that a "tribe of Arabs prevented us from visiting the tower." The tower he was referring to, however, was not Babel. James Rich, British consul general in Baghdad, made detailed notes about a site he presumed to be Babylon[13] but which was in reality again Birs Nimrud, leading all those who followed him into the same error. The list continues until the beginning of the twentieth century, when the site upon which the tower stood was discovered and the descriptions of Herodotus compared to the famous Esagila tablet. On the basis of this data, the tower now exists archaeologically, and Theodor A. Busink's reconstruction, a rectangular plan with eight floors, is generally accepted by all scholars of Assyriology.[14]

But it is precisely in the light of such archaeological certainties that the pictorial variants of the tower's architecture acquire greater interest. The conception of the tower as a circular edifice begins with the panel by Bernardino Jacopi Butinone (1476–1507), is carried on in the engraving by Hans Holbein (1526) and that by Cornelis Anthonisz (1547), until we arrive at the version by Pieter Bruegel the Elder (1563). From this moment until present-day reconstructions, with the sole exception of the version by Fischer von Erlach (1656–1723), the predominant type is a round tower with a spiral staircase. There was, however, a parallel tradition, which consisted of a square or polygonal format, deriving from Byzantine and late medieval models. Two Dutch painters, Marten Jacobsz van Veen, known as Heemskerk (1498–1574), and the "Dutch Vasari" Karel van Mander (1548–1606), in particular, were insistent in rendering the tower with a square base and eight steps (according to Herodotus's tradition). Heemskerk visited Rome in 1532, twelve years after Luther's excommunication; during his three-year stay, he was strongly influenced by Michelangelo and the terrific emotional intensity he instilled in his work. Four years after Bruegel's famous rendition of the Tower of Babel, Heemskerk produced, in 1567, a series of engravings on the theme of catastrophe: in this work, the stepped tower appears as a finished structure, destroyed by a divine bolt of lightning. Van Mander also spent three years in Rome, arriving in 1573. With the conclusion of the Council of Trent in 1563, the Catholic Reformation had ended with the moral and cultural reaffirmation of the Church. As a manifestation of the new security that emanated from the recognition of the Pope's primacy, van Mander's tower is complete, right up to its summit. Its destruction will not be the result of violent retribution from above but will be the outcome of man's exercise of free will, the very thing that Luther argued against. The tower erected upon man's pride gives way at its base, and the building leans perilously to one side.

More than a century passed before theological iconography abandoned the tower to its secular and archaeological destiny. But before it entered Fischer von Erlach's collection of architectural wonders,[15] it was portrayed, perhaps for the last time apologetically, in the *Turris Babel* of the Jesuit Athanasius

Kircher.[16] For Kircher, the tower undoubtedly served as an allegory "rea laesae majestatis divinae," but it was also a historical reality. Kircher was an immobile traveler, as he never left the Collegio Romano, gathering around him accounts from books and the tales of travelers. He left the Dutch engravers free to pursue their images of the tower as a finished, circular structure dominating its surroundings in an ideal city. The theme of ruination or of incompleteness, typical of the Dutch school, was of no interest to Kircher. He rationally demonstrated, aided by the "opinion of excellent mathematicians," that 125 million bricks would have been necessary to build a tower stretching from the earth up to the sky where the moon was: "it thus follows that this tower with his weight exceed the earth by many *parasangs*."[17] Mathematical and static calculations immediately challenged the feasibility of the undertaking, so that destruction by an outside agent would have been unnecessary: as St. Augustine asserted, "Ista civitas quae appellate est Confusio, ipsa est Babylon."[18] This was the problem with which the Jesuit tussled. The Society of Jesus, of which Kircher was an authoritative exponent in the Collegio Romano, had taken upon itself the task of running missions all over the world, controlling a babel of languages, races, and rituals. As a symbol and source of the confusion, the Tower of Babel was an ideal starting point from which to formulate a grandiose universal history capable of embracing all diversity in a unitary scheme of assimilation to Christian doctrine.

To do this convincingly it was necessary to put Thomistic dogmatism aside, applying instead Jesuit flexibility to the question of magical, inexplicable phenomena in order to provide a natural explanation. Purged of empirical outcomes from supernatural explanations, the Renaissance hermetic tradition[19] led pagan magic back to the sphere of natural mysteries, giving verbal legitimization with the phrase "The ends sanctify the means."

Kircher's *Turris Babel* was the last articulated attempt to use the powerful image of the tower as an ideological vehicle for missionary zeal: the circle was thus closed, and from the four corners of the earth the peoples of the world were called back by the Jesuit tower to a renewed linguistic and ideological unification. It was a dream of omnipotence that quickly faded when the Society of Jesus, already shaken by the Chinese Rites controversy and unpopular with European monarchies, was forced by Clement XIV to dissolve on 21 July 1773.

11.5
Byzantine mosaic, c. 1135–1145. Palermo,
Palatine Chapel of the Palazzo Reale.

11.6
Swiss master, miniature from the
Bible of Toggenburg, c. 1411.
Kupferstichkabinett, Berlin.

11.7
English or Flemish miniature drawn from
the Huntingfield Psalter, c. 1180. M. R.
James, *Catalogue of Manuscripts of the
Library of J. P. Morgan* (London, 1906).

11.8
School of Marten van Valckenborch,
Tower of Babel, c. 1533–1612.

11.9
Bernardino Jacopi Butinone (1484–1507),
Christ Disputing with the Doctors, 15th
century. National Gallery of Scotland,
Edinburgh.

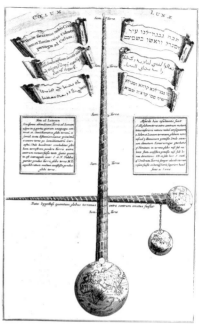

11.10
Frontispiece from Athanasius Kircher, *Turris Babel* (Amsterdam, 1679).

11.11
Demonstration of the impossibility of the tower reaching the moon. Athanasius Kircher, *Turris Babel* (Amsterdam, 1679), page 38.

11.12
Combined table showing the shapes of the characters of the main tongues (angelic, Samaritan, Syrian, and Assyrian). Athanasius Kircher, *Turris Babel* (Amsterdam, 1679), page 157.

Notes

1. For a concise literary, epigraphic, and archaeological documentation, see André Parrot, "La Tour de Babel," *Cahiers d'archéologie biblique* 2 (1953), and the more recent Petra Eisele, *Babylon: die archäologische Biographie der grössten, berühmtesten und verrufensten Metropole des Altertums, zugleich "Pforte der Götter" und "Grosse Hure"* (Bern and Munich: Scherz, 1980), which contains an exhaustive bibliography.

2. Genesis 11:2.

3. "Our brethren have made our hearts melt, saying, 'The people are greater and taller than we; the cities are great and fortified up to heaven'" (Deuteronomy 1:28), and "Hear, O Israel: you are to pass over the Jordan this day, to go in to dispossess nations greater and mightier than yourselves, cities great and fortified up to heaven" (Deuteronomy 9:1).

4. Genesis 9:19.

5. Friedrich Delitzsch, *Babel und Bibel* (Leipzig and Stuttgart: Deutsche Verlags-Anstalt, 1903).

6. On the question of dogma, see André Parrot, *Ziggourats et Tour de Babel* (Paris: A. Michel, 1949), 195–217, and Eisele, *Babylon*, 259ff.

7. Genesis 1:6–8.

8. Perhaps never, as in the case of the Tower of Babel, has a proven historical reality been so continuously subjected to erroneous scientific interpretations. André Parrot reports that, as a symbol of confusion and arrogance, the Tower was attributed with a series of improper uses, above all on the part of theologians (Parrot, *Ziggourats*, 196–200). Christian tradition is based naturally on the certainty of Genesis, but also uses the symbol of the Tower in the litanies of the Virgin (*Turris davidica*, *Turris eburnea*). In pagan tradition, Danae was imprisoned in a bronze tower when she received Zeus's fecund shower of gold, and alchemists used a tower-shaped furnace called *athanor* to transform lead into gold, the weight of flesh into spirit. As a further curiosity, in Peter D. Ouspensky's *The Symbolism of the Tarot* (1913), a tower of tarot cards is described as a construction that "went from the earth to the sky. The summit arose beyond the clouds like a crown of gold." Naturally, it was licked by the usual tongues of fire.

9. It is worth briefly recalling some historical facts: Luther affixed his famous ninety-five theses to the door of the Church of All Saints in Wittenberg on 31 October 1517. On 1 June 1520, Leo X issued the papal Bull *Exsurge Domine* ordering Luther, on pain of excommunication, to retract the forty condemned articles within sixty days.

Luther responded with a sermon written in German on "Good Works" and, among other texts, the important *De captivitate babylonica Ecclesiae*, which constituted the manifestos of the Reform movement. On 3 January 1521, his definitive excommunication arrived in the form of *Decet Romanum Ponteficem*. In 1534 Luther completed and published a translation of the Bible into German, an important contribution to the development of German language and literature.

10. Johann Valentin Andreae, *Turris Babel sive Judiciorum de Fraternitate Rosaceae Crucis chaos* (Strasbourg: Heirs of Lazare Zetzner, 1619). Andreae is known above all for his utopian text *Reipublicae Christianopolitanae descriptio* (Strasbourg: Heirs of Lazare Zetzner, 1615) and for his controversial links with the Rosicrucians. In reality, as Troeltsch asserts, he was one of the most refined of all Lutheran thinkers. A pupil of Maestlin, the teacher of Copernicus, he was associated through his scientific works with the Lutheran circles of Tübingen, and his *Chymische Hochzeit Cristiani Rosencreutz anno 1459* (Strasbourg: Heirs of Lazare Zetzner, 1616), written in 1605 under the pseudonym Christian Rosencreutz, was to influence Goethe's *Faust*. For the involvement of Andreae with the Rosicrucian movement, see, for an opinion that contrasts with that of Yates, John Warwick Montgomery, *Cross and Crucible: Johann Valentin Andreae (1586–1654), Phoenix of the Theologians* (The Hague: Martinus Nijhoff and Brill, 1973). For his utopia, Christianopolis, which might be considered the greatest expression of Protestantism as a social ideal, see Felix E. Held, *J. Valentin Andreae's Christianopolis: An Ideal State of the Seventeenth Century* (Urbana: University of Illinois Press, 1914). Interestingly, *Turris Babel* was dedicated to Heinrich Hein of Rostock, promoter of the utopian *Antilia*, in these terms: "Vide optime Heini, quibus rationibus contra Fraternitatem illam invisibilem utar, Fâma scilicet contra famam," 3. Andreae is referring to the Rosicrucian manifestos published in Kassel in 1614 under the titles: *General Reformation, Fama*, and *Confessio*.

11. Jeremiah 50:13.

12. *Itinerarium Beniamini Tudelensis, in quo res memorabiles, quas ante quadringentos annos totum fere terrarum orbem notatis itineribus dimensus vel ipse vidit a fide dignis suae aetatis hominibus accepit, breviter atque dilucide describuntur* (Antwerp: ex officina C. Plantini, 1575).

13. Claudius James Rich, *Memoir on the Ruins of Babylon* (London: Longman, Hurst, Rees, Orme, and Brown, 1818).

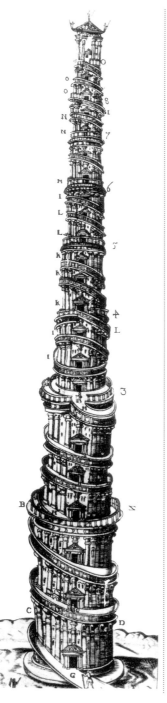

11.13
Anonymous print
(Cologne, 1628).

11.14
Anton Koberger, woodcut,
1493. From Hartmann
Schedel, *Liber chronicarum*
(Nuremberg, 1493).

14. Theodor A. Busink, *De toren van Babel* (Batavia-Centrum: Noordhoff-Kolff, 1938).

15. Johann Bernhard Fischer von Erlach, *Entwurff einer historischen Architektur* (Vienna: Fischer von Erlach, 1721). Fischer von Erlach (1656–1723) makes reference to such sources as Herodotus, Diodorus Siculus, Strabo, Pliny, Justin, and Quintus Curtius; his own description (18v) is detached and partly agrees with that of Herodotus: "Au milieu de cet edifice une Tour quarrée s'elevoit à huit étages, en forme de Terrasses, & lui donnoit un grand éclat. On y montoit par des grands escaliers extérieurs, & tout etoit couronnée par un petit temple, au que on arrivoit commodement par une machine tirés en dedans. Diodore remarque encore, que cette Tour a servi d'observatoire aux Chaldéens. [In the middle of this building, a square tower rose up, eight stories high, in the form of terraces, that gave it a splendid air. One ascended by means of grand exterior stairs, and the whole was crowned by a small temple, to which one gained easy access by a hoist pulled up from inside. Diodorus remarked, further, that this tower was used as an observatory for the Chaldeans.]" The imaginative reference to the lift comes from Strabo.

16. Athanasius Kircher, *Turris Babel sive Archontologia qua primo priscorum post diluvium hominum vita, mores rerumque gestarum magnitudo, secundo Turris fabrica civitatumque extructio, confusio linguarum, et inde gentium trasmigrationi, cum principalium inde erratorum idiomatum historia, multiplici eruditione describuntur et explicantur* (Amsterdam: ex officina Janssonio-Waesbergianna, 1679), 40 (t. A); for Kircher's work, see the excellent book by Dino Pastine, *La nascita dell'idolatria. L'oriente religioso di Athanasius Kircher* (Florence: La Nuova Italia, 1978).

17. Kircher, *Turris Babel*, 39–40. The *parasang* is an ancient Persian measurement corresponding, according to Herodotus, to 6,300 meters.

18. Augustine, *De civitate Dei* 16.4.

19. On this subject, see Pastine, *La nascita dell'idolatria*, and Frances A. Yates, *Giordano Bruno and the Hermetic Tradition* (London: Routledge, 1964).

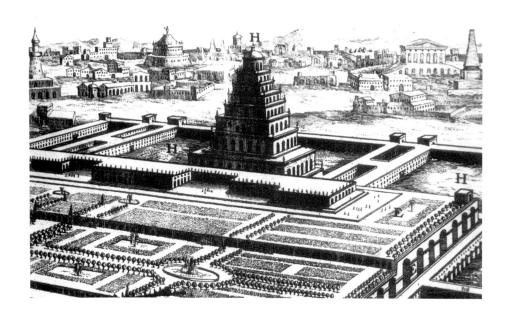

11.15
The square of the Tower of
Babel. Johann Bernhard
Fischer von Erlach, *Entwurff
einer historischen Architektur*
(Vienna, 1721).

INDEX

Branca, Giovanni, 276
Braunfels, Wolfgang, 186, 208, 213
Breasted, James Henry, 93, 97, 100, 105, 127, 165
Bréhier, Emile, 113
Bréhier, Louis, 66, 117
Breithof, Nicolas, 22, 328
Brenzoni, Raffaello, 178
Bresciani, Edda, 95, 96, 100
Bretez, Louis, 158, 243
Briggs, Martin S., 168, 177, 178, 209
Brion-Guerry, Liliane, 120
Broc, Numa, 239
Bronzino (Agnolo di Cosimo Allori), 189
Bruegel, Pieter, the Elder, 358, 363
Brugsch, Heinrich Karl, 99
Brunelleschi, Filippo, 89, 91, 92, 134, 135, 140, 141, 142, 170, 171, 184–213, 238, 273, 284
Brunet, Jean Pierre, 239
Brunetti, Giulia, 208, 210
Bruno, Giordano, 360, 372
Bruno di Ser Lapo Mazzei, 187
Bruschi, Arnaldo, 243
Bucher, François, 170
Buddensieg, Tilmann, 175
Buglio, Ludovico, 344
Buontalenti, Bernardo, 189
Burckhardt, Jacob, 115, 168
Burckhard von Birckenstein, Antoni Ernst, 330
Burns, Howard, 172, 174, 278
Busca, Gabriello, 154, 179, 302, 307, 309
Busink, Théodore A., 363
Butades of Corinth, 126
Buteo. *See* Borrel, Jean
Butinone, Bernardino Jacopi, 363, 367

Caesar, Gaius Julius, 246, 247–248, 313
Calabi, Donatella, 178
Calepino, Ambrogio, 173
Callebat, Louis, 257
Callicles, 247
Callot, Jacques, 189
Calvo, Fabio, 230, 243, 245
Calypso, 57

Camaino di Crescenzino, 195
Cambitoglou, Alexander, 133
Campano da Novara, 132, 235, 242
Capart, Jean, 101
Capobianco, Alessandro, 294, 309, 311
Cappellari, Girolamo Alessandro, 174
Caprara, Otello, 208, 210, 211
Cardini, Franco, 281
Carena, Carlo, 113, 114, 126
Caretta, Alessandro, 118
Caretti, Lanfranco, 305
Carpenter, Rhys, 106
Carra de Vaux Saint-Cyr, Bernard, 253, 258, 260, 279, 283
Carugo, Adriano, 243
Casati, Roberto, 127
Cassander, 111
Cassandra, 60
Cassiodorus, Flavius Magnus Aurelius, 118, 122
Cassirer, Ernst, 133
Castaldo, Giovanni Battista, 306
Castiglione, Giuseppe, 344, 345, 348, 357
Castriotto, Jacomo, 6, 8, 20, 147, 150, 294, 298, 315, 319
Cataneo, Girolamo, 319
Cataneo, Pietro, 151, 177
Catherine II (empress of Russia), 289
Cavalcanti, Giovanni, 192
Cecaumenos, 301
Centorio degli Hortensi, Ascanio, 306
Ceredi, Giuseppe, 275, 310
Cesariano, Cesare, 90, 229–230, 231, 241, 243, 259, 265, 272, 273, 276, 298, 309
Champollion, Jean-François, 53, 94, 98
Charlemagne, 71
Charles IV (duke of Lorraine), 321
Charles V (emperor), 306, 318
Charles VIII (king of France), 287, 301
Charles d'Amboise, 233
Chastel, André, 175, 241
Cheops. *See* Khufu
Cherpion, Nadine, 104
Chevalier de Beaulieu, 316
Chiarugi, Andrea, 213

Desargues, Girard, 3, 13, 15, 30, 232, 303, 341
Descartes, René, 3, 20, 150, 232, 337
Desroches, Christiane, 165, 166
Destrées, J., 304
De Tolnay, Charles, 176
De Ville, Antoine, 156, 318
Diderot, Denis, 20, 182–183
Diels, Otto Paul Hermann, 116, 222, 236
Digges, Thomas, 241
Di Giuseppe, Riccardo, 111
Dijksterhuis, Eduard Jan, 114
Dilke, Oswald Ashton Wentworth, 129, 239
Diocletian (Gaius Aurelius Valerius Diocletianus), 117, 128
Diodorus Siculus, 102, 372
Dionysus, 60, 108
Dioscorides, Pedanius, 122, 125
Djoser, 46, 51, 52, 53, 56, 95, 100, 103, 104, 107, 109, 117
Dodds, Eric Robertson, 113–114
Doesburg, Theo van, 19
Domitilla, 117
Donadoni, Sergio, 107
Donadoni Roveri, Anna Maria, 100
Donatello (Donato de' Bardi), 89, 134, 207
Dondi, Giovanni, 87, 91, 132, 310
Doren, Alfred, 213
Dorman, Peter F., 105
Drabkin, Israel E., 238
Dresden, Arnold, 115
Drioton, Etienne, 101
Dubreuil, Jean, 19, 26, 34, 45, 341
Duby, Georges, 131
Duccio di Buoninsegna, 86
Du Colombier, Pierre, 167, 281
Ducrey, Pierre, 284
Dupain de Montesson, Louis Charles, 317
Dürer, Albrecht, 230, 243, 245, 255, 286, 303–304

Edgerton, Samuel Y., 238
Efesto, 126
Einstein, Carl, 23
Eisele, Petra, 369

Elbern, Victor Heinrich, 167
Elizabeth, St., 346
Empedocles, 116
Engelbach, Reginald, 166
Engelhart, Valentin, 134, 311
Epictetus, 113
Epicurus, 43, 59
Epinoia, 125
Errard, Charles, 303
Errard de Bar-le-Duc, Jean, 318
Ettinghausen, Richard, 44
Euclid, 11–12, 13, 15, 17, 22, 28–29, 30, 31, 34, 43, 44, 65, 78, 88–89, 92, 125, 213, 217, 219–224, 226, 227, 235, 236, 237, 239, 242, 281, 303, 311, 326, 342, 356
Eudoxus of Cnidus, 239
Eugenius of Palermo, admiral of Sicily, 44, 281
Eusebius of Caesarea, 107
Eustace of Thessaloniki, 301
Euthydemos, 165
Evans, Robin, 150, 177, 243

Fabius Maximus, Quintus, 133
Fabriczy, Cornelius von, 210, 211
Falconetto, Giovanni Maria, 230, 241
Falletti, Franca, 211
Fancelli, Salvestro, 141
Fannius Sinistor, 85
Farioli Campanati, Raffaella, 120
Farish, William, 19, 20, 217, 316, 328, 334, 336
Faulhaber, Johann, 311, 312
Federici Vescovini, Graziella, 134, 135, 212
Feldhaus, Franz Maria, 284
Ferdinand I (emperor), 174
Ferdinand I de' Medici (grand duke of Tuscany), 189
Ferdinando I (king of Naples), 171
Fernandez de Enciso, Martin, 240
Ferrari, Giorgio E., 319
Ferri, Silvio, 303
Ferro, Antonio, 181
Fetti, Domenico, 168
Fibonacci, Leonardo, 89, 134–135, 192